BILINGUALISM

Routledge Applied Linguistics is a series of comprehensive resource books, providing students and researchers with the support they need for advanced study in the core areas of English language and applied linguistics.

Each book in the series guides readers through three main sections, enabling them to explore and develop major themes within the discipline.

- Section A, Introduction, establishes the key terms and concepts and extends readers' techniques of analysis through practical application.
- Section B, Extension, brings together influential articles, sets them in context, and discusses their contribution to the field.
- Section C, Exploration, builds on knowledge gained in the first two sections, setting thoughtful tasks around further illustrative material. This enables readers to engage more actively with the subject matter and encourages them to develop their own research responses.

Throughout the book, topics are revisited, extended, interwoven and deconstructed, with the reader's understanding strengthened by tasks and follow-up questions.

Bilingualism:

- introduces students to key issues and themes that include bilingual development and education, and the integration of social and cognitive perspectives
- uses tasks and examples to equip the reader with the necessary skills and insights to assess and interpret research drawn from bilingual populations
- incorporates case studies drawn from a range of countries such as the United States, South Africa, the Netherlands, Australia and Singapore
- gathers together influential readings from key names in the discipline, including Fred Genesee, Richard Bourhis, Elizabeth Peal, Wallace Lambert, Merrill Swain, Jim Cummins and Ellen Bialystok

Written by experienced teachers and researchers in the field, *Bilingualism* is an essential resource for students and researchers of English language and applied linguistics.

Ng Bee Chin is the Coordinator of the Linguistics Programme at Nanyang Technological University, Singapore.

Gillian Wigglesworth is Associate Professor and Head of the School of Languages and Linguistics at the University of Melbourne, Australia.

ROUTLEDGE APPLIED LINGUISTICS

SERIES EDITORS

Christopher N. Candlin is Senior Research Professor in the Department of Linguistics at Macquarie University, Australia and Professor of Applied Linguistics at the Open University, UK. At Macquarie, he has been Chair of the Department of Linguistics; established and was Executive Director of the National Centre for English Language Teaching & Research (NCELTR); and was first Director of the Centre for Language in Social Life (CLSL). He has written or edited over 150 publications and co-edits the new *Journal of Applied Linguistics*. From 1996 to 2002 he was President of the International Association of Applied Linguistics (AILA). He has acted as a consultant in more than 35 countries and as external faculty assessor in 36 universities worldwide.

Ronald Carter is Professor of Modern English Language in the School of English Studies at the University of Nottingham. He has published extensively in the fields of applied linguistics, literary studies and language in education. He has given consultancies in the field of English language education, mainly in conjunction with The British Council, in over 30 countries worldwide. He was recently elected a fellow of the British Academy of Social Sciences and is currently chair of the British Association of Applied Linguistics (BAAL).

TITLES IN THE SERIES

Intercultural Communication: An advanced resource book
Adrian Holliday, Martin Hyde and John Kullman

Translation: An advanced resource book
Basil Hatim and Jeremy Munday

Grammar and Context: An advanced resource book
Ann Hewings and Martin Hewings

Second Language Acquisition: An advanced resource book
Kees de Bot, Wander Lowie and Marjolijn Verspoor

Corpus-Based Language Studies: An advanced resource book
Anthony McEnery, Richard Xiao and Yukio Tono

Language and Gender: An advanced resource book
Jane Sunderland

English for Academic Purposes: An advanced resource book
Ken Hyland

Language Testing and Assessment: An advanced resource book
Glenn Fulcher and Fred Davidson

Bilingualism: An advanced resource book
Ng Bee Chin and Gillian Wigglesworth

Bilingualism

An advanced resource book

Ng Bee Chin and Gillian Wigglesworth

Routledge
Taylor & Francis Group

LONDON AND NEW YORK

First published 2007 by Routledge
2 Park Square, Milton Park, Abingdon, Oxon OX14 4RN

Simultaneously published in the USA and Canada
by Routledge
270 Madison Ave, New York, NY 10016

Routledge is an imprint of the Taylor & Francis Group, an informa business

© 2007 Ng Bee Chin and Gillian Wigglesworth

Typeset in Akzidenz, Minion and Novarese
by Keystroke, 28 High Street, Tettenhall, Wolverhampton
Printed and bound in Great Britain by
The Cromwell Press, Trowbridge, Wiltshire

British Library Cataloguing in Publication Data
A catalogue record for this book is available from the British Library

Library of Congress Cataloging in Publication Data
Ng, Bee Chin.
Bilingualism : an advanced resource book / Ng Bee Chin & Gillian Wigglesworth.
p. cm.
Includes bibliographical references and index.
1. Bilingualism. I. Wigglesworth, Gillian. II. Title.
P115.N49 2007
404.2–dc22
2006100593

ISBN10: 0–415–34386–0 (hbk)
ISBN10: 0–415–34387–9 (pbk)
ISBN10: 0–203–41026–2 (ebk)

ISBN13: 978–0–415–34386–2 (hbk)
ISBN13: 978–0–415–34387–9 (pbk)
ISBN13: 978–0–203–41026–4 (ebk)

Contents

Contents cross-referenced

Series editors' preface

The Routledge Applied Linguistics series provides a comprehensive guide to a number of key areas in the field of Applied Linguistics. Applied Linguistics is a rich, vibrant, diverse and essentially interdisciplinary field. It is now more important than ever that books in the field provide up-to-date maps of what is an ever-changing territory.

The books in this series are designed to give key insights into core areas of Applied Linguistics. The design of the books ensures, through key readings, that the history and development of a subject are recognized while, through key questions and tasks, integrating understandings of the topics, concepts and practices that make up its essentially interdisciplinary fabric. The pedagogic structure of each book ensures that readers are given opportunities to think, discuss, engage in tasks, draw on their own experience, reflect and research and to read and critically re-read key documents.

Each book has three main sections, each made up of approximately ten units:

A: An **Introduction** section in which the key terms and concepts which map the field of the subject are introduced, including introductory activities and reflective tasks, designed to establish key understandings, terminology, techniques of analysis and the skills appropriate to the theme and the discipline.

B: An **Extension** section in which selected core readings are introduced (usually edited from the original) from existing key books and articles, together with annotations and commentary, where appropriate. Each reading is introduced, annotated and commented on in the context of the whole book, and research or follow-up questions and tasks are added to enable fuller understanding of both theory and practice. In some cases, readings are short and synoptic and incorporated within a more general exposition.

C: An **Exploration** section in which further samples and illustrative materials are provided with an emphasis, where appropriate, on more open-ended, student-centred activities and tasks, designed to support readers and users in undertaking their own locally relevant research projects. Tasks are designed for work in groups or for individuals working on their own. They can be readily included in award courses in Applied Linguistics, or as topics for personal study and research.

The books also usually contain a glossary or glossarial index, which provides a guide to the main terms used in the book, and a detailed, thematically organized further reading section, which lays the ground for further work in the discipline. There are also extensive bibliographies.

The target audience for the series is upper undergraduates and postgraduates on language, applied linguistics and communication studies programmes as well as teachers and researchers in professional development and distance learning programmes. High-quality applied research resources are also much needed for teachers of EFL/ESL and foreign language students at higher education colleges and universities worldwide. The books in the Routledge Applied Linguistics series are aimed at the individual reader, the student in a group and at teachers building courses and seminar programmes.

We hope that the books in this series meet these needs and continue to provide support over many years.

THE EDITORS

Professor Christopher N. Candlin and Professor Ronald Carter are the series editors. Both have extensive experience of publishing titles in the fields relevant to this series. Between them they have written and edited over one hundred books and two hundred academic papers in the broad field of applied linguistics. Chris Candlin was president of AILA (International Association for Applied Linguistics) from 1996 to 2002 and Ron Carter was Chair of BAAL (British Association for Applied Linguistics) from 2003 to 2006.

Professor Christopher N. Candlin
Senior Research Professor
Department of Linguistics
Division of Linguistics and Psychology
Macquarie University
Sydney NSW 2109
Australia

Professor Ronald Carter
School of English Studies
University of Nottingham
Nottingham NG7 2RD
UK

and

Professor of Applied Linguistics
Faculty of Education & Language Studies
The Open University
Walton Hall
Milton Keynes MK7 6AA
UK

Acknowledgements

This book would not have been possible if not for the help of a great many people. We are grateful to our students in our various bilingualism classes, both in Australia and in Singapore, who provided us with insights, suggestions and most of all, the impetus to write this book. We are also indebted to the many colleagues and friends who have shared with us their thoughts and experiences on the topics of bilingualism, as well as the challenges of writing a book.

In particular, we would like to express our gratitude to Michael Clyne, Madalena Cruz-Ferreira and Ben Buckland who read and commented extensively on the final draft and gave so generously of their time and effort. Their comments helped us sharpen our focus and clarified many ideas and we can't thank them enough. Naturally, any shortcomings are our responsibility alone.

Finally we would both like to thank our families who patiently provided encouragement and support during the writing process.

We are also grateful to the copyright holders of the following texts for permission to reproduce extracts in Section B:

Charlotte Hoffmann, *An introduction to bilingualism*, pp. 16–17. Pearson Education Limited, 1991, Copyright © Longman. Reproduced with permission.
William Mackey, 'The description of bilingualism', *Canadian Journal of Linguistics/ Revue canadienne de linguistique*, 7 (2), pp. 51–85. Reproduced with permission.
From T.I. Saenz and M.B. Huer, 'Testing strategies involving least biased language assessment of bilingual children', 2003, *Communications Disorders Quarterly*, 24 (4), pp. 184–193. Copyright © 2003 by PRO-ED, Inc. Reprinted with permission.
Ellen Bialystock, *Bilingualism and Development*, 2001, pp. 10–20, copyright © Cambridge University Press, reprinted with permission of the author and publisher.
Jim Cummins, *Language, power and pedagogy*, 2000, pp. 66–71, Multilingual Matters. Reproduced with permission.
Elena Nicoladis and Fred Genesee, 'Parental discourse and code-mixing in bilingual children', *International Journal of Bilingualism* 2 (1) (1998), pp. 85–99. Kingston Press Ltd. Reproduced with permission.
Margaret Deuchar and Suzanne Quay, 'Language choice in the earliest utterances',

Journal of Child Language, 26 (1999), copyright © Cambridge University Press, reprinted with permission of the authors and publisher.

C.E. Johnson and P. Lancaster, 'The development of more than one phonology', *International Journal of Bilingualism* 2 (1) (1998), pp. 265–300. Kingston Press Ltd. Reproduced with permission.

Ellen Bialystok, 'Metalinguistic aspects of bilingual processing', *Review of Applied Linguistics,* 20 (2001), copyright © Cambridge University Press, reprinted with permission of the author and publisher.

Machiko Tomiyama, 'Child second language attrition', *Applied Linguistics,* 2000, 21 (3), pp. 304–332, by permission of Oxford University Press and the author.

Kees de Bot and Saskia Stoessel, 'In search of yesterday's words', *Applied Linguistics,* 2000, 21 (3), pp. 333–353, by permission of Oxford University Press and the authors.

M. Swain and S. Lapkin, 'The evolving sociopolitical context of immersion education in Canada: some implications for program development', *International Journal of Applied Linguistics,* 15 (2), pp. 169–186, 2005, Blackwell Publishing. Reproduced with permission.

R. Aarts and L. Verhoeven, 'Literacy attainment in a second language submersion context', *Applied Psycholinguistics,* 20 (3), 1999, copyright © Cambridge University Press, reprinted with permission of the authors and publisher.

Reprinted from F. Genesee and R. Bourhis, 'Evaluative reactions to language choice strategies: the role of sociostructural factors', *Language and Communication,* 8: 229–233. Copyright 1988, with permission of Elsevier.

Jean Mills, 'Being bilingual: perspectives of third generation Asian children on language, culture and identity', *International Journal of Bilingual Education and Bilingualism,* 4 (6), pp. 396–399, Multilingual Matters. Reproduced with permission.

How to use this book

The main purpose of this book is to introduce readers to key concepts and research in focal areas of studies in bilingualism. Throughout the book, the term 'bilingualism' will be used to include multilingualism. Wherever possible, we have focused on both psychological and sociological explanations of bilingualism. Although it has not been possible to include all facets of the myriad of issues related to bilingualism, we have identified seven main areas which we believe are good departure points for readers interested in this area of study.

As with all the books in the Routledge Applied Linguistics series, this book consists of three sections: Introduction, Extension and Exploration. The Introduction section (Section A) introduces the key concepts central to each topic and develops the reader's understanding of the field by explaining and synthesizing main debates put forward by various researchers. We attend to this by focusing on the analysis of the methodologies and interpretations of the data and research. We believe that careful understanding of the research is necessary before readers can make informed judgements about the research conclusions reached. Throughout this section, we also include reflective tasks and activities which encourage readers to participate actively in forming opinions about the conceptual definitions introduced.

In the Extension section (Section B), we provide readings for each topic. These readings are either seminal papers which shaped the field or readings which clarify a critical idea discussed in Section A. We first present a précis of each reading, contextualizing its significance for the specific topic. In our discussion, we pay attention to the methodology adopted by the researchers and guide readers to draw their own interpretation of the data and discussion. The readings in Section B allow readers to have a guided approach to a more in-depth discussion of each topic and expose them to the research work of significant researchers in the field of bilingualism. The main purpose of this section is to create an awareness of the research process and an understanding of how that is related to the research product.

The Exploration Section (Section C) contains a series of research activities which range from guided exploratory tasks to tasks which require more independent research skills. The tasks are set at different levels of challenge so that readers can gain confidence by attempting the easier and more guided tasks before attempting tasks which require them to develop their own research designs. Generally, the activities in this section require readers to participate actively in research by gathering data on their own. Readers will have a chance to undertake studies which involve different types of data collection (questionnaires, naturalistic, observational, experimental). Guidance on conducting research and data collection is provided throughout.

The target audience for this book is upper undergraduate students who already have some basic understanding of linguistics, and postgraduate students and healthcare professionals who would like to have a better understanding of bilingualism. This book is particularly useful for researchers who need to have a better understanding of research methodology and how this relates to theory building. Bilingualism is a global phenomenon, and consequently we have drawn the case studies which exemplify our discussion from all over the world. Naturally, we are unable to include all the interesting bilingual experiences and research that have been documented. If there are specific reports we have omitted which you feel are critical to our discussion, please write to us and we'll try to include your suggestions or comments on the companion website to the book.

SECTION A
Introduction

Unit A1
Describing bilingualism

What is bilingualism?

What level of competence must you achieve in both languages to qualify as a bilingual?

How do different experiences in acquiring bilingualism affect the degree of bilingualism?

Can there be a single definition of bilingualism?

An often-quoted answer to the question 'What is bilingualism?' is Baetens Beardsmore's comment that 'bilingualism as a term has open-ended semantics' (1982: 1). In other words, the term 'bilingualism' may mean different things to different people as there is no one definition of bilingualism. For the average speaker, bilingualism can be loosely defined as the use of two languages or the native-like control of two languages. The first definition highlights the use of two languages as a key criterion, which may well include speakers who only have rudimentary formulaic expressions, e.g. *greetings*, in the second language. In stark contrast, the second definition imposes a stringent requirement in terms of language proficiency. As is evident, each definition represents a position at different ends of the proficiency continuum even though, in reality, most bilinguals probably fall somewhere in the middle of this continuum. Moreover, often what we read in the literature about how bilinguals should be defined are views of experts which may not reflect the views of speakers themselves.

Though the discussion of how bilingualism should be defined has often centred on the issue of language competence, this focus overlooks other socio-cultural and cognitive factors which are just as relevant when discussing the performance of bilinguals. Hence, the aim of this first unit is to show that bilinguals are part of a wider socio-cultural milieu, and any description of bilingualism needs to account for how bilinguals utilize and interact with the resources in the community. We will show that the impact of social, psychological and cultural variables on the bilingual individual is ultimately central to the experience of being bilingual, and that an understanding of these factors underpins all questions raised in this area of study.

This unit will not attempt to provide an exhaustive definition of bilingualism, as this is widely covered elsewhere (see, for example, Hornby 1979; Skutnabb-Kangas

1981; Baetens Beardsmore 1982; Romaine 1995; Hoffmann 1991; Baker 2006). Instead, the aim is to equip readers with the necessary skills and insight to assess and interpret research drawn from bilingual populations. In order to achieve this, we will first examine how the bilingual experience has been chronicled and examined by various researchers. We will also look at how some factors may exert an influence over our perceptions of bilinguals and how they function. In the course of the discussion, key issues surrounding the description of bilingualism will be highlighted with a view to providing some guidelines which will be useful in engaging with debate and research into bilingualism.

★ Task A1.1

Think about yourself or someone you know who is bilingual:

➤ How did this person become bilingual?

➤ What is this person's proficiency in both languages?

➤ When and where does this person use both languages?

Compare your answer with that of another person in your class:

➤ Can you draw any conclusions about the difficulties which you might encounter if you were asked to provide a single definition of bilingualism?

Consider whether you think someone is bilingual if:

➤ they have a slight non-native accent in one or both languages;

➤ they make occasional errors of syntax in one or both languages;

➤ they do not always know the right words to use in one language;

➤ they may speak both languages fluently but are culturally at ease only in one language.

The topic of how bilingualism can be defined tends to receive universal attention in studies of bilingualism because an understanding of bilingualism in its social, psychological and cultural contexts is an essential initial step before research in this area can be interpreted. This unit is organized around five main issues which are important variables in relation to bilingualism:

■ descriptors which refer to the degree of bilingualism
■ descriptors which refer to the context of bilingual language acquisition
■ descriptors which refer to age of acquisition
■ descriptors which refer to the domain of use
■ descriptors which refer to social orientation.

The first set of descriptors refers to the ways in which we may describe bilingual proficiency. Next, we examine the variables which impact on the contexts in which bilingual acquisition can take place. The third point relates to the age at which the languages are acquired and the possible consequences of this on the degree of bilingualism attained. The fourth issue concerns ways in which we can describe the domains of use of both the bilingual's languages – that is, the circumstances in which the languages are used. Finally, we will discuss how the wider social orientation is also relevant to our understanding of how bilinguals function.

DESCRIPTORS WHICH REFER TO THE DEGREE OF BILINGUALISM

At the heart of the description of bilingualism is the issue of degree of bilingualism. Simply put, *degree of bilingualism* refers to the levels of linguistic proficiency a bilingual must achieve in both languages to be considered a bilingual. Is a bilingual someone who functions like two monolinguals? Or is a bilingual someone who needs only minimal proficiency in one or both languages? These are the views of lay people and they echo the views expressed by experts in the fields, such as Bloomfield (1933), Haugen (1953), Mackey (1962) and Weinreich (1953). Like the general public, experts differ among themselves on this issue, and in many ways the disparities between their views have been seminal in spawning an active debate on how bilingualism should be defined. Let's first look at how bilingualism is conceptualized by specialists in the field.

Bloomfield (1933: 55) defined bilingualism as 'native-like control of two languages', while, in contrast, Mackey (1962: 52) defined bilingualism as 'the ability to use more than one language'. In a similar vein to Mackey, Weinreich (1953) defined bilingualism as 'the practice of alternately using two languages' while Haugen (1953: 7) proposed 'the point where a speaker can first produce complete meaningful utterances in the other language' to be a starting point for defining bilingualism. As can be seen, these definitions range from Bloomfield's rigorous expectations of totally balanced bilingualism to Mackey's, and Weinreich's and Haugen's looser requirements of mere ability or the practice of using two languages. Baetens Beardsmore (1982) described these two extremes as minimalist (Mackey, Weinreich) and maximalist (Bloomfield) in approach. Haugen's view could also be considered minimalist, including as it does the qualification that the utterances have to be 'complete' and 'meaningful' – in other words, the definition will admit someone who is fluent enough to order dinner in a restaurant.

On the other hand, the maximalist approach describes the ideal bilingual who will find no match in reality. If we examine the experience of bilinguals around us, we quickly realize that bilinguals do not, and cannot, function like two monolinguals. In fact, their degree of competence in both languages is greatly influenced by the way each language is used, and this differs greatly from individual to individual.

Moreover, how do we decide who is the ideal representative of a native speaker in each language? This point has become increasingly contentious and will be further discussed in Unit A2.

The maximalist approach is equally unsatisfactory because it fails to make a distinction between those who have only minimal communicative ability in a second language and those who use the language actively in their daily lives in a large range of settings. How, then, can we measure degree of bilingualism?

Macnamara (1969) emphasized the need to discuss the degree of bilingualism not as a unitary component but as degree of competence in sub-components. The sub-components are the four macro skills (speaking, writing, reading and listening). In this schema, competence in bilingualism is seen as a continuum with individuals showing varying degrees of competence in each of the macro skills. A discussion of how this competence can be measured, a critical issue in bilingual studies, will be explored in more detail in Unit A2. Meanwhile, it is important to examine bilingual abilities in various skill contexts and to discuss varying degrees of bilingualism rather than trying to pinpoint a specific level of bilingualism that qualifies one as being bilingual.

 Task A1.2

Rate the competence of your own language(s) in each of the four macro skills: listening, speaking, reading and writing. Use a five-point rating scale (1 = weak, 5 = excellent).

➤ What are some of the factors which impact on your rating?

➤ For each of the macro skills, consider how your rating may change when you are performing different tasks (e.g. reading a book versus reading a newspaper, ordering at a restaurant or making a presentation to your class).

Several terms such as *balanced bilinguals, dominant bilinguals, recessive bilinguals* and *semilinguals* have been used to categorize bilinguals according to the perceived degree of proficiency they have in both languages. As these terms are commonly used, we will review them in the next few sections.

Balanced bilinguals

The term *balanced bilingual* was first used by Lambert et al. (1959) in Canada to describe individuals who are fully competent in both languages. In most instances, when the term balanced bilingual is used, it describes those who are thought to have perfect control of both languages in all settings. Though it is possible to come across bilinguals who are highly proficient in both languages, Baetens Beardsmore (1982) argued that balanced bilingualism is close to impossible to achieve, and is therefore very rare. Even high-level conference interpreters tend to have a preference for one of their languages, and will often specialize in interpreting into their dominant language despite the fact that they are highly fluent in both languages.

Fishman (1972) went further, arguing that bilinguals are rarely equally fluent in both languages in all topics. He argued that sociolinguistic forces demand that bilinguals organize their languages in functionally complementary spheres. For example, a German–French bilingual may be able to speak both languages fluently, but is likely to use German exclusively in certain situations or when discussing specific topics. Fishman emphasized that it is this complementary nature of language functions that assures the continued existence of bilingualism, because any society which produces bilinguals who use both languages with equal competence in all contexts will stop being bilingual, as no society needs two languages to perform the same set of functions. In other words, balanced bilingualism necessarily entails the death of bilingualism.

Dominant bilinguals

The term *dominant bilingual* refers to bilinguals who are dominant in one language. In the context of discussing dominant bilinguals, researchers will often refer to their less dominant language as the *subordinate language*. However, one important criterion to note is that the term 'dominance' may not apply to all domains. So, someone who is dominant in French may not exhibit this dominance in all areas. For example, a French–German computer scientist may speak French most of time except when he is discussing computer science-related topics as he did his training in computer science in German. In cases where specialist jargon (medicine, sports) is required, speakers may consciously choose to speak in the language they normally use when discussing these kinds of topics. For example, an Italian–German teacher may be fluent in both Italian and German, but always discusses soccer in Italian as he mainly plays soccer with his Italian-speaking friends and talks 'soccer' in Italian and not in German. Similarly, a Chinese engineer who was trained in London may prefer to discuss engineering research in English despite the fact that her mother tongue is Mandarin Chinese.

Passive or recessive bilinguals

The term *passive* or *recessive bilinguals* refers to bilinguals who are gradually losing competence in one language, usually because of disuse. As the term 'recessive' seems to have negative connotations, we will use the term 'passive bilinguals' to describe this group of bilinguals. For example, a Dutch migrant in Australia may find himself isolated from the Dutch-speaking community as his daily encounters are with English-speaking Australians (see Clyne 1991). Over time, his proficiency level in Dutch may deteriorate owing to the long period of non-use. As we will see in Unit 5, periods of non-use can have various effects on bilingual competence.

In bilingual communities which are undergoing a shift from one language to another (usually from the home language to the dominant language in the society), it is not uncommon to come across bilinguals who can only understand, but cannot speak, the other language. So, in the Australian context, many older Italians still speak Italian, or an Italian dialect, to their children and grandchildren. However, these second- (children) or third- (grandchildren) generation Italians may reply to their parents or grandparents in English. This is because Italian is gradually being replaced by English for the second- and third-generation Italians (Cavallaro 1998; Bettoni 1985) who are living in an English-speaking community, and being educated in English. Thus, this group of children grows up with an increasingly passive understanding of Italian and often does not use the language actively at all. In such contexts, passive bilingualism, the ability to understand but not produce meaningful utterances, is often contrasted with *active bilingualism*, the productive use of both languages.

Semilinguals, or limited bilinguals

The issue of bilinguals who appear to have limited level of proficiency in both first and second language has dominated some discussions on the issue of degree of bilingualism. The term *semilingualism* was first used by Hansegard in 1968 (cited in Baker 2006: 9) to refer to Finnish-minority students in Sweden who lack proficiency in both their languages. Hansegard described semilingualism in terms of deficit in six language competences:

- size of vocabulary
- correctness of language
- unconscious processing of language (automatism)
- language creation (neologization)
- mastery of the functions of language (e.g. emotive, cognitive)
- meanings and imagery.

According to these parameters, a semilingual is both quantitatively and qualitatively deficient in comparison to monolinguals, and semilingualism has been blamed for the low academic achievement of minority children. Over the years, the term has accumulated pejorative connotations, and researchers who invoked the use of this concept have been widely rebutted (cf. Baetens Beardsmore 1982; Edelsky et al. 1983; Genesee 1984; Spolsky 1984; Baker 2006) for ignoring the socio-political concerns implicit in the existence of semilinguals. These authors argued that semilingualism is rooted in an environment which is not conducive to ongoing bilingualism, where the speakers were socially, politically and economically disadvantaged. Therefore, semilingualism is a situation which is engineered by the environment and not a consequence of bilingualism since a monolingual in the same environment would have faced the same degree of struggle in their academic endeavours. Researchers who highlight the correlation of semilingualism to poor academic achievement without carefully separating the symptoms from the cause only serve to perpetuate the negative stereotype of minority children. Equally critical is how this perception translates into educational policies and curriculum for minority children.

Though the term semilingualism is no longer fashionable, the idea of low-achieving bilinguals who are linguistically competent neither in the first language nor in the second language is still discussed, albeit under a different label. Cummins (1994) acknowledges that labelling someone as a 'semilingual' is highly negative and may be detrimental to children's learning, and proposes an alternative label, 'limited bilingualism', to describe the same condition.

More recently, MacSwan (2000) has criticized further the concept of semilingualism and limited bilingualism. Questioning Cummins's position on defining school-based literacy and academic skills as a component of general language proficiency, MacSwan examined all the evidence put forth for the case of semilingualism and concluded that semilingualism is more a function of socio-economic status (SES) than of language background. In general, MacSwan cautioned against hasty use of labels which do more harm than good for those language learners who are already socially disadvantaged. Baker (2006: 10) sums it up well:

> Rather than highlight the apparent 'deficit' in language development, the more positive approach is to emphasize that, when suitable conditions are provided, languages are easily capable of evolution beyond the 'semi' state.

Though SES is not a trait which is inherently linked to bilinguals, the well-documented interaction between ethnicity and SES is something which we cannot ignore. Studies which carefully control the SES variable have shown that minority children of higher SES do well academically with or without education in their mother tongue (Krashen 1996). In contrast, minority children from lower SES compared unfavourably with mainstream children without language support in their mother tongue. Overall, researchers have shown that the strongest predictor of academic achievement is the number of years of education that the children have received in their first language (see, for example, Krashen 1996; Thomas and Collier 1997). We will return to the issue of how bilinguals are educated in Unit A6 but, in the meantime, it is important to note that external pressures like SES have a significant bearing on the performance and perception of bilinguals. It is for this reason that some bilingual researchers such as Hakuta (1987) carefully control the SES variable in their research on bilinguals. Conversely, in Unit A4, we see that poorly defined bilingual samples led Welsh–English bilinguals from a lower SES to be compared unfavourably to English monolinguals from a higher SES in Saer (1923), a paper which was influential in the thinking on bilinguals for many decades. The unfortunate outcome of such comparisons is that policy-makers often rely on such findings to rationalize programmes which put minority children at a disadvantage.

Task A1.3

➤ Think of bilinguals you know in your community. Are they balanced or dominant or passive? If you have put them in one of the above categories, think about whether this is the case in all domains of activity. What are some of the reasons which influenced your decisions? What are some problems you encountered during your decision-making process?

DESCRIPTORS WHICH REFER TO THE CONTEXT OF BILINGUAL LANGUAGE ACQUISITION

Although bilinguals share the common experience of using more than one language in their lives, the ways in which they acquire their languages vary. Put any number of bilinguals together and the chances are there will not be a perfect match in any of their bilingual experiences. Some will have acquired both languages at home, some through school or university, others through their working environment, or through travel to, or residence in, a foreign country. Within each of these domains (home, school or university, work), there will be further differences. In the home domain, there are a multitude of factors which may impact on the degree of bilingualism which is acquired, including the age at which the language is acquired, the way in which the language is used, to whom the language is used and the frequency with which the language is used. In school and work contexts, similar variables will apply. As can be seen, once the various factors are combined, the permutations are open-ended. In discussing or studying bilinguals, we need to assume that no bilinguals have the same experience even though their profiles may be similar. In this section, we will look at some common parameters used to differentiate the contexts in which bilinguals acquire their languages.

In your readings, you may come across researchers who make the distinctions between *primary contexts* and *secondary contexts*. When used, primary contexts refer to situations where a child acquires both languages in a naturalistic setting without any structured instruction, while secondary contexts refer to the situation when a child acquires one of the languages in a structured setting, usually school. This creates a clear division where one language is acquired in a naturalistic setting and the other is acquired in a formal setting, usually a classroom. This distinction is sometimes referred to as *natural bilingualism* versus *school bilingualism* (Skutnabb-Kangas 1981).

Children who acquire both languages in a primary context acquire the languages as a result of natural input in the environment. This input is usually provided by caregivers, often the parents and/or siblings, when the child is an infant, but as the child enters early childhood, the input can also come from other sources, such as the extended family and the wider community. As we will see in Unit A3, there are many detailed reports on children being raised in bilingual situations like this – often where one parent speaks one language and the other speaks another.

Within the primary context, a further distinction is made between *naturalistic fused* and *naturalistic separate*. In a *naturalistic fused setting*, there is no separation of context for both languages, and the child is exposed to both languages in the same context. So, for example, a Mandarin–English bilingual child may receive input in both languages from each parent, siblings or peers. In such situations, both languages are used by the same speaker. In contrast, a bilingual in a *naturalistic separate* context may hear and use Mandarin only with one parent and English with the other parent. In this context, one language is associated with a specific parent. This latter model is commonly referred to as the one-parent, one-language model. Apart from parents, it is also common for the separation to be made according to other interlocutors such as siblings, peers and grandparents. So, in Singapore, a trilingual child may speak Mandarin to the parents, English to the siblings and Hokkien to the grandparents. More rarely, the physical environment is different, as in the case reported by Ginsberg (1996), where the child spoke to the parents in Spanish exclusively in the home, but in English outside the home; this system of separation was rigidly maintained throughout the child's life. In this case, the child learned to use the physical environment as a cue to switch between the two languages with the same interlocutors.

It is often assumed that language input in the pre-school years takes place in a naturalistic environment. While this is true for most bilinguals, for a large proportion of bilingual children in Asia, for example Singapore, Malaysia and Hong Kong, structured language-focused teaching may begin when the child is as young as two. In Singapore, a child may speak both Mandarin Chinese and English without any formal teaching at birth, but once they start attending childcare, which can be as early as two years of age, it is common for childcare centres to provide structured teaching in both languages. So, in such cases, the distinction between primary and secondary contexts may not be as clear-cut as in other settings.

The issue of primary and secondary contexts is important especially in the study of the language development in bilinguals as there is some debate about whether one context is more beneficial in promoting the desired outcome in the language development of bilinguals. In Unit A3, we will explore the impact of these differences on the language development of bilinguals.

Task A1.4

➤ Do you think we can make a clear distinction between primary and secondary contexts? Can you think of situations when this distinction will be difficult to make? Why do you think researchers make a distinction between these two contexts? (Think about how the two contexts can influence learning behaviour and language use.)

Another distinction made is the difference between *elective bilinguals* and *circumstantial bilinguals*, a distinction proposed by Valdes and Figueroa (1994). Though these terms are not widely used, we feel that they provide a very useful distinction when we are considering different bilingual populations. Essentially, the distinguishing feature is one of volition or choice as some bilinguals actively choose to be bilingual but some just find themselves in a situation where they have no choice but to be bilingual. Elective bilinguals are bilinguals who have some element of choice about learning a second language. This may include children who choose to acquire an additional language in a school setting or someone who learns a new language because their partner speaks a different language. Circumstantial bilinguals, on the other hand, are groups who have no choice when it comes to learning a second language. This may include indigenous groups which have been colonized or groups whose first language is different from the dominant and more prestigious language of the surrounding community. The concept of elective bilinguals and circumstantial bilinguals is particularly critical in the contexts of how bilinguals are measured and therefore is a distinction which we will return to in more detail in Unit A2.

DESCRIPTORS WHICH REFER TO AGE OF ACQUISITION

Age has often been raised as an important descriptor for bilingualism because of the robust research on the relationship between age and language proficiency at various linguistic levels (e.g. Johnson and Newport 1989; Long 1990). Although exceptions and counterarguments have been reported (see Birdsong 1992; Bialystok 1997a; Clark 2003), the bulk of the evidence points towards the advantage of early acquisition for ultimate language attainment. While this is true in general, it appears to be especially the case for phonology, where reports have shown that children who acquired the second language before six years of age were able to achieve native-like competence. On the other hand, mature learners were able to acquire the target language at a much faster rate (Long 1990).

Hence, critical to any discussion of bilingualism is the issue of age as there appears to be what we might call a sensitive age for language learning, which ceases around puberty. The sensitive age is a reformulation of Lennenberg's (1967) critical period hypothesis, which argues that we have a superior language learning capacity early in life which will disappear or decline with maturation. However, the evidence is not totally conclusive as other researchers (see, for example, Birdsong 1992) have shown that native-like acquisition is possible in speakers who were exposed to French after fifteen years of age. In a later study, Birdsong and Molis (2001) found that four of their participants who arrived in the United States after the age of seventeen were indistinguishable in their performance when compared to native speakers. Therefore, the exact age in which the sensitive period operates is controversial, with Birdsong (2005) arguing that there is no clear cut-off point in terms of age at which native-like proficiency cannot be attained.

Age is considered an important factor because there is a strong association between age of acquisition and ultimate attainment of proficiency. Generally, supporters of the sensitive age hypothesis (e.g. Newport 1990) argue that younger children can apply heuristic strategies which are more efficient than adult learners'. However, other researchers (e.g. Bialystok 1997a; Clark 2003) have cautioned that we should not look only at neurological factors when analysing language learning outcomes. In adult learners, other factors such as aptitude, attitude, identity and motivation can significantly affect the learning outcome. Attitudes and motivation, in particular, have been found to impact strongly on the final achievement of the learners' proficiency level (e.g. Gardner 2001; Dörnyei and Clément 2001; Masgoret and Gardner 2003). Apart from attitude, contextual factors such as exposure are also important. In Birdsong and Molis (2001), the amount of English used by their participants at the time of study was a strong indicator of their performance in English.

Another factor we need to bear in mind is that many of the findings in support of the sensitive period hinge on the fact that we have a stable notion of what is a native speaker. In the studies mentioned above, participants were often asked to assess the *nativeness* of a learner's speech or a sample of a learner's writing. With many languages, the issue of what constitutes *native-speakerness* has become more complex with increasing globalization. Many researchers (e.g. Kachru 1987) discuss the difficulties of identifying who native speakers are with the creation of local identities and increasing diversity.

As pointed out by Davies (1991a), the issue of native-speakerness is entwined with identification and social affiliation. Therefore, commonly held assumptions about native speakers have been increasingly challenged at various levels.

Task A1.5

➤ Think about your competence in the four macro skills (speaking, writing, listening, reading) of your native language. Are you equally competent in all four skills? Are there some aspects of writing (e.g. academic writing) which you think may not be as strong as your spoken skills? What would be considered to be 'native-like' proficiency for a learner of English? Generally, what levels of competence do you expect native speakers to have?

➤ It may be useful to consider how you rule someone out as a native speaker. What standards or norms do you use in your assessment? (Which group of native speakers do you have in mind?) Consider the case of someone who is brought up in India and who speaks English as a first language. Would this person be considered a native speaker of English?

Against this backdrop, as we can see, age is a key consideration when discussing or assessing bilinguals and the usual distinction made is between *early bilinguals* and *late bilinguals*. Early bilinguals are those who are exposed to both languages before adolescence and late bilinguals are those who acquire the second language after adolescence. Some researchers also make the distinction between infant bilingualism and early bilingualism (e.g. McLaughlin 1984, 1985), though this distinction is not commonly used.

Apart from its relevance to researchers, the issue of age is important as it can be used to rationalize educational policies and curriculum planning, an issue which we will return to in Unit A6. For example, administrators often ask the questions 'At what age should we introduce the learning of a new language?' or 'Is it futile to introduce language learning at secondary levels?' In addition, understanding how the age factor affects bilinguals may help us to frame expectations of language-learning outcomes in more realistic terms.

DESCRIPTORS WHICH REFER TO DOMAIN OF USE

In answer to the question 'Are you a bilingual?' a bilingual might commonly respond, 'Yes, I speak Greek at home and with my relatives but I generally use English the rest of the time'. Implicit in this response is the notion that languages assume different roles in different settings. This demarcation of functions, more commonly known as *domains*, is central to any discussion of bilingualism. The term 'domain' was first used by Fishman (1972) to describe how speakers compartmentalize their language use. Very simply, domains refer to the different spheres of influence in speakers' lives and for language; Fishman identified family, friendship, religion, education and employment as the main domains. These domains often determine the variety of language as well as the style of language use. However, topic is another factor which can often override the influence of domain. Hoffmann (1991) summarized the most critical domains as the person, place and topic. However, as we will see in Unit B1, these three broad domains can be further refined to capture language behaviour and use accurately.

It is a well-documented sociolinguistic phenomenon that *interlocutors*, or the persons we are speaking to or communicating with, will affect not only our stylistic choice of language but also our language options. Most of the time, bilinguals have a 'special' language relationship with people in their immediate circle. With some people, they predominantly use Language A and with others they may use Language B. For example, one Lebanese–English bilingual may always speak Lebanese to family members and relatives but use English with anyone outside the circle. Another bilingual may use only Lebanese with older relatives and English with younger relatives. However, this same bilingual will use Lebanese with older Lebanese-speaking strangers. A language relationship tends to evolve quite naturally, and often, once a language pattern is set, it is usually not easy to alter this pattern.

Place or *location* can also have a strong impact on language choice. Most multilingual communities have a default language which is used at work, and this home–work dichotomy is a very common one. For example, though most speakers in Singapore are bilingual, the default language for the professional workplace and school is

English and, hence, English is currently the lingua franca in these two domains in Singapore. However, sometimes the *interlocutor*, or person, effect may intersect with the *location* or *place* effect to temporarily disrupt the pervasive use of English. So, although the language commonly in use in the public service sector is English, the service staff serving an elderly Malay woman may switch to Malay if they can speak Malay and their client is unable to speak English.

Apart from work, the physical location itself may give rise to the use of different languages. In Singapore, the language used in Orchard Road, the ritzy side of town frequented by tourists, is often English while the default language for the 'heartland' (residential areas for the majority of Singaporeans) is often Mandarin among the Chinese-speaking majority (which comprises 75 per cent of the population). In the city centre, shop assistants and receptionists will often initiate conversation in English, possibly because the ability to speak English is one of the requisite criteria to work in these establishments. However, in the suburbs, store holders may be middle-aged or elderly Singaporeans who were born before bilingualism in English became the norm. Hence, the situation in the suburbs is highly constrained by the language repertoire of the interlocutors, and a shopkeeper in this context may speak Mandarin or Hokkien to a Chinese customer and English to a Malay or Indian customer. If English is not an available option for the shopkeeper, *patois Melayu* (pidgin Malay) is often used (Li and Milroy 2003).

Topic is another key factor that affects language choice. For many bilinguals, one language receives more structured instruction than the other. For example, a Turkish–English migrant in Australia may speak Turkish with family members all the time while in the home, but have a larger vocabulary and greater expressiveness in English because of the extended time spent studying English in school and university. The increased exposure to English in both written and spoken contexts means that English can be used for a bigger array of topics both technical and non-technical. However, when it comes to discussing topics such as cooking or gardening, the same Turkish–English bilinguals may be more at home using Turkish as conversations about such topics are usually in Turkish. This type of topic specialization when it comes to language choice is, again, extremely common for bilinguals.

Task A1.6

➤ Consider the case of a Korean–English bilingual living in London. If the normal language for interaction at home is Korean, what are some factors which may influence the family members to switch to the use of English within the home context?

DESCRIPTIONS WHICH REFER TO SOCIAL ORIENTATION

The attitudes of bilinguals to their bilingual status, as well as the attitudes of the wider community, are also factors which contribute to our understanding of bilingualism. The relationship between attitude, identity, motivation and individual bilingualism will be discussed in detail in Unit A7. In this section, our focus is on how influences within the society can impact on how bilinguals perceive themselves and how bilinguals are perceived.

To understand this fully, we first have to make a distinction between bilinguals in a bilingual or monolingual context and bilinguals in a multilingual context. We also need to recognize the difference between bilingual contexts which receive high levels of infrastructure and administrative support in terms of funding and recognition, and bilingual contexts which receive minimal support of this kind.

Many bilinguals live in places where the home language is different from the language spoken outside the home, and this is common in countries such as the United States, Australia and Britain. In this context, bilingual children generally receive little or no school support for their home language and, more often than not, going to school entails learning the language of the wider community. In Australia, bilingual children do receive some official support for their home language as up to 47 languages are accredited for the end of high school examination and they can receive instruction in a government School of Languages on Saturdays (Clyne 2005). However, in reality the logistic difficulty of incorporating the home languages in the school curriculum of these minority children means that, on an individual level, language maintenance is relegated to something that is pursued outside the school contexts. In the literature, this situation is often perceived as one of *subtractive bilingualism* as learning a new language may mean losing competence in the first language (Lambert 1974). In other instances, subtractive bilingualism has been narrowly defined as the replacement of the first language by the second language (Cummins 1976: 20). Cummins further argued that many bilinguals in subtractive bilingual learning situations may not develop native-like competence in either of their two languages. However, many bilinguals are able to 'successfully' replace their first language and become highly proficient in the newly adopted language. Though this is achieved at the expense of the mother tongue, the success of such bilinguals is clear evidence that subtractive bilingualism does not necessarily result in limited bilingualism (see Krashen 1996; Thomas and Collier 1997).

In view of the negative connotations attached to subtractive bilingualism, a more neutral term like '*differential bilingualism*' may be more appropriate for this phenomenon. Instead of a simple replacement of L1 by L2, differential bilingualism highlights the differential development of the bilingual's first and second language. Without academic support or instructional input, it is natural to expect that the first language cannot develop at the same rate and have the same range of functions as the second language. In many contexts, differential bilingualism also refers to a situation where the two languages spoken by the bilinguals are of unequal status.

In multilingual contexts, as opposed to bilingual contexts, there is the potential for problems of a different nature. Many multilingual communities (e.g. Singapore, Malaysia, Switzerland, Belgium, Canada) have policies which explicitly endorse the use of more than one language in official domains – the most critical being the school. In places like Switzerland and Belgium, multilingualism is based on territorial considerations and this can create conflict. However, the constitution protects the rights of individuals to learn their mother tongue on top of other official languages in the country. In such contexts, the languages spoken by bilinguals are usually visible in the educational domain, though visibility in social domains may be correlated with the status of the language within the community. For example, although Tamil is an official language in Singapore and receives equal support and funding in the school system, its visibility in terms of use and relevance socially is much lower than that of Mandarin. This could be because of the smaller demographic concentration as Tamil speakers make up only 6 per cent of the population. When languages enjoy official patronage, there is an implicit political will to ensure language maintenance in such situations, and there is usually very high instrumental motivation to maintain high degrees of bilingualism as learning an additional language provides a skill which enhances the individual's opportunities in life. This conducive language environment is referred to as *additive* bilingualism where learning a new language is seen as a form of enrichment or an asset widely desired by the community.

Some multilingual societies are so diversified that often certain languages, usually the vernaculars (languages used in informal settings), are sacrificed as bilingual policies promote languages which are not the mother tongue of the speakers. For example, in Tanzania, Swahili and English are official languages despite the fact that the indigenous population may speak a different vernacular (Mkilifi 1978). Similarly in Singapore, Mandarin is taught in schools despite the fact that the home language of many Chinese Singaporeans may be a vernacular such as Hokkien, Teochew or Cantonese. In India, where English and Hindi are both official languages of the central government, English is still the preferred language in the South. This situation presents a more complex picture as, at one level, the official languages are developed in an additive environment but the vernaculars do not receive any official recognition. In Singapore this has led to the gradual disappearance of such vernaculars in Chinese homes (Ng, in press).

Task A1.7

➤ Bilingual children growing up in a monolingual English context often find their home language oddly irrelevant in their lives outside the home. If you were working in the town council of a community with a high percentage of Spanish–English bilinguals, what are some strategies that you could implement within the community to make Spanish more visible and therefore more relevant to the bilingual children's lives?

Summary

We have discussed five variables:

- degree of competence
- context
- age
- domain
- social orientation.

Although these are crucial departure points when thinking about bilingualism, there are many more factors which can influence the bilingual experience. These include self-identity, attitude towards the community, demographic factors and hypothetical mental organization of the two languages. As we work through the literature on bilingualism, we will no doubt come across more variables which will allow us to see bilingualism in a new light. However, we believe that these five variables serve as the basic starting points to frame our enquiries about bilingualism and bilingual research.

We hope that our discussion of these variables has served to show that bilingualism is not a concrete entity that can be quantified or dissected. Though trying to pin down what constitutes bilingualism is a slippery task, this does not mean that the phenomenon defies categorization. We have tried to show that, in place of trying to arrive at a definition of what is bilingualism, it is more productive to describe bilinguals according to the descriptors discussed in this unit. These descriptors help us understand the phenomenon we work with and guide us to frame our queries in the right contexts. Most importantly, it helps us avoid drawing erroneous conclusions that have been based on mistaken premises. The descriptors will help us develop profiles of individual bilinguals as well as the bilingual communities we work in, and this is the critical first step in any bilingualism research.

In subsequent units we will return repeatedly to the issues raised in this unit. These descriptors not only help us understand the phenomenon of bilingualism, but are also at the core of studies of bilingualism.

In Unit B1, we briefly consider a short extract from Hoffmann (1991) describing the variability in the conditions under which people become bilingual. The second extract is from a seminal paper by Mackey (1962) which details the complexities of describing bilingualism.

Unit A2
Measuring bilingualism

What does it mean to know a language?

What does language knowledge consist of, and how do we measure it?

Should a bilingual's two languages be measured against the single language of a monolingual?

How do we measure the language knowledge of native speakers?

As you can probably infer from the discussion of the complex nature of defining bilingualism in Unit A1, the measurement of bilingual language skill is far from simple. We have seen that the range of what can constitute a definition of bilingualism falls anywhere along a continuum from full competence in one language plus limited knowledge of a second, to apparent full competence in all skills in two or more languages. In addition to this, as we saw, we need also to be aware of the importance of identifying the range of variables which impact on bilingual language use – such factors as the age of acquisition, the various domains of language use (which may be different for both languages), and the socio-cultural contexts in which the languages are used.

In this unit, we will begin with a discussion of whose bilingual skills we are measuring. Not everyone comes to bilingualism by the same route, and, as we will see, this has implications for both the kinds of measures we use and how we think about language knowledge. The first group we will consider are those people who for some reason choose to learn another language and thus move towards bilingualism. We will examine the kinds of testing instruments that are used for this group and this will introduce a number of concepts which are central to the understanding of the measurement of language.

Next, we will look at issues in testing linguistic minorities living in situations where their home language is different from that of the wider community. In particular, we will discuss the importance of using appropriate testing instruments both for educational assessments and for the identification of language difficulties (or specific language impairment) in children, and introduce the ways in which bilingualism is measured by researchers. As we will see in more detail in Unit A4, researchers need to assess the bilingualism of individuals in order to further our understanding of the range of effects of bilingualism on individuals. In the next few sections, we will focus in particular on the assessment of children's language since this has been a major area of study.

WHOM ARE WE TESTING?

Tests of all kinds are generally developed for specific populations. Because of the very varied nature of bilingualism and the myriad different ways that people acquire some degree of bilingualism, it is helpful to delineate the circumstances under which we assess the language of people who are bilingual. Very roughly, we can consider classifying bilingual speakers into three different groups:

- developing bilinguals
- stable bilinguals
- attriting bilinguals.

Stable bilinguals are generally people for whom bilingualism is a way of life, and for whom the daily use of two languages is the norm rather than the exception. They may be either *elective* bilinguals or *circumstantial* bilinguals, although they are probably more likely to come from the latter group. They may use both languages in different contexts – for example, they may speak Language A at home and Language B at work, or they may use both languages in a variety of contexts. Alternatively, they may live in a multilingual community where two or more languages are used routinely.

Attriting bilinguals consist of those individuals who are, for some reason, suffering from some aspect of language attrition. This may result from lack of contact and lack of use of one of their languages (and this is often the case with elective bilinguals), or it may be the result of pathological factors either associated with age or as a consequence of some kind of accident. This general area of language attrition will be dealt with in more depth in Unit A5.

For the purposes of this unit, we will concentrate on the issues that surround the measurement of the language of what we term *developing* bilinguals.

 Task A2.1

➤ Drawing on the people you know, try to think of some examples of people who are:

- developing bilinguals
- stable bilinguals
- attriting bilinguals.

➤ Is it possible to be a member of more than one of these groups?

Developing bilinguals

We focus on this group because it is the largest and the most widely assessed group. As we discussed briefly in Unit A1, Valdes and Figueroa (1994) divide this group into two: *elective bilinguals* and *circumstantial bilinguals*. This is a useful division, and one which we will use to structure this unit. Each group has quite different characteristics, as shown in Table A2.1 (adapted from Valdes and Figueroa (1994: 13–14).

Table A2.1 Characteristics and examples of elective and circumstantial bilinguals

Elective bilinguals	Circumstantial bilinguals
Characteristic of individuals	Characteristic of groups
Choose to learn another language	Second language required to meet needs of new circumstances
Communicative opportunities usually sought artificially (e.g. in classroom)	Communicative needs may relate to survival, or success; communicative needs will vary across individuals
First language will usually remain the dominant language	Two languages will play a complementary role and the stronger language may vary depending on the domain
Examples of elective bilinguals	**Examples of circumstantial bilinguals**
A child raised with a French-speaking mother and Italian-speaking father in an English-speaking environment	Children raised in families where two languages are spoken both inside and outside the home
A Japanese student who has learned English in order to study for a Master of Arts degree in Australia	Immigrant groups who have moved to a country where another language is spoken
An American man who learns Russian because he has married a Russian woman and moved to Russia	Indigenous groups living in countries which have been colonized
A diplomat who learns Mandarin Chinese for her job	Groups whose first language is different from the prestige language of the surrounding community. (A prestige language is one which has higher status in the community than other languages spoken, usually because it is the language of education and government.)

As we saw in Unit A1, the major difference between elective bilinguals and circumstantial bilinguals is that, for the former, there is generally some element of choice about learning a second language, while the latter are obliged to learn another language as a result of the circumstances in which they find themselves. Although these circumstances may be chosen, as in the case of choosing to emigrate to another country, they are frequently not a result of choice – for example, people forced to flee their country of origin as a result of war or famine, or indigenous people in countries whose language is not used as a result of colonization.

The implications for the assessment of bilingualism turn out, in fact, to be quite different for these two different groups. While these two groups will be used to structure our discussion of bilingual assessment, it is important to point out that although this distinction is a useful one as a framework for the discussion of bilingual assessment, it is not necessarily as clear-cut as Table 2.1 above implies.

Task A2.2

➤ Try to think of some examples of people who are 'elective' bilinguals and people who are 'circumstantial' bilinguals.

➤ Can an individual move from one group to the other?

➤ Can you be a member of both groups at the same time? How? Try to give an example of a person who would be considered to be both an elective bilingual and a circumstantial bilingual (assuming that this person is at least trilingual!).

➤ Would you yourself qualify for membership of one of the groups? Which one?

Assessing bilingual proficiency

The assessment of bilingual language proficiency is difficult in part because we are immediately confronted with the question of 'what is a bilingual', or, as Bialystok (2001a: 10) puts it, '*When is enough enough?*':

> The problem of knowing who is bilingual conceals a more basic question: how much is enough? Who among us does not know pieces of some other language – words or phrases, perhaps a rule or two, and some social routines for greeting, toasting drinks, or asking directions? These fragments hardly count as competence in the language, but how much more is required before some implicit threshold is reached? Accepting the standard assumption that no bilingual is ever equally competent in both languages, how much language is needed before we agree that a person is bilingual?

> The answer depends on how we define language proficiency. We talk about language as though it had concrete existence and could be measured by scientific instruments. We describe the acquisition of language as though we move irrevocably from a state of innocence to one of mastery along a predictable path. We identify language impairment, language delay, and language precocity without ever specifying the standard against which these

cases are to be judged. We use 'language' in research designs as both a dependent and an independent variable, choosing fragments to serve as stimuli but concluding truths that define the domain. But what is the norm for language competence? What do we mean by language proficiency? What are its components and what is the range of acceptable variation? Although these questions may seem to be prior to any use of language as a research instrument or conclusion about language ability in individuals, they rarely if ever are explicitly addressed.

What constitutes language proficiency is a difficult question. When we want to measure the language of bilinguals, we are often (though not always) concerned not only with measuring one language but with measuring both languages, and with measuring the interrelationships between these two languages. These issues will be discussed in more detail below.

We have used the distinction between elective and circumstantial bilinguals to help us respond to Bialystok's question of when 'enough is enough'. By drawing this distinction between the two groups, we will argue that for elective bilinguals we almost never assess both languages. Rather, we assume the speaker's proficiency in their first language, and assess only their proficiency in their second. For circumstantial bilinguals, however, the situation is rather different. This is because often we *should* be concerned with assessing both languages because circumstantial bilinguals use language in different contexts and to assess only one may not give us a full picture of the individual's overall language ability. Mills (1995: 144–145) provides a good example illustrating that children will not necessarily know the word for a concept in both their languages:

> I encountered Kuldip (age six) who was a Panjabi-speaker and had been in the UK for six months. It became evident Kuldip did not know the names of the shapes 'square' and 'rectangle' in Panjabi, but *did* know them in English.

As we will see, there are often factors which make it either difficult or impossible to appropriately assess a child in both languages. Equally, while we can recognize that we *should* be assessing the interrelationship between the two languages, this is not always an easy prospect.

Task A2.3

➤ A child who goes to school at five has considerable linguistic knowledge, and, if the child is bilingual, the child has considerable linguistic knowledge in both languages. Think about the language knowledge children develop during their primary or elementary school years. Can you identify some areas in which the child might develop linguistic knowledge in the school language, but not the home language?

ASSESSING THE BILINGUAL PROFICIENCY OF ELECTIVE BILINGUALS

In the examples of elective bilinguals given in Table A2.1 (with the possible exception of the first situation of the child growing up in a simultaneously bilingual environment), it is clear that each of the individuals mentioned is a native speaker of one language, and is learning another language as a second language. In each case, the individual has elected to learn the other language and is motivated to learn it. For this group of individuals (i.e. elective bilinguals) we can almost always identify quite easily the language of which the individual is a native speaker. However, we generally do not seek to assess the proficiency of their native language. As we will see below, this marks a substantial difference in the way in which we think about assessing elective bilinguals compared with circumstantial bilinguals. Thus, when we are assessing the language of an elective bilingual, we are almost always concerned with assessing their second language: the role of their first language (the one of which they are a native speaker) does not generally come into consideration except inasmuch as it might impact on their acquisition of the second language. This is because we tend to accept native speakers as proficient speakers of the language even though, as native speakers, they may have greater or lesser vocabularies, and may each have slightly different grammars (Davies 1991b; see also Unit A1). Certainly not all native speakers speak identically, but when we talk about native speakers we tend to think about an idealized native speaker who demonstrates full competence in the language. In the discussion below, then, we focus on what we need to measure when we think about measuring the second-language proficiency of those people who, largely through choice, elect to learn another language.

Measuring language

The measurement of any phenomenon requires that initially we have a clear definition of the bounds of the phenomenon that we want to measure. With physical objects in the world this is considerably less problematic than with psychological constructs because physical entities generally (though certainly not always) are relatively clearly defined – we know where they begin and where they end. In order to be able to measure the object, in addition to knowing where it begins and ends, we need to have some kind of gauge that is meaningful, and with which we can expect to be able to make reliable evaluations. If we decide to measure the length of a table, we will probably use a tape measure of some kind. The scale of the tape measure may be either in centimetres or in inches. When we look at the table we can see its length, and we know that we need to measure from one end to the other, and note the length. Obviously, the measurement of much larger physical objects, such as the height of buildings, or much smaller physical objects, such as atoms, poses more complex problems. However, they are more complex problems because of their size, either their largeness or their smallness, which may mean that instruments need to be developed specifically, or that mathematical procedures, such as triangulation, will be required to complete the measurement.

While we can relatively easily identify physical objects, then, that we want to measure – the table, the building or the atom – this is not so clearly the case with language. Language, like intelligence, cognitive ability and personality, is a psychological construct, and its measurement can involve the assessment of many different aspects of language (e.g. broadly, the four macro skills of speaking, reading, writing and listening). In order to be able to begin to measure language knowledge, then, we need to know what language consists of; in other words, we need to have a model of language; we need to *define the language construct.*

Task A2.4

➤ Think about what it means to know a language. What do you need to know to be able to speak and use a language? Clearly, you need to know how the grammar works, how to pronounce the language, and the vocabulary of the language. But what else do you need to know?

Defining the language construct

What do we mean when we say that someone knows how to use a language (Spolsky 1985)? This is something to which language testers have given considerable thought because before measures can be developed, we must know what the construct is – in other words, we need to know what, exactly, it is that we are measuring.

Language is a complex phenomenon, and there are many different aspects which can be assessed. This can include the four skills – speaking, reading, writing and listening – and, more specifically, particular aspects of language – pronunciation, intelligibility, syntax, vocabulary and discourse skill, to name but a few. Another important aspect of testing that needs to be considered is that, when we are testing a person's language, we can only elicit samples of their language performance. It is never possible to do more than this, since we cannot hope to be able to sample anyone's language in all possible circumstances. In other words, in evaluating a person's linguistic performance, we have to make inferences about their ability to use the language in other contexts from those which we are able to sample in the test. It is, therefore, as Bachman and Palmer (1996: 66) argue, crucial to define what it is we mean by language ability:

> If we are to make inferences about language ability on the basis of per-formance on language tests, we need to define this ability in sufficiently precise terms to distinguish it from other individual characteristics that can affect test performance. We also need to define language ability in a way that is appropriate for each particular testing situation, that is, for a specific purpose, group of test takers, and TLU [test language use] domain. For example, we may want to focus on test takers' knowledge of how to organise utterances to form texts for one particular testing situation, while

in another we may be more interested in their knowledge of appropriate politeness markers. The way we define language ability for a particular testing situation, then, becomes the basis for the kinds of inferences we can make from the test performance.

 Task A2.5

➤ Think about the kind of language skills you need to have to complete an arts degree at university successfully. Make a list, in order of importance, of the language skills you believe would be required. How would the list differ if the degree were in engineering?

Probably the most widely cited model in language testing has been that of Bachman (1990), further developed in Bachman and Palmer (1996), who have proposed models of communicative language ability that take into account both *language knowledge* and *strategic competence*. *Language knowledge* includes the knowledge which is required to use language appropriately in particular contexts, and is made up of several components (Bachman and Palmer 1996). *Organizational knowledge* refers to the formal properties of language required for understanding and producing language, as well as organizing language into longer stretches. It consists of grammatical knowledge and textual knowledge:

> **Grammatical knowledge** is involved in producing or comprehending formally accurate utterances or sentences. This includes knowledge of vocabulary, syntax, phonology, and graphology.

> **Textual knowledge** is involved in producing and comprehending texts . . . *spoken or written* – that consist of two or more utterances or sentences. There are two areas of textual knowledge: knowledge of cohesion and knowledge of rhetorical or conversational organization.
> (Bachman and Palmer 1996: 68)

Pragmatic knowledge relates utterances, sentences or texts to the communicative goals of the people using the language and to the setting in which it is used. It can be divided into *functional knowledge* and *sociolinguistic knowledge*. Functional knowledge is made up of:

> *Knowledge of ideational functions* [which] enables us to express or interpret meaning in terms of our experience of the real world. These functions include the use of language to express or exchange information about ideas, knowledge or feelings. Descriptions, classifications, explanations, and expressions of sorrow or anger are examples of utterances that perform ideational functions.

> *Knowledge of manipulative functions* enables us to use language to affect the world around us. This includes knowledge of the following:

1   *instrumental functions*, which are performed to get other people to do things for us (examples include requests, suggestions, commands, and warnings)
2   *regulatory functions*, which are used to control what other people do (examples include rules, regulations, and laws); and
3   *interpersonal functions*, which are used to establish, maintain and change interpersonal relationships (examples include greetings and leave takings, compliments, insults, and apologies).

Knowledge of heuristic functions enables us to use language to extend our knowledge of the world around us, such as when we use language for teaching and learning, for problem-solving, and for the retention of information.

Knowledge of imaginative functions enables us to use language to create an imaginary world or extend the world around us for humorous or esthetic purposes; examples include jokes and the use of figurative language and poetry.

(Bachman and Palmer 1996: 69–70)

Finally there is *sociolinguistic knowledge*, which allows us to use language appropriate to the context in which it is being used – this may include knowledge of the most appropriate dialect to use in a particular situation, or when to use different registers, such as when to use a formal register versus when to use more informal registers.

This understanding of language in theoretical terms is critically important in testing because it is from this model of language that we develop our test construct – the abstract theoretical concept that is reflected in test performance. In order to test language, therefore, we need to (1) know how to *describe* language, and (2) know how to *operationalize* it in terms which are precise enough to allow it to be measured. This means we need to be able to break down language into measurable units as, generally, language competence is an invisible attribute. Obviously we cannot realistically measure every aspect of the language itself. Thus, we are inevitably going to *infer* language ability on the basis of what we are able to observe. In order to do this, we first need to identify what the abilities are that we want to measure.

In any assessment, there are two central concepts which are crucial to interpreting the outcome of the measurement. The first is *validity*. Validity refers to the extent to which the measurement instrument (e.g. the language test) is an appropriate measure of the phenomenon itself – in this case, language. For example, a vocabulary test could not be considered a valid measure of communicative ability in a language, but a rating of an oral interview would probably provide a more valid measure. The second is *reliability*. Reliability refers to the extent to which something is measured consistently. There are various ways of measuring reliability – for example, a test may be given twice to the same group of people to see the extent to which the scores are consistent across the two occasions. These issues are discussed in more depth in Fulcher and Davidson (2007).

Types of test

When we are measuring second-language proficiency (as we have defined elective bilingualism), there are various purposes for which tests can be used. Henning (1987) discusses a range of types of test, of which the following are probably the most commonly used:

- *Proficiency tests*: designed to measure a person's language ability irrespective of the type of language experiences the person may have had. These are tests of general language proficiency where the required language proficiency is specified by a set of expectations of the types of activities the candidate would be expected to be able to do with language in order to be considered a proficient speaker of that language. Two well-known proficiency tests are the IELTS (International English Language Testing System) and TOEFL (Test of English as a Foreign Language).
- *Achievement tests*: designed to evaluate the language learned in a specific language instruction programme; such tests relate specifically to the curriculum of the course and will be designed to evaluate either progress or the final achievement of the learners.
- *Diagnostic tests*: designed to identify areas of language strength and weakness, generally for the purposes of providing additional and appropriate assistance at a later time.
- *Placement tests*: designed to identify the most appropriate placement for learners in classes where classes of varying proficiency levels are available.

Both in language learning situations and in the testing and assessment of languages, we often think in terms of the four macro skills – speaking and writing (the productive skills) and reading and listening (the receptive skills) – and traditionally tests have often been designed to specifically evaluate each of these skills. Recently, however, there has been an increasing focus on the development of more integrated tasks which go beyond the notion of assessing each skill independently and require candidates to perform tasks in which more than one skill is tested (e.g. reading a text and then writing a summary of it tests both reading and writing skills) (Wigglesworth, in press).

 Task A2.6

It is often the case that individuals do not demonstrate the same levels of competence in each of these four skills.

➤ Under what circumstances might individuals develop their skills in one area more than in another? See if you can think of some examples.

➤ Under what circumstances might you decide that:

- testing one or two skills is **more important** than to test another?
- testing one or two of them **might not** be necessary at all?

➤ Provide examples and give reasons for your choices.

Tests can vary on a number of different dimensions, and these dimensions have implications for both the validity and the reliability of the tests. While we cannot discuss these in any detail here, those interested in exploring the concepts under-lying testing and assessment are directed to Bachman and Palmer (1996), Brown (2004), Henning (1987), Hughes (1989) and Fulcher and Davidson (2007). While all of these provide relatively in-depth treatments, a brief and accessible overview of testing concepts can be found in McNamara (2000).

Tests may be:

- direct or indirect
- scored objectively or subjectively
- criterion- or norm-referenced.

Direct tests test the actual skill under investigation, while *indirect tests* measure the abilities which underlie the skill in which we are interested (Hughes 1989). To illustrate this difference, Hughes uses the example of writing an essay. In a direct test, we would ask the candidate to write an essay, which would then be scored; in an indirect test, we might devise a set of grammar correction items in which the candidate was required to identify the incorrect item and revise it. While this would not be a direct test of the candidate's ability to write an essay, such skills are strongly correlated with the ability to write an essay.

Tests can be scored either *objectively* or *subjectively*. Objective scoring does not require any judgement on the part of the assessor. An example is a multiple-choice item in which the correct item has to be selected from a set of distractor items. In this case, the answer is either right (where the correct item is chosen) or wrong (where it is not). Subjective scoring refers to the type of assessment where judge-ments need to be made by a rater, which usually involves some measure of judgement and expertise. Written texts and spoken discourse are usually subjectively scored by a rater using a rating scale which defines different levels of proficiency. Rating scales may be either *holistic* – where the mark is assigned on the basis of a holistic evaluation of the candidate's speech or writing – or *analytic* – where several scores are assigned on the basis of different aspects of the speech or writing. For example, in an analytic rating scale for a speech sample, the rater might be asked to assign three scores, one for grammar, one for intelligibility (pronunciation and stress patterns) and one for breadth of vocabulary. Thus, a candidate's written essay or their response to an interviewer's questions would be examples of the type of activity which would be subjectively scored. *Reliability* is always of concern in subjective scoring since raters tend vary in their harshness (Upshur and Turner 1999) and in the way they interpret the rating scale (Lumley 2002). Rater training attempts to address problems with rater consistency and to ensure that raters assess as fairly as possible. In some cases, statistical analyses can be used to contribute to identifying rater bias (Wigglesworth 1993; McNamara 1996), but, because raters do tend to vary, best practice in testing would require each text to be scored by more than a single rater.

Any kind of measurement implies a comparison: this may be with other members of the group or cohort, where measurements are made and compared across the group, often in relation to a standardized set of results, or the comparison may be with some definition of ability, or criterion. The former is known as *norm referencing*, and the latter as *criterion referencing*.

Performance-based testing

A performance-based test is 'a test in which the ability of candidates to perform particular tasks, usually associated with job or study requirements, is assessed' (Davies et al. 1999: 114). These kinds of test are designed to measure a candidate's productive language skills through performances on tasks which allow the candidate to demonstrate the type of language skills which it is expected they will be required to use at some later stage. Thus, a central tenet of performance tests is authenticity, where tasks are designed to be authentic representations of the types of activities candidates will perform in the real world; however, the degree to which it is possible to make inferences based on the language elicited by particular test tasks as a reflection of the candidates' ability to manage the task in a subsequent real-world context remains a matter for debate (Wigglesworth, in press).

In many ways, performance tests appear to enhance validity by eliciting samples of the type of language that will be required in future situations, but Darling-Hammond (1994) offers a cautionary note about such tests, pointing out that performance-based assessments do not inherently mean that testing will be more equitable. She argues that we still need to apply rigorous standards and be very careful that such assessments really are fair and valid forms of assessment. These types of assessment may be seen as preferable because they are essentially seen as more authentic: they are based on the kind of real-world tasks that students may normally be expected to participate in, and evaluated on criteria which assess the actual performance, rather than the multiple-choice type, or discrete type test items which have traditionally been administered. However, as Darling-Hammond points out, we must still be vigilant with many of the traditional concerns with any kind of testing: for example, determining that they avoid bias, evaluating how they resolve concerns about subjectivity versus objectivity, and how they influence curriculum and teaching – that is, the washback effect that such assessments may have.

Alternative types of assessment

There are also alternative ways of making assessments about language knowledge, and these include portfolio assessments where individuals collect a number of samples of their work which demonstrate their language ability. As Diaz Rico and Weed (1995) suggest, such portfolio assessments may include written work, self-assessments, reports, dictations, audio recordings etc. and are designed to show the learner's progress over time. There are also competency-based assessments where language knowledge is evaluated in relation to the learner's ability to perform particular task competencies under various conditions. In these cases, although assessment may often be done formally, it is generally embedded within the curriculum. For example, in the Adult Migrant English programme in Australia, assessment is competency-based, and so learners may be required to complete a role-play activity in which they are asked to make a complex request (such as asking to change an interview time), or they might be asked to write a short report, for example on a memorable day in their lives.

Task A2.7

➤ Consider the following options for assessing the writing proficiency of a class of twelve-year-old second-language learners and then respond to the questions below:

Type 1   Portfolio assessment (consisting of three drafts of two essays of 500 words; two drafts of two argumentative essays; a journal; a weekly dictation; material collected over one term)

Type 2   An exam-based assessment consisting of two essays, one descriptive, one argumentative, of around 300 words, written under exam conditions

Type 3   A test of grammar, a cloze test and a spelling test conducted under exam conditions (a cloze test is a written test in which sentences or paragraphs are provided in which certain words have been deleted. The test candidate is required to fill in the spaces, e.g. 'Yesterday Mike ____ to the market and bought some carrots'

➤ Which type of assessment do you think:

- ■ would be the most *valid* (in other words, the most accurate in predicting the proficiency level of the children's language ability)?
- ■ would be the most *time-consuming*?
- ■ would be the most *reliable*?
- ■ would be the one the *children* preferred?
- ■ would be the one the *teacher* preferred?

➤ Which would you choose in this situation? What are the advantages and disadvantages of each?

While more communicative models of language testing are currently prominent, there is also a move towards more holistic, qualitative assessment. These alternative modes of assessment offer more qualitative assessments of the learner's abilities on the whole, but also involve a more time-consuming commitment on the part of the assessor and the learner, and do not provide comparable data in the way that more traditional types of tests offer. They may also not be as equitable, and fairness and ethical concerns need to be taken seriously (McNamara 1996, 1998).

We have now briefly overviewed a range of considerations relevant to the ways in which language can be assessed formally. On the whole, language tests and language assessments are designed for elective bilinguals: that is, they evaluate the language of second-language learners against the norm of a native speaker of that language (Valdes and Figueroa 1994). Circumstantial bilinguals fall into a rather different category, and the question of whether they should be evaluated against native-speaker norms is one which has been widely discussed. Grosjean (1989) in a seminal article argued strongly for the view that a bilingual should not be seen as the sum of two monolinguals. Taking the point further, De Groot and Kroll (1997: 2) argue that bilingualism cannot be viewed as simply the sum of two monolingual minds but that we need to take account of the interaction between the two languages. Further, they argue that this interaction is a complex one, the investigation of which will require detailed understanding of monolingual knowledge of language as well as of the bilingual knowledge of the languages. This means that the issue of the relationship between the bilingual's two languages becomes one of paramount importance. As we will see below, these issues are very complex ones.

ASSESSING THE LANGUAGE OF CIRCUMSTANTIAL BILINGUALS

When we are assessing the language of elective bilinguals, we are not really concerned with their competence in their first language (or, in other words, the language of which they are a native speaker). When we turn to look at the situation with respect to circumstantial bilinguals, the situation – particularly with children – is rather different. We have chosen to focus on the assessment of children because of both the complexity and the importance of doing so – for example, 11 per cent of all primary, and 9.1 per cent of all secondary, schoolchildren in the UK come from non-English-speaking backgrounds (Strand and Demie 2005).

In Unit A1, we discussed extensively the concept of the 'domain' of the bilingual's two languages. This is an important distinction which often differentiates the elective bilingual from the circumstantial bilingual. As we have seen above, an elective bilingual is by nature a native speaker of a language. This means that generally this person is a native speaker of a language and that this language will be spoken across all domains – at home, in the kitchen, with family, with relatives, at work, on the phone for giving lectures or presentations, in conferences, on the factory floor, in the community, at the shops, at social events, at the children's school etc.

When we are considering assessing circumstantial bilingual language, we need to think in terms of domains of language use. While these domains will not be linguistically differentiated for the monolingual speaker, it is frequently the case that they are differentiated for the circumstantial bilingual. With adult circumstantial bilinguals, we might want to consider whether they have been educated in one or both of their languages – and, related to that, what level of educational attainment has been achieved, and whether this was equivalent in both languages. It is, in fact, quite unusual for circumstantial bilinguals to use both languages in exactly equivalent domains, or for exactly equivalent functions. This point, therefore, needs to be taken into consideration. Many bilinguals, for example, may use only one of their languages in their professional or work life, while the other is used exclusively at home. In these cases, one of the languages may be dominant over the other.

Alternatively, it may be that one of the languages is more dominant in certain domains, while the other language is dominant in a different set of domains. Thus, a university lecturer may lecture in English on a topic (say geography) in an English-speaking country, but speak Japanese exclusively at home and in the community. This does not mean that if requested to give a lecture on geography in Japanese, this speaker will necessarily be able to do so with any ease. These language functions occur in different domains, and the skills required for one are not necessarily instantaneously transferable to the other (for example, particularly in a case like this where specialized vocabulary is required, the speaker may not have available this vocabulary in the 'home' language). This issue of the domain of language use is clearly one which needs to be taken into consideration since a circumstantial bilingual may not have equal competence in the performance of both their languages in all domains available. We saw in Unit A1 the importance of different domains of language use for bilinguals, so it is important that any measurement of the language use pertains to the domains in which those languages are used.

ASSESSING THE LANGUAGE OF CIRCUMSTANTIALLY BILINGUAL CHILDREN

In the last section of this unit, we are going to focus specifically on assessment issues as they pertain to children growing up in situations of circumstantial bilingualism. As Table A2.1 (p. 21) shows, children growing up as circumstantial bilinguals are generally children who come to school speaking a minority language of the country in which they are living. When they arrive in school, they may have had only limited access to the language of education in the community in which they are living. However, the importance of appropriate assessment of the needs of such children cannot be overestimated. This is because these children now make up a substantial proportion of the school population. Mahon et al. (2003) point out that one in eight schoolchildren in the UK come from a minority ethnic background. In the US, the number of limited-English-proficient (LEP) students attending school increased by 65 per cent in the ten years from 1994 to 2004, with approximately one in ten schoolchildren now coming from such backgrounds. This is in striking contrast to the situation in many other countries, where there is enormous variation in language backgrounds, approximately 80 per cent of these LEP children report Spanish as their native language (Batalova 2006). Clearly, this makes the assessment of both languages a much more accessible goal.

The work on assessing the language of circumstantially bilingual children comes from two main sources. One is the assessment of such children in the educational system, where there is often quite substantial standardized testing of content material. The other is the assessment of children who may have specific language impairment, which should be diagnosed as early as possible so that they may be provided with appropriate treatment. We will deal with these issues briefly below. In Unit B2, we will consider in more depth those issues that we need to take into consideration when assessing bilingual children in the school situation.

The use of norm-referenced tests is widely recognized as being problematic for assessing children being raised in situations of circumstantial bilingualism (Genishi and Brainard 1995; Gutierrez-Clennen 1996; Thomas and Collier 1997), because such tests have generally been normed on populations which do not include bilingual children. For this reason, bilingual children who are tested with these instruments may be seriously disadvantaged and assessed as not only linguistically limited but also cognitively deficient (see Unit A4 for a more detailed discussion of how this has impacted on views of bilingualism and cognitive function).

The importance of appropriately assessing circumstantially bilingual children has been widely recognized because of the potential for language problems to result in poor school performance, and subsequently to limit life choices. Cummins (1979, 1984) makes a distinction between *basic interpersonal communicative skills* and *cognitive academic language proficiency* (more recently termed *conversational language proficiency* and *academic language proficiency* respectively in Cummins 2000). This view has been the subject of considerable discussion and controversy. Romaine (1995: 268) argues that the model is too simplistic, and empirically difficult to test, while Hamers and Blanc (2000: 99) maintain that it lacks explanatory adequacy since it does not address the issue of simultaneous bilingualism, nor does it explain why children fare differently. None the less, the model remains a useful one given the fact that as children go through the formal educational system, they need to acquire very different language skills from those that they are using routinely at home. The distinction between basic conversational proficiency and academic language proficiency is a very important one because, while children may reach basic conversational fluency within two years, it takes between five and seven years to attain academic language proficiency (Strand and Demie 2005). Thomas and Collier (1997) report on two earlier studies which suggest that these estimates may be rather conservative:

The student samples consisted of 1,548 and 2,014 immigrant students just beginning their acquisition of English, 65 percent of whom were of Asian descent and 20 percent of Hispanic descent, the rest representing 75 languages from around the world. These students received 1–3 hours per day of ESL instructional support, attending mainstream (grade-level) classes the remainder of the school day, and were generally exited from ESL within the first two years of their arrival in the U.S.

We limited our analyses to only those newly arriving immigrant students who were assessed when they arrived in this country as being at or above grade level in their home country schooling in native language, since we expected this 'advantaged' on-grade-level group to achieve academically in their second language in the shortest time possible. It was quite a surprise to find a similar 5–7 year pattern to that which Cummins found, for certain groups of students. We found that students who arrived between ages 8 and 11, who had received at least 2–5 years of schooling taught through their primary language (L1) in their home country, were the lucky ones who took only 5–7 years. Those who arrived before age 8 required 7–10 years or more! These children arriving during the early childhood years (before age 8) had the same background characteristics as the 8–11-year-old arrivals. The only difference between the two groups was that the younger children had received little or no formal schooling in their first language (L1), and this factor appeared to be a significant predictor in these first studies.

(Thomas and Collier 1997: 33)

Task A2.8

➤ Can you think of what types of activities children around the age of five would be involved in at home and make a list of them (e.g. playing, watching children's programmes on television, shopping at the supermarket etc.)? What kind of language do you think would be required for these kinds of activities?

➤ When children begin to attend school, they must both behave in a different way and use language in different ways. List the kinds of activities children partic-ipate in at school which are different from those at home (e.g. learning a range of academic skills including numeracy and literacy, sitting at tables or on mats in groups for a reasonable period of time, listening to detailed instructions about activities). Can you describe the kind of language that would be required for these kinds of activities?

ASSESSING BILINGUAL CHILDREN FOR SPECIFIC LANGUAGE IMPAIRMENT

At any one time, 10 per cent of the population of normal children entering the school system will be affected by some sort of speech disorder; from this it follows that a similar proportion of bilingual children will be affected (Holm et al. 1999). The likelihood is that when children or their parents are advised that the child should see a speech pathologist they may encounter a number of difficulties. These include the high chance that the speech pathologist will not be familiar with at least one of the child's languages, and standardized (or any other kind of) assessment instruments will not be available in at least one of their languages. Where assessment instruments are available, they may not be in the child's dominant language, and there may be very limited norms available for bilingual children.

This potential for bias in language assessment for linguistic and cultural minority students has been widely recognized (Valdes and Figueroa 1994). Saenz and Huer (2003) point out that second-language students routinely score lower than their monolingual peers despite the appearance of fluency at the conversational level. While the standardization procedure may include some children from minorities, they are none the less biased, usually towards the middle-class monolingual English children who constitute the majority of the population upon whom such tests are standardized. Furthermore, Pert and Letts (2003) argue strongly for the importance of ensuring that when children are being tested for language impairments, all the languages the child uses are tested. This is because using English-only procedures will not be adequate to assess the child's full linguistic repertoire, and this is particularly the case where the child has had only limited opportunities to learn English. Pert and Letts describe the kinds of problems which are encountered:

> Even if a therapist is bilingual, they are unlikely to speak all the languages they encounter (Lahey, 1992), and the lack of normative data means that diagnosis will be based on subjective decision making. Clinicians have been severely hampered by the lack of assessment materials available in languages other than English, and often by lack of access to appropriate language speakers who possess the skills to administer an assessment. The latter problem has been overcome in some areas by the employment and training of bilingual co-workers, without whom an effective service for non-English first language students would be impossible to sustain. Co-workers can also provide information about the languages they speak, which will help the therapist make judgements about the normality or otherwise of any particular child's language skills. In the absence of test materials, the clinician can use spontaneous speech sampling, aided by a co-worker, to form an impression of the child's expressive skills when speaking his or her first language. However, in contrast to English, there is no guarantee that the therapist will have access to developmental stages and norms for the target language. Without a body of research on which to base decisions about developmental stages, the therapist who is

professionally committed to providing an accurate assessment and to planning intervention is effectively attempting to do the impossible.

(2003: 268)

The study undertaken by Pert and Letts tries to address these issues, and they raise a number of points which must be taken into consideration when testing children from bilingual backgrounds, as well as highlighting the complexities involved in this kind of testing. In discussing the development of tests of expressive language in three different Asian languages widely used in their region of the UK, they point out a few of the difficulties which may be encountered in attempting to address these issues. The first is that if the home, or first, language is not considered to carry much prestige with it, then parents may not report it as a language they use. They also point to the problem of identifying different dialects which may have very similar names. Finally, Martin et al. (2003) suggest that the 'standard variety' of the language spoken in the original home country may not be the same as that spoken by second- and third-generation migrants now living elsewhere.

Assessments used with children also need to be age-appropriate, and should not be confronting for the child. Hasselgreen (2005) points out that there is now general consensus on the features that assessment activities for young children should encapsulate. These are:

- Tasks should be appealing to the age group, interesting and captivating, preferably with elements of game and fun
- many types of assessment should be used, with the pupil's, the parents' and the teachers' perspectives involved
- both the tasks and the forms of feedback should be designed so that the pupil's strengths (what he or she can do) are highlighted
- the pupil should, at least under some circumstances, be given support in carrying out the tasks
- the teacher should be given access to and support in understanding basic criteria and methods for assessing language ability
- the activities used in an assessment should be good learning activities in themselves.

(Hasselgreen 2005: 338–339)

SELF-ASSESSMENTS OF BILINGUAL PROFICIENCY

There are two ways in which we can obtain information about a bilingual's language from self-assessments. One approach is through the use of language background scales, such as the one given in Task C1.4 (pp. 271–273) in which bilinguals are asked to provide information about their language use with a series of questions which investigate to whom they speak each of their languages, and how often they do so. Baker (2006: 33–34) points out that these kinds of scales necessarily have some limitations because they are generally not exhaustive of targets (people) or of domains (contexts). Language activity with uncles and aunts, discos, correspondence, organizations, hobbies and travel are not included, for example. The choice of items included in such a scale is somewhere between an all-inclusive scale and a more narrow sample of major domains. At first glance, it may appear the more inclusive a scale is the better. There is a problem, illustrated by Baker & Hinde (1984: 46): 'A person who says she speaks Welsh to her father (mostly away at sea), her grandparents (seen once a year), her friends (but tends to be an isolate), reads Welsh books and newspapers (only occasionally), attends Welsh Chapel (marriages and funerals only) but spends most of her time with an English speaking mother and in an English speaking school might gain a fairly high "Welsh" score'.

 Task A2.9

➤ Refer to the language background questionnaire provided in Task C1.4. How well would this work with the person described in the example above? How might these limitations be addressed without ending up with an exhaustive, but massively long, questionnaire? To do this it will help to think about ways in which you might prioritize questions about particular people or activities.

While language background scales of the type discussed above have been used extensively in bilingual research, they do not purport to measure the proficiency of speakers, rather their patterns of language use across a variety of domains. Proficiency can, however, be measured through self-assessment questionnaires, and although these have limitations they can serve a useful purpose. Little (2005: 321–322) argues that there are three main reasons for using self-assessments: firstly, for learners to be able to assess their progress in terms of the curriculum they are learning; secondly, to encourage learners to regard assessment as a shared responsibility; and thirdly, to allow learners to identify occasions in which the target language can be used for additional explicit language learning. While self-assessment of language skill is generally related to curriculum concerns, and closely tied to it (see Ross 1998 for a detailed discussion of this), the Council of Europe has now developed a self-assessment instrument called the European Language Passport as part of the European Language Portfolio. This allows speakers to evaluate their language skills in terms of understanding (reading and listening), speaking (spoken interaction and spoken production) and writing. Skills in each of the five areas are assessed on a six-point scale (A1, A2, B1, B2, C1, C2) where A is advanced, B intermediate and C beginner. At the end of the process, the 'Language Passport' can be downloaded (see http://europass.cedefop.europa.eu). 'Dialang' (www.dialang. org) is another site where you can test your proficiencies in fourteen different languages.

In this introduction to the complexities of measuring bilingualism, we began with an overview of the various types of bilinguals we might want to assess. We focused on the evaluation of the language firstly of elective bilinguals, where our interest will be on assessing them in their second language. We then looked at the more complex question of assessing the language of circumstantially bilingual individuals, specifically considering the difficulty of assessing children in these situations.

In the Extension part (Unit B2), we will build on the discussion in this unit by reading three extracts; the first, by Saenz and Huer (2003), posits a variety of alternative forms of testing, showing the advantages and disadvantages of each, focused particularly on speech pathologists. The second reading, by Bialystok (2001a), discusses the issue of proficiency and what it means in different circumstances. The third focuses on a widely cited theoretical model proposed by Cummins (2000) designed to raise our awareness of the kinds of factors which need to be taken into account in assessing children's language in educational systems.

Unit A3
Bilingual acquisition

Is it more difficult for a child to learn two languages than to learn one language?

Does learning two languages affect the rate at which language is acquired?

At what point does the child differentiate between the two languages?

In this unit, we focus on children who grow up learning two languages simultaneously. That is, we are concerned only with the situation where the child acquires two languages from very early on – bilingual first-language acquisition (BFLA) (De Houwer 1995) – and not with cases where the child first acquires one language, and then a second is introduced – even though this may occur at a relatively young age. We will discuss the issue of what a 'relatively young age' means below. Bilingual first-language acquisition is the learning of both languages in a naturalistic setting, in which both the formal aspects and the social conventions of the languages must be acquired. Thus, the child must learn about the phonological properties of both languages, how the morphological system works, how sentences are constructed, as well as how meaning is encoded and discourse is constructed. In addition to this, however, there are also sociolinguistic aspects of language which must be learned. Just as there are rules which govern the formal properties of languages, so there are rules which govern the social and pragmatic uses of language which may vary across the two languages to which the child is being exposed. We will explore some of these issues in more depth in Unit B3.

ACQUIRING TWO LANGUAGES

The range of possibilities for raising children bilingually is both enormous and extremely variable, and there are many factors which may impact upon the successful acquisition, or not, of two or more languages. Language is not neutral. This means that some types of behaviour are likely to influence the child's attitudes towards the two languages in either negative or positive ways. Although all normally functioning children will learn the language of their parents and community in a monolingual setting without difficulty, this is not necessarily the case for bilingual children, and not all children learning two or more languages are raised in bilingual communities. Thus, growing up bilingual cannot be assumed, and there are many factors which contribute to its success.

Task A3.1

➤ What sorts of factors do you think might contribute to a child's successfully learning two languages from an early age? Think about the kind of environment the child might be growing up in, and assume that the child has two parents who speak different languages. Consider the implications of the language the parents speak to each other. Make a list of those factors which you feel might contribute to successful bilingual acquisition, and those factors which you feel might detract from its success.

Among the factors which affect the acquisition of two languages simultaneously are the quality and the quantity of the interaction. This is particularly important in situations where one language is a minority language and where the child needs to be encouraged to talk in the minority language. What may be critical to the long-term success of the child's bilingualism is a positive attitude towards the minority language, together with plenty of opportunities to use it. Most of our knowledge about the ways in which children learn two languages comes from detailed studies of single children acquiring two languages (e.g. De Houwer 1990; Hoffmann 1985; Lanza 1997; Leopold 1947, 1949a, 1949b) or small groups of children (e.g. Döpke 1992; Zentella 1997). With these children, it is often the case that one of their languages is the minority language and the main input for this language is from one parent. However, while these are the best-documented studies of bilingual acquisition, in fact the majority of children in the world today grow up bilingually in bilingual environments, where the use of two languages in the community is the norm. The complexity surrounding bilingual child language acquisition cannot be overestimated, and in this unit we will examine the major issues which have been raised, and continue to be raised, in the substantial literature which addresses this topic.

Teasing out the generalizations from bilingual language-acquisition research is often difficult because of the variability inherent in any such study. For each study of a bilingual child, the child is learning two languages (which may be different from the two languages any other child is learning), in an environment which may also be different from any other child's environment. Added to this must be the fact that even in monolingual first-language acquisition, children exhibit substantial amounts of individual variation. Children acquire language at greatly varying rates and adopt different strategies and approaches in the process. These differences are compounded when the child is becoming bilingual. However, in general, it appears that bilingual children acquire both their languages at a similar rate and in a similar manner (see, for example, Petitto et al. 2001) to monolingual children.

In the following sections, we will begin by considering briefly what we mean by bilingual first-language acquisition. From this point, we will move on to the complex environment in which bilingual children grow up, and consider how this may affect their acquisition of their two languages. Next we consider the point at which children differentiate their two languages. This will also raise the issue of whether we can realistically compare bilingual children's acquisition to monolinguals', and, if we cannot, what standards we should use instead. We will also discuss the complex relationship of language input to bilingual acquisition, and discuss what this means for the child, a topic we will again explore further in Unit B3. While we will discuss the ways in which children acquire two languages, we should point out that this is in no way meant to negate the experience of the many children in the world who, for various reasons, grow up in multilingual environments learning more than two languages – in some cases three or even four.

DEFINING BILINGUAL FIRST-LANGUAGE ACQUISITION

The term *bilingual first-language acquisition* is now fairly widely used to refer to children in a bilingual environment acquiring two languages simultaneously from birth (see De Houwer 1995). This term can be compared to bilingual second-language acquisition where the child is learning a second language after learning the first – also known as sequential acquisition. However, no matter what terminology we may choose to adopt, it is important that the term is appropriately and adequately defined so that we are able to determine whether the children referred to in the studies we examine meet the criteria for bilingual first-language acquisition. This issue is not trivial. McLaughlin (1984) used the term to refer to children learning two languages under the age of three. Köppe and Meisel (1995) adopted the same definition. However, there are problems with this definition, particularly because by the age of three the first language is generally relatively well established.

 Task A3.2

➤ Think of a child you know aged about three. Make a list of the kinds of thing that the child is able to do with language at this age. Can s/he speak in sentences? How complex are these sentences? How broad is the child's vocabulary? What kinds of questions does the child ask? What range of grammatical structures (e.g. demonstratives, imperatives) does the child use? Does the child use appropriate terms (e.g. address terms) in speaking to different people, and does the child make appropriate choices as to which language to use depending upon whom s/he is speaking to?

Children at this age speak relatively fluently, are developing rapidly in terms of their knowledge and use of syntax and morphology, and demonstrate rudimentary awareness of the social and pragmatic constraints of the language they are acquiring. As we will discuss below, there is now little doubt that bilingual children differentiate their two languages pragmatically (i.e. they know which language to use to whom and for which different purposes) by at least the age of two.

The most straightforward definition of bilingual first-language acquisition is one where the child has access to both languages from birth. Clearly, this is the least arbitrary definition available. However, it is also somewhat limiting. Intuitively we might also wish to categorize as simultaneous acquisition the case of the child who has access to both languages from six months, or eight months, or perhaps twelve months – in other words, before the child begins to speak, which is on average around the age of ten to fourteen months. However, we must take into consideration the fact that even if we adopt this rather more lenient definition of simultaneous acquisition to include children who may not have been exposed to one of their two languages until the age of twelve months, the definition fails to take into account the substantial amount a child learns about language before the first word is even spoken. Despite these caveats, it is this definition we have chosen to adopt. Thus, in the discussion which follows, it may be assumed, unless otherwise stated, that the studies discussed relate to children who had access to two languages prior to their first birthday.

THE COMPLEX LINGUISTIC ENVIRONMENT OF THE CHILD

Surprising though it may seem to those of us who live in largely monolinguistic and monocultural societies, the majority of children are born into social and cultural situations where they have access to more than one language (see Bhatia and Ritchie 2004). Children who are born into bi- or multilingual societies will naturally develop two or more languages since this is the norm in such communities – almost everyone speaks more than one language. While this is probably the most common environment for the acquisition of two first languages, it also tends to be the least investigated (Romaine 1995).

Fewer children will develop their two languages in a situation in which the surrounding community is monolingual, although this is the group which tends to be the most studied – largely because the majority of the detailed case studies of bilingual language acquisition are the result of linguists studying their own children. In these contexts, children learn two languages for a variety of reasons. It may be that their parents have migrated to a country where the language is different from their own first language. Others will develop their bilingualism because their parents speak different languages from each other, but reside in the country of one of the parents. A small minority will develop their bilingualism as a result of a decision by their parents to introduce the children to more than one language because they have the capability to do so. This may occur where, for example, one parent speaks a second language with native-like or near-native competence (see, for example, Saunders 1982, 1988), and makes the decision to use this language with the child in the home. Harding-Esch and Riley (2003) offer a series of sixteen case studies of different bilingual circumstances.

The degree to which the child will become a successful bilingual is determined by a number of variables. These include both individual factors and societal factors.

From the extensive research on (monolingual) first-language acquisition, we know that all children with normal cognitive and physical functions will acquire the language of the family and community group they are born into, provided they have adequate exposure to the language, and have the opportunity for interaction in it. There is substantial individual variation in the specifics of the path the child may adopt (Shore 1995) and there are commonalities in the developmental patterns of specific languages (see Slobin 1985–1997). So, while children learn language at greatly varying rates and in a variety of different ways, these differences are compounded when the child is becoming bilingual. In general terms, as we will see, there is little evidence that bilingual children acquire either of their languages more slowly than monolingual children, despite having to cope with two different systems. However, we need to bear in mind that

> bilinguals rarely use their languages equally frequently in every domain of their social environment. Rather they use each of them for different purposes, in different contexts, and in communicating with different partners. Consequently, their abilities and skills in using each of these languages reflect their preferences and needs in the multifaceted social context in which they interact with others.
>
> (Meisel 2004: 93)

To become bilingual, a child must grow up in a bilingual environment. The question, though, of what constitutes a bilingual environment is a difficult one because the bilingual environments to which the child is exposed can vary enormously. Romaine (1995: 183–185) outlines a number of different bilingual environmental dimensions determined by three criteria, each of which may impact on the eventual success of the child's bilingualism:

■ the language(s) which the parents speak and whether they are the same or different
■ the language which is spoken in the community in which the family lives, and whether this community is monolingual or bilingual
■ whether the language(s) spoken are the same as or different from those of the parents, and the strategies the parents adopt in speaking to the child.

The complex interplay of variables which affect the bilingual child's acquisition of the two systems can be illustrated by comparing the linguistic input of monolingual children to that of bilingual children. While individual languages differ in terms of structure, phonology, pragmatics, socio-cultural norms, etc., despite these differences monolingual children receive linguistic input which is homogeneous in a number of important ways:

■ It consists of one language only.
■ Both parents speak that language to the child.
■ The language of the community around them is the same as the language spoken at home.

■ When they enter into formal childcare and/or educational institutions, the language they have learned is the one that is used in the institutional setting.

For children born into bi- or multilingual families (or communities), this is not the case. There is an additional layer of variability at each level of input, which means that these children are inevitably going to be a much more heterogeneous group. This can be evidenced by a direct comparison with each of the points related to input for monolingual children. Bilingual or multilingual children will experience some or all of the following:

■ linguistic input that consists of more than one language
■ each parent speaking a different language to them
■ the language of the community differing from either one or both of the languages they speak at home
■ the language in formal childcare and/or educational institutions not being one of the languages to which they have been exposed.

Before we go on to evaluate what we know about bilingual language acquisition, let us consider the ultimate expectations we have for the child who is growing up bilingually.

Task A3.3

➤ When somebody tells you they are bilingual, consider what your expectations of this are. What do you expect that the person can do with their two languages? Do you expect them to be equally fluent in both languages? Do you expect them to be able to read, write, listen and speak in both languages? Do you expect them to be able to interact in exactly the same ways in both languages in the same sorts of environments? Make a list of what you would expect a person to be able to do with two languages if they were bilingual.

As we saw in Unit A1, if you ask ten people what they think of when they hear that someone is 'bilingual', they will almost certainly say that this means that the person concerned can speak two languages fluently. They may also add that the person would sound like a native speaker of both. However, any concept of bilingualism is relative – while bilinguals certainly do speak two languages and may sound native-like in both, it is rare to find an individual who does not have one language which is more dominant than the other, particularly in functional terms.

This differentiation among functional competencies in the two languages is an important one, because although we tend to think of bilinguals as people who speak two languages (i.e. they are like two monolinguals put together in one person), they are not, in fact, the same as two monolinguals in one person (see Grosjean 1989 for a discussion of this issue). For almost all bilinguals, their languages will be functionally separated. The view of the bilingual as two monolinguals has, in fact, tended to disadvantage bilingual children whose acquisition has been the focus of investigation. For example, as Romaine (1995) points out, although there are studies that have argued that bilingual children tend to lag behind their monolingual peers in vocabulary acquisition, a rather different picture emerges if the vocabulary acquisition in both languages together is considered. If this is done, we find that bilingual children's total vocabulary is comparable in size to that of monolingual children (see Pearson et al. 1993).

ONE SYSTEM OR TWO?

One of the most pervasive questions in bilingual child language acquisition has been the issue of whether the child begins with one linguistic system or two. In other words, is the child initially unable to differentiate between the two systems, and if this is the case, how early, and at what stage, do the two linguistic systems become differentiated? This question has motivated a substantial volume of research.

The importance of this question resulted initially from the view, largely held within monolingual language communities, that exposure of children to two languages could be detrimental. Bilingualism was considered to be a possible source of confusion for children, so that if children were to begin with two languages, it would make learning both languages more difficult. The concern, then, was that they might end up with deficiencies in both languages (Barreña 2001; see also the discussion of cognitive effects in Unit A4). The issue of how bilingual children acquire their two languages, and how this compares to the acquisition of those same languages by monolingual children, has thus been of both theoretical interest, because of the contribution such knowledge will make to our understanding of children's language acquisition processes, and practical interest for families and communities who want to raise their children bilingually.

Evidence for the idea of a single system was empirically supported by examples of language mixing which were reported in early bilingual acquisition (e.g. Lindholm and Padilla 1978; Redlinger and Park 1980). This unitary language system assumed an underlying undifferentiated subsystem for each of phonology, lexicon and syntax (Genesee 1989). In other words, it was suggested that the child did not initially have differentiated systems for the language to which s/he was exposed. Volterra and Taeschner (1978) proposed a three-stage model of bilingual language development in which they argued that, initially, the child is unable to distinguish two different systems. According to this model, the child begins with a single linguistic system which is gradually separated into two. In the first stage of the model, the child's system consists of a single lexical system which includes words from both languages. In other words, this entails the idea that the child has only a single word for any lexical item or concept. Thus, if a French–English bilingual child has the word 'chair' in English, according to the model s/he would not additionally have the word 'chaise' in French. In the second stage of the model, the child separates the two lexicons, but maintains a single set of syntactic rules for both languages. In the third stage, the child has two different codes but associates each language with specific people – that is, the child demonstrates pragmatic differentiation of the two languages. Volterra and Taeschner's model was developed from their study of three children. Hildegarde was the English–German bilingual daughter of Leopold (1947, 1949a, 1949b), who kept a highly detailed diary of his daughter's bilingual language development. Lisa and Giulia were Italian–German bilinguals who were studied over an extensive period by their linguist mother (Taeschner 1983). Volterra and Taeschner's claim for the first stage is based on the notion that the language the child uses depends not on the language spoken to her, but on what she wants to say – this may involve two- to three-word constructions which use a mixture of words taken from both languages, where the syntax is difficult to assess. In the second stage the child has two lexical systems – that is, the child may use two words for the same object but use the same syntactic system for both languages. In the third stage the child is able to differentiate two systems but reduces the complexity of the task by labelling people as speakers of one or two languages.

The alternative hypothesis, the independent development hypothesis, claims that children acquiring two languages separate the languages from a very early age. Genesee (1989), for example, argues that children do, in fact, differentiate their languages functionally from a very young age. Genesee argues that most claims that are made for the unitary hypothesis are inadequate; for example, although Vihman (1985) claims that a child uses English in an Estonian context (when the rest of the English-speaking family are around), she does not show that Estonian is used in the English-speaking context despite the fact that this would be expected if the child was using a single system. As Genesee (1989) points out, one of the important issues which has to be addressed here relates to the different ways in which interpretations of children's use and misuse of words can be made, depending upon whether these analyses are being conducted on the speech productions of bi- or monolingual children.

In the bilingual acquisition literature, much of the mixing reported in the bilingual child's speech has been reported as restricted use of specific lexical items, or overuse of the other language. This issue with analysis occurs also in first- (mono-) language acquisition, but here it is reported as being either an underextension (where the item or word is used is very limited in context) or overextension (where the item or word is used in a wider variety of situations than is appropriate). An example of the first would be a child using the word 'dog' to refer only to the family dog but no other dog. An example of the second would be using the word 'dog' to refer not only to dogs but to all other four-legged animals as well.

Task A3.4

➤ Can you think of a young child you know, probably between the ages of twelve and twenty-four months, who uses a word or words in this way? For example, at fifteen months the daughter of one of the authors overextended the word 'dog' to refer to all four-legged animals for a brief period, and would point at a field of cows and say 'doggie, doggie'!

It is well established that bilingual children of different languages have different time lines in their acquisition of specific features of syntax, and that both frequency, saliency and typological factors will influence the rate of acquisition in both languages in just the same way as they do in the monolingual child acquiring a single language. It may well be the case, then, that the bilingual child uses his or her bilingual resources to best effect by expressing something in one language which the child is yet to acquire in the other. Genesee (1989: 174) concludes:

> In sum, I have argued that, contrary to most interpretations of bilingual development, bilingual children are able to differentiate their language systems from the beginning and that they are able to use their developing language systems differentially in contextually sensitive ways. As well, I have suggested that more serious research attention needs to be given to parental input in the form of bilingual mixing as a possible source of influence in children's mixing. Evidence that children's mixing may indeed be related to mixed input by parents was presented. This evidence, however, was limited to lexical mixing, and more attention to phonological, morpho-logical and other kinds of mixing by parents and children is clearly needed. The available evidence is obviously inadequate to come to confident conclusions regarding these points, and my re-examination of other researchers' transcriptions must be regarded as preliminary and tentative pending more adequate research. What is clear from this review is that the case for undifferentiated language development in bilingual children is far from established.

In Unit B3, we will consider these issues in more detail. Now, by way of introduction, we turn to examine parental strategies and their role in the emerging bilingual competence of their children.

PARENTAL STRATEGIES AND THE SOCIOLINGUISTIC CONTEXT

Essential to an understanding of how the bilingual child's language develops are documented records of the amount and type of input the child receives in his or her different languages. There are methodological problems associated with gathering and evaluating this type of information, and we will be examining some of these problems in more detail in Unit B3.

As we have indicated before, most of the children who are the subjects of the detailed bilingual acquisition studies reported in the literature are the children of linguists, or those studied by linguists. The amount of data provided on their language input varies enormously. For example, Test (2001) reports that the English–Arabic bilingual child she studied was spoken to in English by the mother, and Arabic by the father. The father spent three days a week at home, while the mother spent four days a week at home, and each parent spoke only their own language with the child. The parents were living in Sweden, and Swedish was the language they spoke outside the home, but they communicated with each other in English. In this study, Test was interested in the extent to which clues available from gesture (for example, pointing, waving, raising an eyebrow) in the infant's input might contribute to the child's ability to differentiate the two languages at a very early stage, and this was the focus of the study. It was therefore important to have accurate information regarding the exposure to the input languages. The findings from this study supported, albeit tentatively, the possibility that

> the parents, through differences in their gesture and language use, seem to have created a prelinguistic social communicative context which would support the child seeing the two communicative systems as separate systems both gesturally and verbally. During the limited amount of time that the child was studied here, it seems that this child perceives these differences in the gestural system and reflects these differences in his own use of gestures.
>
> (Test 2001: 172)

As we have seen, in evaluating the amount of input that bilingual children receive, there are a variety of factors which need to be taken into account. These include both language use and other, non-linguistic, factors. Other considerations relate to, for example, self-report data (that is, the parents reporting about the extent to which they communicate in a particular language with their child), which may be quite unreliable. Goodz (1994), for example, found that despite parents' apparent commitment to a strict one-parent, one-language policy, all the parents in her study spoke both languages to their children at various times. How strictly parents maintain the one-parent one-language approach may also, of course, vary over time. Documentation of the context of bilingual language acquisition is essential to an understanding of bilingual language acquisition itself. This has been thoroughly addressed by Lanza (2004), who examined the question of language mixing in bilingual children. Her overarching argument is that language mixing in bilingual children is not a reflection of the child confusing the two languages but, rather, may reflect the way language is used by the parents. Lanza suggests that there are five basic types of discourse strategies which parents may adopt in response to their children's language mixing and that these strategies occur on a continuum which reflects the ways the monolingual or bilingual context can be negotiated. Figure A3.1 (Lanza 2004: 268) illustrates this.

The first two strategies used by the parent are essentially requests for clarification. For example, if we assume that the child is acquiring two languages, A and B, and is in a context with the parent who speaks Language A, then, when using the *minimal grasp strategy*, the parent will respond to the child's utterance in Language B by

Monolingual context				Bilingual context
Minimal grasp	Expressed guess	Adult repetition	Move-on strategy	Code switching

Figure A3.1 Parental discourse strategies (from Lanza 2004: 268)

requesting clarification in Language A. Similarly, with the *expressed guess strategy* the parent will make a guess (using Language A) at the child's meaning (in Language B). Both these responses are likely to encourage the child to use Language A since they do not necessarily imply full understanding by this parent of Language B.

The *adult repetition strategy*, in which the adult repeats in Language A the child's utterance provided in Language B, may encourage the child to speak in Language A. However, this strategy also demonstrates to the child that the parent understands Language B. This point is important since this may indicate to the child that use of Language B, while perhaps not preferred, is certainly acceptable. Similarly, with the *move-on strategy*, the parent is demonstrating that the child's utterance has been understood simply by allowing the conversation or activity to continue. Thus, these two strategies both imply that the parent has a good understanding of Language B. They do not necessarily encourage the child to think in terms of having to use Language A exclusively. The strategy of *code mixing* is where the parent switches from Language A to Language B in response to the child's code mix, thus implicitly accepting the child's code switching (Lanza 1997, 2004).

The different strategies can be used to examine parental discourse strategies in interacting with their bilingual children, and, as can be seen, the parents' understanding of how they interact with their bilingual child will allow them to make choices, either consciously or unconsciously, about whether to encourage a monolingual or bilingual context of interaction. Lanza (1992, 1997) used this system to explore the bilingual acquisition of two children being raised in Norway by an English-speaking mother and a Norwegian father. Her highly detailed study of the language acquisition of the two children being raised in this family suggests that 'In family bilingualism parental strategies are decisive for establishing active bilingualism, particularly the strategies of the minority language-speaking parent' (Lanza 2004: 326).

OTHER FACTORS IMPACTING ON BILINGUAL ACQUISITION

One factor which needs to be taken into consideration is the status of the minority language in the family. In a situation where one of the parents speaks a minority language, and the other speaks the language of the outside community, it may be quite challenging to ensure that the child receives adequate input from the minority language to enable the child to become bilingual in both languages. Juan-Garau and Pérez-Vidal (2001) examine the parental strategies used with a child acquiring Catalan and English in a Catalan-speaking situation in order to identify the types of input strategies that were used which enhanced the child's ability to speak both languages. They argue that in a situation in which the minority language is spoken by one parent, the strategy of using code mixing by the speaker of the more dominant language may illustrate an attempt by this parent to promote the use of the minority language. They also show that a change in strategy by the father (the speaker of the minority language) when the child turned three was successful in developing and extending the child's communicative competence in this language. Their findings, they suggest, are in agreement with those of Goodz (1989). She found that fathers tended to have higher expectations of their children's linguistic abilities in their interactions with their children once the children had acquired a level of language competence which allowed this.

A further consideration may relate to the location in which the languages are used. Quay (1998) provides a detailed outline of the input a child growing up bilingually receives from both her parents, where both of them speak both languages. She discusses the different strategies they adopt. Initially, the mother speaks English to the child when alone with her, but Spanish when the father, who always speaks Spanish to the child, is present. However, when the child is one year old, the mother changes strategies, speaking Spanish to the child at home all the time, except when monolingual English-speaking visitors are present, when English is spoken. The child also attends a crèche where only English is spoken. Quay reports that the child would speak Spanish at home and on the journey to the crèche, but would switch to English while talking to her mother upon entering the crèche gate. Upon leaving, the child spoke English until she got into the car, whereupon she spoke Spanish. This phenomenon, where language is associated with specific situations, is not unusual. Quay argues that it is important for parents to be flexible in their language use with their children to ensure that children being raised bilingually grow up with appropriate awareness of appropriate bilingual behaviour in different linguistic contexts.

Our current understanding of the way in which children acquire two languages simultaneously derives largely from the substantial number of detailed case studies of children growing up in 'one-parent, one-language' situations (such as De Houwer 1990; Lanza 1997; Deuchar and Quay 2000). In these situations, the input to the child is controlled by one parent speaking one language to the child, while the other parent uses a different language. This means that there is generally clear functional differentiation between the two languages.

However, in many situations where the community is bilingual (or even multi-lingual), people may move from one language to another in the same conversational turn, or even in the same sentence. This shift from one language to another is known as code switching, and where children are growing up in these environments, the languages they are learning may be much less well differentiated than is the case in many of the studies we have looked at so far where the languages are kept much more separate. Generally there has been much less of a focus on the kinds of developmental patterns which may occur in situations where children are growing up bilingually (or multilingually) but where the input they are receiving is variable (people may use their different languages in differing amount) and mixed (people may code switch routinely in conversation).

In these contexts, the input directed to children can be expected to reflect this complexity, and children will receive highly variable input, which may include several languages and/or dialects in addition to considerable code switching from the individuals who provide these children with the major source of their input. While research suggests that children growing up in bilingual situations develop both languages at a similar rate to their monolingual peers (Oller et al. 1997), these results have tended to come from studies in which the language input is differentiated by person and/or context. For example, in many Indigenous communities in central Australia, code switching is the normal way of talking in the community. Adults may use a variety of different codes, ranging from more or less acrolectal (English-like) to basilectal (less English-like) creoles, and may incorporate more or fewer tokens of the traditional language into their speech. Children raised in these communities grow up hearing a variety of different speech from adults at different ages (McConvell et al. 2005) where language choice is used for expressive purposes (McConvell 1988). Thus, in these central Australian communities code switching is a normal way of life. We are only just beginning, however, to understand how children in communities of this type acquire language from the complex input that surrounds them.

Summary

In this unit we have discussed a range of issues which are important to the developing languages of the bilingual child. We have limited this discussion to those children about whom the most research is available – those children growing up with parents who speak two different languages. It is important, however, to remember that for many children growing up with two languages, the different languages are not always as clearly differentiated as much of the research indicates. Many children hear two or three languages in their community from birth, and often the speakers of these languages code-switch regularly in conversation.

In Unit B4 we will explore three studies in more depth. The first study focuses on the input characteristics of the parents' language spoken to the child and the kinds of strategies that they adopt, and what this means for the child's developing languages. The second study looks at the choices the child makes in terms of languages early on in the acquisition process. The final study examines the phonological development of two languages in a single child. This last study is important because it may throw some light on the stage at which the two languages are clearly differentiated by the child.

Unit A4
Bilingualism and cognitive ability

Is bilingualism likely to interfere with a child's general overall development?

Is bilingualism beneficial to a child's mental development?

Will learning two languages be confusing for a child?

Despite the fact that bilingualism is the way of life for the majority of the world's population, the question of whether or not bilingualism should be encouraged is often asked in countries where the population is predominantly monolingual. Where countries which are multilingual are concerned, the question is sometimes asked when the second or third languages involved are those that do not enjoy official patronage. The people who are most concerned with these questions are generally parents and educators who wish to raise their children in the best possible language environment.

Over the years, research has evolved from a predominantly pessimistic view of bilingualism to one of optimism as the beneficial effects of bilingualism on both the social and the cognitive abilities of bilinguals have become more widely documented. From a practical point of view, knowing two languages simply means gaining access to two different worlds and having twice the opportunities. The majority of people in the world in fact grow up bilingual in situations where two or more languages are constantly being used in both educational and social contexts. For this group of bilinguals, the benefits of bilingualism are plainly obvious and they hardly need to be convinced, as there is strong instrumental motivation to maintain their bilingualism. Unfortunately, the same cannot be said for bilinguals who live in societies with a single dominant language such as, for example, Britain, the United States and Australia, where the documented benefits have not filtered down to the general public. In such places, the fear that bilingualism or multilingualism may somehow contribute to cognitive deficits is a further disincentive and an enduring social and psychological obstacle to the growth of multilingualism.

The objective of this unit is to evaluate the cognitive ramifications for those who have embarked on a bilingual way of life. We will begin by tracing the historical development of attitudes and research on bilingualism and cognition, and address the assumptions embedded in these studies, particularly the earlier ones. Following that, we will examine 'cognitive flexibility' and 'metalinguistic awareness', two commonly reported positive effects of bilingualism on cognition. Finally, we will briefly summarize the implications of these findings for the social and educational experience of bilinguals and isolate the circumstances or situations which are conducive to promoting the positive effects of bilingualism.

 Task A4.1

➤ If you were an Indonesian parent bringing up a child in a place where English was the dominant language used in schools and in other public domains, what concerns might you have about:

- ■ not being able to give the child enough English input at home before the start of school?
- ■ encouraging your child to spend more time learning and using Indonesian?
- ■ the impact of your child's Indonesian on her/his English competence?

The questions posed in Task A4.1 are general but common concerns, which most parents have when choosing to bring up their children bilingually. As all parents want the best for their children, such concerns are understandable. To be able to address these concerns, however, we need to first know about the impact of speaking a second language on the child's general development. We will begin by tracking the main developments in this area of research and by reviewing the terms and concepts encountered. The vast literature in this area of study can be broadly divided into three main categories:

- ■ studies which demonstrated detrimental effects of bilingualism
- ■ studies which demonstrated no negative or positive effects of bilingualism
- ■ studies which demonstrated enhancing effects of bilingualism.

The question 'Is bilingualism bad?' is one that has been around for a long time, and the many years of positive research reports on this topic have not been enough to dispel this notion among educators and lay people alike. Although it is encouraging to hear people espouse the idea of bilingualism, it is also common to hear doubts and reservations expressed about the potential harm of exposing a child to two or more languages. Parents who have chosen to bring up their children bilingually or trilingually are often asked the seemingly innocuous question 'Isn't it confusing for the child to learn so many languages?' When people ask this question, it is often because they are making assumptions about language and how language affects our minds. For example, a commonly held assumption is that speaking too many languages leads to speakers confusing one language with another, leading to the inability to learn any one language successfully. Another assumption is that it is impossible to be good at two languages, and that one is likely to suffer should children insist on retaining, for example, the home language. As Grosjean (1982) pointed out, while we never doubt that the study of mathematics or the pursuit of music is good for our general development, the learning or use of an additional language

– an innocent enough activity – seems to attract close scrutiny. Historically, bilingualism has been scrutinized, particularly in contexts where a bilingual is seen to be failing or floundering in academic contexts or is suffering from a language-related impairment such as stuttering or hearing loss. In such situations, it is understandable that learning a second language will be a low priority for parents already battling with other more serious issues. However, there is no research to indicate that bilingualism will adversely affect stuttering, or that a second language will be detrimental to those who are hearing-impaired. Although Crutchley et al. (1997) found that bilingual children with SLI (Specific Language Impairment) performed worse than their monolingual counterparts, their findings were contradicted when sampling variables were accounted for. Instead of classifying bilingual SLI children as one generic group, Paradis et al. (2003) isolated French–English bilinguals with SLI who acquired both languages simultaneously, and compared them to their French and English monolinguals who have SLI. When these careful sample selection procedures were put in place, they found no difference between the severity of language impairment in bilingual as compared to monolingual SLI children. This underscores the importance of adequately describing bilingual samples under study. Paradis et al.'s (2003) findings are indeed reassuring to parents whose bilingual children have some form of language disability. Up to now, there is no evidence to suggest that bilingualism is negatively associated with language impairment.

When it comes to children in special populations, the problems are manyfold. One of the main problems is to do with measurement as, traditionally, these children are assessed only in one language, for a variety of reasons (see Unit B2). When Thordardottir et al. (1997) experimented with using both the languages of the bilingual children in their treatment, not only did they find that no adverse effects can be attributed to the use of bilingual intervention but they concluded that bilingual intervention is desirable as it avoids negative aspects that can result from using only one language from a child's bilingual environment.

While mathematical skills and musical skills are seen to enhance mental ability and, therefore, mental space, language learning has always been seen as something that occupies mental space. When it comes to languages, the brain is seen as a finite space for which language or languages must jostle for room. Unfortunately, this myth is something that has been perpetuated by bilingual researchers themselves. Over the years, it has been claimed that in terms of vocabulary acquisition, bilinguals lag behind monolinguals but they catch up at a later age, an assumption that, as we have found in Unit A3, is negated when we cease to see bilinguals as two composite monolinguals. In the following sections, we will trace the various developments in this area of research and tease out the factors which have led to assumptions about bilingualism in both past and current practice.

THE EARLY YEARS: BILINGUALISM HAS DETRIMENTAL EFFECTS ON COGNITIVE FUNCTIONING

While bilingualism itself has a long history, it was not till the mid nineteenth century that possible harmful effects of speaking a second language were formally expressed by Humboldt (1767–1835), who argued that it is only through monolingualism that we can preserve the essence of each individual language. Though Humboldt's idealization of monolingualism did not help in affirming the status of bilingualism, it was the 'hard' evidence from social science that delivered the most damage.

The earliest documented empirical work on the detrimental effects of bilingualism came from three articles published by Saer and his colleagues between 1922 and 1924 (Saer 1923; Saer et al. 1924), which found mainly negative effects for bilingualism. These studies were crucial in influencing decades of subsequent research. In an extensive study, Saer (1923) compared 1400 seven- to eleven-year-old bilingual and monolingual children from Wales (Task C1.2 explores this article in more detail). Children were given a range of tests, including an IQ test, from which Saer concluded that bilingual children were significantly inferior to monolingual children, and that this difference became more pronounced with increasing age. However, there were significant methodological problems with Saer's research in both his sampling procedure and the type of measurements he took. First and foremost, he was comparing middle-class monolingual children with working-class bilingual children, and the reliability of the tasks he used in terms of what these tasks say about cognitive ability of bilinguals was also questionable. Saer also translated standard tests from English to Welsh, a practice (as we saw in Unit A2) which is known not to produce accurate results. Other studies in the same period echoed Saer's findings. Pintner and Keller (1922) compared the performance of English-speaking children and 'foreign' children on IQ scores and a series of other cognitive tests. Parentage was mainly used to categorize children as bilinguals or monolinguals in this study, and as a result the English-speaking groups consisted of Anglo-Celtic Americans, Afro-Americans and Americans of Jewish descent. The foreign group consisted mainly of children of Italian and Spanish parentage. Pintner and Keller found that foreign children scored poorly on IQ tests in comparison with other non-verbal tests of intelligence.

Despite severe methodological flaws, a whole series of studies confirmed the inferiority of bilinguals in both verbal and non-verbal tasks. In some studies, they were found to perform poorly only on tests of non-verbal intelligence (see Darcy 1953 for a comprehensive review). These studies spanned four continents and involved 26 different cultural groups including Chinese, Japanese and Hopi Indians. Though more than 50 per cent of the studies indicated weak levels of language competence in English for the bilingual population, English was the medium used for testing. There is no doubt that being tested in the weaker language is one of the reasons why the bilinguals performed poorly in the experimental tasks.

Task A4.2

➤ How do you ensure that your bilingual and monolingual samples are comparable? If you have to choose monolingual and bilingual children from the general population to investigate the effects of bilingualism on cognitive development, what guidelines would you choose to select your participants?

➤ Socio-economic status (SES), is an important variable in social science research. What do you think are some of the concrete effects of SES on the daily experience of bilingual and monolingual children?

Despite their methodological flaws, these studies had considerable influence, and by the middle of the twentieth century the opinion that bilingualism is detrimental to cognitive functioning was firmly established. This was so despite the fact that several contemporary studies had found no significant positive or negative impact of bilingualism on mental functioning.

For example, Bere (1924) found that the outcomes were affected by the home language of the children. Her tests also strongly indicated that children who spoke English at home did better in the tests. This confirmed the 'language handicap' hypothesis put forward by other researchers who had reported negative findings. This observation was further supported by the finding that foreign children's scores on the Kuhlmann–Binet Scale (a test of general cognitive ability) increased after receiving at least one year of exposure to English in school (Arthur 1937). More notably, in a carefully controlled but small study by Arsenian (1937) where bilingual children aged between nine and fourteen were carefully screened and matched with monolinguals for SES and age, no differences were found in measures of intelligence used. Other studies such as Jones and Stewart (1951) reported that lower scores for non-verbal skills in the bilingual population of their study could be due to SES rather than to linguistic background. The importance of SES in underscoring performance results was also highlighted by other researchers (cf. McCarthy 1930; James 1960).

Generally, the studies between 1922 and 1943 used an assortment of intelligence quotient (IQ) tests as standard tools to measure the cognitive abilities of bilinguals. Some of the tests used were language-based and some were not. These studies indicate that once the language component was factored out of the tests, bilinguals were not inferior to monolinguals in performance. It is obvious that the results of such tests are going to be only as reliable as the instrumentation or type of tasks used. As we noted above, several studies in this early period used translated tests, and, as we discussed in Unit A2, translated tests should never be considered as equivalents of the original tests.

Another issue of concern is whether the various IQ tests used were valid measures of intelligence. This is a contentious topic which is beyond the scope of the discussion here. It is widely recognized, however, that such tests do not measure innate abilities; instead, they contain inherent cultural bias which may place bilingual children at a distinct disadvantage. Needless to say, using a culturally biased set of instruments on a bilingual and bicultural population is methodologically questionable. Furthermore, traditional IQ tests measure only *convergent thinking* – that is, arriving at a single solution after assessing a series of problems. This excludes *divergent thinking*, which has been linked with creative intelligence.

 Task A4.3

➤ In studies where outcomes are related to the status of monolingualism or bilingualism, it is clearly important that the researchers are clear about how 'bilingualism' is defined and measured. This is a problem faced by most researchers working in the area of bilingualism, and there are no easy answers. However, if you were to do a study in which 'bilingualism' was a variable, how would you:

   ■ define your bilingual participants?
   ■ determine the degree of bilingualism in your participants?

➤ It may be helpful to think about a target bilingual sample that you might want to work with. You may also want to review some of the issues raised about measuring bilinguals in Unit A2.

The most severe criticism of studies from this early period concerns the inadequate definition of bilingualism and the confounding of SES and ethnicity variables. Most of the studies in this period fail to control adequately for the effects of SES, with bilingualism frequently being severely confounded with low SES. In a detailed analysis of preceding studies, McCarthy (1930) reported that more than half of the bilingual schoolchildren in such studies came from typical working-class backgrounds. In contrast, the English monolinguals were from educated middle-class homes. Furthermore, how bilingual proficiency was measured in the bulk of the early studies was problematic. As discussed in Unit A2, the measurement of bilingual proficiency is a highly complex process and unless it is done well, the findings drawn from such studies will always be questionable. After four decades of inconclusive findings, the turning point came in 1962, when Peal and Lambert published their ground-breaking paper on this topic.

BILINGUALISM ENHANCES COGNITIVE FUNCTIONING

Despite inconclusive evidence about the negative effects of bilingualism, up until the 1960s bilingualism was not a concept that was associated with anything positive. In the first documented case study of a bilingual, Leopold (1949a) cited his bilingual daughter Hildegarde's metalinguistic awareness as evidence of the enhancing effects of bilingualism. He noticed that she was precociously aware of rhymes and would deliberately destroy rhymes in word play. Leopold argued that bilinguals were able to detach sound from meaning because of the constant early exposure to two languages. So, from a very young age a bilingual child is constantly aware of two competing forms for one meaning. This, he stressed, puts a bilingual child in a position of advantage over a monolingual child.

Although Leopold is fondly cited by researchers these days, a single case study in the midst of a robust body of work pointing to the contrary was bound to have little impact. In this respect, Peal and Lambert's (1962) study, which re-examined the issue of the relationship of bilingualism to intelligence, marked a major watershed in the history of bilingual research. Although it will be given detailed attention in section Unit B4.2, we will briefly summarize it here.

Peal and Lambert (1962) strictly controlled the SES and language background of the 364 bilingual and monolingual participants in their Canadian study. They screened their sample with great care, matching the children on SES, sex, age, language, intelligence and attitude. Their study found that once SES and language competence variables were controlled, bilinguals outperformed monolinguals in IQ tests. Moreover, bilinguals were also found to have more positive attitudes towards French-speaking communities than their (English or French) monolingual counterparts had.

Another interesting question arose as bilinguals in Peal and Lambert's study were found to be not categorically better on all measures of non-verbal tasks. Such tasks can be divided into two subgroups, one requiring spatial and perceptual processes and the other requiring symbolic manipulation. In spatial and perceptual processes, the emphasis is on spatial acuity and perceptual speed, whereas symbol manipulation tasks require understanding of abstract relations, concepts and factual information. The Raven Progressive Matrices, developed by Raven (1998), are one example of this type of test which requires symbolic manipulation. In such tests, the participants must form a concept or discover relations between elements, which cannot be done without some level of cognitive reorganization. The test consist of 60 matrices or designs of varying complexity from which a part has been removed, and participants are required to choose the missing insert from a set of eight alternatives. These items are often seen in IQ tests and a very similar example can be found in Aiken and Groth-Marnat (2006: 137).

Task A4.4

➤ The issues of what constitutes general intelligence and how intelligence should be measured are widely debated. Try out one of the many IQ tests available online and see if you can identify the items that measure non-verbal intelligence and those that measure verbal intelligence.

In Peal and Lambert's study, bilinguals were found to be better in the symbolic manipulation types of non-verbal tasks but performed the same as the monolinguals in the non-verbal tasks requiring spatial and perceptual processes. Peal and Lambert called this ability 'mental or cognitive flexibility' and proposed that bilinguals' early awareness of two different codes, and their ability to associate two words with one object, may have enhanced the development of an increased cognitive flexibility. Peal and Lambert's study is extremely significant because it gave the next generation of researchers the ideological backdrop underpinning the methodological guidelines with which to investigate more rigorously the relationship between bilingualism and the mind.

BILINGUALISM AND INTELLIGENCE

On the surface, Peal and Lambert's landmark study laid to rest previous claims of monolingual superiority in IQ tests. However, the first challenge that Peal and Lambert faced was the criticism that their bilingual subjects were somehow more intelligent to start with, and that this was why they were so efficiently bilingual. By stringently controlling the level of bilingualism in their subjects, they might have in effect precluded those of lower intelligence from participating in their study. This is not an insignificant point as previous studies (e.g. Gardner and Lambert 1959) had shown a positive correlation between language aptitude and intelligence. One may ask whether the more intelligent children, as measured by non-verbal intelligence tests, are the ones who become bilingual, or whether bilingualism itself has a favourable effect on non-verbal intelligence.

Peal and Lambert's own exploratory analysis seemed to indicate that some level of intelligence is essential for bilingualism. However, this does not rule out the fact that bilingualism may in some ways be a positive influence on non-verbal abilities. This thorny 'chicken first or egg first' issue was finally resolved by Hakuta and Diaz (1985), who conducted a longitudinal study which tracked the relationship between cognition and bilingual proficiency. By assessing both the language proficiency and the cognitive level of bilinguals over time, Hakuta and Diaz presented findings which conclusively supported the hypothesis that it is bilingual proficiency that exerts an influence on cognitive functioning and not the other way round. By confirming the positive causal relationship between intelligence and bilingualism their study marks another key turning point. However, in a later study, Hakuta (1987) reanalysed the longitudinal data and argued that, while the degree of bilingualism was a better predictor of cognitive ability, the reverse was also true, although the effect was not quite as strong. He also reported another set of results, which indicated that there was no relationship between increased bilingual proficiency and the metalinguistic awareness for the bilingual sample, who were drawn mainly from lower socio-economic backgrounds. In his discussion, Hakuta argued that the context in which bilinguals function must be taken into account. In this case, the bilinguals were bilingual in a subtractive setting. As we discussed in Unit A1, the social environment of the bilingual often has important implications for the shaping of the bilingual experience.

Task A4.5

➤ Given that balanced bilinguals are not very common, what language should bilinguals be tested in? What are some of the practical problems which researchers have to overcome when working with bilingual samples in terms of:

■ the language the test is designed in?
■ the language used by researchers when conducting these tests?

CURRENT VIEWS ON THE EFFECTS OF BILINGUALISM

The direction of research following Peal and Lambert's study took an about-turn. Since 1965, a stream of papers have highlighted the positive effects of bilingualism and marked a change in research focus. Instead of making a general search for IQ superiority, the new generation of researchers have been far more specific in their enquiry. Various researchers found that bilinguals were superior to monolinguals on tasks requiring *cognitive flexibility* and *metalinguistic awareness*, while others argued that special conditions have to exist before bilinguals can enjoy the cognitive benefits. These conditions are usually related to the level of proficiency attained in the two languages. As mentioned in Unit A2, it has been hypothesized that bilinguals have to achieve certain thresholds in their language competence before reaping the cognitive rewards. In the next few sections, we will review some of the literature in this area and try to draw out the common issues uncovered in the different studies.

Cognitive flexibility

Loosely defined, *cognitive flexibility* is used to mean creativity or ability to use divergent thinking, such as the ability to generate multiple associations from one concept, or the ability to mentally reorganize the elements of a problem or situation. How is cognitive flexibility measured? What type of tasks measure divergent thinking? The answer is varied. For example, in Scott's (1973) study, she asked her participants to generate as many possible uses for paper clips as they could. In a different study, Feldman and Shen (1971) used a Piagetian Object Constancy task in which pre-school children were presented with a paper plate which was destroyed in their presence. After this, they were presented with an identical plate and asked, 'Is this plate the same as the plate I showed you just now?' According to the study, bilinguals were more likely to answer 'no' in comparison to their monolingual counterparts. Feldman and Shen concluded that bilinguals arrived at an object constancy developmental stage earlier than monolinguals because of their exposure to two languages.

Landry (1974) and Cummins (1977) both reported that learning a second language in elementary school might increase divergent thinking. Using an Embedded Figure

Test – a specific task for measuring cognitive flexibility which involves detecting simple objects embedded in larger, more elaborate figures such as the search for multiple hidden objects in the *Where's Waldo?* picture book – bilingual children were found to perform significantly better than monolingual children (Balkan 1970; Cummins and Gulutsan 1973).

Metalinguistic awareness

As indicated by Leopold in 1949, bilinguals have an advantage when it comes to analysing language forms owing to their early exposure to two different linguistic codes, since such exposure promotes a more analytic orientation to linguistic operations. As a result, bilinguals are metalinguistically more aware than monolinguals, a trait which Cummins (1977) defined as the development of children's awareness of certain properties of language including their ability to analyse linguistic input.

Broadly defined, metalinguistic awareness is the ability to focus on different levels of linguistic structures such as words, phonemes and syntax. This ability to analyse language more intensely has been the subject of many studies (see Bialystok 2001b for a review). Metalinguistic awareness and bilingualism is a burgeoning area of study, with researchers working on a number of different aspects, some focused on the phoneme level, some on the word level and some on the sentence level. Generally, these studies have targeted the following aspects of linguistic structure:

- word awareness
- phonological awareness
- sentence awareness
- semantic awareness.

In the following sections, we will briefly discuss metalinguistic awareness studies for each of these linguistic structures.

Word awareness

There are two interpretations of *word awareness*: the ability to recognize that the speech stream is composed of discrete units called words, and the awareness that the relationship between words and their meaning is arbitrary. Traditionally, researchers working on word awareness in bilingual populations have adapted word awareness tasks developed for the monolingual population. (See Bowey and Tunmer 1984 for a discussion of word awareness in the context of monolingual children.)

The awareness of word as a discrete unit

In a series of studies, Bialystok (1986a, 1986b, 1987a, 1987b, 1988) compared the performances of Grade 1 English monolingual and French–English bilingual children on tasks such as sentence segmentation (word count) and word judgements. The children were read sentences which were either intact or scrambled and asked to count the number of words in each utterance. The number of syllables and morphemes were also manipulated to further examine the child's concept of word. In these studies, bilinguals consistently outperformed monolinguals except in the case of sentences consisting entirely of monosyllabic words.

Yelland et al. (1993) found word awareness in Grade 1 children who were learning Italian as a second language to be higher than among those who were not receiving language classes. Even more interesting is their finding that higher word awareness was also correlated with heightened reading skills, though this advantage disappeared at the end of Grade 1. Their finding was supported by Campbell and Sais (1995), who compared the performance of 15 English monolingual and 15 English–Italian pre-schoolers on a range of word awareness tasks and found that the bilinguals performed better than the monolinguals. As word awareness is implicated in phoneme awareness, the authors concluded that exposure to a second language in the pre-literate stage can only serve to enhance the development of literacy. In a more generic study, Goncz and Kodžopelijć (1991) also reported that children with bilingual pre-school experience exhibited more developed reading skills such as concentration, synthesis and abstraction than monolingual children.

Task A4.6

➤ Yelland et al.'s (1993) study is intriguing as they found that even minimal exposure to a second language can have positive outcomes in terms of meta-linguistic awareness. If exposure to a second language promotes word awareness and this has been found to be indicative of heightened reading skills, what implications does this research have for early and primary education?

The awareness of the arbitrariness of language

The very basis of metalinguistic awareness requires the understanding that language is essentially symbolic and that the relationship between form and function is completely arbitrary. In studies by Ianco-Worrall (1972) and Ben-Zeev (1977), children were asked to play a game involving some symbolic manipulation. One task required a simple symbol substitution that tested the children's acceptance of the arbitrariness of language. For example, they were asked if it was all right to switch names for 'turtle' and 'plane'. They were then asked to play a game where they had to say 'turtle' when they meant 'plane'.

This is named *plane*, right? (The experimenter holds up a toy aeroplane.)

In this game its name is *turtle.*

Can the *turtle* fly? (Correct answer: yes.)

How does the *turtle* fly? (Correct answer: with its wings.)

In other tasks, the substitution involved violating grammatical rules of the language. For example, children were told to replace 'the boy' with 'pencils' when given the sentence 'The boy sings loudly'.

Here, the bilingual children were first pre-tested with Berko's (1958) Wug Test. (The Wug Test is a morphological test which tries to find out if children are able to generalize simple morphological rules such as rules for forming the past tense, using novel words.) Only children who scored 70 per cent and above for the Wug Test were selected. (Information and jpeg versions of the Wug Test can be downloaded from *Wugs-Online* on http://childes.psy.cmu.edu/topics/.) This was to ensure that violation of grammatical rules in the task was voluntary and not due to the children's lack of grammatical competence in the test language.

Bilinguals are expected to do better in such tasks as they are more aware of the arbitrariness of language. Hence, they are more likely to reject the notion that one object can only have one name. The Afrikaans–English children in Ianco-Worrall's study and the Hebrew–English children in Ben-Zeev's study both performed better than their monolingual comparison groups in this task. However, Ben-Zeev did not find a bilingual advantage in her Spanish–English bilinguals. She concluded, however, that the lower SES of her Spanish–English bilingual subjects in comparison to the monolingual group could be the reason for the failure of the bilingual group to perform better in such tasks.

In a slightly different task with Irish–English bilinguals, Cummins (1978) asked children drawn from Grades 3 and 6 of middle-class Dublin schools to justify their responses to questions. The children were asked, 'Suppose you were making up names for things, could you then call the sun "the moon" and the moon "the sun"?' and were then required to justify their response. The children's justifications fell into three categories:

- *empirical justifications.* For example, 'The names could be interchanged because both the sun and the moon shine.'
- *rigid conventional justifications.* For example, 'They are their right names so you couldn't change them.'
- *arbitrary assignment responses which recognized the arbitrary relationship between form and function.* For example, 'You could change the names because it doesn't matter what things are called.'

The findings indicate that bilinguals were significantly more likely to respond with an appeal to the arbitrariness of language and that this tendency was even more pronounced among the children in Grade 6.

Task A4.7

➤ These studies on arbitrariness require children to violate semantic and grammatical rules. The ability to violate rules is seen as an indication of metalinguistic flexibility. Can you think of possible arguments against this assumption?

Phonological awareness

Phonological awareness is the ability to recognize that speech is composed of distinct units of sound. In phonological awareness tasks, children are required to isolate relevant phonological segments as the basis of their analysis. For example, they may be asked to identify the 'odd one out' (e.g. in groups such as '*pat, pan, pal and pet*') or they may be asked to provide minimal pairs (e.g. 'Give me another word that sounds like *hat*') or supply rhyming words etc. (e.g. 'Take away the first sound of *pat* by substituting the first sound of *mop*'). All such tasks test the children's ability to segment sounds into discrete phonological units.

Using an assortment of such tasks, Davine et al. (1971) found that bilingual children in elementary school in Canada performed better than monolingual children in distinguishing phonological differences. Rubin and Turner (1989) reported a similar advantage that extended into reading and writing skills in their cohort of French–English bilinguals. In an extensive and carefully controlled study by Bruck and Genesee (1995), French–English bilinguals were given a battery of phonological awareness tests in both kindergarten and first grade. Their performance was compared to that of age-matched monolingual English speakers. The findings indicated that bilinguals were better in certain phonological tasks such as syllable counting, while monolinguals were better at phoneme counting.

Sentence awareness

Sentence awareness is the ability to recognize utterances which are grammatically acceptable within the language. In sentence awareness tasks, the children are often asked to detect, correct and explain errors. Studies on monolingual children indicate that they have difficulty noting and correcting errors of this kind before the age of 5;6 to 6;0, even though such errors are not present in their speech. However, Galambos and Goldin-Meadow (1983) reported that Spanish–English bilingual children who were proficient in both languages picked out such errors more easily as young as 4;6 years of age. While young monolingual children focused on the message conveyed, bilingual children readily focused on the structure. For example, when provided with a grammatically correct but semantically anomalous sentence like 'Apples grow on noses', bilingual children were more likely to ignore the semantic distraction and focus on the structure. In a subsequent study, Galambos and Hakuta (1988) found that more proficient bilinguals performed better at the tasks than bilinguals with lower levels of proficiency. These findings were again supported, but qualified by a different study by Galambos and Goldin-Meadow (1990), which examined the performance of English monolinguals, Spanish monolinguals and English–Spanish bilinguals who were required to correct, detect and explain a series of grammatical errors. In this study, bilinguals were better than monolinguals at noticing and correcting errors but showed no advantages when they had to explain the errors. The results indicate that bilingualism accelerates metalinguistic awareness but does not change the awareness qualitatively.

 Task A4.8

> Studies on sentence awareness seem to indicate that language proficiency is a factor which may affect the outcome of the results. What implications does it hold for the general claim that bilingualism has positive influences on cognition?

Semantic awareness

There is an assortment of tasks which qualify as semantic awareness tasks even though the researchers who used these tasks did not label them as 'semantic aware-ness' tasks. The Semantic-Phonetic Preference tasks were used in several studies (Ianco-Worrall 1972; Ben-Zeev 1977; Cummins 1978), and bilingual and mono-lingual children's ability to focus on semantic similarity rather than phonetic similarity was compared. In the test trials, the children were given sets of words, such as *cap*, *can* and *hat*. They were then asked, 'Which is more like *cap*, *can* or *hat*?' The choice of *hat* indicated a semantic preference and the choice of *can* indicated a phonetic preference. The bilinguals in Ianco-Worrall and Ben-Zeev's studies were found to give more semantic responses than phonetic responses. In both studies, semantic preference is seen as a more 'sophisticated' choice as it is a prefer-ence which increases with age. Ianco-Worrall (1972) argued that this preference shows that the child is more able to focus on the meaning and is not tied to the form of the words. However, such an interpretation is curious given that a phonetic preference could also be interpreted as a sign of increased phonetic awareness. While the semantic–phonetic preference may be an inadequate measure of semantic awareness, it would be interesting to uncover the motivating principle behind the preference.

Other studies of semantic awareness look at the children's ability to form a semantic hierarchy and organize objects into superordinate or subordinate categories. There is some evidence (Cummins 1978) to show that bilinguals may have some advantage in this kind of mental organization.

Task A4.9

➤ Can monolingual children become metalinguistically more aware without exposure to another language?

Overview of studies on metalinguistic awareness

Overall, the studies on metalinguistic awareness have shown the general superiority of bilinguals in word awareness tasks, though some researchers have instead found that bilinguals do not outperform monolinguals in some specific metalinguistic tests. For example, in phonological awareness tasks, the effect is more task-specific. The various attempts to explain the discrepancy in the research have resulted in two strands of argument. The first is the Threshold hypothesis proposed by Cummins (1976) and the second is the Analysis and Control hypothesis proposed by Bialystok (2001a).

THE THRESHOLD HYPOTHESIS

Cummins attempted to resolve inconsistencies in this area by proposing that lower levels of proficiency attained could explain the lack of advantage found for some bilingual populations. He hypothesized that there are minimum levels of competency which have to be attained before the benefits of bilingualism can set in. In this hypothesis, Cummins proposed two thresholds of language competence. He argued that to avoid negative effects from bilingualism, the lower threshold must be attained and that children at this first threshold will not experience negative or positive benefits from bilingualism. In Cummins's framework, the cognitive growth of children who fail to reach the first threshold will be adversely affected. Those who attain the second threshold (high levels of bilingual competence) will enjoy all the enhancing effects of bilingualism.

The Threshold theory has found support from studies by Bialystok (1988), Dawe (1983), Galambos and Hakuta (1988), Ricciardelli (1992) and Clarkson and Galbraith (1992). All these researchers found that the performance of bilinguals improved with increased language proficiency. Bialystok (1988) and Galambos and Hakuta (1988) found that the proficiency levels of their subjects were crucial in determining the outcome of the findings.

The main problem with the Threshold theory is the difficulty in establishing what these thresholds are in concrete terms. Assuming that an objective quantification of a bilingual's linguistic competence is possible, it is still impossible to determine where one should draw a line for each threshold. Edelsky et al. (1983) aptly point out that the Threshold theory is a post hoc explanation of the bilingual phenomenon and it needs direct empirical investigation with rigorous replications across linguistic and cultural groups. However, given the opaqueness of the concepts, the Threshold hypothesis cannot be clearly defined or empirically tested. This is the main reason why reactions to the Threshold hypothesis have been cautious (see Baker 2006: 144 for a detailed critique).

Furthermore, there are the additional social issues of the context in which one would find children who fail to achieve the lower threshold of competence. There is a strong overlap between situations leading to lower threshold competence and bilingualism in subtractive contexts. Hence, the threshold hypothesis is confounded with social variables, which have not been considered. Moreover, several studies, especially Yelland et al.'s (1993), indicate that high levels of competence are not necessary for the facilitating effects of bilingualism to take place. As evidenced in Yelland et al.'s study, minimal exposure to a second language was enough to give the children an edge in word awareness tasks and reading superiority even though the effect was short-lived.

ANALYSIS AND CONTROL HYPOTHESIS

In Unit A2, we saw that there is a need to take into account the different types of tasks when we are measuring language proficiency. By focusing on the difference in task demands, Bialystok (1988) proposed a model whereby bilinguals, irrespective of their degree of bilingualism, may be more advantaged at tasks which place greater demands on the *control of linguistic processing*. However, bilinguals who have attained high levels of proficiency in both languages are also advantaged at tasks that require more *analysed linguistic knowledge*. Drawing on theories from cognitive processing, Bialystok identified two cognitive processes, control of attention and analysis of representational structure, which she argues are able to explain the different demands in the tasks. In tasks requiring higher levels of analysis, participants have to use their knowledge to work out relationships between concepts and ideas, while in tasks requiring higher levels of control, participants are required to attend to some features while ignoring or inhibiting their response to other distracting features.

In Bialystok's model, examples of tasks which require control of linguistic processing are *word length* and *symbol substitution*, while tasks like *word discrimination*, *word print* and *word order corrections* require the analysis of linguistic knowledge. In the *word length* and *symbol substitution* tasks, the children have to ignore distractors and attend only to key elements, such as the length of the word, as opposed to the picture or the substitution and the violation of the grammar. The *word discrimination, word print* and *word order corrections* tasks all require the children to assess and evaluate their knowledge about that domain, and form judgements based on what they know. Analysis and control are not necessarily mutually exclusive as it is quite possible that tasks which are high in control are high in analysis as well.

The central thesis in Bialystok's (2001a) proposal is that the enhanced metalinguistic awareness effect operates differently for different linguistic structures. She argues that bilingualism does not have a general effect on a domain of knowledge such as metalinguistic awareness. Rather, the effect is on the underlying cognitive processes that are activated in the different tasks. More recently, the bilingual advantage in control of linguistic processing tasks has been found to disappear in young adulthood only to reappear again at a later stage (Bialystok et al. 2005). This framework presents a useful way of resolving the discrepancies in research findings.

So far, all the studies discussed have focused on a restricted set of Indo-European languages. More cross-linguistic studies focusing on languages with typologically different orthographies will allow us to better assess the relationship between phonological awareness and bilingualism. What is significant in these studies is the suggestion of the potential link between bilingualism and phonological and word awareness skills. The fact that both sets of skills are implicated in early literacy (cf. Tunmer and Myhill 1984) means that the role that bilingualism plays in enhancing literacy development in early childhood needs to be taken into account. In other words, if it could be conclusively shown that bilingualism is a crucial variable in promoting or accelerating early onset of literacy, it would have major implications for bilingual educational policies.

Summary

Apart from cognitive flexibility and metalinguistic awareness, bilingualism has also been found to enhance other types of cognitive skills (see Cummins 2000). It has been found to help in metaphor processing and has even been found to exert positive influences on the development of mathematical reasoning and logical deduction skills. In a Theory of Mind study which looks at young children's understanding of mental verbs such as 'think' and 'believe', Goetz (2003) found Mandarin–English bilinguals to be more advanced than monolinguals. There is also some evidence that bilingualism can have an enhancing effect on the learning of a third language, as various researchers such as Bild and Swain (1989) have reported that Grade 8 students from heritage (non-English immigrant) language backgrounds who were enrolled in a French–English bilingual programme performed better than an English-background group in the same programme. In a different study, Swain and Lapkin (1991) compared the French proficiency of four groups of students and found that children who had literacy skills in their heritage language performed better in their third language. Clyne et al. (2004) have similarly reported bilinguals to be more effective and persistent learners of a target language than monolingual learners. Apart from their general language learning abilities, bilingual children were also found to acquire pragmatic skills more efficiently in a third language (Jorda and Pilar 2003).

In sum, the evidence that bilingualism per se does not cause any harm has been firmly established. The literature in this area is far too robust for anyone still to maintain that bilingualism is detrimental to cognitive functioning. Most of the articles that reported negative findings were either methodologically or theoretically flawed. Instead, there is substantial evidence to suggest that bilingualism may have cognitively enhancing effects. More specifically, bilinguals perform better in tasks requiring cognitive flexibility and are also superior in certain metalinguistic skills, though this last observation is not universally held, nor is it drawn from studies which are methodologically flawless.

Generally, armed with a more informed understanding of the phenomenon of bilingualism, the newer generation of students and researchers are more cautious in interpreting findings. This does not obviate the fact that often the tasks used to measure the same constructs under investigation vary widely. And although researchers are now more careful about measuring proficiency levels of bilinguals, different studies use very different measures. It is thus important that we extrapolate trends from these studies with careful consideration.

While we can confidently bury the 'bilingualism is bad' precept, we can only hypo-thesize that 'bilingualism is good' under certain conditions and in certain contexts. If bilingualism is positive, why are the effects not categorically visible across all bilingual groups? What are these specific conditions and what are the specific contexts which are necessary before we can consistently and confidently predict beneficial effects of bilingualism? These are some questions which we will continue to explore in Unit B4 through reading Peal and Lambert (1962), which ushered in a methodological rethink which saw a spurt of research illustrating positive effects as well as a refinement of explanations and justifications. The second article, by Bialystok (2001b), refined how we understand the relationship between cognition and bilingualism by focusing on the ways in which bilingualism affects different aspects of metalinguistic awareness. These articles are iconic papers from these two periods.

Unit A5
Language attrition in bilinguals

What happens to your language skills if you do not use the language for a period of time?

Do we forget first the things we learned first? Are you likely to lose skills in a language more rapidly if you stop using it at a younger age?

Will increased competence in the language make attrition less likely? Can language attrition be reversed?

Many of us learn a language at school, college and/or university. Some of us may gain considerable proficiency in the language through spending time either as an exchange student, or through work or even on holiday in a country in which that language is spoken. Often, for some reason, we cease to maintain this kind of contact with the language. Then, at some later stage, when we resume contact, we might find that our language abilities are not what they once were. In other situations, people may move from one country to another and, as a result, lose some proficiency in the first language. This is, unfortunately, too often the case with children, especially if they are very young when they move. The focus of this unit is *language attrition*, which refers to the process whereby an individual's ability to speak and understand a language is reduced. The term used for loss of language at a community level, which we will touch on only briefly here, is *language shift*.

Task A5.1

➤ Consider your own experience of learning a language. How well do you consider you knew this language when you were at your most competent?

➤ Make a note of the environments in which you still have contact with the language. If you have had no further contact, try to recall when this contact finished.

➤ In what ways has your competence in the language changed over time?

LANGUAGE ATTRITION AND LANGUAGE SHIFT

While language attrition, or forgetting (Hansen 2001), is for the most part a psycho-linguistic process which takes place at an individual level, it is strongly influenced by a number of social variables. Language shift, however, occurs at the societal level and is usually the result of language contact. Across the world, large numbers of languages have been lost as a result of contact between two or more languages, particularly where one language is dominant and is considered to be the prestige language. In such situations (for example, where the first language of an immigrant group is used alongside the language of the adopted country), there is always a danger that the minority language will be lost. To some extent this is related to individual language attrition as, when a community ceases to use its traditional language and no longer passes it on to its children, there is imminent danger of the language being lost. In some cases (such as the immigrant example given above), this will not necessarily result in language death since the immigrant language will presumably continue to be spoken back in the home country.

In other situations, however, there is the danger of the language being lost altogether. For example, in Australia, many Aboriginal languages have now disappeared and many more are in a period of transition from the traditional language to some form of creole (a hybrid language resulting from contact between English and the traditional language). This process is speeding up in many Indigenous communities as children are no longer learning the traditional language as a first language. This is largely a result of the arrival of English-speaking immigrants (and more recently speakers of other languages), where English has a prestige status as a result of its use in education, business and technology.

What both language attrition at the individual level and language shift at the societal level have in common is lack of use:

> in language loss, sociolinguistics and psycholinguistic processes interact, and . . . in this interaction language use is the crucial and pivotal issue, both in intragenerational attrition and intergenerational shift. Language use is considered as the single most important variable in both acquisition and language loss.
>
> (De Bot 2001: 66)

In this unit, we are going to focus on the processes involved in language attrition at the individual level, and begin to consider the questions of *what* is lost and *why* it occurs. Firstly, we will examine the factors which may affect language attrition – such as age, motivation, education and attitude. This will allow us to evaluate factors which affect language attrition, and the extent to which the language is forgotten. Secondly, we will consider the ways in which language competence is reduced – what features of language disappear first and at what stage in the attrition process this occurs. Owing to limitations of space, we will not consider the complex question of *how* language attrition occurs, although interested readers are referred to

Köpke (2004) for a review of the nature of the mechanisms, both psycholinguistic and neurolinguistic, which underlie language forgetting.

TYPES OF LANGUAGE ATTRITION

Van Els (1986) identified four types of attrition, determined by two dimensions – firstly, *what* is lost, and secondly, *the environment* in which it is lost. This can be depicted diagrammatically (Figure A5.1). Examples of a possible situation in which each type of loss may occur are also provided.

Where it is lost	What is lost	
	First language	*Second language*
First-language environment	E.g. loss of the first language as a result of ageing and/or some pathological conditions (e.g. dementia or trauma)	E.g. loss of a foreign or second language upon return to the first-language environment, or through lack of contact with the second language owing to end of schooling, moving etc.
Second-language environment	E.g. loss of the first language as a result of emigrating to a country in which a different language is spoken; especially likely to apply to children who emigrate with parents	E.g. language loss late in life after emigrating to a country in which a different language is spoken (may also be related to pathological conditions)

Figure A5.1 Types of language loss

The most common types of language attrition are in the two shaded boxes: the loss of a second language in a first-language environment, and the loss of a first language in a second-language environment. In these situations, attrition occurs naturalistically in environments in which another language or languages are dominant (Olshtain 1989). This contrasts with attrition which results from the effects of age, trauma or pathological decline of some sort, which, although important, will not be the focus in this unit (see Paradis 2004 for an extensive treatment of these issues).

Task A5.2

➤ Consider how the following factors might compromise one's language ability after a period of non-use:

- age at time of discontinued use
- proficiency at time of discontinued use
- level of literacy in the language
- number of years since language was last used.

Think about whether you would you expect both comprehension and production to be affected in the same way. If you think they might be affected differently, what leads you to this conclusion?

HYPOTHESES ABOUT LANGUAGE ATTRITION

There are various hypotheses that attempt to explain language attrition, with the earliest being the Regression hypothesis. This was first proposed by Jakobson (1941) in the context of aphasia, and postulated that language attrition was the reverse of the process of language acquisition. In other words, the hypothesis proposed that what was last learned, in terms of language, would be first lost in the process of attrition. Although Jakobson's hypothesis was designed to explain language attrition in aphasics, aphasic language attrition is not progressive and the hypothesis has not been empirically supported. While the Regression hypothesis has been investigated more broadly in studies of attrition (see De Bot and Weltens 1991, 1995), support for the hypothesis has been somewhat limited because, as Tomiyama (2000) pointed out, it is clear that other factors such as frequency of input and the saliency of the linguistic items under study impact on whether or not a specific linguistic feature is lost.

To some extent the issue of frequency of use has been addressed by the Activation Threshold hypothesis (Paradis 1997), which takes into account the frequency with which a linguistic item is used. As Gürel points out, this theory predicts that an individual's ability to access a particular linguistic feature is use-dependent, such that if an item is not used frequently, it will be more difficult to activate (that is, it will have a higher activation threshold). In a situation in which the L1 is being used only minimally, the activation threshold for L1 features will become higher, while that for L2 features, which are being used regularly, will be lower. Thus, it

> specifies the relation between the frequency of use of a linguistic item and its activation and availability to the language user. The more an item is activated, the lower its activation threshold is. The threshold of activation raises if the item is inactive, i.e. unselected (and disused). It is more difficult to (re)activate an item with a high activation threshold. In other words, when a particular linguistic item has a high activation threshold, more activating impulses are required to reactivate it.
>
> (Gürel 2004: 55)

Gürel's (2004) empirical study investigated the effects of L2 English on the pronominal system of L1 Turkish speakers, and she argued that the Activation hypothesis framework is able to predict which linguistic features are most likely to be subjected to attrition. This comes about as a result of the competition these particular features in the L1 are in with features in the other language (the L2) which have a lower activation threshold. Thus, if a form which occurs in the L1 is not available in the L2, competition does not set in, and the form will be less susceptible to attrition. Where this is not the case, and the features from the L1 and L2 compete with each other, attrition is more likely to occur. To summarize:

> When an L1 linguistic element or rule has no equivalent form in the L2, the L1 is not in competition with the L2. In such situations, the L1 element does not compete with an L2 element that has a lower activation threshold. Thus, interference or attrition does not occur in such contexts.
>
> (Gürel 2004: 75)

In the following section, we will consider some of the empirical findings in relation to language attrition, by examining the extent to which different variables impact upon language attrition. We begin by looking at second-language loss in a first-language environment, before turning to look at first-language loss in a second-language environment.

SECOND-LANGUAGE LOSS IN A FIRST-LANGUAGE ENVIRONMENT

As we saw with language acquisition, there are numerous cognitive and social factors which may impact on the degree of attrition of an individual's language. One of these is age. When it comes to language attrition, age appears to be a clear advantage. Examining the English attrition of younger (five- to eight-year-olds) and older (eight- to fourteen-year-olds) children who returned to Israel (a Hebrew-only-speaking context) after living for a minimum of two years in an English-speaking environment, Olshtain (1989) found attrition to be more rapid for the younger group than for the older group. However, she argued that there are a number of other factors which may have impacted on this result. The older learners had learned English both naturalistically and at school in ESL classes, whereas the younger children had learned exclusively in naturalistic settings at pre-school. The older group also had access to greater levels of literacy upon leaving their English-speaking environments, and reported continued reading in English after returning to Israel. In other words, the two groups are not exactly comparable because their differing experiences could have impacted on the degree to which they maintained contact with their second language and in turn contributed to their ability to retain, or not, the language.

Cohen (1989) investigated his own children's loss of their third language, Portuguese, when they returned to Israel at the ages of nine and thirteen (their other two languages were Hebrew and English). His findings correlated with those of Olshtain in that he found that the younger child's language loss was more rapid than that of the older child. Cohen was interested in particular in the attrition of the productive lexicon, pointing out that there are four aspects of vocabulary that can contribute towards the forgetting of a particular lexical item (Cohen 1986). These are the *form* of the word, the *position* of the word, the *function* of the word and the *meaning* of the word (p. 146). Cohen was able to test this hypothesis in the study of his own children, testing them at the end of the first month, third month and ninth month after their return to Israel. He found that although they were unable to *produce* the same number of words at nine months that had been present at one and three months, they were able to *identify* these words from a word list at eleven months. Cohen concluded that there are differences in the ways in which receptive vocabulary and productive vocabulary are lost, with receptive vocabulary appearing less vulnerable to attrition than productive vocabulary. Cohen argued that the issue is thus more related to lexical access than to actual memory loss. As he points out, one of the factors which may have impacted on the older child's ability to retain language better than the younger child may be that the older child had better literacy skills in the language.

 Task A5.3

> Why do you think literacy skills may slow down the progress of attrition? Consider the enrichment that literacy skills may bring to the life of an average speaker who has lost contact with a speech community.

One very fruitful area for research into language attrition has proved to be the study of Japanese children who have spent varying periods of time living in English- (or other) speaking countries with their Japanese parents, and who subsequently return to Japan. Hansen (1999), in her edited volume, reports three studies of children who have lived in English-speaking countries with their parents and then returned to Japan. These studies document the process of attrition of their English using a variety of methodologies to elicit the data. For example, Reetz-Kurashige (1999) used storytelling and retelling from a picture book and examined English verb usage (following an earlier study by Olshtain 1986). She elicited data from three groups of nine-year-old children:

■ 18 Japanese returnees who had spent an average of 2.4 years living in the US
■ a baseline Japanese group who were living in Honolulu
■ a group of native English-speaking children resident in the US.

The language of the returnee children was evaluated two or three times over a 12- to 19-month period following their return to Japan. Her findings supported those of the earlier Olshtain (1986) study, finding similar patterns of attrition in the verbal system, where irregular verbs were regularized in later data collection periods (e.g. 'ate' became 'eated' and 'woke' became 'waked'), and phrasal verbs were replaced with single verbs (e.g. 'turn off' became 'close' or 'shut'). She also found that proficiency level appeared to be a factor in attrition, with more proficient speakers having lower levels of attrition. As Reetz-Kurashige argues, this supports the inverse hypothesis, which proposes that 'the higher the subject's proficiency, the lower the degree of attrition' (1999: 41). As she points out, these findings contradict the earlier findings of Bahrick (1984) and Weltens (1989), which had suggested that proficiency and the amount of attrition which occurred were independent. She explains this contradiction:

> The answer . . . lies in the study designs. First, this study measured speaking skills, whereas most of Weltens's and much of Bahrick's measured reading and listening. Productive skills, as research has shown, are more susceptible to attrition than recognition skills. Second, this study focused on children whose L2 competency was much below Weltens's college students' or Bahrick's adults'. Third, this study reported individual loss patterns through tracking the same subjects over time, whereas Weltens and Bahrick both measured attrition by comparing groups. Thus, a closer look at task, subject characteristics, and measurement design resolves the apparently contradictory findings of this study and Weltens's and Bahrick's.
>
> (Reetz-Kurashige 1999: 41)

Reported in the same volume, Yoshitomi (1999) used a variety of data collection techniques in her longitudinal study of four girls returning to live in Japan after three to four years in the US. She collected storytellings as well, but she also collected samples of the girls' language in free interaction and samples of planned speech, and conducted listening comprehension tests, as well as interviewing the girls and their parents. There were four data collection points evenly spaced over a one-year period. Yoshitomi had three main findings as a result of her study. The first was that she found less attrition than she had expected. Secondly, she found that the girls' abilities to combine their language subskills reduced over time (so that, for example, more errors were made in complex sentences than in simpler sentences; there was a decrease in fluency over time). Thirdly, she found that language attrition, as one would expect, appeared to take place to a greater extent when the children had few opportunities for interaction with native speakers.

Task A5.4

➤ Yoshitomi also found that once the data collection for this study had begun, the girls' attrition appeared to reduce. Do you find this surprising? What factors do you think might have been responsible for this outcome?

➤ Before reading further, see if you can work out what effects this regular testing of the girls' language abilities might have had on their awareness of their own language proficiency.

Yoshitomi argued that the testing of the girls' language made them aware of the fact that they were suffering from some language attrition, and that this acted as a motivational factor which encouraged them to work on maintaining their language. Such affective factors in language attrition, of which motivation is one, have also received some attention.

Gardner et al. (1987) examined the second-language attrition of a group of students learning French as a second language and tested them both on their proficiency levels and on a battery of tests which assessed their attitudes and motivations. This study, however, found little relationship between the rate of retention of language and motivation, but found that level of proficiency was important, with less loss where learners were more proficient. This is not, however, necessarily at odds with the findings of Yoshitomi (1999). Yoshitomi was speculating about the role that conscious knowledge of one's reducing access to the language might play in relation to motivation to prevent attrition. Gardner et al. (1987), on the other hand, were focusing on the kinds of variables which might be able to predict vulnerability to attrition. However, as we will see in Unit A7, the attitudes of bilinguals interact with language use and proficiency in a complex manner which cannot be easily summed up.

In general, then, we can see that there are many interacting factors that contribute to an individual's second-language loss upon return to the first-language environment. These include age (older is better), proficiency (more is better), and motivation to maintain the language (which may be related to recognition that the language is being forgotten). We also saw that comprehension tends to remain, even where production is lost.

FIRST-LANGUAGE LOSS IN A SECOND-LANGUAGE ENVIRONMENT

Younger bilinguals

As we saw above, there is now considerable evidence to indicate that with second languages, the language knowledge of younger children (particularly those below the age of about eight or nine) appears to be more at risk than the language knowledge of older children and adults. There is some support for the view that this outcome applies also to the attrition of a first language in a second-language environment. Such attrition is not an uncommon experience in these days of large-scale migration, and in this section we will consider some of the studies which have investigated children's first-language attrition, usually as a result of immigration to another country.

 Task A5.5

➤ It is now common for children to move with their families to live in countries where the language spoken is other than that they have grown up with, or are learning as young children. It is not unusual for these children to lose their first language in favour of their second language. What environmental factors do you think might contribute to this outcome?

Isurin (2000) documented the loss of Russian by a nine-year-old child who was adopted and moved to the US. This detailed longitudinal study focused on vocabulary loss by the child once she no longer had access to her native language while having extensive exposure to English. Three different types of picture-naming task were used. In one task, the child had to name the picture in Russian and then English; in another, the language used for picture naming was not specified; and in the third task, picture naming was in Russian, but the stimuli were labelled in English. Reaction times – that is, the amount of time taken to say the response – were also measured. There were seven data collection points over a nine-month period dating from when the child started school. The focus of the study was on the relationship between L1 attrition and L2 acquisition. Clearly, the results of the study need to be treated with caution since this was a longitudinal study of only one child; however, they do indicate an association between the attrition of the first language and the acquisition of the second. The study found that nouns tended to be lost and acquired more rapidly than verbs, which underwent a slower transition, and that, in particular, high-frequency words, cognates and semantically convergent pairs were the most vulnerable group (p. 163). Isurin explained this finding, which is contrary to most other attrition studies, which find that low-frequency words are most vulnerable to attrition, by arguing that in this case there was no longer any access to the L1 by the child, whereas most studies take place in situations where there was continual access to L1, so the low frequency of words in the L1 may contribute to their attrition. In concluding, Isurin argued (p. 164) that

> The general conclusion derived from the results of the present case study is that in a pure attrition situation, where a person loses any contact with L1, the process of L1 forgetting might be directly determined by L2 acquisition, and the accessibility of lexical items in L1 might be affected by the acquisition of L2 equivalents for the same concepts.

Task A5.6

➤ Consider how Isurin's findings relate to the Activation Threshold hypothesis discussed earlier.

Isurin's study was of one child who no longer had any access to her first language. A more usual situation is one in which the child maintains access to the first language, while living in a second-language environment. In just such a case, Anderson (2001) followed two L1 Spanish-speaking siblings over a two-year period, beginning approximately two years after they had moved with their parents to the United States. The parents continued to speak to the children in Spanish, but allowed them to respond in English. They attended an English-speaking school, and played with English-speaking playmates. At the time of the move, the children were 1;6 and 3;6; they had lived for several years in the United States at the time of the study, and were both attending elementary school. They were recorded interacting with their mother, in Spanish, for about 30 minutes every one to two months, for a period of 22 months. The focus of the analysis was on verbal inflectional morphology – Spanish verbs inflect for person, number, mood, tense and aspect, usually as suffixes. A number of aspects of verbal usage were examined, including the number of errors, variety of verbs used and use of regular and irregular verbs. Differences were found in the attrition rates of the two children, with the younger child's language appearing to be more susceptible to attrition than that of the older child. The younger child also tended to use more English in the recorded sessions, and appeared more reluctant to use Spanish, while the older child expressed a desire to develop her Spanish skills. It is possibly the case that these attitudinal factors may have had an impact on the results.

These studies examined the loss of language by children living in a second-language environment. With the amount of immigration to other countries there is in the world today, children are often educated in a language which is not their first, and their peers are often native speakers of the immigrant children's second language. However, it is important to note that although children may lose productive skills in their first language, the maintenance of a passive knowledge of the language, even if they do not speak it, does appear to correlate positively with first-language recovery when they are provided with the opportunity (Uribe de Kellett 2002). In Unit B5, we will examine two studies which indicate that even after many years without contact, there are advantages to having learned a second language even when it is believed to have been lost.

 Task A5.7

➤ Why do you think that receptive language ability in children (comprehension) might be less liable to attrition than productive ability?

➤ Consider the implications of this for the measurement of bilingual ability.

Older bilinguals

Studies of language attrition must, by their nature, be longitudinal, and there have been several such studies of immigrant populations which have focused on the degree of attrition over a long period of time. One example is the study by De Bot and Clyne (1994), which examined longitudinal data collected over a 17-year period from Dutch–English bilinguals in Australia. In this study, data which had been collected earlier (1971 and 1987) were used for comparative purposes, and were examined at the lexical level, the morphosyntactic level and the textual level. They found that there had been remarkably little attrition in this population of Dutch speakers. They pointed out that this may indicate that if there is little attrition in the first ten years, then it is likely that this situation will maintain in later years. This is because the Dutch speakers tested in 1994 were those who were fluent speakers in both 1971 and 1987 (in other words, they had maintained their fluency over that period).

As people get older, their ability to access specific lexical items at the time they want to use them tends to reduce, and there will be occasions when they have a word on the 'tip of their tongue' but cannot immediately recall it. Goral (2004) pointed out the importance of understanding this phenomenon in normal language attrition in healthy ageing adults, suggesting that there are likely to be similar processes at play in relation to language attrition in ageing monolinguals, as well as language attrition in ageing bilinguals. However, for bilinguals there are a number of additional factors which impact on their language abilities, which include the interactive effects between the two languages, the competition for processing capacity between the two languages, and transfer between the two languages (Goral 2004: 45).

Many of the studies of language attrition that are reported in the literature are case studies of single individuals, or small numbers of individuals. Each of these individuals is likely to have had very different experiences both in learning their languages in the first place and in their later attrition and the reasons for it. It needs to be borne in mind that studies of language attrition by their nature have to be longitudinal, following participants over a period of time to investigate increasing attrition in a language. For this reason, and given that each individual case in which language attrition takes place tends to be different from all others, these studies are necessarily time-consuming and highly detailed. As a result, language attrition studies almost always involve small sample sizes, and it is, therefore, difficult to control the range of different variables which may impact on the outcomes of these studies, and comparison across different cases and different studies is difficult.

Summary

As we have seen, language attrition involves a series of complex cognitive processes related to the ways in which we access our linguistic knowledge, which interact with a large number of social variables, and it is difficult to separate out the ways in which these variables affect language attrition. As has been demonstrated from the above discussion, although attrition appears less severe for older speakers, there are other variables which interact with age. For example, literacy skills do not usually begin to develop until children attend school, and once this happens it is difficult to disentangle the extent to which age is a variable independent from literacy. Similarly, children's proficiency in the language improves with age. Motivation, closely related to attitude, is also recognized to be a significant factor affecting the extent to which a language is maintained. As children grow older, their attitudes to their language or languages may be influenced by all kinds of different experiences and exposures, including peer group pressure. Thus, older children are likely to have more entrenched attitudes, which may be either negative or positive towards one or more of their languages. Exposure, of course, is another key factor that affects language attrition, and this varies enormously in different contexts.

None the less, as Köpke (2004) argues, language attrition in children is more severe than is the case in adults, and she points out that there have now been several studies which indicate quite clearly that age on departure is the most important predictor for language attrition. She goes on to point out that while this is the case for children, with adults attrition tends to be much more limited despite the fact that they may have spent long periods of time in second-language environments.

In Unit B5, we will examine two studies which focused on children who stopped using a language because of relocation. The first study illustrates how different levels of skills attrite differently over time, and in the second study we see how a language can still leave residual traces despite 30 years of non-use.

Unit A6
Education and literacy in bilingual settings

What is bilingual education?

Are some models of bilingual education more successful than others?

Do children learn to read better if they initially acquire literacy skills in their first language?

How do children develop literacy in two languages?

There is a broad range of different models which all come under the general term *bilingual education*. Baker (2006) distinguishes between three major approaches to bilingual education:

- monolingual forms of education for bilinguals
- weak forms of bilingual education for bilinguals
- strong forms of bilingual education for bilingualism and biliteracy.

Hamers and Blanc (2000: 321), however, restrict their definition of bilingual education to 'any system of school education in which, at a given moment in time, and for a varying amount of time, simultaneously or consecutively, instruction is planned and given in at least two languages'. In other words, for Hamers and Blanc, only Baker's third category would constitute *bilingual education*. This distinction between strong forms of bilingual education and the weak and monolingual forms outlined above is important because it discriminates between *subtractive* educational practices and *additive* educational practices. In both monolingual and weak forms of bilingual education, the programmes are *subtractive* in the sense that the second language is developed at the expense of the child's first or native language, whereas *additive* approaches foster the development of both the first and the second language (Brisk 2006: 46).

In this unit, we will begin by briefly considering Baker's first two categories of bilingual education, the monolingual and the weak approaches. This will be followed by a discussion of strong forms of bilingual education with reference to specific bilingual programmes. Next we will examine the development of biliteracy and children's demonstration of early literacy awareness. Finally, we will examine the debate on whether literacy skills can be transferred across languages and discuss the implications of the findings for the education and assessment of bilinguals.

Task A6.1

➤ Are you aware of any bilingual education programmes in your local community or school district? Have you ever participated in a bilingual programme or have you had contact with one?

➤ If so, how much input was there in each of the two languages? Did it change in different year levels? Why do you think this was the case?

MONOLINGUAL AND WEAK FORMS OF BILINGUAL EDUCATION

Monolingual and weak forms of bilingual education are designed for minority-language children. The main aim of such programmes is to assimilate children into the mainstream (monolingual) educational system as soon as possible. Programmes of this type are not designed to foster the children's first or native language(s). Where parents decide this is important, it must be done outside the mainstream school curriculum, and to address this need, Saturday and after-school programmes are often designed for this purpose.

Monolingual forms of bilingual education

Following Baker's (2006) categorization, in monolingual forms of education children are mainstreamed into normal classes and *submersed* immediately into their second language. There are various ways in which the children may be given language tuition in the majority language, among which are the following:

■ They may receive a period of intensive majority-language tuition before entering the mainstream classes.
■ They may initially receive intensive majority-language tuition in specific classes separate from the mainstream classes.
■ They may spend half a day, or some other proportion of the day, in a majority-language class and the remainder of the day in mainstream classes.
■ They may be placed in a mainstream class but with additional assistance from a specialist majority-language teacher working in the classroom.
■ They may be withdrawn from the class for specific periods of time for majority-language classes.
■ They may be placed in a mainstream class with no additional support other than the general classroom teacher. In this context, as Baker (2006: 216) puts it, 'students will either sink, struggle or swim'.

Generally, in the situations described above, where majority language support is provided, it is limited in duration.

Task A6.2

➤ Think back to Cummins's (1979, 1984) distinction between *conversational language proficiency* and *academic language proficiency* as discussed in Units A2 and B2, where conversational language proficiency took up to two years to develop, while academic language proficiency took between five and seven. If support in learning the majority language is only provided for a year or two, to what extent are Cummins's concerns likely to be realized with this type of educational approach?

Weak forms of bilingual education

Bilingual transitional education is another term used for 'weak' forms of bilingual education. In this model, children begin school with some language support in their first language. This generally takes the form of school content, such as mathematics, literacy and other subjects, which are taught in the first language, with a gradual and increasing move to teaching in the second language. By way of example, Urow and Sontag (2001) describe a bilingual programme in which language arts are taught throughout in both languages, with maths, science and social studies being initially taught in Spanish (the minority language), and then in both languages from Grade 5. Thus, science materials and mathematics are taught earlier in the second language while literacy-based subjects are taught in both languages. To some extent, this model requires a relatively homogeneous group of language minority children, a situation which is much easier to achieve in some places than others. In the US, where Spanish speakers are a large proportion of the population overall, transitional education is mandated in some states. As Thomas and Collier (2002: 123) report:

> Since all elementary schools in Houston are required by state law to offer a bilingual program for limited-English-proficient (LEP) students in Grades PK-5 whose home language is spoken by 20 or more students in any single grade in the entire school district, the large majority of elementary schools provide at least transitional bilingual education for Spanish-speaking LEP students.

Bilingual transitional programmes vary in both the amount of L1 education and the length of time over which it is provided. Thomas and Collier's (2002) extensive study, which reports on outcomes in terms of academic achievement by minority-language learners in the US, includes two models of transitional education. The first, termed the 90–10 model, involves 90 per cent of instruction in the first language in the lower grades with gradually increasing instruction in the second language to fourth grade, whereas students in the 50–50 model receive 50 per cent of their education in each language for the first three to four years before moving into the mainstream (Thomas and Collier 2002). The Thomas and Collier study is probably one of the most comprehensive evaluations of the different range of bilingual programmes currently available, and we briefly summarize some of the major findings below:

- Dual-language and immersion programmes (see below) achieved the best results in L1 and L2, and had the lowest dropout rate.
- Minority-language learners who initially attended remedial, segregated programmes did not close the achievement gap after integration into the mainstream, and the gap was either maintained or widened in later years.
- Short-term programmes of one to three years for students with no proficiency in English were inadequate; the length of time taken to reach grade-level performance was a minimum of four years.
- The strongest predictor of L2 achievement for language-minority student achievement was the amount of formal schooling in L1.
- Children who had bilingual schooling outperformed monolingually schooled students in all subjects after four to seven years of dual-language schooling.
- While minority-language students who exited into mainstream English programmes initially outperformed those in bilingual programmes when tested in English, by the high school years the bilingually schooled children outperformed the monolingually schooled children.

These findings, based on a five-year study which included five school districts across the US, point to the advantages of dual-language or immersion programmes, but warn that any programme, whether bilingual enrichment or ESL,

> must meet students' developmental needs: linguistic (L1–L2), academic, cognitive, emotional, social, physical. Schools need to create a natural learning environment in school, with lots of natural, rich oral and written language used by students and teachers (L1 and L2 used in separate instructional contexts, not using translation); meaningful, 'real world' problem-solving; all students working together; media-rich learning (video, computers, print); challenging thematic units that get and hold students' interest; and using students' bilingual–bicultural knowledge to bridge to new knowledge across the curriculum.
>
> (Thomas and Collier 2002: 335–336)

The findings of this report demonstrate the importance of appropriately designed programmes which meet the students' linguistic needs in both languages in order to avoid the potential problem of children ending up with limited competence in both of their languages – or subtractive bilingualism.

 Task A6.3

> Ideally, we might want to educate all children in their first language, and to introduce the second language as well. What kinds of practical challenges can you think of which would make this difficult to manage in many situations?

Can you think of ways in which you could design a simple programme based on what you learned above which maximizes the advantages while minimizing the costs?

Given the positive findings as to the benefits of bilingual education indicated by Thomas and Collier, we will now consider in more detail those programmes in which all instruction is in two languages.

STRONG BILINGUAL EDUCATION PROGRAMMES

In these bilingual educational programmes, two languages are routinely used for the purposes of teaching content material. As we will see below, there are a number of different models that can be adopted in situations in which bilingual education is required. For example, Baker (2006) distinguishes ten different types of bilingual education programmes, which included heritage-language maintenance programmes. Brisk (2006), however, identifies eleven different programmes, but her list excluded both heritage maintenance and programmes taught only in one language (even when used with bilingual children). Thus, there are many different ways in which bilingual programmes can be classified. Below, we will discuss three major types of bilingual programmes, and will focus on programmes which are designed specifically to foster both bilingualism and biliteracy. These programmes are:

- *immersion programmes for majority children* where children coming from the same first-language background are educated in a second majority language
- *dual-language programmes* (or two-way immersion programmes) in which mixed groups of majority-language and minority-language children are educated in the two languages
- *programmes designed to maintain or revitalize indigenous languages* of bilingual minority children where children are educated in both the majority language and the minority language with the specific aim of maintaining, or in some cases revitalizing, the minority language.

The major difference between these bilingual education programmes and the monolingual and weak bilingual programmes discussed in the previous section is that the three approaches to bilingual education outlined above promote additive bilingualism. In programmes of this type, a major aim is to ensure that both the L1 and the L2 are maintained and developed. This compares to the subtractive approaches discussed earlier in which the major aim is assimilation and integration into both the language and the culture of the majority.

Immersion programmes for majority children

Immersion education is distinguished from two-way or dual-language education by the fact that for the majority of children, teaching is in their second language (although, as we will see in Unit B6, increasingly it may be the third or the fourth language). By comparison, in dual-language programmes the two languages in which teaching is conducted are each the first language of approximately half of the children enrolled in the programmes. Immersion programmes, therefore, are specifically designed to educate majority children in a second language which they have generally had no contact with prior to entering the school system.

Probably the best known of the immersion programmes are those which were introduced into Canada in the late 1970s with the goal of promoting bilingualism. However, immersion programmes can now be found in many countries across the world, including Australia, Austria, France, Germany, Hong Kong, Hungary, the US and Spain (Johnstone 2001). Bostwick (2001) provides an account of an English immersion programme in Japan (and Kanagy 2001 reports on a Japanese immersion programme in Oregon in the US).

Our focus will be on the programmes in Canada, which are now widespread and to varying degrees exist in every province (Allen 2004), and which have been the subject of extensive research and investigation. These programmes were designed for English-speaking children to enable them to attend schools in which they would receive the majority of their education through the medium of French. The aim is for the children to develop bilingualism as well as biliteracy in both English and French. There are various different approaches taken within immersion models. These include early (kindergarten) immersion, and late (year 5 or 6) immersion. While some programmes involve total immersion, others use partial immersion. Programmes which begin early tend to adopt a total immersion approach in the second language for the first two to three years. Mid-way through primary school the children's first language is reintroduced and used for teaching some content subjects. An important aspect of immersion programmes, and one which distinguishes them from the submersion programmes discussed above, is that in such programmes there is overt support for the first language of the children, and this is generally achieved through bilingual teachers. This is a crucial aspect of the immersion programme, which is designed to ensure that additive, as opposed to subtractive, bilingualism is the result. However, as we will see in Unit B6, changes to Canadian demographics are heralding some changes in the core principles of these programmes.

The Canadian immersion programmes, as we say, have been the subject of intense research activity. One of the most pervasive findings has been that despite their intensive language input, students lack knowledge about some of the formal aspects of French (Harley et al. 1990), which, as a consequence, requires specific attention with instruction which focuses specifically on the form, or grammar, of the language (Lightbown 1990). Studies by Swain and colleagues have focused on the use of content-based tasks which encourage a focus on form (e.g. Swain 2001; Lyster 2004). Other studies have investigated differences in attitudes towards speaking French by students enrolled in immersion and other types of programmes (Baker and MacIntyre 2003; Kissau 2003), and the effect on the teaching of content subjects in the second language (D'Entremont and Garneau 2003; Turnbull et al. 2001; Laplante 2000). A report by Allen (2004) on reading levels in Canadian schools revealed that fifteen-year-old English-speaking students enrolled in French immersion programmes outperformed students enrolled in non-immersion programmes in almost all provinces when tested in English. However, other factors may have contributed to this result. For example, girls comprised 60 per cent of the enrolments in immersion programmes and have been found to outperform boys in reading more broadly in reading assessments, and students enrolled in the immersion programmes tended to come from higher socio-economic backgrounds in general, and hence the findings probably cannot be solely attributed to immersion education (Allen 2004).

Task A6.4

➤ As we have seen, in immersion programmes such as those in Canada the children entering the programme all speak English and their classes are all conducted in French. While the children might speak to each other in French in the school grounds, on the whole they do not get language input from their native French-speaking peers. Can you think of any ways in which this lack of peer native-speaker input might affect the children's language comprehension and production in different domains? You might want to refer back to the discussion of different domains of language use in Unit A1.

In the next section, we look at a different type of immersion programme where children from two different language backgrounds attend the school, and teaching is provided in both languages.

Dual-language or two-way immersion programmes

Dual-language programmes are a specific type of programme in which students from two different language backgrounds attend the programme in roughly equal proportions. As an alternative to educating minority-language children through submersion in the majority language or through bilingual transitional programmes, the underlying philosophy of dual-language programmes is to engender both bilingualism and biliteracy. In addition to this, in such programmes

> a deep respect for the target (minority) language and its speakers is fostered which leads to increased self-esteem and ethnic pride among language minority students and improved intercultural relations between the two groups of students. Thus, language minority students receive not only linguistic support, but also cultural, psychological and social support in their academic development. At the same time, language majority students are immersed in a foreign language which they gradually and easily acquire, as the value of their first language and ethnic identity is never questioned.
>
> (Rolstad 1997: 43)

Two-way programmes are, therefore, an additive and positive way of educating language-minority students because there is an emphasis on teaching in the minority language rather than relegating it to a status in which it is the home language only. While all two-way immersion programmes have a similar underlying philosophy (bilingualism and biliteracy in both languages), classroom implementation varies in detail across different schools. Urow and Sontag (2001), mentioned above, report on a Spanish–English two-way programme in which teaching is 80/20 in Spanish/English in the first six years (pre-kindergarten to Grade 4), 60/40 in Grade 5, and 50/50 in the next three years. In the first two years of schooling, children are taught literacy skills in their first language, and from Grade 2, children have formal language instruction in both languages. Maths and science-based subjects are taught in Spanish until Grade 5, after which both languages are used. All teachers in the school are bilingual, but rigorously adhere to the language assigned to their teaching period. Selection of children into the school is done carefully to ensure a mix of ethnicity and language backgrounds, which include Spanish-dominant, English-dominant and Spanish–English bilingual children. A reflection of the programme's success, which draws children from all over the Chicago area, is its substantial waiting list, and the fact that most of the teachers send their children to the school.

Calderón and Slavin (2001) discuss a slightly different model of two-way immersion in Texas in which all the students come from Latino backgrounds, mostly from low socio-economic backgrounds, with approximately equal parts of English-only speakers, Spanish-only speakers and bilingual Spanish–English speakers. In this school, the curriculum is taught 50 per cent in Spanish and 50 per cent in English throughout, and the school places particular emphasis on the development of literacy skills in the early years, including one-to-one tutoring for first-graders who are having difficulty with reading. A measure of the school's success is reflected in the fact that in the three school years from 1998 to 2001, the school population increased from approximately four hundred to over eight hundred students.

Rolstad (1997) reports on a rather different model of two-way immersion from Los Angeles in which children are taught in Korean and English. Approximately half the children attending the programme are from Korean-language backgrounds, but this programme differs from many two-way immersion programmes in that, while the majority of the remaining children come from Tagalog- or Spanish-speaking backgrounds, most were proficient in English when they began school. For these children, therefore, Korean is their third language. The programme begins with 90 per cent of instruction in Korean in the first year, gradually reducing the amount of teaching in Korean by 10 per cent each year until instruction is 50/50 by fifth grade. Rolstad's empirical study followed four children for five years, and five children for six years. The findings suggest that children enrolled in such two-way programmes in which they are learning a third language do not suffer detrimental effects in terms of self-concept, in their ethnic identity or in either academic or linguistic achievement. This study is discussed further in the extract by Swain and Lapkin (2005) in Unit B6.

In sum, two-way immersion education can be seen as a positive experience for children experiencing either their second or their third language. However, since a crucial element of these programmes is that there are equal numbers of children from the two different language backgrounds, they will be limited to particular communities with large numbers of minority-language children from the same language background.

Task A6.5

➤ Two-way immersion supports the language of minority children and the language of majority children by providing equal input in both. This means that both languages are represented in the school community as being equally valued, which has benefits for the children in terms of both their linguistic skills and their self-esteem and self-concept. Reflect on the differences in perception of the minority language in a two-way immersion programme and a minority language transition programme.

Programmes designed to maintain or revitalize indigenous languages

Indigenous languages across the world are being lost as children no longer learn them as their first language. Krauss (1998), for example, points out that of the original 175 indigenous languages spoken in the United States, only 20 are now being acquired by children. Similarly, McCarty (2002) argues that of the 210 indigenous languages still spoken in the US and Canada, only 34 are spoken by all generations, suggesting that 84 per cent will be lost in the next two generations since children are no longer learning these languages. In the Australian context, McConvell and Thieberger (2001) argue that, at the current rate of loss, it is potentially the case that there will be no indigenous Aboriginal languages spoken in Australia by the year 2050 (although they point out that it is likely that the current trend will even out, leaving a small number of languages still spoken at that time). These rather dire predictions are certainly borne out in a number of communities where children are not learning the traditional language, but rather creoles (known as Kriol in Australia) (Disbray and Wigglesworth, in press; McConvell et al. 2005) or mixed languages (Meakins and O'Shannessy 2005).

Language revival programmes, often similar in design to those discussed above, can help redress these types of situations where indigenous and heritage languages are losing ground to mainstream and often more prestigious languages. Smith (2003) stresses the importance of the impact of language and education policies on such programmes with respect to minority languages. She argues that

> Approximately 95% of the world's linguistic groups speak a minority language, although state funded education frequently remains monolingual

(in the official language of the state). The selection of the dominant language of education is inextricably linked to the survival of the culture of the linguistic group concerned. The language of education is usually the language of bureaucracy, knowledge of which is essential for those wishing to progress in the society in which they live. The adoption of bilingual education policies using the official language and the minority language is one key to the survival of the lesser-used language.

(Smith 2003: 129)

Bilingual education for indigenous minorities was a policy in the Northern Territory in Australia from 1972 to 1998, and during this time English and Australian Aboriginal languages were used side by side in classrooms to teach literacy and numeracy (Nicholls 2005). The end of this bilingual policy had widespread implications. McConvell and Thieberger (2001) summarize the effects of this on Aboriginal languages:

The end of bilingual education in the Northern Territory represents a serious setback for Indigenous languages . . . Not only have some language programs and positions related to Indigenous language programs been lost but the status of Indigenous languages has been downgraded significantly within the education system.

Nicholls (2005) points out that the preference for Aboriginal communities them-selves is to retain bilingual education for three major reasons. The first is that of maintaining and developing a sense of identity. In Australia, Aboriginal children were often punished for speaking their own languages in school, and in some cases were removed from their families so that they grew up speaking English monolingually. As a result:

it is little wonder that the language/identity nexus is so strongly and passionately upheld in Indigenous Australian communities. It is widely recognised in Australian Aboriginal communities that language plays a critical role in the process of children's identity formation and in their socialisation in the more general sense.

(Nicholls 2005: 164)

The second reason is the educational benefits which result from allowing children to learn initially in their first language and, thus, to understand what is going on around them as they enter the new environment of the school. The third reason, Nicholls argues, pertains to human rights, in the sense that children should have the right to become literate initially in their own language. McCarty (2003: 148) argues that language loss is a human rights issue since 'through our mother tongue, we come to know, represent, name, and act upon the world', thus pointing out that the 'indigenous languages cannot be divorced from larger struggles for democracy, social justice and self-determination'.

Working towards the reversal of language loss is important and must be done in a limited time frame, and evaluations of these programmes designed specifically to revitalize indigenous languages are increasingly reported in the literature. Stiles (1997) discusses four such programmes in four different countries with a view to identifying those features which engender success. None of the languages involved in these programmes was being learned by the younger generation, and it was a primary language for only a limited number of older people. In all cases, English was replacing the indigenous language as the primary means of communication in the communities.

The first programme reported on by Stiles (p. 148) is the Cree Way Project developed in the north of Canada and designed to immerse students in Cree in the early years of primary school as a way of using

> Cree language in the schools to validate Cree culture and create a Cree tribal identity. The program also aims to make reading and writing more impor-tant within their previously oral culture, to create a curriculum reflecting Cree culture and the Cree conceptual framework, and to implement that curriculum in the public schools

The Cree language is used exclusively up to Grade 4, after which half the programme is in English or French, and half in Cree. The Cree programme is enhanced by two camps a year which provide important experiences in the transmission of cultural traditions, and these include the teaching of a range of activities such as trapping, beading and making snowshoes which the children then write about, in Cree, in their journals. The programme receives support from a range of sources, which include the government, the availability of Cree teacher certification, and regular staff development workshops.

Near the Grand Canyon in the US, the Hualapai Bilingual/Bicultural Education Program is committed to developing true bilingualism and uses computer, video and television technologies to enhance learning in a mainly immersion programme. Once again, community support has been a crucial aspect of the success of the programme, as has staff development with respect to the language, which help staff to develop materials and curriculum in the language. This programme has produced a practical orthography and grammar of the Hualapai language, as well as certified Native American teachers. Furthermore, the programme has resulted in significant gains for the students on standardized as well as local assessments, in addition to improved attendance and graduation rates (McCarty 2003: 152).

In New Zealand, where 15 per cent of the population is Maori, a full immersion programme to revitalize te reo Maori (the Maori language) has developed from Kohanga Reo (language nests) first established in 1982, where the philosophy underlying Kohanga was one of full immersion to ensure a central principle of 'He korero Maori' (speaking in Maori) (May and Hill 2005: 377). These programmes exposed children to the te reo Maori from birth through to about eight years in homelike atmospheres (Stiles 1997: 151). In some cases, there were te reo Maori primary schools for the children to continue into, although generally there were too few to meet demand. This has resulted in a growth in Maori immersion programmes at primary and secondary levels (Rao 2004). An important aspect of te reo Maori immersion programmes has been the level of immersion, with May and Hill (2005) reporting that in New Zealand, Maori immersion is associated with 80–100 per cent immersion in the language, arguing that such high levels of immersion are 'entirely appropriate for the wider goal of revitalising te reo Maori, and the more specific goal of fostering the highest levels of language proficiency possible among students in te reo Maori, if the school or programme have the appropriate staff and resources to accomplish this' (p. 393). Indeed, May and Hill go on to point out that what has been achieved through Maori-medium education in the last twenty years has been quite remarkable (p. 400).

The final programme discussed by Stiles (1997) is the Punana Leo programme in Hawai'i, designed to promote the Hawai'ian language through bilingual and biliterate education. The programme is an immersion programme which children attend ten hours a day. Only Hawai'ian is spoken in the school grounds, and parents are also required to attend weekly language classes. The success of the programme has been reflected in statewide immersion programmes through both elementary and secondary school. In the 1999–2000 academic year, 1800 students attended a Hawai'ian immersion programme in 17 public schools on several islands, and demand for bilingual education increases with each year (Yamauchi and Wilhelm 2001).

Stiles (1997) argues that there are several key issues which contribute to the success of these programmes. They need to come from within the indigenous culture and not be imposed from outside. Not only language but understanding and learning about cultural traditions need to be integrated into the programmes. It is therefore important that indigenous people themselves are involved in the programmes and can address these needs. The programmes not only must begin at a young age but, as May and Hill (2005) among others point out, must continue throughout the majority of primary schooling in order to allow literacy to develop fully. Lastly, community support and parental involvement are also important aspects which contribute to the success of the programmes (see also Hickey 1999, who argues for the importance of parental support in relation to immersion programmes in Ireland in support of Irish).

In the context of the United States, where native American languages, as we saw above, are in serious decline, McCarty (2003) addresses two questions in relation to immersion programmes designed to revitalize indigenous languages, asking both whether such immersion schooling can promote success at school and whether such programmes can serve to revitalize a language. On the basis of an analysis of 25 years of related research, she concludes positively in response to both questions, but warns about the importance of full immersion education in situations where language loss is severe.

BILITERACY: A DEVELOPMENTAL PERSPECTIVE

In tandem with the issue of bilingual education is the question concerning biliteracy provision for bilingual children in bilingual programmes. What kinds of issues are pertinent to bilingual children on the cusp of acquiring literacy? We have seen earlier, in Unit A4, that being bilingual does enhance some aspects of bilingual children's metalinguistic skills, which are found to be positively related to literacy skills. So, are bilingual children somehow privileged when it comes to acquisition of literacy? On the other hand, there was some evidence that bilingual children score lower on vocabulary tests in comparison with their monolingual peers; and, as vocabulary knowledge is implicated in literacy development, will bilingual children's literacy development be adversely affected? In the next two sections, we will examine how biliteracy is developed – a topic which is integral to any discussion of the outcome of bilingual education.

Given that literacy is such a critical component of education, there is a robust literature addressing the issue of literacy development in the first language. Parents and educational authorities alike are immensely concerned about literacy development in children. This is because success or failure in developing literacy is critical to a child's academic future.

Much of the research on biliteracy has focused on the impact of pedagogical frameworks, curricula and environments on the acquisition of biliteracy (e.g. Glynn et al. 2005), the socio-cultural practice of biliteracy in different settings (Hornberger 2004) and the cognitive issues surrounding the acquisition of literacy in two languages for individual bilinguals. The discussion on biliteracy will focus mainly on the cognitive issues concerning the acquisition of literacy in two languages. The following sections will discuss the literacy issues faced by bilingual children when they start school and the extent to which being bilingual equips them with the prerequisites for reading and writing. In this context, we will also discuss the issue of script and orthography differences and the transference of literacy skills across languages.

WHAT IS BILITERACY?

Hornberger (2004: 156) defined biliteracy as 'any and all instances in which communication occurs in two (or more) languages in or around writing'. Reiterating the same idea in a more elaborate way, Pérez and Torres-Guzmán (1996: 54) described biliteracy as the 'acquisition and learning of the decoding and encoding of and around print using two linguistic and cultural systems in order to convey messages in a variety of contexts'. What is important in these two descriptions is that biliteracy goes beyond reading and writing, and that it also encompasses an understanding of the cultural systems the children interact in.

Very literally, when we study biliteracy we are concerned with the development of reading and writing skills in both the child's languages. Some researchers (e.g. Brisk and Harrington 2000) have a narrower application of the term 'biliterate', as they make the distinction between just having the proficiency to read and write in a particular language and being able to function as a literate person in either language. Brisk and Harrington give the example of someone who can read at Grade 6 in one language, but only at Grade 1 in the other language, as not being biliterate. So, for them, being biliterate implies the ability to maintain literacy skills at equivalent levels in both languages. This stringent description is reminiscent of the concept of balanced bilinguals, a view which has been widely questioned.

Our approach to biliteracy is more akin to Hornberger's (2004) model, which, instead of using proficiency in literacy as a limiting variable, views biliteracy as affected by four variables:

- contexts of biliteracy
- the development of biliteracy
- content of biliteracy
- media of biliteracy.

She refers to this as the *continua of biliteracy*. In this model, bilinguals' biliteracy is described in terms of their experience along the proposed continua rather than their proficiency in a set of skills. Therefore, the focus here is not on bilinguals who are biliterate in the Brisk and Harrington sense of the word but on bilinguals who engage in reading and writing at any level and in any context in both languages.

 Task A6.6

➤ This is a question you could ask yourself if you are a bilingual. Otherwise, you may want to talk to some bilinguals around you and find out:

- if they read and write in both languages
- if they read and write in both languages in roughly equal proportions
- if the content of what they read and write is the same in both languages.

➤ For the first two the answer is most likely to be 'No'. If so, ask how the two languages are used differently.

LITERACY ISSUES FACED BY BILINGUAL CHILDREN IN SCHOOL

Bialystok (2004: 577) comments that when dealing with bilingual children, educational authorities often make the assumption that 'children have one mind, one conceptual system and one language'. However, the reality is quite the contrary. In the last five units, there has been a recurrent theme around the difficulty of categorizing and assessing bilinguals because of the highly diversified nature of the bilingual population. The issues are very similar when it comes to classifying the literacy skills of bilinguals.

Bilinguals arrive in the school setting with vastly different levels of language proficiency. Some may speak only one minority home language and some may speak a few minority languages, none of which is a standard variety. Some may have a degree of proficiency in the school language, while others may have proficiency in both the school language and the home language. The degree of exposure to literacy also typically varies from child to child. For a large proportion of children in the world, it is not uncommon to enter school without any knowledge of the language used in the school setting. In such situations, as discussed above, without the support of bilingual education, assimilation into the majority language is often the aim, and the result will be literacy only in the majority (or school) language.

Task A6.7

➤ Do you remember your first day at school? Were you able to read and write? What stage were you at in your literacy development? For example, were you able to recognize letters and numbers? Were you able to read labels and notices on doors? Imagine the confusion of not being able to recognize simple signs such as 'Entrance', 'Exit', 'Washroom' or 'Do not enter'. If you were an English child attending a Chinese school, you would have found the following signs 安静 'Silence', 厕所 'Toilet', 闲人免进 'Do not enter', undecipherable. Now, imagine not being able to recognize these signs as well as not being able to understand the language spoken around you. This is the bewildering experience of many bilinguals who are placed in a submersion programme where they are learning through L2, a language they are totally unfamiliar with.

The Interdependence hypothesis

One of the major questions in biliteracy development relates to the extent to which some components of literacy are common to both languages. This is a crucial question which speaks to the issue of whether literacy skills transfer across the two languages. The proposal that best addresses this issue is Cummins's Interdependence hypothesis (1979).

Cummins's Interdependence hypothesis proposed that CALP (Cognitive Academic Language Proficiency) is transferred from one language to another. The hypothesis predicted that any increment in CALP in one language would lead to an increment in CALP in the other language and that this effect would be bidirectional. Hence, improvement in L1 reading or writing skills would feed into the L2, and improvement in L2 skills would feed into the L1. Since 1979, the Interdependence hypothesis has found support in many studies. Mainly, these studies found high correlations between children's language skills in L1 and L2 (e.g. Wagner et al. 1989; Baetens

Beardsmore and Swain 1985; Huguet et al. 2000; Abu-Rabia 2001). However, the correlation between languages that do not share the same orthography (e.g. Mandarin and English) was significantly lower than for language pairs such as Spanish and English. This issue of orthography influencing outcomes of studies on reading and processing has been widely reported and we will return to discuss this issue later on.

With the exception of languages which have different orthographies, the empirical data support Cummins's Interdependence hypothesis that L1 learning facilitates L2 and vice versa. Cummins (1981) referred to this shared knowledge base as *Common Underlying Proficiency*. The concept of a Common Underlying Proficiency has both theoretical and practical implications for the bilingual population, as a related question is whether the development of literacy for bilinguals is different from that of monolinguals since they may have the opportunity to transfer skills from one language to the other. In the following sections, we will address the following questions: Is there a set of basic skills which are shared across two languages before children become literate? Will bilinguals develop or utilize these skills in different ways?

 Task A6.8

➤ Consider the practice of reading a news item of current interest in your local papers. What are some reading processes which are likely to be similar regardless of which language you read in?

THE PREREQUISITES FOR READING AND WRITING

Bialystok et al. (2005) identify two reasons why literacy development may be different for bilinguals when compared to monolinguals. The first is the difference in the background of the bilinguals' literacy skills, which developed differently from those of monolinguals; the second is the possibility that skills acquired in one language may be transferred to another.

Bialystok et al. (2005) note three specific prerequisite skills critical to literacy which may have developed as a result of the different backgrounds of bilinguals. They are:

■ oral proficiency
■ metalinguistic awareness
■ general cognitive development.

Oral proficiency has been widely reported to be associated with children's acquisition of literacy and is the most common test used to diagnose literacy development (Geva 2000). Oral vocabulary, in turn, has also been correlated with oral proficiency (cf. Adams 1990; Garcia 2003). As there are several studies (see, for example, Umbel et al. 1992) which show that pre-school bilingual children have a smaller set of vocabulary compared to their monolingual peers, Bialystok et al. (2005) speculated that bilingual children's development in literacy may be disadvantaged by their smaller vocabulary size.

In Unit A4, we reviewed several studies which found bilinguals to be meta-linguistically more aware in certain tasks. That is, bilinguals were able to analyse some levels of linguistic structure more intensely. More pertinently, some researchers (Yelland et al. 1993; Bruck and Genesee 1995; Campbell and Sais 1995) have reported a temporary bilingual advantage in phonological awareness for five-year-olds that disappears by age six. As phonological awareness has been widely acknowledged as a good predictor of alphabetic reading ability (Geva and Wang 2001) and there is a suggestion that bilinguals are advantaged in this area, this might be an area where bilinguals are privileged over monolinguals.

The third skill concerns the way orthographies or script type may influence the working memory by either constraining or facilitating the transfer of information. To test the role these three skills play in determining biliteracy, Bialystok et al. (2005) compared three groups of Grade 1 bilinguals, Spanish–English, Hebrew–English, Cantonese–English, and a monolingual English group. All the three language pairs vary in terms of similarities. If oral proficiency is a factor, all three groups of bilinguals should be similarly affected. Using a series of tasks designed to assess vocabulary, working memory and phonological awareness, they found that there was an effect for script, and we discuss the details of this in the next section.

LEARNING TWO DIFFERENT SCRIPTS

All over the world, children regularly learn how to write in more than one script when they go to school. However, in English-dominant countries, biliteracy can sometimes be portrayed as a liability. Kenner et al. (2004) observed that mainstream teachers in England tended to be concerned that their bilingual pupils might become confused when dealing with different scripts. Kenner and her colleagues (2004) undertook a study which goes some way towards mitigating such concerns. In this study, bilingual children as young as four years of age showed high levels of meta-linguistic awareness. In a role-playing game, they were able to explain to their classmates differences between the English writing system and those of their languages – Mandarin, Arabic and Spanish. Hence, the researchers concluded that bilingual children are able to integrate two scripts into their early literacy experience without confusion (Kenner et al. 2004).

Furthermore, Kenner (2004) reports that five-year-old bilingual children in her study looked for connections between the two scripts and exploited the similarities as well as differences. The following quotation from Kenner (2004: 51) describing a demonstration of the Arabic script to his classmates by Yazan, an Arabic–English bilingual, indicates a conscious transference of knowledge across languages and systems.

> For example, when Yazan wrote his name in Arabic in a peer teaching session, his classmate Imrul commented 'You writed a three, didn't you?' (One element of Yazan's name resembled the English number 3). Yazan's response was simply 'No'. But later, when Imrul suggested that another part of Yazan's name could be a 'U', Yazan replied 'No – yeah!', expressing his recognition of the particularity of the Arabic letter in the this context, and of the possibility of dual representation because part of the letter did indeed resemble an English 'U'.
>
> Later in the same session, when Yazan was writing an Arabic word using his Saturday school work as a model, he commented on various parts of the word as he wrote, saying 'this look like a zero and this look like a U and this look like a one', all of which were possible comparisons. Yazan's use of the phrase 'look like' (rather than 'is') showed that, for him, both meanings of the symbols could co-exist simultaneously across alphabetic systems or across letter-number systems.

Kenner points out that this ability of bilingual and biliterate children to use two graphemic systems as reference points sets them apart from their monolingual peers. Biliterate children have an early understanding that written signs are arbitrary and carry different meaning in different languages.

 Task A6.9

> ➤ When were you first aware of different scripts? Did you remember noting their unusual qualities and comparing them to a system you are more familiar with?

The effects of different scripts

The process of learning how to read involves many steps; the key step is breaking the code of the orthographic system. There is great variation in how languages represent the spoken word in the written form, which we will refer to as *script*. The script used in English, Spanish, French and German, all Indo-European languages, is alphabetic and represented with the Roman alphabet. Arabic, Greek and Russian have their own scripts.

Apart from the use of different scripts, the way each language has conventionalized the sound–letter representation or *orthography* also varies. A transparent orthography has a simple one-to-one correspondence between the written representation and sound, and in an alphabetic writing system transparency is enhanced by one-to-one correspondence between letter and sound. In this regard, Italian is orthographically transparent in comparison to a language like English, which has a considerably more opaque letter–sound correspondence. For example, the *rough/dough* pair differ in one letter but the pronunciation is entirely different, and we can find many such examples in English.

Task A6.10

➤ How regular is the letter–sound correspondence in English? Take the letter 'c' and draw up a list of 20 words with 'c' in various positions (at the beginning of the word and in the middle of the word). Note the way the letter 'c' is pronounced in each instance. Do you see a direct letter–sound correspondence?

At the extreme end of the opaque continuum, we have languages like Mandarin, which uses a different writing system – logographs. Logographs are not based on phonological representations, and in Chinese, each character represents a unit of meaning: learning how to read a character or grapheme does not help in reading another character which carries a similar sound. For example, the character 月 'moon' is read as *yuè* and so are the following characters: 越 'to pass', 跃 'leap' and 阅 'read'. This contrasts sharply with sound-based systems such as English, where it is still possible to retrieve the sound despite the opacity of the writing system. So, when we compare scripts across cultures, we see that there are systems which are comparatively easier to crack and others which require a substantial amount of effort to work out. In this section, we will discuss the different scripts and orthographies and the impact they have on the literacy development of bilingual children.

Essentially, there are two hypotheses about the effect of orthography on reading. One hypothesis is script-dependent, claiming that reading varies across languages, and reading development should vary with the transparency of a particular orthography. With transparent orthographies, children should be able to develop accurate word recognition skills a lot faster. Conversely, with less transparent orthographies, children will take a longer time to master the learning of the system. In a study comparing incidence of dyslexia, Lindgren et al. (1985) found higher incidence of dyslexia in the United States than in Italy. They argued that the lower prevalence of dyslexia in Italy is directly related to the higher transparency of the writing system in Italian. In contrast, the more complex phoneme–grapheme relationship in English places heavier demands on cognitive processes than that of Italian does.

In contrast, the central processing hypothesis proposes that reading is an independent skill which is not constrained by the type of orthography. Instead, literacy acquisition is dependent on common underlying cognitive processes such as 'working memory, verbal ability, naming, and phonological skills', and deficiencies in these processes are more likely to affect literacy acquisition (Veii and Everatt 2005: 240). Though the central processing hypothesis and the Interdependence hypothesis stress a common underlying source, the central processing hypothesis is different from the Interdependence hypothesis framework, as the central processing hypothesis refers specifically to the processing of script and reading, whereas the Interdependence hypothesis refers to the broader notion of general communicative skills. (For a summary of the script-dependent hypothesis and the central processing hypothesis, see Geva and Siegel 2000 and Veii and Everatt 2005.)

Geva and her colleagues (e.g. Geva and Siegel 2000; Gholamain and Geva 1999) conducted a series of studies comparing languages of different scripts and found that their results supported both the script-dependent hypothesis and the central processing hypothesis. In a study comparing bilingual Persian–English children, Gholamain and Geva (1999) found that children learn to decode Persian (Farsi) faster than English despite limited exposure to Persian. This, according to Gholamain and Geva, has to do with the fact that, in comparison to English, Farsi is a more phonologically transparent script, thus supporting the script-dependent hypothesis. However, they also found general reading ability between Farsi and English to be highly correlated and they argue that this is because of higher-order skills involved in reading.

Returning to the study by Bialystok et al. (2005), recall that the study examines reading skills in four groups of children, three groups of bilinguals and one monolingual group. The writing systems in the bilingual groups differ in level of transparency and types of scripts. The Spanish–English bilingual group represents the group with the most similar language pairs (both are Indo-European and both are written alphabetically in a Roman script). The languages are different for the Hebrew–English bilingual group as, though both are alphabetical, the scripts are different and the two languages are from typologically different language groups (Semitic and Indo-European). The third bilingual group (Chinese–English) has the most dissimilar languages. Not only are the languages typologically different, they also use totally different writing systems.

The purpose of the careful selection of the language pairs is to test two hypotheses:

> The first is that the prerequisites to literacy that develop differently in monolinguals and bilinguals will lead to an advantage for bilingual children on reading measures once these measures have been controlled but the advantage will be greater if the two languages use the same writing system. The second is that the writing systems will determine the extent to which the skills developed in one language will transfer to the bilinguals' other language.
>
> (Bialystok et al. 2005: 47)

The findings found support for facilitation and transfer of reading skills across languages for the Hebrew–English and Spanish–English bilingual children, whose two languages shared a writing system. Moreover, the Hebrew–English and Spanish–English bilinguals have a clear and significant advantage when compared to the monolinguals, but the Chinese bilinguals were not significantly different from the monolinguals in all the tasks. However, the researchers note that the Chinese–English bilinguals were also profiting from their bilingualism, considering the fact that they started literacy instruction with reduced English proficiency. What is significant is that having a smaller vocabulary has not disadvantaged bilinguals in any way.

Geva and Siegel (2000) found that both hypotheses can be invoked to explain the development of biliteracy. The general awareness of phonological processes is a common underlying skill which can be transferred from one language to another, especially when the grapheme–phoneme match of the script is transparent. However, if the language is orthographically complex, the script-dependent hypothesis will apply as well. Furthermore, they argue that correlation between two languages is likely to be higher with general reading skills as they involve higher-level skills such as syntactic and semantic analysis. Other factors essential to reading, such as scanning, skimming and making inferences from prior knowledge and contexts, have also been found to be less affected by orthographic variations.

Implications

Transference of skills across languages is evident in most languages and, more importantly, there is evidence that biliteracy in different scripts, if mastered, brings beneficial cognitive effects such as enhanced learning of a third language (Clyne et al. 2004). Swain et al. (1990) also found evidence that literacy in one language contributed to a higher proficiency in the immersion language of bilingual immigrant children in their study of literacy attainment in immersion education. A critical implication of studies on biliteracy is that we can teach literacy in one language via another language. As Clyne et al. (2004: 49) point out:

> Once a child can read one language, they do not need to start from scratch to learn to read another language. There are some component skills of literacy, such as:
>
> ■ recognition of the structure of a word;
> ■ recognition of the structure of a sentence;
> ■ recognition of sound patterns possible in a language and ability to manipulate structural features of spoken language. Such recognition leads to prediction.

The findings are an indication that in developing the literacy curriculum for language pairs with different script systems and orthographies, educators should take into account the types of challenges that children in these groups may face. Educators could exploit languages with more transparent writing systems by stepping up the literacy input in that language in the early years, since there is clear indication that transfer does take place. What we do not know is whether introducing literacy in the orthography that is more transparent would be more facilitative. In the cases of languages with vastly different orthographies (e.g. Chinese and English), we have yet to determine strategies which would increase the facilitation between the two different writing systems.

If different orthographies impact on how literacy is developed, they also have significant implications for how bilinguals are assessed and evaluated. Veii and Everatt (2005) report on a series of studies where learning difficulties in one language did not manifest in the other language. For example, they cite the case of someone with a reading problem in Hebrew but not in English and that of a child who was dyslexic in English but not in Japanese. In a larger-scale study, Miller-Guron and Lundberg (2000) report on several children who showed deficiency in their literacy skills in Swedish but were able to demonstrate advanced phonological skills (widely linked to literacy acquisition). However, these children had no problems in English. These examples point to the need to test bilinguals in both languages. As discussed in Unit A2, when tests for developmental disabilities are conducted in one language (usually English), bilinguals run the risk of falling through the gap and missing out on treatment when they really need it.

Summary

Bilingual education comes in many shapes and forms, but here we have been conservative in our definition, taking as bilingual only those programmes in which two languages are used for teaching the curriculum. Since programmes which do not foster the development of both of the child's languages (thus educating children to be both bilingual and biliterate) are not included, our definition highlights the difference between submersion education and immersion education. This points to the important differences between 'submersion' and 'immersion', and 'subtractive' and 'additive' bilingualism. The empirical evidence suggests that submersion programmes are more likely to lead to subtractive bilingualism whereas immersion programmes are more likely to lead to additive bilingualism. We have also seen that it is important for immersion programmes to continue for at least seven or eight years to ensure that children have the time to develop full academic proficiency in both languages. However, even with languages as diverse as Mandarin and English some cross-language facilitation does take place.

The ability of bilingual programmes to reduce or reverse community language loss is perhaps one of the most exciting aspects of bilingual education in recent times. When carefully managed, supported and encouraged by indigenous communities, programmes in which students are immersed in an indigenous language can be successful, and, as with dual-language or two-way programmes for minority students, bilingual programmes can contribute to the children's sense of self-worth and self-esteem.

Our discussion of biliteracy centred on the literacy development of the individual. Unlike general oral proficiency, the development of literacy is a skill that requires concerted effort as it does not happen spontaneously. So far, we have examined only phonological transfer without considering transfers in other levels of linguistic knowledge. Up until now, not much research has been done in this field but there seem to be some suggestions that although transfer was found at the level of pragmatics, phonology and literacy skills, this effect was very limited at the level of lexicon and syntax (Verhoeven 1994). From a theoretical point of view, this seems to suggest that some skills (e.g. phonological processes) are more permeable than others. What implications does this have for the way we learn? Are there special teaching techniques that one could adopt to facilitate the transfer of skills across languages? The questions concern simultaneous acquisition of two literacy systems, a field that will see much growth in coming years.

In Unit B6, we will read two extracts. The first, from Swain and Lapkin (2005), concerns bilingual immersion programmes in Canada, and examines the ways in which the changing demographics, and the increasing population of immigrants from non-English-speaking backgrounds, have brought about changes to the core principles and values of immersion programmes and the implications these core values have for bilingual education in general. The second, from Aarts and Verhoeven (1999), is a study of Turkish children's biliteracy skills in a submersion context. In this extract, we will take a closer look at the methodology used in the evaluation of literacy of Turkish children in the Netherlands and examine the impact of submersion on the literacy maintenance of the bilingual children.

Unit A7
Attitudes and bilingualism

What is language attitude?

What role does it play in bilingual and multilingual contexts?

What impact does it have on bilingual proficiency, bilingual language choice, bilingual identity and the survival of bilingual communities?

Attitude is a concept central to bilingualism and has given rise to innumerable studies in the field of social psychology and even more in the description and analysis of bilingual and multilingual communities. In most studies, speakers are found to have specific attitudes to speakers of different languages, dialects and accents. As speakers themselves are unaware of these attitudes, there is a tendency for them to form stereotypes based on these attitudes. This, in turn, exerts a strong influence on social perceptions – the process through which we seek to understand others around us (Baron and Byrne 1997).

In the bilingual context, attitude has been linked in various ways to the language proficiency, use of the bilingual's two languages and bilinguals' perception of other communities and of themselves. It has also been linked to the vitality of bilingual communities and, finally, to the loss of language within that community. Attitude is a potent force that underscores both the experience of being bilingual and the way members of a minority group contribute to the maintenance of a minority language (Hamers and Blanc 2000).

The intricate link between attitudes and language use is succinctly captured by Baker (1992), who points out that policy implementations cannot afford to ignore prevailing language attitudes as they provide social indicators of changing beliefs. He argues that 'in the life of a language, attitudes to that language appear to be important in language restoration, preservation, decay or death' (Baker 1992: 9). For some communities, this is particularly significant. For example, Adegbija (2000), citing the tumultuous linguistic history of West Africa, argues that attitudes and beliefs associated with language form the fundamental fabric of social networks.

Task A7.1

➤ List three to five languages you hear around you in your community (e.g. French, Cantonese, Italian, Vietnamese, Khmer, Fijian, Lebanese Arabic). Next, ask yourself what your instinctive feeling is for each of the languages. You might like to note down any adjectives that come to mind for each language. Do your responses give you some indication about the attitudes that you may have to each of the languages?

Traditionally, studies which attempt to measure language attitudes have evaluated the language attitudes of speakers towards different languages, dialects and accents, and they do so by comparing them in the same society – for example, attitudes to English and French in Quebec, English and Spanish in the US, or Minnan and Mandarin in Taiwan. Other studies have looked at attitudes to different varieties of the same language such as the various dialects of English in England, or different varieties of German in Switzerland.

These studies generally examine attitudes to language from four main perspectives. A large proportion of the studies focused on speech styles or varieties and their perceived status in the community. These studies may involve both bilingual or monolingual speakers and communities and may discuss how 'prestige' accents, such as that of so-called *received pronunciation* (*RP*) in the UK, compare with accents from Birmingham, Devon or Yorkshire (Giles 1970, 1971; Hiraga 2005). Another group of researchers has examined how attitudes affect language choice and use. The focal groups under study are mainly bilingual or multilingual communities, which often have to make a choice between using a standard language – often the language of the dominant group – and the language of their own community. These studies typically explore the attitudes of bilinguals towards both their first language, and the languages used in their community. Linked to the studies on language choice and use, some researchers have focused on the impact of language attitudes on language maintenance and language policies. Lastly, another group of researchers investigate how attitudes affect second-language learning. In these studies, researchers explore the various attitudinal features which they claim may correlate with successful and non-successful second- or foreign-language acquisition. In this unit, we will draw upon studies from the first three groups as these are the most relevant to explaining bilingual language choice and behaviour.

As an overview, we will discuss how attitude is studied and measured in socio-linguistics and social psychology. A key issue is how the experience of being bilingual can alter a person's perceptions of their social environment. For example, several studies have demonstrated that bilingual education can change the attitudes of those who participated in the programme in measurable ways. In addition, bilinguals are also affected by how speakers from outside the bilingual community perceive them. We will also examine how the attitudes of individuals, such as parents or teachers, and institutional policies impact on the development of bilinguals. Throughout, we will discuss how attitude, consciously and unconsciously, influences communication patterns, language choice or language use.

METHODOLOGY USED IN LANGUAGE ATTITUDE STUDIES

How attitude is defined

Our idea of what constitutes language attitude has been greatly influenced by developments in social psychology. Cargile et al. (1994) interpret language attitudes as a disposition to react favourably or unfavourably to a situation, an object or an event. More importantly, to social psychologists, attitude is part of the mental schema which we use to perceive the world and to guide social relationships (Baron and Byrne 1997). In essence, these mental schemata allow us to rely on cognitive shortcuts to process social information efficiently.

It is within this framework that various studies on language attitude have attempted to measure the attitudes of people towards speakers of different languages, dialects and accents. While most researchers widely acknowledge the critical role played by attitudes and beliefs in the vitality of language in multilingual societies, pinning down a common definition of attitude is not easy. The issue of how attitude should be defined has generated substantial discussion, but the following commonalities across different researchers, identified by Agheyisi and Fishman (1970: 139), provide a useful guide. Language attitudes are:

- related to the perception of speakers of different language varieties
- learned from the individual's experience
- of an enduring, rather than momentary, nature
- related to behaviour, although it is difficult to make categorical statements about this relationship.

Using this as a backdrop, we will adopt Baker's (1992: 13) definition of attitude as comprising the three major components of *cognition, affect* and *readiness for action*. In Baker's model, a distinction is made between cognitive and affective components of attitude, and this distinction parallels what the individual may say about the language compared to what they feel about the language. This distinction is based on the belief that overtly stated attitudes may hide covert beliefs. In the example given by Baker to illustrate this point, an Irish speaker may express a very positive attitude to the Irish language and believe in the importance of continuity of Irish and its value in the transmission of the Irish culture. However, this speaker's affective feeling for the language, the culture or literature may be contrary to the overtly positive views expressed. That is, the affective component may not be congruent with the cognitive component. We believe this is an important distinction even though most studies have studied only the cognitive aspects (Cargile et al., 1994). As Baker (1992) points out, the *readiness for action* component evaluates whether feelings or thoughts in the cognitive and affective components translate into action.

Thus, in the same example, the person with a favourable attitude to Irish might say that they would send their children to a bilingual school. This three-way distinction proves to be a very useful way of understanding the research in this area.

Task A7.2

➤ Drawing on the three components – cognition, affect and readiness for action – described by Baker (1992), how would you account for the attitude of an Italian–English bilingual who is very positive about Italy and Italians, and feels that Italian is a crucial aspect of an Italian person's identity, but who does not speak Italian to his children and has not been back to Italy in the last 20 years (despite the fact that he can afford it)?

WAYS OF EVALUATING AND MEASURING ATTITUDES

A variety of different methods have been used for measuring language attitude. A useful distinction is between *direct* and *indirect* methods (Fasold 1984).

Direct methods

One way of investigating a bilingual's attitude towards a speaker or a situation is through direct questioning in which participants are asked to state their opinions about language or languages using a questionnaire, or through an interview. In direct investigations of language attitudes, the participants may be asked specific questions about their attitudes to language groups, to the language itself or to issues or features associated with the language, such as its uses or cultural associations (Baker 1992).

In this context, some questions can be more direct than others. For example, a question such as 'Do you think speaking Swahili is useless when you can already speak English?' is direct, whereas a question such as 'What do you think of someone who speaks Spanish in an environment where everyone speaks English?' is more indirect. An example of the use of a direct method is Garret et al. (2005), who asked their participants in the US, New Zealand and Australia to name eight English-speaking countries, apart from their own. The participants then had to describe how the English spoken in each country strikes them when they hear it spoken.

Another popular method is to get participants to rate a range of statements such as 'French speakers are inefficient' or 'English speakers are arrogant' on a Likert scale from 'strongly agree' to 'strongly disagree'. An example of a study which employed a combination of both methods is the study by Gibbons and Ramirez (2004), who interviewed English–Spanish bilingual teenagers in Sydney. They were asked questions such as:

How do you feel about Spanish?

What do you think are the chances that the Spanish language will survive in Sydney?

How do you feel about English?

Following that, they were each asked to fill in a closed-ended questionnaire by rating the following statements on a Likert scale (agree/disagree):

Spanish will not be very useful internationally in the future.

Spanish is a beautiful language.

I really like being around people when they are using Spanish.

You only need English in the modern world.

 Task A7.3

➤ To what extent do you think speakers are likely to be completely honest when answering questions of this type? Can you think of some reasons why some speakers may not wish to divulge their real opinions?

Alternatively, a semantic differential scale can be used to evaluate language attitudes. In studies using semantic differential scales, pairs of bipolar adjectives are used to assess the profile of a group or individual speaker. The following are examples of semantic differential scales for six adjectives drawn from Baker (1992: 18). These scales could be used to assess the response to a statement like: 'Rate Turkish speakers on the following scales':

1————2————3————4————5
Unmusical   Musical

1————2————3————4————5
Ugly   Beautiful

1————2————3————4————5
Difficult   Easy

1————2————3————4————5
Old fashioned   Modern

1————2————3————4————5
Useless   Useful

1————2————3————4————5
Weak   Strong

Though direct methods are commonly used, it is widely acknowledged that such methods are unlikely to be able to measure attitudes precisely. As Baker (1992) has argued, speakers may respond to an attitude by providing socially desirable answers so that they can appear more conforming or prestigious, depending on the image they wish to portray. They could also be influenced by the researcher's verbal and non-verbal cues and the perceived leanings of the researcher conducting the study. With direct measurements, we are able to assess only the cognitive aspects of the attitude component, and not the affective aspects.

Indirect methods

Indirect methods seek to measure language attitudes without letting the participants know that it is their language attitude which is under study. A method pioneered by Lambert et al. (1960) called the matched-guise (MG) technique is now widely used in language attitude research. In a typical MG study, speech samples of fluent bilingual speakers are recorded, with speakers speaking in both languages. Researchers using MG tasks usually control the guises (the speech samples of the bilingual) by ensuring that both speech samples are neutral in content. These guises are then played to participants, who are asked to rate 'each' speaker on a range of semantic differential scales, such as perceived degree of intelligence, honesty, education etc. The purpose is to gather subjective reactions to the speakers, but not to the language. In these situations, the taped speech sample is stripped of all cues except the language, hence the participants are responding to variations in language, as the speakers of both guises are the same person. The MG technique is the most common indirect method used to measure language attitude. There is now a proliferation of studies using variations of the MG tasks.

Task A7.4

➤ Critics of MG have argued that real-life communication provides far more cues than an MG task. What are some of these cues? Can you think of ways in which you could modify the MG task to increase its authenticity?

Apart from the use of questionnaires, interviews and MG techniques, one could also use observations as a way of unobtrusively assessing attitudes. In this case, attitudes are inferred from observed behaviour. However, the validity of this assumption is questionable as observations are susceptible to a wide range of subjective interpretations.

Generally, whether language attitude can be objectively measured is a controversial issue, and the various methods used have been comprehensively reviewed and critiqued in the last two decades (e.g. Agheyisi and Fishman 1970; Fasold 1984; Potter and Wetherell 1987; Cargile et al. 1994). Regardless of the methodological flaws identified, there is no denying that language is not a neutral entity and, more importantly, that language is a very potent form of self-identification (Ingram 1980). As such, despite the criticisms of language attitude studies, research in this field has persisted as there is a consensus that, elusive as it is, attitude is not a dimension that can be ignored. In the following section, we will review some studies on language attitudes within bilingual communities.

BILINGUAL ATTITUDES TO SELF AND OTHERS IN THE COMMUNITY

Lambert et al. (1960) and Lambert (1967) were among the first to study language attitudes in a bilingual community. In a pioneering study, Lambert et al. (1960) pointed out that the behaviour of bilinguals is strongly influenced by their attitude towards the language and the motivations they have for using the language. Using the MG technique, speakers who could pass as native speakers in English and French were recorded speaking a short paragraph in both languages. Both English Canadians and French Canadians listened to the tape and were then asked to rank the different speakers on a number of different personality traits such as *height, looks, intelligence, dependability, leadership, sociability, likeability, self-confidence* and *character.* Lambert et al. found that the English guise was judged more favourably than the French guise in terms of personality traits such as *intelligence, self-confidence, friendliness* and *dependability* by both English and French Canadians. The French guise, on the other hand, was judged more positively on *religiosity* and *kindness.*

The MG technique demonstrates that language serves as a cue for attitudes and has subsequently been applied to other languages and other sociolinguistic situations. Generally, there is agreement that the MG technique is a very useful tool for identifying the unequal status of languages in society. Most of the semantic differential scales in MG studies measure two factors: status and solidarity. Traits such as *intelligence, leadership, dependability* and *confidence* are more related to status, whereas traits such as *sociability, kindness* and *likeability* are more associated with solidarity. In MG studies, a language can be rated along four dimensions. Languages can be high in status and high in solidarity, high in status and low in solidarity, low in status and high in solidarity or low in status and low in solidarity.

 Task A7.5

➤ Think of the languages spoken around you that you identified in Task A7.1. Categorize them into the four 'status' and 'solidarity' categories discussed. Explain your decision for placing the language(s) in each of the categories.

Early studies suggested that in a bilingual language pair there is a tendency for the language that enjoys higher prestige to be ranked lower in status and higher in solidarity. For example, in the Montreal context in the 1960s, French Canadians were ranked higher on one of the solidarity traits (kindness) (Lambert 1967). This pattern was also found in a study with Peruvian Indians. Wölck (1973) found that Quechua speakers were rated higher on *good looks* and *kindness*, while Spanish speakers were rated higher on status-related traits, e.g. *level of education* and *social class*. Similarly, a study set in Morocco found that French guises were associated with sophistication while those speaking Moroccan Arabic were perceived as being informal and intimate (Bentahila 1983). In Hong Kong, the same trend was found for English and Cantonese (Lyczak et al. 1976), where English was associated with increased status whereas Cantonese was rated highly on solidarity traits.

Most of these MG studies are collected in formal contexts such as schools and tertiary institutions, and we need to be cautious about interpreting the findings collected in such formal contexts. As pointed out by Carranza and Ryan (1975), more careful separation of contexts can yield significantly different results. In their sample, Spanish was rated higher than English in both solidarity and status in the home context, but lower than English in the school context. As Lawson and Sachdev (2000) indicate, school, after all, is generally a status-stressing environment that may bias respondents to pay attention to status features only. This *diglossic* perception of languages, a phenomenon discussed in the next section, is quite pervasive, and over time one language gains social prestige. This inevitably will have an influence on language attitudes, a topic we will discuss in the next section.

Task A7.6

➤ Most studies have been collected in formal contexts such as schools and universities. Can you think of examples of informal contexts where alternative data might be collected?

➤ What kinds of problems do you envisage with conducting language attitude research in the informal contexts you have identified?

LANGUAGE PRESTIGE AND LANGUAGE ATTITUDES

The observation that languages within a community may relate to prestige in a specific way was first made by Ferguson (1959). He first used the term *diglossia* to describe a situation where two related languages in a community, for example, are allocated different functions. The High variety usually attracts wider social prestige while the Low variety is used in the home environment and for in-group communication. The most cited example is the use of Modern Standard Arabic (the High variety) alongside other regional varieties of Arabic (Low varieties). Modern Standard Arabic is used for formal purposes such as literary works, religious ceremonies and public speeches. The Ferguson model of diglossia is often referred to as *classic diglossia* (Myers-Scotton 2006). Other examples of classic diglossia are the co-existence of Swiss German and Standard German in Switzerland, and

Katharevousa and Dhimotiki in Greece. However, in the case of Greece, Dhimotiki, the Low variety, is now widely used as politically driven language reforms in the last few decades have led to its use in formal domains such as law, media and education.

The concept of diglossia was extended by Fishman (1972) to language pairs which are not related in bilingual communities. In a typical Fishman *diglossic* situation, the two languages within a community enjoy different status and prestige and are allocated different functions. Although Fishman's extension of diglossia to include unrelated languages in bilingual communities has been debated (see Hudson 2002), it is a very useful framework, as status and prestige continue to be very salient features when describing language use in bilingual communities. For example, in much of China, Putonghua (Mandarin) is used in the workplace and school, and other regional languages (usually referred to as 'dialects' or *fānyán* even though some varieties are not mutually intelligible) are used in homes and public places. Accordingly, Putonghua is perceived to be the language which will provide an economic advantage whereas the regional languages are associated with speakers' cultural roots (Li and Lee 2004). In African nations, colonial languages such as French, Portuguese and English are widely perceived to be associated with success. Adegbija (2000: 88) notes that:

> in virtually all official circles in West African countries, indigenous languages tend to be mostly restricted to informal and non serious contexts, whereas European languages tend to be used frequently in strictly formal and serious contexts. The usage pattern further enhances the esteem of European languages.

Though the quotation refers to West African states, it could just as easily apply to other African states, e.g. Tanzania or South Africa (Kembo 1991; Kamwangamalu 2004).

Although both classic diglossia and Fishman's variation of diglossia assign language use into two separated spheres of influence, there is a fundamental difference between them. As Myers-Scotton (2006: 87) points out:

> Under classic diglossia, at least everyone in the community speaks the same L variety as a home language. That is, the L variety is everyone's L1. The High variety is always a variety that is learned through special study; it is not simply acquired as part of a natural process in the home. So sufficient schooling is the gateway to potential power. Under extended diglossia, everyone in the community speaks his or her L1, of course, and it is acquired in the home. But here's the catch: For some people the L1 is also the H variety, but for others, their L1 is only an L variety. Thus, by the accident of family, some people have more access to participating in status-raising interactions.

Myers-Scotton further adds that stable diglossia in the extended situation is difficult to preserve as it involves maintaining L1 as a Low variety alongside L2, which is a prestige (High) variety. There is some evidence that in such diglossic situations, the low variety is more susceptible to shift as the low status and prestige of the low variety ultimately influences the attitudes of the speakers towards the use of the language in a negative way. Clyne (2006) identifies diglossia in the home country of migrants to be a factor which contributes to language shift in immigrant communities.

The relationship between language prestige and language attitudes is not always a straightforward one. Villamil Touriño (2004) reports that Galician spoken in Madrid is poorly maintained even though the Galician speakers' self-report data indicate extremely positive attitudes to Galician. Villamil attributes the lack of language maintenance to the low prestige of Galician in comparison to Spanish. However, in such cases the overt attitude may be high but the covert attitude is none the less low. While Galician speakers may outwardly support the idea of retaining Galician, their practice of not using Galician with their children speaks otherwise. In a different study in Paraguay, Choi (2003) made similar observations that, despite very positive attitudes to Guarani (an indigenous language) in the community, it was not being used or, therefore, transmitted to children, and the language shift from Guarani to Spanish across generations was, therefore, likely to be rapid. These studies demonstrate the importance of maintaining a distinction between a separate *readiness for action* component identified by Baker (1992).

Task A7.7

➤ Can you conceive of a situation where intense negative orientation towards a language is not matched by the practice in reality? (For example, parents who dislike English but send all their children to English immersion programmes?) Why would such a negative attitude produce action contrary to what one would expect?

IDENTITY AND LANGUAGE ATTITUDE

Language is commonly used as an identification to separate one community from another. In these cases, high ratings for solidarity features could also indicate that the language holds a strong identity marker for the community (Fasold 1984). Woolard's (1984) study of attitudes towards Catalan and Castilian (Spanish) speakers in Barcelona found that not only was Catalan rated highly on prestige but when the Catalan speakers were speaking Castilian, they were penalized and rated lower than Castilian speakers. Here, language identity with Catalan is so strong that using Castilian, the language of the outgroup, is perceived as 'linguistic betrayal' (Woolard 1984: 70). In Taiwan, language attitudes were found to correlate strongly with language use. Participants who were Minnan-Taiyu- (Mandarin) speaking bilinguals were more likely to actively use Minnan if they rated pro-Minnan maintenance statements highly (Van den Berg 1988). Not surprisingly, this attitude extended to perceptions of Han (Mandarin) scripts in comparison to Taibun (Minnan) scripts. In a study comparing attitudes to these two varieties of scripts, Chiung (2001) found that Minnan speakers were more likely to rate Taibun highly. The author also claims that the general acceptance of Taibun is an indication of the rising sense of a need to establish a national identity for Taiwan.

The issue of how language works as a marker of identity in bilinguals is a topic which is well researched and we will examine this in more detail when we examine what minority languages mean to a group of young English–Punjabi bilinguals in the extract by Mills (2001) in Unit B7.

 Task A7.8

> ➤ Researchers working on uncovering language attitudes always stress how important it is to be aware of their own preconceived ideas about other languages. Why do you think such self-awareness is important?

THE EFFECT OF BILINGUALISM ON LANGUAGE ATTITUDES

Apart from documenting subjective reactions to languages, MG studies have also been used to examine whether the experience of being bilingual can alter perceptions and attitudes. In such studies, bilinguals' reactions to MG speech samples were compared with those of monolinguals. Peal and Lambert's (1962) comparison of the attitudes of French–English bilingual children with those of French mono-lingual children in Montreal found that being bilingual did alter the French–English bilinguals' perceptions of the English speakers in the community. The bilinguals showed no differences in their evaluations of both English and French samples, while the French monolingual children rated the English speech sample more negatively than they did the French sample.

Since 1962, there have been several studies (MG as well as studies using other methods) that have attributed significant changes in attitude to bilingualism. A study by Lambert and Tucker (1972) showed fairly similar and positive effects of bilingualism except for the fact that the attitude changed from being positive to being neutral over time. After surveying majority children in immersion pro-grammes in Canada, Genesee (1995) concluded that the effect on attitudes towards other languages was positive. More importantly, this finding was achieved without negatively affecting their feelings towards their own home culture, a point which is a source of concern for some parents.

Positive effects on attitudes after attending an immersion programme have also been reported in studies outside the Canadian setting. For example, Imhasly (1977) demonstrated that English-speaking children who had attended a Spanish–English bilingual programme had claimed more positive attitudes towards Mexican culture.

In a study which involved 247 Japanese children in an English immersion programme in Japan, Downes (2001) found that, apart from showing a stronger sense of cultural identity than the comparison group, Japanese children in the immersion programme also showed a stronger attraction towards Western culture, and a more positive attitude towards English. In addition, he also found that these immersion students showed a stronger identity with Japan and more heightened awareness of the Japanese language in comparison to Japanese children not in immersion programmes. Downes described these traits as indications of the enhancing effects of bilingual immersion as the children were positively attuned to both cultures.

Apart from immersion classes, exposure to language classes alone is sometimes enough to trigger positive attitudinal responses. In a study comparing two communities in Spain, Baix Segre (Catalonia) and Baix Cinca (Aragon), Huguet and Llurda (2001) found that generally children in Baix Segre, where Catalan has a bigger functional range and is a school language, are more positive about Catalan than the children in Baix Cinca, where the school language is Castilian (Spanish). This is hardly surprising, but what is intriguing is the comparison of Baix Cinca children who attended some Catalan classes as part of the curriculum to Baix Cinca children who did not have the same exposure. The findings indicate that this subset of children were just as positive towards Catalan when compared to the children in the Baix Segre group. In fact, the results indicate that the children with the highest overall language attitude scores were this particular group of children, who appeared to be positively oriented to both Catalan and Castilian.

Although education appears to play a pivotal role in transforming perceptions, we are not suggesting that education alone, or just being bilingual, can neutralize hostilities or rivalry between groups. As pointed out by Oyetade (1996), increased bilingualism in Yoroba and Nupe in Nigeria did not correlate significantly with positive attitudes towards each other's culture. Oyetade attributed this to the age-old economic struggle between the two groups. Ultimately, other socio-cultural, economic and political factors can constrain language attitudes. On this topic, we will read a special case comparing Montreal and Quebec City in Unit B7. There is no doubt, however, that bilingual education programmes are a factor which impacts on how we view other community groups.

Task A7.9

➤ In the studies cited above, studying a language can somehow positively modify a learner's orientation towards the community of the target language. What are some aspects of language learning which can contribute to this transformation?

ACCOMMODATION THEORY

Studies on language attitudes have clearly established that individuals' responses to languages and language choices are not neutral. Consequently, there is now a substantial body of research which focuses on how attitudes influence language choices made by bilinguals towards members from the bilingual speaker's community (*ingroup*) and members from outside the speaker's community (*outgroup*). Initially known as Social Accommodation Theory (Giles 1977), this concept has been refined and researched extensively over the last few decades and has evolved into what is now referred to generally as Communication Accommodation Theory (CAT) (Sachdev and Giles 2004), extending Social Accommodation Theory to all aspects of communication. CAT proposes that individuals use communication to indicate their attitudes towards each other, and they do so by adapting their communicative behaviours to those of their interlocutor, accommodating to and becoming more like the interlocutor. Alternatively, individuals can also distance themselves from the interlocutor by refusing to modify their original communication style.

Adaptation towards the other speaker is known as *convergence* and the reverse is known as *divergence*. In CAT, convergence tends to be identified through language features such as accent, language choice, speech rate, pauses and utterance length. Non-verbal features such as smiling and gaze also contribute to its identification. This movement towards and away from others is called *accommodation*.

Myers-Scotton (2006) points out that though both convergence and divergence are probably unconscious acts, divergence can be more deliberate and conscious than convergence. For example, Bortoni-Ricardo (1985) found that her Brazilian Portuguese speakers consciously used a more conservative form of the Portuguese spoken in north-eastern Brazil to resist identifying with the urban Brazilian Portuguese spoken around them. Similarly, Aikenvald (2003) reports that Tariana speakers, a small community living in the Brazilian jungle, consciously avoided the use of Tucano, a more dominant language, as Tucano is perceived as the language of the invaders.

CAT has proved to be a very useful concept for studying bilingual attitudes as it provides researchers with a powerful way to infer attitudes from observations of actual behaviours. The fact that we accommodate our speech style is uncontroversial and there are numerous studies on this topic. In the next section (Unit B7), we will read an extract by Genesee and Bourhis (1988), who used accommodation theory as a framework to study how French and English Canadians relate to each other in Quebec City.

THE RELATIONSHIP BETWEEN LANGUAGE ATTITUDE AND SELF-REPORT DATA

Though language attitudes have been found to play an important role in second-language acquisition, proficiency and attrition (see Gardner 1985; Dörnyei and Clément 2001), the role they play in moderating the proficiency of circumstantial bilinguals is still unclear. This may have to do with the fact that in studies of circumstantial bilinguals, the use of self-report data in place of objective measures of bilingual proficiency is more common. The issue of attitudinal orientation is a topic that has been explored more thoroughly in the second-language setting except for a handful of studies which focused on the relationship between proficiency and language attitude. Peal and Lambert's (1962) study indicates that positive orientation and identification with the target language group was more important for the monolinguals than for the bilinguals when it came to predicting proficiency. Hakuta and D'Andrea (1992) explored the three-way relationship between self-report data, actual proficiency and attitudes. Firstly, they found that there were two main types of attitudinal clusters: *positive orientation* towards maintenance and *subtractive orientation* towards maintenance. There was a third cluster which they loosely identify as 'pragmatic value underlying language use' (Hakuta and D'Andrea 1992: 78). The first two clusters will be examined as they are more relevant to the discussion here.

As in the direct method described earlier, participants were asked to rate a set of statements using a Likert scale. Examples of statements relating to both orientations can be found in Task C7.2. Interestingly, Hakuta and D'Andrea found that attitudinal features did not predict proficiency but did predict the language choice made by the participants about whether they would use Spanish in contexts other than the parental home. More precisely, subtractive orientation towards maintenance predicts a shift away from Spanish, and positive orientation towards maintenance predicts the reverse. They surmised that if the choice is not to use Spanish outside the parental home, transmission of Spanish would ultimately be affected.

Furthermore, they found a positive correlation between proficiency ratings in the self-report data and maintenance. Here, positive orientation towards maintenance leads to higher self-report proficiency, and, conversely, subtractive orientation leads towards lower self-report proficiency. They concluded that, in fact, the self-report data can be used indirectly as a measure of attitudes. This finding is significant as a substantial body of research in bilingualism is based on such data.

CODE SWITCHING, CODE MIXING AND LANGUAGE ATTITUDES

As we discussed in Unit A1, an integral part of being a bilingual is the ability to control the two languages in any given situation because a bilingual has to make pragmatic decisions about what language to use and when. Often the decision will be to use both languages in the same conversation. This phenomenon is referred to as code switching. (Note: code switching and code mixing have been variously defined to mean the use of two (or more) languages inter- or intra-sententially.)

An example of inter-sentential code switching is the following English–Mandarin sample from Singapore:

> *Hey, this is getting really boring. Zhè yàng làn de jiemù hai yào wǒmén kàn.*

> 'Hey, this is getting really boring. Why are we asked to watch such a lousy show?'

In inter-sentential code switching, there is no switching within the sentence or clause. Another example of code switching, this time between clauses in English–Swahili, is provided by Myers-Scotton (239–240).

> *Have some vegetables, nipe kabeji hizi.*

> 'Have some vegetables, give me these cabbages.'

Compare this to intra-sentential code switching where the switching is intra-clausal:

> *Nǐ shěnme shíhòu yào go shopping?*

> 'When are you going shopping?'

Though some researchers (e.g. Kachru 1978; Bokamba 1988) make the distinction between inter-sentential and intra-sentential code switching, preferring to describe the latter as code mixing, others (e.g. Myers-Scotton 2006) have treated the phenomenon under the general term of code switching. Here we will use the term *code switching* for both types of code switching.

Code switching relates to attitudes because it elicits strong affective responses from both bilinguals and monolinguals, so that any discussion of bilingual language attitudes needs to account for attitudes to code switching. Several studies have shown that attitudes in this context are often associated with language maintenance, shift and loss.

Despite the fact that code switching has been accepted as a natural and systematic aspect of bilingualism by sociolinguists for many years, there is a tendency for the general public to still view it negatively. Lawson and Sachdev (2000: 1345) cited findings from studies undertaken in Nigeria, Morocco and Hong Kong that report negative remarks such as 'still colonized' (for Morocco), 'verbal salad' (for Nigeria) and 'very irritating' (Hong Kong) to describe the phenomenon of code switching.

Ritchie and Bhatia (2004) made the distinction between covert (unconscious) attitudes and overt (conscious) attitudes. They argued that in some cases, overt negative attitudes (e.g. expressions of dislike for code switching) may not match up with actual behaviour (covert expression). For example, in the case of Hong Kong, Gibbons (1987) found that despite the Hong Kong speaker's overt dislike for code switching in Cantonese and English, such behaviour (at that time) is seen as a bridge between the more Westernized English-speaking world and the more traditional Cantonese-speaking Hong Kong. Romaine (1995) also reported that using Punjabi loan words when speaking English was viewed both positively and negatively by Punjabi–English bilinguals as it could signal either the prestige of knowing English words or the intrusion of contaminating elements. Others, like Lawson and Sachdev (2000), argue that, in fact, code switching may attract some level of covert prestige. In their study of code switching in Tunisia by Arabic–French bilinguals, Lawson and Sachdev (2000) found that the negative attitudes of the participants to code switching were not congruent with their actual usage as most of the participants reported a high level of code switching in the diary they were required to keep.

In Rampton's (2005) study (conducted in a town in the south Midlands of England), which adopted a more ethnographic approach, he found the use of Punjabi, Creole and stylized Indian English to be conditioned by a multitude of social factors. These factors interacted in a complex manner to create social identity for the youths in the study and carried symbolic social meanings. For example, the stylized Indian English was negatively stereotyped as an intergroup language but used widely in the presence of authoritative adults as a way of subverting their authority.

Generally, it seems that reactions to code switching do not follow a consistent pattern across language pairs. In the case of Italian–English bilinguals, Bettoni (1985) reported that code switching was rated very negatively by Italo-Australian speakers themselves. This is also the case for English–French bilinguals from Ottawa and Flemish–French bilinguals in Brussels. In Ottawa and Brussels, English–French bilinguals and Flemish–French bilinguals kept code switching to a minimum because of the intense negative reaction it attracted from the community. As pointed out by Grosjean (1982), the lack of tolerance for code switching in the Flemish–French community could be due to the historical linguistic rivalry and conflict within the group resulting in a clear separation of languages. On the other hand, Puerto Rican–English bilinguals consistently viewed code switching favourably and in their speech code switching occurred as much as 97 per cent of the time (Poplack 1987).

However, the case of Puerto Rican bilinguals is more the exception than the rule. Ritchie and Bhatia (2004) noted that the reaction of the general public (mono-linguals and bilinguals alike) to code switching is usually negative. Code switching is often seen as a sign of the linguistic death of both the participating languages, and bilinguals who mix their languages are often perceived as speakers who are unable to speak either of their languages well, though, as we have seen in Unit A1, the notion of semilingualism has been widely criticized. An interesting fact is that the most severe critique of code switching has often come from bilinguals themselves. Bilinguals often 'consider code-switching to be a sign of "laziness", an "inadvertent" speech act, an "impurity", an instance of linguistic decadence and a potential danger to their own linguistic performance' (Ritchie and Bhatia 2004: 350). More critically, it is not uncommon to find bilinguals deprecating their language proficiency, and they often cite code switching as a reason for not being bilingually competent. Lawson and Sachdev (2000), reviewing the evidence, suggested that bilinguals who have negative attitudes to code switching may under-report their proficiency in self-report data. Earlier, we discussed how positive attitudes can lead to better self-report of language proficiency; this is an example of how negative attitudes can have the reverse effect.

What is the impact of such negative responses to code switching on bilinguals? If code switching is a natural part of being bilingual, its stigmatization will gradually lead to the avoidance of code switching, which in turn may lead to attrition in the less dominant language. Moreover, denigration of code switching could also contribute to negative self-identity in bilinguals and, in a bid to preserve the 'purity' of languages, bilinguals may run the risk of marginalizing their own bilingual experience. Furthermore, as pointed out by Ritchie and Bhatia (2004), code switching can be promoted if mixing becomes the mark of cultural or social identity, which could in turn lead to positive identification with being bilingual, a socially desirable outcome. Bhatia and Ritchie (2004) further note that the creativeness of code switching has been widely exploited globally in advertising, and this seems incompatible with the general negative attitudes code switching tends to attract. This observation gave the authors reason to believe that the covert prestige of code switching may in fact still be very high.

Sometimes, the reasons could be instrumental. For example, code switching between standard English and 'Singlish', a variety of Singapore English generally perceived as non-standard by the government authorities, is highly stigmatized and discouraged. Despite concerted efforts by the authorities to ban the use of Singlish, it was featured prominently in the SARS campaign produced by government bodies during the 2004 SARS pandemic. In a bid to reach out to the public and educate them about the dangers of SARS, the government body resorted to the language that has the most 'appeal' in its promotional materials, thus providing an indirect recognition of the covert prestige enjoyed by code switching.

 Task A7.10

➤ Listen in on the conversation of bilinguals speaking to each other. Do they use one language consistently or do they code-switch? What are some motivations for the code switching instances you observed? For example, Rampton (2005) noted that Punjabi-speaking teenagers code-switched to English in the playground when they did not want the teachers to understand their discussion. In the classroom, they might code-switch to stylized Indian English, pretending they did not have enough language competence to understand or to carry out a task.

PARENTS, TEACHERS, HEALTHCARE PROVIDERS AND LANGUAGE ATTITUDES

As we know, early childhood and adolescence are a critical part of an individual's life and it is during this period that a child is more vulnerable to outside influences. In this section, we will explore how attitudes from parents, teachers and healthcare providers can facilitate or hamper the development of bilinguals.

Parents

Parents naturally exert a strong influence over their children. It is, therefore, reasonable to predict that positive attitudes to bilingualism will correlate with higher levels of language maintenance. Indeed, some studies have confirmed this hypothesis. For example, Hamers (1994) conducted a large-scale study to explore the role of social networks in maintaining the mother tongue of immigrant children in Canada, and identified the positive attitudes of the family towards bilingual competence, cultural contexts and identity as playing a critical role in promoting L1 maintenance. She found the effect to be more pronounced for fathers in her cohort. However, as we saw earlier in our discussion of diglossia, overt positive attitudes may not necessarily correlate with language use or maintenance. In a study of Sicilian–Italian–English trilinguals in Sydney, there was a deliberate choice not to use Sicilian with the next generation despite strong positive orientation towards that dialect of the Italian language (Cavallaro 1998).

To understand the impact that parents may have on the bilingual development of a child, it may be necessary to look at behaviour rather than at overt attitudes. In a study looking at loss and maintenance of first-language skills, Guardado (2002) examined four Hispanic families in the United States who were all positively oriented to the maintenance of Spanish. Despite the positive attitudes, only two families could be considered to be successful in providing a conducive bilingual environment. Guardado drew up a profile of parenting styles which are conducive to supporting language maintenance. In this profile, she suggests that the more successful parents were more positive and encouraging, and that they tended to use more entertaining methods in developing an interest in their language. At the same time, they devoted more time to cultivating the children's Hispanic identity.

On the other hand, parents can also be instrumental in aiding the children's shift to a language of greater utilitarian value. In South Africa, the majority of mothers interviewed in a study by De Klerk (2000) preferred their children to learn English rather than Xhosa. Opinions about the necessity of maintaining Xhosa ranged from 'Xhosa is just a language. I'm not really attached to it' to 'It's fine to let [Xhosa] die. We have never teach our son any Xhosa' to 'I don't know if it is worth it – if you get educated in Xhosa, up to the tertiary level – what then? Who can you communicate with? Nobody else will understand you' (De Klerk 2000: 209). This intensely utilitarian view of language contrasts with the interview data gathered from Mills's study in England which we will read in Unit B7.

Teachers

There is no doubt that teachers are central in the lives of young children, and their attitudes, positive or negative, towards the bilingual children's language use are likely to have an impact on their language behaviour and choice. Dorian (1978), for example, reported on an extreme case where teachers went around to the homes of bilingual pupils asking parents to stop using Scottish Gaelic in the home as this interfered with the children's learning of English. In Singapore, where there is strong support for bilingualism, the support is for bilingualism in English and Mandarin and not for bilingualism which involves the use of any of the local vernaculars such as Hokkien, Teochew, Cantonese or Hainanese. Schools still actively discourage children of Chinese background from speaking anything other than English and Mandarin. This started with the 'Speak Mandarin Campaign' in 1979. By 2006, the campaign had successfully atrophied trilingualism within the Chinese community and, increasingly, young Chinese Singaporeans are growing up bilingual only in Mandarin Chinese and English. Very few can understand or speak the local vernacular languages.

Cruz-Ferreira (2006: 226) discusses how the parents of one trilingual child studying in an international school in Singapore, Sofia (six years old), were told by teachers that the root of Sofia's behavioural problems, which ranged from 'refusal to learn' to 'aggressive behaviour', was her inability to cope with the many languages she was speaking. Sofia was referred to a special needs class and labelled 'unstable', and her parents were told to stop using languages other than English at home! This is despite the fact that Sofia's academic ability was not in question as she had excellent grades in science, maths and any subject involving handicraft. As Cruz-Ferreira points out, there are unfortunate consequences for the child and for multilingualism in general when labels like 'unstable' and 'refusal to learn', and the illogical attribution of multilingualism as a cause for any behavioural problem, are kept in official records to be inherited by future form teachers.

Thus far, there have been no comprehensive studies that focus on teachers' attitudes to bilingual children and on how these attitudes concretely affect the development of bilinguals. However, several studies have confirmed that teachers working with bilingual children do have beliefs and attitudes which predispose them to being either supportive or unsupportive of bilingualism (Leek 2001; Cotacachi 1996). In a study of attitudinal differences among elementary teachers towards the use of the native language, Garcia (2001) reported that teachers with bilingual training certification were more positive to Spanish speakers and they were also more likely to value children who spoke Spanish. An ingroup effect was also found, as Latino bilingual certified teachers had the most positive attitudes.

Healthcare professionals

There is relatively little research that focuses on how healthcare professionals such as doctors, nurses, psychologists and speech therapists perceive and view bilinguals, often referred to CLD (Culturally and Linguistically Diversified) clients in this field of research. However, there are several anecdotes that suggest that some may view bilingualism as a form of interference with normal development. For example, Saunders (1982) recounts his own experience of having his doctor warn him against the 'risk' that speaking two languages might pose to his son's development of English. Romaine (1995) cites cases in which bilingual parents in a South Asian community in Britain were advised by school psychologists against speaking two languages to the children as this might confuse them. Romaine attributed such reservations about bilingualism to the prevailing thought that language mixing is harmful.

The most recent study which explicitly explored the role of attitude in healthcare professionals is the study undertaken by Döpke (2003), who surveyed 99 speech pathologists living in the metropolitan area of Victoria, Australia. Döpke (2003) reports that 30 per cent of the speech therapists in her Australian sample discouraged the use of a language other than English. Out of these, 17 per cent expressed an overt concern that exposure to another language might jeopardize the development of English. Her findings also indicated that speech pathologists with more CLD clients had more positive attitudes and beliefs about bilingualism and were more likely to encourage parents to continue using a language other than English. They were also more likely to provide advice on different aspects of bilingual development and were also more likely to invest time and effort in professional development which would help their CLD clientele.

Access to professional development with CLD populations is important, given the widely acknowledged difficulty of distinguishing difference from disorder in CLD children (Li et al. 2005). In the United States, a survey conducted by Roseberry-McKibbin (1994) reported that only 25 per cent of speech pathologists received training on working with CLD children. As pointed out by Döpke (2003), decisions for or against a language disorder in CLD children depend on the clinician's knowledge of what is normal development of the languages involved and other socio-pragmatic factors which are culture-bound. This lack of training impacts on two areas: the cultural knowledge of the CLD children and the use of traditional methods of assessments as discussed in Unit A2.

The importance of language and cultural knowledge has been asserted frequently in the literature on CLD children (see, for example, Brice 2002; Cline 1998; Hammer

1998). Brice (2002) advised that speech pathologists should familiarize themselves with the language and culture with the population they are working with. Li et al. (2005: 200) note how the cultural difference in the interpretation of silence could lead to misdiagnosis:

> Variation also exists in the uses to which language is put and its role in society. One particular aspect of this which could easily lead to mis-diagnoses of language disorder is the use of silence. In Britain and North America, generally, to be verbally fluent, though not verbose, is socially prestigious, while to be silent, especially when introduced to someone for the first time, when a relationship/situation is ambiguous, or at parties, would be impolite and interpreted as rudeness, disinterest or distress. In the bilingual assessment context it may be misinterpreted as non-comprehension or as inability to respond. Testers would need to be assured that the subcultural acceptable silence was not masking a true language disorder.

Li et al. (2005) further emphasize the importance of the attitude to language variation in distinguishing between difference and language disorders. This is more complex as code switching is the norm in CLD contexts. They point out that some healthcare professionals still regard a normal speaker as one who has perfect know-ledge of both or all the languages and never mixes them in conversation. Hence, they caution that 'Speech and language pathologists must see language variation as a normal phenomenon and not as an indicator of communication disorder' (Li et al. 2005: 201).

As it is often difficult to identify what is developmentally normal, several steps have been suggested to prevent misdiagnosis. Some of these steps (Li et al. 2005: 203) are:

1   familiarization with cultural, social and cognitive norms of the individual's speech community
2   familiarization with linguistic and communicative norms of the individual's speech community
3   the selection of appropriate, unbiased, standardized and criterion-referenced tests
4   preparation of culturally appropriate natural elicitation procedure.

There is no doubt that it is more demanding to work with CLD children in terms of time and resources. Most of the above suggestions, especially those involving the modification and creation of alternative tests for CLP children, need time and specialized training. Most healthcare professionals would need to be especially motivated to invest the time in professional development programmes for such training. The fact that such training is needed is highlighted by Hand (2001), who found that despite the consistent message reiterating the importance of gathering data on language and culture in the therapy session, the speech pathologists in her study did not exploit this aspect in their interviews with CLD parents. Instead, the sessions were characterized by monosyllabic answers even when the CLD parents themselves raised the issue of language, offering the opportunity for the clinician to collect data on the children's language development. In a different context, Isaac (2001, 2005) identifies the importance of cultural knowledge when speech pathologists use interpreters in their therapy sessions. In her study, she notes the communication barriers between interpreters and clinicians, which were in part due to the lack of familiarity with the CLD client's background. Naturally, communication breakdowns in such situations interfere with the effectiveness of the clinical session. With training, these clinicians will be able to gain better insights into the children's home language and home culture and hence will be more able to choose successful strategies in their treatment programme.

The issue of accurate diagnosis is critical with CLD children as the research shows that CLD children are underrepresented in speech pathology services. Crutchley (1999) and Yavas and Goldstein (1998) hypothesize uncertainties about assessment and interventions to be the reason why these children are not referred to speech pathology services. Furthermore, those who are identified with speech disorders tend to present with more severe language problems than monolingual children (Crutchley 1999). Hence, hesitation and confusion about CLD children can lead to costly misdiagnosis which results in these children missing out on timely treatment.

Parents, teachers and healthcare professionals are likely to take their cues from a wider and more influential source such as government bodies. In the next section, we will briefly review how language policies can leave indelible marks on the bilingual landscape.

THE IMPACT OF LANGUAGE POLICIES ON LANGUAGE ATTITUDES

As pointed out by Sachdev and Bourhis (2001), there is no doubt that dominant ideologies expressed in official language policies influence bilingual communication. In South Africa, Kamwangamalu (2004) reported that English was adopted as the official language to avoid 'tribalism'. The promotion of English as the official language has in turn led to negative attitudes towards the mother tongue and affected decisions parents made about language transmission. In this case, decisions about maintenance are not made by speakers alone but are strongly influenced by government and community support. The case of South Africa is emblematic of many multilingual countries. Singapore is also a prime case where language planning and policies shape the linguistic practices of Singaporeans, changing a multilingual population to one that is bilingual in English and one of the other officially sanctioned languages: Mandarin, Malay or Tamil (Kwan-Terry 2000). Apart from in Singapore, overt language policies are often used for managing and manipulating language behaviours in multilingual settings such as India, China, Indonesia, the Philippines and countries in Latin America and Africa.

During the process of language planning, some languages are usually accorded more status than others. As pointed out by Dorian (2004), this has immense ramifications for the speakers of languages without official status. The irreconcilable power difference between speaking a language with status and one without has enormous linguistic and social impact on the maintenance of these languages.

Apart from overt language policies, other practices – for example, the introduction and wide application of the Stanford–Binet Test in the education system in North America in the 1950s – were instrumental in curbing the flourishing of bilingualism for many decades (Mackey 2004). This is because the Stanford–Binet Test disadvantaged bilingual children, who performed poorly in comparison to their monolingual peers, and their poor performance led to public fear and condemnation of bilingualism. Consequently, parents were discouraged from using their native language, and the acculturation of immigrant children was accelerated. As Shohamy (2006: 98) points out, tests serve as powerful means of determining the status and power of specific languages in society as an effective tool for 'assimilative agendas'.

Given the pressure to assimilate, bilinguals were reticent about their ethnicity, as any overt expression of ethnic pride was likely to be interpreted as unpatriotic. The heightened nationalism and patriotic fervour added to the pressure of assimilation. The pressure to assimilate was reinforced by immigration policies in the United States at the turn of the twentieth century which actively encouraged assimilation by giving preference to migrants from well-assimilated groups (Mackey 2004). So, in effect, the socio-political climate in the United States up to 1960 was not conducive to the expression of cultural diversity and multilingualism, and it was only through active bilingual policies at the Federal level in the 1960s that the status of bilingualism was improved.

 Task A7.11

> What are the official languages in your country? Are these languages used in schools? Are there any languages spoken in the community which have not been given official status? Are the official languages also the languages that are used in shops, restaurants and homes?

Summary

In this unit, we have discussed studies which confirm that bilinguals have varying attitudes towards the languages of the wider community and, more importantly, studies in which the wider community responds differently to bilinguals in ways which may or may not facilitate bilingual development. Moreover, we saw how the mere exposure to bilingualism can enhance a bilingual's acceptance and understanding of other ethnic groups.

Generally, we see that there are several layers of influence on bilingualism ranging from that of the wider society such as schools and other government institutions, to the significant roles played by teachers, parents and healthcare professionals in providing or not providing support for bilingualism. All these factors contribute to the moulding of the bilinguals' self-identity, and bilinguals draw on this sense of this identity to negotiate and create symbolic links with people they come in contact with. Naturally, positive attitudes to bilingualism help promote cultural diversity while negative attitudes work against the creation of a heterogeneous society. However, language attitude within an individual or a community is a dynamic process and is constantly changing in response to changes in the socio-political contexts. Enlightened language policies, coupled with supportive educational environments, can transform and greatly enhance the bilingual experience.

SECTION B
Extension

Unit B1
Describing bilingualism extended

In Unit A1, we discussed the problem of describing and classifying bilinguals, and we also highlighted the relevance of applying descriptors such as context, domain, age, socio-economic status and proficiency when describing bilingualism. In this section, we will begin by examining cases of the bilingual experience and review in more detail some of the descriptors we introduced in Unit A1.

IDENTIFYING BILINGUALS

All over the world, people become bilingual for various reasons. Hoffmann (1991) lists immigration, migration, close contact with other language groups, schooling and growing up in bilingual families as possible sources of bilingualism. To this list we would also like to add *multilingual societies* where individuals are expected to be proficient in two or more languages. In Task A1.1, you were asked to identify someone who is bilingual and to create a profile by examining the ways in which they use both languages. Here, we will present a list of likely scenarios of bilingual experience from Hoffmann (1991).

C. Hoffmann (1991) *An introduction to bilingualism,* **New York: Longman, pp. 16–17.**

Text B1.1
C. Hoffmann

The three definitions mentioned so far say nothing about how well the languages need to be known, whether both have to be mastered in all sorts of skills, whether they must be used in similar or different situations, or about any particular requirements regarding the uses to which the languages are put. Yet such considerations would probably be relevant in deciding whether any, or all, of the following should be considered as bilinguals:

(1) the two-year-old who is beginning to talk, speaking English to one parent and Welsh to the other;

(2) the four-year-old whose home language is Bengali and who has been attending an English playgroup for some time;

(3) the schoolchild from an Italian immigrant family living in the United States who increasingly uses English both at home and outside but whose older relatives address him in Italian only;

(4) the Canadian child from Montréal who comes from an English-speaking back-ground and attends an immersion programme which consists of virtually all school subjects being taught through the medium of French;

(5) the young graduate who has studied French for eleven years;

(6) the sixty-year-old scholar who has spent a considerable part of her life working with manuscripts and documents written in Latin;

(7) the technical translator;

(8) the personal interpreter of an important public figure;

(9) the Portuguese chemist who can read specialist literature in his subject written in English;

(10) the Japanese airline pilot who uses English for most of his professional communication;

(11) the Turkish immigrant worker in . . . Germany who speaks Turkish at home and with his friends and work colleagues, but who can communicate in German, in both the written and the oral forms, with his superiors and the authorities;

(12) the wife of the latter, who is able to get by in spoken German but cannot read or write it;

(13) the Danish immigrant in New Zealand who has had no contact with Danish for the last forty years;

(14) the Belgian government employee who lives in bilingual Brussels, whose friends and relatives are mainly Flemish speakers but who works in an entirely French-speaking environment and whose colleagues in the office (whether they are Flemish or not) use French as well;

(15) the fervent Catalanist who at home and at work uses Catalan only, but who is exposed to Castilian Spanish from the media and in the street and has no linguistic difficulty in the latter language.

So what *is* bilingualism? Many specialists would say that all the above individuals could be classed as bilinguals; but public opinion, and at least some of these people themselves, would probably disagree. It is possible to think of a number of explanations for the difficulties involved in arriving at a precise definition.

 Task B1.1.1

➤ So what *is* bilingualism? How can we answer the question posed by Hoffmann? Can you come up with possible answers by using context, domain, age, socio-economic status and level of competence as guiding parameters? (See discussion on descriptors in Unit A1.) When you have tried to do this, think about the following points:

▪ Does applying these descriptors help you in sorting out the bilinguals from the non-bilinguals?

▪ Do you need more information for each of these cases? If so, what kind of information would you require to help you?

▪ Can you present an argument for prioritizing these descriptors?

▪ In what way do you think the descriptors are helpful or unhelpful in understanding the difficulties facing researchers when they describe bilinguals?

THE COMPLEXITIES OF DESCRIBING BILINGUALISM: DEGREE OF COMPETENCE

In every area of study, there are a number of 'must read' articles, and Mackey's (1962) 'The description of bilingualism' is one such article when we are talking about definition of bilingualism as it is one of the earliest articles to articulate fully the complexities of studying the phenomenon of bilingualism. Prior to this, many researchers used the term loosely to include anyone who showed any proficiency in another language. There was a general lack of concern or understanding about how bilinguals are defined or classified, and in many cases bilinguals were tested in their weaker language, which affected their performance negatively. This was often based on the assumption that bilingualism entails equal competency in both languages, which in turn led to misconceptions about bilingualism, such as the claim that bilinguals were cognitively less adept at various tasks, or that bilinguals were less capable academically. The full extent of this impact has been explored in more detail in Unit A4.

At the time of publication, Mackey's paper served the critical function of providing a framework to investigate the phenomenon of bilingualism, and we have included his paper because some of the conundrums he identified are just as relevant today as they were in 1962 when the article was published. In this article, Mackey comprehensively explores the various descriptors discussed in Unit A1, as well as other factors which may impact on bilingualism such as memory, aptitude and intelligence and how the two languages may interfere with each other. His paper was also a departure from other publications on bilingualism in this period as he focused on issues other than competence such as the domain of use, and the socio-cultural environment of the bilinguals. In the extract below, Mackey discusses the discussion of 'degree (of competence)' and 'functions'. These terms refer to the concepts we discussed in Unit A1, but in Unit A1 we used the term 'domains' rather than 'functions'.

As you read this article, bear in mind that it is well over forty years old, and there are certain turns of phrase which may appear rather old-fashioned. Note also that we have not changed Mackey's use of the generic 'he'; its use reflects the degree to which our expectations of appropriate language have changed over the years. Furthermore, as the extract is lengthy it has been presented in short separate sections.

William Mackey (1962) The description of bilingualism. *Canadian Journal of Linguistics*, **7**: 51–85.

Text B1.2
W. Mackey

. . .

Degree

The first and most obvious thing to do in describing a person's bilingualism is to determine how bilingual he is. To find this out it is necessary to test his skill in the use of each of his languages, which we shall label A and B. This includes separate tests for comprehension and expression in both the oral and written forms of each language, for the bilingual may not have an equal mastery of all four basic skills in both languages. He may indeed be able to understand both languages equally well; but he may be unable to speak both of them with equal facility. Since the language skills of the bilingual may include differences in comprehension and expression in both the spoken and written forms, it is necessary to test each of these skills separately if we are to get a picture of the extent of his bilingualism. If, however, we are only interested in determining his bilingualism rather than in describing it, other forms of tests are possible: word-detection tests, word-association and picture-vocabulary tests, for example, have been used for this purpose (Peal and Lambert, 1962).

The bilingual's mastery of a skill, however, may not be the same at all linguistic levels. He may have a vast vocabulary but a poor pronunciation, or a good pronunciation but imperfect grammar. In each skill, therefore, it is necessary to discover the bilingual's mastery of the phonology (or graphics), the grammar, the vocabulary, the semantics, and the stylistics of each language. What has to be described is proficiency in two sets of related variables, skills, and levels. This may be presented as in Table B1.2.1.

Table B1.2.1 Degree

	Levels									
	Phonological		**Grammatical**		**Lexical**		**Semantic**		**Stylistic**	
Skills	A	B	A	B	A	B	A	B	A	B
Listening										
Reading										
Speaking										
Writing										

If we consider Table B1.2.1, it is easy to see how the relation between skills and levels may vary from bilingual to bilingual. At the phonological and graphic level, for example, we have the case of the Croatian who understands spoken Serbian but is unable to read the Cyrillic script in which it is written. At the grammatical level, it is common to find bilinguals whose skill in the use of the grammatical structures of both languages cannot match their knowledge of the vocabularies. At the lexical level it is not unusual to find bilinguals whose reading vocabulary in Language B is more extensive than it is in Language A, and far beyond their speaking vocabulary in either language. At the semantic level a bilingual may be able to express his meaning in some areas better in one language than he can in the other. A bilingual technician who normally speaks Language A at home and speaks Language B indifferently at work may nevertheless be able to convey his meaning much better in Language B whenever he is talking about his specialty. Finally, a bilingual's familiarity with the stylistic range of each language is very likely to vary with the subject of discourse.

Text B1.2
W. Mackey

To get an accurate description of the degree of bilingualism it is necessary to fill in the above framework with the results of tests. Types and models of language tests have now been developed. On these models it is possible to design the necessary tests for each of the languages used by the bilingual in the dialects which he uses.

In the above extract, Mackey demarcated our language ability into the four basic macro skills, and our language competence into five discrete levels for analysis. Through these analyses, he demonstrated that the competence of bilinguals in either language can vary across the four basic macro skills, as well as the five discrete linguistic levels as shown in the examples.

Task B1.2.1

Imagine that you are a Greek–English bilingual and you have to assess your own suitability for a course on Greek–English translation.

➤ How would you go about assessing your own language ability?

➤ How reliable would you consider the methods you used?

Now imagine you have to assess the bilingual competence of Greek–English bilingual college students to gauge their suitability for the same course.

➤ What difficulties are you likely to run into?

➤ What factors may affect the reliability of your assessment?

As you have probably seen from this exercise, assessing the degree of competence in bilinguals is quite complex. Imagine how these factors can be further compounded when you add a third or fourth language. In the next section we will explore the *domain* or *function* of bilingualism in more detail.

THE COMPLEXITIES OF DESCRIBING BILINGUALISM: FUNCTION

In Unit A1, we discussed person, place and topic as the main factors governing language choice. Mackey discusses the same concepts using the term 'function'. (An equivalent term used in Unit A1 is 'domain'.) He makes the distinction between external functions and internal functions, as well as detailing the various pressures that speakers experience which result in specific language choices, as well as the role of language levels. Mackey identifies five major domains, the *home, community, school, mass media* and *correspondence*, and further distinctions are made in each domain. For example, in the 'home' domain, interactions with each parent, siblings, other relatives and domestic helpers are studied separately. In the 'community' domain, he looked at the neighbourhood, ethnic group, church group, occupation group and recreation group.

In Mackey's model, each of these domains is affected by a list of variables such as *duration, frequency* and *pressure*. 'Duration' basically refers to the length of each contact. 'Frequency' refers to how often a particular domain is relevant in the bilingual's life. Mackey also identifies a cluster of other 'pressure' variables such as *economic, administrative, cultural, political, military, historical, religious* and *demographic* which may influence the bilingual to use one language over another. It may be that not all these pressure factors are relevant to the situation you have mind, so you may modify this model to suit your purpose.

Using this detailed template, Mackey plotted the individual's use of two languages, subdividing each language into *comprehension* (passive ability) or *expression* (productive ability).

Text B1.2
W. Mackey

Function

The degree of proficiency in each language depends on its function, that is, on the uses to which the bilingual puts the language and the conditions under which he has used it. These may be external or internal.

External functions

The external functions of bilingualism are determined by the number of areas of contact and by the variation of each in duration, frequency, and pressure. The areas of contact include all media through which the languages were acquired and used: the language-usage of the home, the community, the school, and the mass media of radio, television, and the printed word. The amount of influence of each of these on the language habits of the bilingual depends on the duration, frequency, and pressure of the contact. These may apply to two types of activity: either comprehension (C) alone, or expression (E), as well. These variables plotted against the areas and points of contact give Table B1.2.2.

If we examine Table B1.2.2 we note that it lists a number of contact areas and points, each of which appears opposite a number of columns of variables. Let us first consider the contacts.

Contacts

The bilingual's language contacts may be with the languages used in the home, in the community, in the school, in the mass media of communication, and in his correspondence.

Home languages

The language or languages of the home may differ from all or any of the other areas of contact. Within the home the language of the family may differ from that of its domestics and tutors. Some families encourage bilingualism by engaging a domestic worker or governess who speaks another language to the children. Others send their children as domestic workers into foreign families for the purpose of enabling them to master the second language. This is a common practice in a number of bilingual countries. Another practice is the temporary exchange of children between families speaking different languages. There are even agencies for this purpose. Some families who speak a language other than that of the community insist on keeping it as the language of the home.

Table B1.2.2 Variables plotted against areas and points of contact

Contacts	Variables				Pressure															
	Duration		Frequency		Economic		Administration		Cultural		Political		Military		Historical		Religious		Demography	
	A	B	A	B	A	B	A	B	A	B	A	B	A	B	A	B	A	B	A	B
	CE	CE	CE	CE	CE	CE	CE	CE	CE	CE	CE	CE	CE	CE	CE	CE	CE	CE	CE	CE
1. Home Mother Father Siblings Other relatives Domestics, etc.																				
2. Community Neighbourhood Ethnic group Church group Occupation group Recreational group																				
3. School Single medium Dual Media: Parallel Divergent Subjects: Private tuition Group Individual Self																				
4. Mass media Radio Television Cinema Recordings Newspapers Books Magazines																				
5. Correspondence																				

Within the family itself the main language of one member may be different from that of the other members. This language may be used and understood by the other members; or it may simply be understood and never used, as is the practice of certain Canadian Indian [i.e. Native American] families where the children address their parents in English and receive replies in the native Indian language of the parents.

In families where one of the parents knows a second language, this language may be used as one of two home languages. Studies of the effects of such a practice have been made by Ronjat (1913), Pavlovitch (1920), and Leopold (1939–49) to test the theory that two languages can be acquired for the same effort as one. Each experiment used Grammont's formula 'une personne' 'une langue' (Grammont, 1902), whereby the same person always spoke the same language to the child, the mother limiting herself to one of the languages and the father to the other.

Community languages

These include the languages spoken in the bilingual's neighbourhood, his ethnic group, his church group, his occupation group, and his recreation group.

1. *Neighbourhood*: A child is surrounded by the language of the neighbourhood into which he is born, and this often takes the place of the home as the most important influence on his speech. . . .
2. *Ethnic group*: The extent to which the bilingual is active in the social life of his ethnic group is a measure of the possibility of maintaining his other language. This may be the most important factor in a community with no other possible contact with the language.
3. *Church group*: Although church groups are often connected with ethnic groups, it is possible for the bilingual to associate with one and ignore the other. Although he may attend none of the activities of his ethnic group, he may yet bring his children to the foreign church or Sunday school, where sermons and instructions are given in a language which is not that of the community.
4. *Occupation group*: The bilingual's occupation may oblige him to work with a group using a language different from that which he uses at home. Or, if he lives in a bilingual city like Montreal, the language of his place of work may be different from that of the neighbourhood in which he lives. Or, if he is engaged in one of the service occupations, he may have to use both his languages when serving the public.
5. *Recreation group*: A bilingual may use one of his languages with a group of people with whom he takes part in sports, in music, or in other pastimes. Or he may attend a club in which the language spoken is not that of his home or his neighbourhood. Or the foreign children in a unilingual school may be in the habit of playing together, thus maintaining the use of their native language.

These domains emphasize the importance of individual bilinguals as members of specific speech communities. The extent to which an individual is involved in the community of the language spoken has been found to be positively correlated with the use of the language. Clyne (1991) reported that Greek–English bilinguals in Melbourne who maintained strong ties with the Greek community and social networks were more likely to show stronger levels of language maintenance in Greek than those who did not. This was not only limited to the individual bilingual but was often extended to their immediate families. Bilingual communities which are able to maintain vibrant community lives are often described as communities with high *ethnolinguistic vitality*. By comparison, Clyne (1996) found that the Dutch–English bilingual community in Melbourne was far less successful in maintaining Dutch and this was because its members' social networks with other Dutch speakers were extremely weak.

While links with communities are not the only measures which can predict bilingual language maintenance and use, these measures are useful for examining the 'health' of a bilingual community. They also underscore the importance of a speech community and the need to ensure that bilingual communities remain visible and have activities that enable speakers to see the relevance of the language and cultural skills at regular intervals.

Task B1.2.2

➤ Phanh and Hong are Vietnamese parents bringing up three children (five, ten and fifteen years old) in a predominantly English-speaking country where there is a vibrant, and large, Vietnamese community. At home they speak to their children in Vietnamese but have noticed that recently all three children have been speaking less Vietnamese, and they have been speaking to each other in English. Phanh and Hong are concerned that the children may soon stop speaking Vietnamese altogether. What advice would you give Phanh and Hong? What kind of resources would you expect them to be able to access in their community?

A factor which has a significant impact on both bilingual ability and the sustainability of bilingual communities is the school. This is because when it comes to schooling we have to adhere to the norms set by the relevant governing bodies. In multilingual countries, education often involves the political and sensitive act of selecting the language to be used in schools. For example, in India, the southern Indians (whose native language may be Tamil, Malayalam or Kannada) prefer to use English as a second language in school even though the language of the political elite in Delhi is Hindi. In many communities (e.g. Indigenous communities in Australia) where there are many different Indigenous languages, it may not be possible to provide language instruction in all the different languages.

In monolingual contexts, bilinguals often do not have any support for their minority languages in mainstream schools. In such situations, some communities mobilize their own resources to provide additional language programmes, for example Saturday Greek classes for Greek children in Australia. In fact, all over the world, a substantial portion of bilinguals go to school and receive formal instruction in only one of their languages. For such bilinguals, the language which is not being used in the school context will tend to develop differently. We referred to this as differential bilingualism in Unit A1. In some cases (e.g. Canada), the administration has sometimes made provision for bilingual programmes which allow bilinguals to be educated in both their languages. In Australia, bilingual children do receive some official support for their home languages in that many of these languages are accredited through examination at the end of high school, and instruction in these languages can be obtained through attendance on Saturdays at a government-funded School of Languages (Clyne 2005).

Naturally, the ideal school system for bilinguals is one where the bilinguals receive input and instruction in both languages which is equivalent in quantity and quality. A bilingual education that accords equal importance to both languages is unfortunately not the norm, even in countries where there are two official languages. The issue of bilingual education will be further examined in Unit B6. Here, we will focus on some basic issues which bilinguals have to face when they start going to school.

**Text B1.2
W. Mackey**

School languages

A person's language contact in school may be with a language taught as a subject or with a language used as a medium of instruction. Both may be found in three instructional media: single, dual, and private.

1. *Single medium*: Some parents will go to a lot of trouble and expense to send their children to a school in which the instruction is given in another language: schools in foreign countries, foreign ethnic communities, or bilingual areas (Mackey, 1952).

In bilingual areas, the language of single-medium schools must be determined by the application of some sort of language policy. This may be based on one of the four following principles: nationality, territoriality, religious affiliation, or ethnic origin.

According to the principle of nationality, a child must always take his schooling in the language of the country, regardless of his ethnic origin, religious affiliation, or of the language which he speaks at home. This is the policy of most of the public school systems in the United States.

According to the principle of territoriality, the child gets his schooling in the language of the community in which he happens to be living. This is the practice in Switzerland, for example.

The principle of religious affiliation may be applied in countries where linguistic divisions coincide to a great extent with religious ones. A sectarian school system may take these language divisions into account. In Quebec, for example, there are French Catholic schools, English Protestant schools, and English Catholic schools, The French Protestants in some areas may not be numerous enough to warrant a separate school system, in which case a French Protestant family might send their children to an English Protestant school rather than to a French Catholic one.

The principle of ethnic origin takes into account the home language of the child. In countries where bilingual communities are closely intermingled the policy may be to have the child do his schooling in the language which he normally speaks at home. This is the policy, for example, in many parts of South Africa.

2. *Dual media*: The bilingual may have attended schools in which two languages were used as media of instruction. Dual-media schools may be of different types. In their use of two languages they may adopt a policy of parallelism or one of divergence.

Parallel media schools are based on the policy that both languages be put on an equal footing and used for the same purposes and under the same circumstances. The parallelism may be built into the syllabus or into the time-table. If it is part of the syllabus, the same course, lesson, or teaching point will be given in both languages. This has been the practice in certain parts of Belgium. If the parallelism is built into the time-table, the school makes exclusive use of one of the languages during a certain

Text B1.2
W. Mackey

unit of time – day, week, or month – at the end of which it switches to the other language for an equal period, so that there is a continual alternation from one language to the other. This is the practice of certain military and technical schools in Canada. Another type of dual-media school is governed by a policy of divergence, the use of the two languages for different purposes. Some subjects may be taught in one language, and some in the other. This is the practice in certain parts of Wales. In describing the influences of such practices on a person's bilingualism it is important to determine which subjects are taught in which language. If one of the languages is used for religion, history, and literature, the influence is likely to be different from what it would be if this language were used to teach arithmetic, geography, and biology instead (Mackey and Noonan, 1952).

3. *Private tuition*: Schooling may be a matter of private instruction, individually or in small groups. This may be in a language other than that of the community. The second language may be used as a medium of instruction or simply taught as a subject. Some people may prefer to perfect their knowledge of the second language by engaging a private tutor in the belief that they thus have a longer period of direct contact with the language than they would otherwise have. Finally, there is the bilingual who tries to improve his knowledge of the second language through self-instruction. This may involve the use of books and sound recordings (see below).

Task B1.2.3

Think about your language learning experience in your school years.

➤ How many hours of language study did you do each week?

➤ What levels of language competence did you finally achieve?

➤ Do you think increasing the number of hours in the curriculum in the second language would have been sufficient to improve your language proficiency?

➤ Were any of the content subjects taught in the language that you were learning?

More than any other domain, the mass media help bilinguals to keep abreast with the cultural and linguistic developments in the source country. Culture and language are both dynamic products that evolve and change with times, and it is only through the currency of television, newspaper, magazines and movies that bilingual communities can stay informed.

Mass media

Text B1.2
W. Mackey

Radio, television, the cinema, recordings, newspapers, books, and magazines are powerful media in the maintenance of bilingualism. Access to these media may be the main factor in maintaining one of the languages of a bilingual, especially if his other language is the only one spoken in the area. Regular attendance at foreign film programmes and the daily reading of foreign books and magazines may be the only factors in maintaining a person's comprehension of a foreign language which he once knew. Reading is often the only contact that a person may have with his second language. It is also the most available.

Correspondence

Regular correspondence is another way by which the bilingual may maintain his skill in the use of another language. He may, for business reasons, have to correspond regularly in a language other than the one he uses at home or at work. Or it may be family reasons that give him an occasion to write or read letters in one of his languages. The fact that immigrants to the New World have been able to correspond regularly with friends and relatives in Europe is not to be neglected as a factor in the maintenance of their native languages.

Task B1.2.4

➤ Most cities these days are relatively multicultural. Think about the city you live in, or one that you are familiar with. Make a list of some of the languages which you have heard spoken there. Try to rank your list in order of quantity. Next, compare your list with the demographic distribution of the city. (Note: you might be able to find this kind of information on the Internet.) Do you hear all the languages in the list spoken? Is there a correlation between population density and the most widely spoken language?

➤ Look at the schedule of television and radio programmes in the city or town where you live. What languages are they in? How well do the programmes reflect the composition of the inhabitants in the city?

➤ Given the technological advances in the last few decades, what can you add to the mass media and correspondence sub-domains? What impacts do these new carriers of information have on the development of bilingualism?

Duration and *frequency* are both important variables which interact with the domains in which the language is used. So, for example, someone who goes to the German-speaking church twice a week for one hour each time will score higher for *contact* than someone who goes to church only at Christmas and Easter for three hours each time. These two variables look at the *intensity* levels in which the bilingual engages with each of the domains. The measures *comprehension* and *expression* are also important for examining the type of interactions in which bilinguals participate.

Variables

Contacts with each of the above areas may vary in duration, frequency, and pressure. They may also vary in the use of each language for comprehension (C) only, or for both comprehension and expression (E).

Duration

The amount of influence of any area of contact on the bilingualism of the individual depends on the duration of the contact. A 40-year-old bilingual who has spent all his life in a foreign neighbourhood is likely to know the language better than one who has been there for only a few years. A language taught as a school subject is likely to give fewer contact hours than is one which is used as a medium of instruction.

Frequency

The duration of contact is not significant, however, unless we know its frequency. A person who has spoken to his parents in a different language for the past 20 years may have seen them on an average of only a few hours a month, or he may have spoken with them on an average of a few hours a day. Frequency for the spoken language may be measured in average contact-hours per week or month; for the written language it may be measured in average number of words.

. . .

This extract demonstrates how deeply embedded a bilingual can be within the network of his or her community. In many ways, to understand or describe bilinguals, one needs to have an insight into their lives. Mackey's detailed discussion about the necessity of paying attention to how languages are used in the various domains demonstrates a key idea expressed in his opening paragraph – that 'bilingualism is the property of the individual'. Each individual creates a unique 'print' of his or her bilingual world. It is the individual's interactions with the wider community that create the phenomenon of bilingualism. Therefore, in defining bilinguals it is not possible to leave the wider society out of the equation. In fact, Mackey's extract reinforces the fact that describing bilinguals out of their social context is a meaningless exercise.

Task B1.2.5

➤ If you were asked to collect data about language use, duration and frequency in a bilingual household with three generations (grandparents, parents, three children), what do you think would be the most effective way for you to collect the data? What types of questions would you ask? What kinds of measures can you think of to assess duration and frequency?

It is common procedure nowadays in sociolinguistics to collect extensive background data to explore the function of language use in studies focusing on bilingualism. Such data are useful in providing information on the language-use patterns of bilinguals in all aspects of their lives. A common method used by researchers to find out information about *function* is by collecting self-report data. In this method of data collection, bilingual participants are often given a questionnaire to complete about their language use. These questionnaires are usually simplified versions of the items listed in Table B1.2.2 above. See the example (Table B1.2.3) extracted from Baker (2006: 21).

Table B1.2.3 Baker's Language Background Scales

> Here are some questions about the language in which you talk to different people, and the language in which certain people speak to you. Please answer as honestly as possible. There are no right or wrong answers. Leave an empty space if a question does not fit your position.

In which language do YOU speak to the following people? Choose one of the answers

	Always in Spanish	*In Spanish more often than English*	*In Spanish and English equally*	*In English more often than Spanish*	*Always in English*
Mother					
Father					
Brothers/ sisters					
Friends in the classroom					
Friends outside school					
Teachers					
Friends in the playground					
Neighbours					

In which language do the following people speak to YOU?

	Always in Spanish	*In Spanish more often than English*	*In Spanish and English equally*	*In English more often than Spanish*	*Always in English*
Mother					
Father					
Brothers/ sisters					
Friends in the classroom					
Friends outside school					
Teachers					
Friends in the playground					
Neighbours					

As you can see, you can draw various items from Mackey's Table B.1.2.2 and develop a questionnaire for a study which looks at language use.

Task B1.2.6

> Can you foresee any possible problems with using the self-report method? What are the advantages of self-report data? What other methods of data collection can you think of? Comment on the advantages and disadvantages of each of the methods you come up with.

THE COMPLEXITIES OF DESCRIBING BILINGUALISM: THE ENVIRONMENT

Bilinguals actively assess their sociolinguistic environment and make decisions on how to deploy or limit their language resources every day, and negative external pressures can lead to involuntary replacement of one language with another. More and more, sociolinguists have become keenly aware that bilinguals negotiate their way through these subtle demands from day to day. In each of the areas of contact, there may be a number of pressures which influence the bilingual in the use of one language rather than the other. These may be economic, administrative, cultural, political, military, historical, religious or demographic. Not all the *pressure points* mentioned are relevant but some, like religion, can play a significant role in promoting assimilation or pluralism. For example, working in the Australian context, Clyne (1991) argues that religion has served to aid both assimilation and transition to the dominant culture, as well as help maintain bilingualism in other contexts. However, recent census data point towards waning of impact from the religious sectors as the community becomes increasingly secular (Clyne 2003). In this extract, Mackey examines the outside pressures which influence how bilinguals use both their languages.

1. *Economic*: For speakers of a minority language in an ethnic community, the knowledge of the majority language may be an economic necessity. Foreign parents may even insist on making the majority language that of the home, in an effort to prevent their children from becoming economically underprivileged. Contrariwise, economic pressure may favour the home language, especially if the mastery of it has become associated with some ultimate monetary advantage.

   Text B1.2
   W. Mackey

2. *Administrative*: Administrative workers in some areas are required to master a second language. A bilingual country may require that its civil servants be fluent in the official languages of the country. Some countries may require that foreign service personnel be capable of using the language of the country in which they serve. A few governments have been in the practice of granting an annual bonus to the civil servant for each foreign language he succeeds in mastering or maintaining; this is the case in some branches of the German Civil Service.

3. *Cultural*: In some countries, it may be essential, for cultural reasons, for any educated person to be fluent in one or more foreign languages. Greek and Latin

Text B1.2
W. Mackey

were long the cultural languages of the educated European. Today it is more likely to be French, English, or German. The quantity and quality of printed matter available in these languages constitute a cultural force which an educated person cannot afford to ignore.

4. *Political*: The use of certain languages may be maintained by the pressure of political circumstances. This may be due to the geographical contiguity of two countries or to the fact that they are on especially friendly terms. Or the pressure may be due to the influence of the political prestige of a great world power. Political dominance may result in the imposition of foreign languages, as is the case for certain colonial languages. After many years of such dominance the foreign colonial language may become the dominant one, develop a regional standard, and be used as the official language of the country.

5. *Military*: A bilingual who enters the armed forces of his country may be placed in situations which require him to hear or speak his second language more often than he otherwise would. People serving in a foreign army must learn something of the language which the army uses. The fact that two countries make a military treaty may result in large-scale language learning such as that witnessed in Allied countries during the Second World War. Military occupation has also resulted in second language learning, either by the populace, by the military, or by both.

6. *Historical*: Which languages the bilingual learns and the extent to which he must learn them may have been determined by past historical events. If the language of a minority has been protected by treaty, it may mean that the minority can require its children to be educated in their own language. The exact position of the languages may be determined by the past relations between two countries. The important position of English in India is attributable to the historical role of Great Britain in that country.

7. *Religious*: A bilingual may become fluent in a language for purely religious reasons. A person entering a religious order may have to learn Latin, Greek, Coptic, Sanskrit, Arabic, or Old Church Slavonic, depending on the religion, rite, or sect of the particular order into which he enters. Some languages, also for religious reasons, may be required in the schools which the bilingual may have attended; Latin and Hebrew are examples of such languages.

8. *Demographic*: The number of persons with whom the bilingual has the likelihood of coming into contact is a factor in the maintenance of his languages. A language spoken by some five hundred million people will exert a greater pressure than one used by only a few thousand. But number is not the only factor; distribution may be equally important. Chinese, for example, may have a greater number of native speakers than does English; but the latter has a greater distribution, used, as it is, as an official and administrative language in all quarters of the globe.

 Task B1.2.7

➤ What is or are the national language(s) of the country you come from or the place you are living in now? In what ways do official policies on languages hinder or support bilingualism or multilingualism?

So far, we have examined how bilinguals interact with the environment and the influences which the environment can have on bilinguals. Mackey, however, also took into consideration the internal world of bilinguals and asked questions such as 'What languages do bilinguals choose to use in their internal dialogue?' This demarcation of internal and external functions has now been widely used in collecting information about patterns of language use in bilingual research. This mode of investigation has been particularly useful in assessing the vitality of languages in the community. In particular, it provides a very good indication of possible language maintenance and language shift.

Internal functions

Bilingualism is not only related to external factors; it is also connected with internal ones. These include non-communicative uses, like internal speech, and the expression of intrinsic aptitudes, which influence the bilingual's ability to resist or profit by the situations with which he comes in contact.

Text B1.2
W. Mackey

Uses

A person's bilingualism is reflected in the internal uses of each of his languages. These may be tabulated as in Table 1.2.4. Some bilinguals may use one and the same language for all sorts of inner expression. This language has often been identified as the dominant language of the bilingual. But such is by no means always the case. Other bilinguals use different languages for different sorts of internal expression. Some count in one language and pray in another; others have been known to count in two languages but to be able to reckon only in one. It would be possible to determine these through a well-designed questionnaire.

Table 1.2.4 Internal uses

	Auto-language	
Uses		
Counting	A	B
Reckoning	A	B
Praying	A	B
Cursing	A	B
Dreaming	A	B
Diary-writing	A	B
Note-taking	A	B

Task B1.2.8

➤ Which of the functions (both internal and external) do you think is critical to maintaining the bilingual's positive attitudes towards the community? Which of the functions do you think would be important if the aim is to increase bilingual language proficiency and use in the community? Identify a bilingual community in your midst and discuss how the various pressures discussed in Mackey's paper work to either support or suppress the vitality of this community.

Summary

Though domains (or functions) are critical in describing bilingualism, domains alone are not the primary factors influencing language choice. Sankoff (1972) identified *interlocutor* as a variable which plays a critical role in influencing language choice. Role-relationships such as parent–child, teacher–student, priest–church-member all exert an influence on code choice which may take precedence over other domain factors. Sankoff also suggested that the 'medium' of interaction is significant as some bilinguals may use one language when talking face to face with someone but choose another language when they have to speak on the phone.

These extracts demonstrate how complex an issue it is to define bilingualism, given the numerous variables to attend to. Over the years, researchers have become more careful in their selection of bilinguals for their research samples, and have also become more prudent when extending their findings to the general population. Researchers are now concentrating on exploring, critiquing and extending the framework used to talk about bilinguals.

However, despite a general heightened sense of awareness, there are still some who dispense with the careful procedural considerations when it comes to matching their bilingual sample. In Unit C1, we will analyse a few of these studies and look at the extent to which they have followed guidelines which we discussed in this chapter.

Unit B2
Measuring bilingualism extended

In Unit A2, we considered some of the key concepts which need to be taken into consideration when we assess languages. We discussed the importance of identifying different groups of bilinguals and considered also the ways in which we could assess an individual's developing bilingualism. We looked at this differently depending on which of two different types of bilinguals we were concerned with assessing: elective or circumstantial bilinguals. In this Extension section, we are going to consider in more depth some of the concerns that we have been discussing in relation to assessing the language of bilingual children in a range of circumstances.

ASSESSING THE LANGUAGE OF BILINGUAL CHILDREN

We will focus on children because the assessment of children's language is required in many contexts. One reason for assessing a child's language can be to identify whether there are any inherent problems in the child's language development which may require attention for the purposes of remediation. We will begin with a reading in which this issue is considered further. Children's language also often needs to be assessed for educational purposes. In the second article, we consider how language proficiency may impact on children both educationally and cognitively, and in the third reading we examine the role of language proficiency in the classroom and the ways in which it may be assessed.

In Unit A2, we discussed some of the difficulties with developing appropriate assessments for children who may have developmental delays in both of their languages. In the following extract, Saenz and Huer (2003) discuss some of the practical approaches that can be taken to alleviate this problem. We saw that there was a serious potential for bias in the testing of bilingual children, and this first extract considers the advantages and disadvantages of a variety of alternatives to standardized tests, with a view to moving towards less biased testing practices for children who speak minority languages. While the extract focuses on children with potential developmental speech delay, many of the points raised are as relevant to more educationally oriented testing as they are to the identification of delays or difficulties in language development.

Saenz and Huer (2003) discuss in some detail the kinds of approaches that can be taken to ensure that bilingual children are having their language assessed by the least biased means possible. They do this by adopting various methodologies which can be used in the assessment process for bilingual children. The approach selected will depend on a range of factors and the practicalities of adopting one approach over another. *Renorming*, for example, in which a standardized test is administered to a different, and more appropriate, group from that on which it was originally standardized, may be a relatively expensive option since it involves considerable administration and analysis costs, whereas dynamic testing may well prove a cheaper option but requires a considerable time commitment for each individual tested.

Text B2.1
T.I. Saenz and
M.B. Huer

T.I. Saenz and M.B. Huer (2003) Testing strategies involving least biased language assessment of bilingual children. *Communication Disorders Quarterly*, 24 (4): 184–193.

Renorming

Renorming a standardized test using the target population at issue has been advocated as an alternative to using norms based upon the population of the United States. The issue of establishing appropriate norms is an important one. Genesee and Upshur (1996) stated that an appropriate norming group should include individuals of the same ethnic and cultural backgrounds, linguistic background, age, gender, and educational level and type. The group on which the test is normed should also be relatively homogeneous. . . .

Renorming a test has several advantages. In a large and relatively homogeneous school district like Santa Ana, large numbers of bilingual pupils share the same cultural and linguistic backgrounds and economic status, making the time and effort expended in renorming potentially worthwhile. When the performance of particular students in the district is compared to that of their peers, speech-language clinicians can be relatively confident that students who score in the low range on the test rank substantially below peers of the same background.

Renorming also possesses a number of disadvantages. The process requires substantial coordination and time to assess enough typically developing children to provide meaningful norms. In a small or relatively unpopulated geographical area or highly diverse school district, there may not be enough speech-language pathologists or students sharing the same cultural/linguistic backgrounds to collect meaningful local norms. In addition, applicability of the norms is limited to the population upon which it has been renormed (Blevins, personal communication, November 7, 2002).

Tests that are both translated and renormed also should have their reliability and validity established for the intended uses (Baker et al., 1998). The difficulty in finding exact equivalencies for English words and concepts may change the absolute and relative difficulty of test items, seriously compromising a test's reliability (Kayser, 1998; Roseberry-McKibbin, 2002). Translated items also may not correspond as clearly with pictured items on a vocabulary test as the original English vocabulary words. In addition, grammatical structures in different languages may not be equivalent or may be acquired at different ages. Finally, differences in life experiences may not easily translate from one culture to another (Roseberry-McKibbin, 2002).

Another concern about local norms is that they frequently are lower than the norms for the samples tested during a test's initial standardization (Brice, 2002). Although such norms may be considered appropriate for local use, individuals rightly may be concerned that separate publication of norms for different cultural or linguistic groups may (a) give the impression that some groups are not as linguistically capable as others and (b) be used to question the competency of students from different backgrounds.

One factor in lower scores is the familiarity of the testing task to the children who are being tested and the way in which test items are presented. Peña, Quinn, and Iglesias (1992) discovered that low-income Puerto Rican children in the United States often were not taught labels of objects, making labeling an unfamiliar task. Peña and Quinn (1997) also found that Puerto Rican and African American children performed significantly better on the Comprehension subtest of the *Stanford–Binet Intelligence Test* (Thorndike, Hagen, & Sattler, 1986), which required descriptions, than on the *Expressive One-Word Picture Vocabulary Test* (EOWPVT; Gardner, 1979), which required object labeling. The more familiar description task was better than the labeling task at differentiating between children with typical skills and children with language disorders.

Consequently, lower performance on renormed language tests by children who are culturally or linguistically diverse may be due to a variety of factors, including family income, difficulties with translation, familiarity and presentation of tasks, and fluency in English. A test that attempts to provide differential diagnosis thus may have a number of confounding factors that affect a child's score. Although children should not be identified as having a disability based on linguistic, cultural, or economic factors, the influence of each may be difficult to calculate.

Text B2.1
T.I. Saenz and
M.B. Huer

Task B2.1.1

➤ Recall from Unit A2 that the immigrant population in the United States (which is where Santa Ana is) is much more homogeneous than the immigrant populations of many other countries because approximately 80 per cent of the children from a minority background are Spanish speakers. Why might renorming a test for a homogeneous population be more appropriate than for a heterogeneous one?

Dynamic assessment

A second proposed solution to the issue of least biased assessment is dynamic assessment (Bain & Olswang, 1995; Brice, 2002; Goldstein, 2000; Jacobs, 2001; Kayser, 1998; Lidz & Peña, 1996, Peña & Quinn, 1997; Peña et al., 2001; Peña et al., 1992; Tzuriel, 2001). This method typically involves a sequence of testing, including pretesting, teaching, and posttesting. A child is first pretested using a standardized test or informal task. Following administration of the test, the evaluator works with the child as a coach or mentor on tasks similar to those on the pretest, teaching the child test strategies and techniques and working with the child on problems and concepts. The aim of this intervention phase is to teach the child techniques or concepts that will enable him or her to perform well on the posttest. Such components as the amount of examiner effort needed to help the student, the rapidity with which the child changes responses following teaching, and the generalization of task performance to other tasks can be measured (Goldstein, 2000). Following this phase, the child is

Text B2.1
T.I. Saenz and
M.B. Huer

retested, using the same test as the pretest. The child's scores on the pretest and posttest can also be compared to determine the child's degree of transfer. According to the theory of dynamic assessment, children with typical language ability and poor pretest results may score substantially higher on the posttest because they have a typical ability to learn the test's concepts or procedures when given adequate exposure and effective teaching (Peña et al., 1992).

Dynamic assessment has a number of advantages (Peña et al., 2001; Peña et al., 1992; Ukrainetz et al., 2000). For example, after implementing a program introducing Puerto Rican preschoolers to labels, Peña et al. (2001) found that the mean scores of nondisabled Puerto Rican preschoolers on the EOWPVT rose from 1 standard deviation below the mean to within normal limits. Children with speech or language disorders, however, made far more modest gains, confirming the value of dynamic assessment techniques to differential diagnosis. Similarly, in a study of Native American preschoolers, Ukrainetz and colleagues discovered that children's categorization skills markedly improved after an intervention phase. In addition, because test administration is not modified, standardized test scores can be reported, and the students' rise in test scores, as well as their test scores following teaching, may be considered as important as initial test results (Peña et al., 2001).

Dynamic assessment does have some disadvantages, the greatest of which may be time (Brice, 2002; Peña, 1996). In most cases, using dynamic assessment involves pretest, posttest, and teaching phases, rather than one test administration. If the evaluator chooses a high-structure, standardized approach to dynamic assessment, he or she may need to develop intervention activities and cues for the intervention phase that are designed to teach the tasks measured by each test (Peña, 1996). Furthermore, the evaluator can use triple or more the time expended for one administration of the test in performing dynamic assessment, although innovations such as incorporating teaching procedures and graduated prompts into administration may reduce the time required (Bain & Olswang, 1995; Jacobs, 2001).

The amount of time and effort spent in teaching tasks in the intervention phase may be hard to justify for some tests. For example, both Peña et al. (1992) and Ukrainetz and colleagues (2000) selected skills important to academic achievement – labeling and categorization. Both skills had implications for children's success in school settings and thus would interface well with the current emphasis upon teaching skills relevant to classroom success. In contrast, the frequently used *Clinical Effectiveness of Language Functioning–Third Edition* (CELF-3; Semel, Wiig, & Secord, 1995) has six subtests for every age group tested, some of which test skills seldom directly used or taught in speech-language interventions. Because the most important score on the test is based on a combination of all six subtest scores, an individual attempting to perform dynamic assessment might need to provide interventions for each subtest. Consequently, dynamic assessment may be an effective measure of students' speech and language disorders, but time constraints may make it difficult to implement dynamic procedures with many tests or many students.

Other issues with dynamic assessment include reliability and validity. In low-structure, prescriptive approaches to dynamic assessment, cueing may not be standardized; therefore, increases in scores from pretest to posttest may not be comparable to those of other students (Peña, 1996). In such cases, the results of dynamic assessment may be better used to prescribe interventions than to determine if a child has a speech or language disorder.

Task B2.1.2

➢ Dynamic assessment, because it involves a teaching phase, is a rather time-consuming approach to assessment. However, its great strength lies in its ability to assess the potential for learning of individual children. Given this, see if you can think of a couple of circumstances under which it might be a useful approach.

Other nonstandardized measures

Text B2.1
T.I. Saenz and
M.B. Huer

A third proposed alternative to standardized testing involves nonstandardized measures other than dynamic assessment, and researchers have proposed a variety of these. For example, parent interviews, questionnaires, and/or checklists (Cheng, 1991; Roseberry-McKibbin, 2002) may be used to obtain information about parental perspectives regarding a child's language disorder. Restrepo (1998) also found that parental report of a child's speech and language problems, number of errors per T unit,[1] family history of speech and language problems, and mean length of T unit are useful in discriminating between Spanish-speaking children with language deficits and Spanish-speaking children with typical language skills. The first two factors are especially useful in identifying children with language deficits.

Ethnographic assessment (Brice, 2002; Goldstein, 2000) involves the observation of a child in different contexts with different communication partners and is used to study the child's language abilities in naturalistic situations. Additional information may be obtained from interviews with parents, teachers, and aides in which the interviewee is encouraged to describe his or her experiences with and opinions about the child's speech and language skills (Westby, Burda, & Mehta, 2003). *Transdisciplinary Play-Based Assessment* (Linder, 1993), used with children up to age 7 years, includes some aspects of ethnographic assessment in a team approach. One member of the assessment team facilitates play with the child and elicits different behaviors while another member interviews the parent, using questions similar to those employed in ethnographic interviewing. A third team member videotapes the interaction, and all of the additional team members observe the facilitator–child interaction while using checklists to identify relevant behaviors.

. . .

A number of tasks related to classroom competencies have also been suggested as possible assessment alternatives. Gutierrez-Clennen (1998) found narratives and complex syntax and formulation tasks to be useful in eliciting the type of language common to classroom discourse. Criterion-referenced testing (Goldstein, 2000) has been used to analyze a child's mastery of key language behaviors instead of comparing the child's performance to that of other children. The key language behaviors selected for analysis may include tasks used in the curriculum. Portfolio assessment (Goldstein, 2000; Kayser, 1998) involves the collection over a period of time of a body of the child's work that represents different tasks and assignments. Portfolios may include samples of reading and writing abilities. Curriculum-based assessment (Baker et al., 1998; Shinn, Collins, & Gallagher, 1998) involves the use of tasks that

---

1 A T-unit is a standardized measure of language defined by Hunt (1966: 735) as 'one main clause plus whatever subordinate clauses happen to be attached to or embedded within it'. [Editors' note]

Text B2.1
T.I. Saenz and
M.B. Huer

are similar to those used in the classroom to assess the skills necessary for success in school.

Informal measures have a variety of advantages. They frequently involve tasks that are more naturalistic than those performed in standardized tests and, consequently, are more directly related to success in the classroom. Because they are non-standardized, informal measures may be modified without substantially changing their validity, and they also can be designed and administered to effectively assess individual students' areas of strength or weakness.

Informal measures also have a variety of potential drawbacks. Because there are no norms, a student's performance cannot be quantitatively compared with that of other students. Reliability also may be an issue. Although research may establish some expectations for the acquisition of speech-language skills at specific ages, these expectations are typically based upon the performance of monolingual children. Consequently, the speech-language pathologist must rely on clinical experience to make a differential diagnosis. A speech-language pathologist who has extensive experience with children from a specific socioeconomic, linguistic, and cultural group may be able to make seasoned and appropriate clinical judgments; however, a less experienced speech-language pathologist – or one with little experience with a specific linguistic or cultural group – may have difficulty comparing a student's performance to the performances of other children from the same background (Langdon & Saenz, 1996). In addition, examiner bias may affect students' performance. Problems in this area include an overinterpretation of the student's abilities based on a small sampling of behavior, a lack of familiarity with linguistic and cultural issues that may affect the student's performance, and low expectations that result in not providing the student with sufficient opportunities to respond (Roseberry-McKibbin, 2002).

. . .

 Task B2.1.3

In the preceding paragraph, the following points are identified as potentially problematic in informal testing of children:

- reliability
- comparing bilingual children with monolingual children
- differential experience of speech pathologists
- lack of familiarity with cultural and linguistic issues affecting student performance
- low expectations.

➤ Can you think of any ways in which some of these concerns might be mitigated?

Text B2.1
T.I. Saenz and
M.B. Huer

Test modification

The final alternative to standardized testing is test modification (Brice, 2002; Erickson & Iglesias, 1986; Goldstein, 2000; Kayser, 1998; Langdon & Saenz, 1996; Mattes & Omark, 1991; Roseberry-McKibbin, 2002). Based in part upon the idea that some bilingual students' lower performance on standardized tests is due to a lack of familiarity with testing tasks, test modifications are designed to provide further instruction in and information about the task to enable the student to perform more effectively. Erickson and Iglesias, Mattes and Omark, Langdon and Saenz, Kayser, and Brice have advocated a variety of modifications of testing. Langdon and Saenz adapted Mattes and Omark's suggestions and made the following recommendations:

Text B2.1
T.I. Saenz and
M.B. Huer

1. Make sure that students have had experience with content or tasks assessed by the test.
2. Reword or expand instructions.
3. Provide additional time to respond.
4. Test beyond the ceiling.
5. Record all responses and prompts.
6. Provide credit for responses that use a different dialect or language from Standard American English.
7. Use additional demonstration items.
8. Allow students to label items in receptive vocabulary tests to determine appropriateness of stimuli.
9. Have students explain incorrect answers.
10. Ask students to identify actual objects or items if they have had limited experience with books and pictures.

Although norms cannot be used in modified testing, proponents believe that test modifications can act as an abbreviated form of intervention and enable students who perform poorly on a standardized administration of the test to perform better on a modified version.

One of the main advantages of test modification is its time efficiency. Evaluators can choose to administer a test using standardized, and then modified, administration procedures. Alternatively, they may opt to use only modified administration procedures if norms are not to be used. One of the disadvantages is that unlike dynamic assessment, the second administration of a test cannot be scored using norms, because of the modification of testing procedures. Only the discrepancy between first and second test administration may be considered. In addition, many of the modifications also may need to be developed prior to test administration, necessitating an additional expenditure of time. Yet another disadvantage is that the efficacy of using test modifications has not been formally validated.

As you have seen from the extract, there are a variety of alternatives to using standardized and normed tests which address the issue of bias in the testing of children from linguistically and culturally diverse backgrounds. As is the case with any form of testing, however, nothing is perfect and each alternative has advantages and disadvantages. Which test to be adopted will depend on the purpose of the test, the time available for testing, and which alternative the clinician or educator considers is the most appropriate under the circumstances. As you can imagine, the assessment of children from linguistically and culturally diverse backgrounds is a sensitive issue because testing, by its nature, provides a measure of performance at a specific time and place, and may carry with it an element of error.

Task B2.1.4

➤ Imagine you had a friend who was raising their three-year-old child bilingually and who was worried about their child's language development. What kind of advice would you give your friend to help them to find an appropriate place to have their child's language assessed?

We began with this extract from Saenz and Huer (2003) for two reasons. It provides a useful practical checklist of the range of factors which need to be taken into consideration when testing bilingual children in both clinical and educational settings. Bearing in mind the concerns raised above, from this point we are going to move beyond such practical concerns about the assessment of children's language to a focus on some more theoretical considerations. In the next two extracts, we will examine some of the ways in which different levels of proficiency might impact on children both in terms of their cognitive development and in educational settings.

THE ROLE OF BILINGUAL PROFICIENCY

The next extract, from Bialystok (2001a), considers the ways in which different levels of language proficiency may impact on educational attainment. This extract not only raises and discusses some important conceptual considerations in relation to bilingual proficiency but will also provide a background to the concepts and considerations encountered in Unit A4 on cognitive development. Bialystok's interest is in the cognitive and linguistic development of bilingual children, and in the extract below she discusses the role of proficiency, building on Cummins's work and the relationship of his model to academic success. The Threshold hypothesis (Cummins 1979) postulated that there are minimum levels of competency which have to be attained before the benefits of bilingualism can set in. He proposed two thresholds of language competence and argued that, to avoid negative effects from bilingualism, the lower threshold must be attained. Children at the first threshold would not experience negative or positive benefits from bilingualism. The cognitive growth of children who failed to reach the first threshold would be adversely affected. Those who attained the second threshold (high levels of bilingual competence) would enjoy all the enhancing effects of bilingualism.

Text B2.2
E. Bialystok

E. Bialystok (2001) *Bilingualism and development: Language, literacy, and cognition.* **Cambridge: Cambridge University Press, pp. 226–231.**

There are two dimensions on which proficiency is pertinent to the development of bilingual children. The first is the *absolute* level of proficiency in each language, that is, a judgment of the child's competence relative to native speakers; the second is the *relative* level of proficiency across the two languages, that is, an estimate of the command of each of the bilingual's languages with respect to the other. Both of these have been investigated, although the distinction between them has not always been made clear.

Text B2.2
E. Bialystok

The threshold hypothesis proposed by Cummins (1979) is a formal attempt to incorporate proficiency levels into predictions about the effects of bilingualism. The hypothesis is primarily driven by absolute levels, but it is framed within a context that places some significance on relative proficiency. The dependent variable of the hypothesis is academic success. Three types of bilingualism, based on both the relative and absolute mastery of the two languages, are identified. In limited bilingualism, the child lacks age-appropriate skills in both languages. In partial bilingualism, the child has achieved age-appropriate proficiency in one of the two languages. Finally, proficient bilingualism is marked by normal levels in both languages. He argues that limited bilingualism leads to cognitive and academic deficits but that proficient bilingualism results in cognitive advantages.

Cummins claims that no consequences follow from partial bilingualism, but it is on this point that absolute and relative proficiency levels make different predictions. For the measures that Cummins examines, primarily academic achievement, the most critical element is that children have age-appropriate levels in one of their languages and that this language gives them access to the abstract concepts that are the currency of schooling. Therefore, the relevant contrast is between children who have such facility in at least one language (partial bilingualism and proficient bilingualism) and children who do not (limited bilingualism). In contrast, research into cognitive, but not necessarily academic, consequences of bilingualism has used more subtle and arguably more arcane instruments of assessment. In this research, the important question is whether bilingualism adds benefits beyond those enjoyed by comparable children, not those at risk. The relevant contrast groups here are bilingual children with age-appropriate language skills in one language (partial bilingualism) versus bilingual children with age-appropriate language skills in both languages (proficient bilingualism). None of these children is at risk of academic failure, as Cummins rightly points out. Nonetheless, their bilingualism has had different impacts on subtle aspects of their developing cognitive profiles.

This is an important point as Bialystok here makes a very useful distinction which we can relate to both the different circumstances and different environments in which bilingual children are raised. Cummins's concern (children with limited bilingualism versus children with more proficient bilingualism) is with children in the school situation, the majority of whom will come from circumstantial situations, and for whom limited bilingualism can be a serious risk. Bialystok's concern is more research-oriented, focusing on the extent to which bilingualism in children can impact on cognitive development, and in this situation the focus is on partial versus proficient bilingualism. These concerns are taken up and explored in greater detail in Unit A4.

Text B2.2
E. Bialystok

Some research with bilingual children who are not balanced in their relative language proficiency but are sufficiently skilled in one of the languages (cf. partial bilinguals) has sometimes reported positive cognitive effects for these children (e.g., Bialystok, 1988; Cromdal, 1999; Hakuta & Diaz, 1985; Yelland, Pollard, & Mercuri, 1993). In fact, Hakuta and Diaz (1985) showed that the greatest gains to cognitive and metalinguistic insights came in the earliest stages of being bilingual, when proficiency in the two languages was most asymmetrical. None of this research contradicts the point made by Cummins regarding the essential need for language proficiency to minimally place children in the domain of having access to academic language skills. The important point is that children have not been found to suffer any disadvantages from learning and using two languages, even in academic settings, providing that one of their languages is established to a level appropriate for children their age. McLaughlin (1978) even claims that there may be no negative consequence if the instruction is carried out in the child's weaker language, the one that is not developed to age-appropriate levels (contradicting the warnings of Macnamara, 1966), as long as the level is *sufficient* to function in the instructional setting.

Task B2.2.1

➤ Consider the point made by McLaughlin (1978) that there may be no negative consequences for the child if the instruction is in the weaker language '*as long as the level is sufficient to function in the instructional setting*'. What do you think are the implications of this statement for children arriving in their new country at different ages?

Text B2.2
E. Bialystok

A related question is how skills developed in one language can be transferred to the other. The question is particularly important for children who have one stronger and one weaker language, and even more crucial when schooling is in the weaker language. Again, it is Cummins (1991) who has contributed significantly to this question. He reviews a large number of studies that compare the oral and academic language proficiency of children in their first language and the level of skill they acquire in each of these domains in their second language. These studies cover many language pairs and many instructional models. For academic uses of language, such as reading, there tend to be moderately strong correlations between the level of skill attained in both languages. Cummins attributes these relationships to the underlying cognitive involvement in development of these skills. For oral uses of language, the correspondence between children's competence in the two languages depends more on individual child attributes, such as personality and interaction style.

Part of the explanation for the transfer of skills across languages, as well as their lack of transfer, can be found again in the threshold hypothesis. Cummins' (1979) review of the literature shows that the detrimental effect of the lower threshold (lack of adequate competence in both languages) on academic achievement is well established. The reason is that there is no language in which children are able to establish the cognitive systems that are at the base of academic functioning. Even setting up these concepts in one language would permit their transfer to the other. The principle is the same whether the child is learning one or two languages: cognitive structures require the establishment of particular concepts, and these concepts require linguistic support.

These relations may appear circular but they illustrate that both absolute and relative proficiency levels are decisive in determining how the bilingual experience will affect children's academic and cognitive development. The positive cognitive consequences of bilingualism emerge when children control a reasonably balanced and competent mastery of the two languages. Although some cognitive processes have been shown to be enhanced from asymmetrical configurations of language competence, these effects are less reliable than are those that accompany regular and equivalent use of two languages. These effects of balance between languages appear more decisive than does the effect of time, namely, whether the two languages were

Text B2.2
E. Bialystok

acquired together. Admittedly, however, no research has established this. As long as children ultimately master the two languages across the relevant contexts of use (home, school), it should not matter that they learned one before the other. Even under ideal conditions, bilingual children go through different periods of favoring one or the other of their languages. Therefore, to some extent the notion of simultaneity in the acquisition of two languages is irrelevant.

The point that Bialystok raises here is in relation to whether children learn both their languages simultaneously (i.e. from birth) or not. In the next unit, we will be looking in some detail at the acquisition of language bilingually and we will be focusing on children learning their languages simultaneously. However, as Bialystok points out, often we are not concerned with how children have acquired their bilingual state; 'a child of six or seven years old who becomes bilingual is a bilingual child' (Bialystok 2001a: 226). It does not matter whether children have learned two languages from birth, or whether they have learned one language and then the other sequentially.

Text B2.2
E. Bialystok

For education to either profit from children's bilingualism or escape impairment because of it, the absolute proficiency level of at least one language is crucial. Considering only educational outcomes, the balance between the two languages is less critical than is the need for one of them to be developed to a level that is sufficient for schooling. But again, the timing for achieving that proficiency does not seem to matter.

Timing and proficiency, therefore, are two dimensions that distinguish among some of the configurations in which children learn two languages. Timing, the question of whether the languages should be learned one at a time or together, is probably not very important in the long run. Proficiency, however, does matter. Therefore, we can return to the question of the likely impact on a child who is moved to a different country and begins school in a different language from that spoken in the home. The child's weaker language may be either the one spoken at home or the one used in school. It is improbable that any academic consequence would follow from having some, even minimal, competence in a language that was not the language of schooling, but it is very consequential to consider the effect of having limited competence in the language of school.

Bialystok (2001a: 229) argues that in situations where children speak two languages at home and are educated in one of those languages (which is well established), there are never disadvantages for bilingualism, although there may only be advantages in specific situations. However, as we have seen, this is not always the case. In the next section she considers children in bilingual education programmes.

Text B2.2
E. Bialystok

Consider the following situation: An educated middle-class family living in Berlin is about to move to Los Angeles because of a career opportunity for the mother. (Let's assume she was offered an important chair at a famous university and her husband has agreed to find work as a sales clerk or, better still, to stay at home and take care of the house). Their only child is four years old and speaks only German. The parents will continue to speak German at home because that is what is natural, but the child will enter school and begin to learn English. What will happen to the child and what should the parents do?

The indications are that the child will do just fine. She will learn English from the environment (because she will likely socialize with English-speaking children), from television, and from kindergarten. Kindergarten will require sufficient English to build the academic foundation for her education. By the time she starts first grade, she will probably have enough English upon which to build an academic base, although her English skills will be weaker than those of her native-speaking class-mates. While her classmates are learning about letters, numbers, and the names of dinosaurs, she will additionally be learning the forms and structures of English, but the burden will not be onerous. If it is, or if she is slightly older and has not had the time to master English to levels appropriate for the grade, then some ESL train-ing would be helpful. The parents will, of course, be worried that the child's English places her at a disadvantage and possibly consider imposing English as the language of the home.

★ Task B2.2.2

➤ As Bialystok goes on to say, given the environment in which the child lives, and with the educational circumstances she is in, there is no reason to believe that the child's English will not develop 'in due course' or that it will in any way detract from her being academically successful. If you were talking to her parents, what reasons would you give to support this view?

The learning latency

But what does 'in due course' mean? How long should it take children to acquire a level of proficiency in the school language that allows them to function and thrive in an academic environment? Many of our attitudes, expectations, and policies are based on some implicit notion of how long it is prudent to allow children to gain language proficiency before we judge them by the standards set out for the system. During that time, we make allowances and evaluate them by relative rather than absolute standards, accepting progress itself as the measure of success. This is the difference between the standards set by norm-referenced and criterion-referenced assessments . . . But school success is ultimately determined by the absolute (criterion-referenced) standards of the institution. Parents want their children to do well; they do not want them to do well *for an immigrant*.

A large-scale study by Hakuta, Butler, and Witt (2000) examined this question for immigrant children in California. They tested children in two school districts that had high proportions of nonnative English-speaking children. The two districts also differed in their socioeconomic standing, one being more middle-class (district A) than the other (district B). In district A, the more affluent of the two, the study included all the children who had been designated LEP (limited English proficiency) when they entered kindergarten and were between first and sixth grades at the time of testing. This sample included 1,872 children. In district B, a sample of 122 children in grades one, three, and five were selected according to the same criteria, namely, that they entered the school district in kindergarten and were designated LEP. Unfortunately, the testing instruments used in the two districts were not the same so direct com-parison between the two districts can be made only cautiously. Still, the design had merits that are largely absent in other evaluations of this type, especially more informal ones. Notably, assuring that all children entered the school district in kindergarten controlled the age at which English was introduced. If there are any effects of age on the ability and success of learning another language, they were not influencing the results of this study. Minimally, then, the study provides a means of assessing the length of time it took children to reach levels of English that were comparable with native speakers. As a secondary issue, some insight into the role of social class could be gleaned.

The results for the two districts were comparable although the learning latencies were different. In district A, children's test scores were compared with the norm achieved by the native English-speaking students in the same district. By the end of grade four (representing five years of schooling), over 90 percent of the LEP students had achieved oral English proficiency that was comparable to their native-speaking peers. The range of time needed to arrive at this level was two to five years. Academic English proficiency took longer; the 90 percent criterion was not reached until the end of grade six and the range of time needed was four to seven years. The tests used in district B compared children's performance to native speaker norms rather than to classmates in the school district. The LEP children in this board had a more difficult time reaching criterion and the gap between their performance and native speakers actually widened throughout the period examined. In grade three, they were about one year behind the norm in various reading measures, but by grade five they were two years behind. Many differences between the districts, however, prevent a direct comparison of these achievement levels. Some of the factors are economic levels, types of programs available, and nature of the tests used. The general conclusions from this study are that children can reach both age- and peer-referenced norms for English but that it takes time. The first two or three years are a time of rapid growth, but the curve rises at a slower rate for many years after.

Hakuta (1999) states: 'When strict comparisons are made that control for the background factors, children learn English at the same rate regardless of the kinds of programs they are in, i.e., instruction through the native language does not slow down student acquisition of English. It takes most students 2 to 5 years to attain a level of English that does not put them at a disadvantage in regular instruction. Their rate of acquisition of English depends on the level of development of native language – children with strong native language skills learn English rapidly. Motivation to learn English is uniformly high both among parents and the students.'

These empirical findings, despite their limitations, provide considerable support for Cummins's (1979) distinction between *basic interpersonal communicative skills* (BICS) and *cognitive academic language proficiency* (CALP), which has been discussed, developed and criticized extensively in the literature ever since. BICS referred to the kind of language that was used for interpersonal communication in everyday types of situations, whereas CALP referred to the type of language which was required to manage more academic endeavours, and which was required to succeed at school and in the workplace. More recently, Cummins (2000) has used the terms *conversational language proficiency* and *academic language proficiency*. The terms are useful in reflecting the fact that as they go through the formal educational system, children need to acquire very different language skills from those that they are using routinely at home. Cummins's main point is that while children who attend school take approximately two years to achieve conversational language skills, they take much longer – between five and seven years – to acquire the level of language required for the increasingly demanding academic tasks they will need to perform as they move through the school system.

Cummins was particularly interested in children in circumstantial bilingual situations. This is a substantial group in many countries where there is widespread immigration, such as the US, Canada and Australia, and in many countries in Europe. But it is also a matter of serious concern in many other countries where multilingualism is normal and where the language of education is often different from the language(s) that children learn in their home environment. For example, children growing up in Java, Indonesia, learn Javanese at home, but their education will be in Bahasa Indonesian – the lingua franca of education in Indonesia. Children growing up in New Caledonia learn their indigenous languages at home, but are educated in French. Indigenous children in many countries learn a different language at home from that of their education (e.g. many Indigenous children in Australia do not learn standard English at home – they may learn either a creole, a traditional language or a mixed language – but most will be educated in standard Australian English when they go to school).

Cummins argues that when children begin to attend a school system where the language of education is other than their first language, they will often develop conversational language proficiency relatively quickly. However, academic language proficiency takes much longer to acquire. In other words, children entering school with a first language other than the language of education may rapidly learn the language and be able to communicate quite effectively at a surface level (i.e. they might attain conversational proficiency) but they will not necessarily have the skills to manipulate the more academic language required for long-term success in school. Although Cummins's model does not go uncriticized, it can be useful for evaluating the types of tasks and activities that children in school will encounter and need to be able to manage. The model provides helpful guidelines about both evaluating the language skills required and observing the children's abilities to manipulate these language skills.

In Text B2.3 below, Cummins outlines a framework for assessing language skills, in which he emphasizes the importance of the social context of language use. Cummins points out the importance of recognizing the context for which the framework was developed, arguing that the framework was designed for one particular socio-cultural context – that of schooling. Cummins emphasizes the importance of using it only for evaluation within this specific context.

J. Cummins (2000) *Language, power and pedagogy: Bilingual children in the crossfire*. Clevedon: Multilingual Matters, pp. 66–71.

Cognitive and contextual demands

The framework outlined in Figure B2.3.1 is designed to identify the extent to which students are able to cope successfully with the cognitive and linguistic demands made on them by the social and educational environment in which they are obliged to function in school. These demands are conceptualized within a framework made up of the intersection of two continua, one relating to the range of contextual support available for expressing or receiving meaning and the other relating to the amount of information that must be processed simultaneously or in close succession by the student in order to carry out the activity. While cognitive demands and contextual support are distinguished in the framework, it is not being suggested that these dimensions are independent of each other. In fact, as Frederickson and Cline (1990) point out, increasing contextual support will tend to lessen the cognitive demands – in other words, make tasks easier.

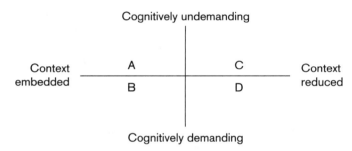

Figure B2.3.1 Range of contextual support and degree of cognitive involvement in language tasks and activities

Situating the framework

Before describing the framework, it is important to place it in an appropriate context of interpretation and to define some of the terms associated with it. In the first place, the framework, and the associated conversational/academic language proficiency distinction, focuses only on the sociocultural context of schooling. Thus, we are talking about the nature of language proficiency that is required to function effectively in this particular context. The framework was not intended to have relevance outside of this context.

Related to this is the fact that language proficiency and cognitive functioning can be conceptualized only in relation to particular contexts of use. Just as sociocultural or Vygotskian approaches to literacy emphasize that 'literacy is always socially and culturally situated' (Pérez, 1998a: 4) and cannot be regarded as content-free or context-free, language proficiency and cognitive functioning are similarly embedded in particular contexts of use or *discourses* which are defined by Pérez as the ways in which 'communicative systems are organized within social practices' (1998b: 23). Thus, the social practice of schooling entails certain 'rules of the game' with respect to how communication and language use is typically organized within that context. In short, in the present context the construct of *academic language proficiency* refers not to any absolute notion of expertise in using language but to the degree to which an individual has access to and expertise in understanding and using the specific kind of language that is employed in educational contexts and is required to complete academic tasks. Drawing on the categories distinguished by Chapelle (1998), academic language proficiency can be defined as the language knowledge together with the associated knowledge of the world and metacognitive strategies necessary to function effectively in the discourse domain of the school.

. . . [T]his perspective is consistent with an interactionist perspective on language ability 'as the capacity for language use' (Bachman & Cohen, 1998: 18). Current theoretical approaches to the construct of language proficiency have shifted from viewing proficiency as a trait that individuals possess in varying degrees to seeing it as inseparable from the contexts in which it will be manifested. Thus, Bachman and Palmer (1996) use the term 'ability-task' to refer to the unity of ability and task (context) characteristics. Chapelle (1998: 44) similarly notes that a construct such as 'vocabulary size' 'cannot be defined in an absolute sense but instead is a meaningful construct only with reference to a particular context'. Thus, in the context of schooling, discussions of greater or lesser degrees of language proficiency or 'adequacy' of an individual's proficiency refer only to the extent to which the individual's language proficiency (CALP) is functional within the context of typical academic tasks and activities. As noted above and elaborated below, the characteristics of instruction (context) will determine the functionality or 'adequacy' of an individual's proficiency in the language of instruction as much as the degree of proficiency in any absolute sense.

In this regard, it is helpful to introduce the notion of *register* which will be elaborated further in subsequent sections. Register is defined in the *Concise Oxford Dictionary of Linguistics* (Matthews, 1997: 314) as 'a set of features of speech or writing characteristic of a particular type of linguistic activity or a particular group when engaging in it . . . journalese is a register different from that in which sermons are delivered, or in which smutty stories are told'. Registers are the linguistic realizations of particular discourse contexts and conventions. Academic language proficiency thus refers to the extent to which an individual has access to and command of the oral and written academic registers of schooling.

In summary, as students progress through the grades, the academic tasks they are required to complete and the linguistic contexts in which they must function become more complex with respect to the registers employed in these contexts. Not only is there an ever-increasing vocabulary and concept load involving words that are rarely encountered in everyday out-of-school contexts but syntactic features (e.g. passive rather than active voice constructions) and discourse conventions (e.g. using cohesive devices effectively in writing) also become increasingly distant from conversational uses of language in non-academic contexts. The framework outlined in Figure B2.3.1 presents an analytic scheme for mapping in a general way how the construct of language proficiency can be conceptualized in terms of the intersections of cognitive (or information-processing) demand and contextual support in academic situations.

Task B2.3.1

➤ Think about the kinds of activities children are required to do at school and how these change as children go through the school system. On a piece of paper, label three columns each with one of the following age groups: five, nine and fourteen. In each, list one or two speaking, reading and writing tasks that you might expect a child to encounter at school at each of these ages.

➤ What are the different language requirements of these tasks?

Description of the framework

Text B2.3
J. Cummins

The extremes of the context-embedded/context-reduced continuum are distinguished by the fact that in context-embedded communication the participants can actively negotiate meaning (e.g. by providing feedback that the message has not been understood) and the language is supported by a wide range of meaningful interpersonal and situational cues. Context-reduced communication, on the other hand, relies primarily (or, at the extreme of the continuum, exclusively) on linguistic cues to meaning, and thus successful interpretation of the message depends heavily on knowledge of the language itself. In general, as outlined in the previous section, context-embedded communication is more typical of the everyday world outside the classroom, whereas many of the linguistic demands of the classroom (e.g. manipulating text) reflect communicative activities that are close to the context-reduced end of the continuum [in Figure B2.3.1].

The upper parts of the vertical continuum consist of communicative tasks and activities in which the linguistic tools have become largely automatized and thus require little active cognitive involvement for appropriate performance. At the lower end of the continuum are tasks and activities in which the linguistic tools have not become automatized and thus require active cognitive involvement. Persuading another individual that your point of view is correct, and writing an essay, are examples of Quadrant B and D skills respectively. Casual conversation is a typical Quadrant A activity while examples of Quadrant C are copying notes from the blackboard, filling in worksheets, or other forms of drill and practice activities.

The framework elaborates on the conversational/academic distinction by highlighting important underlying dimensions of conversational and academic communication. Thus, conversational abilities (Quadrant A) often develop relatively quickly among immigrant second language learners because these forms of communication are supported by interpersonal and contextual cues and make relatively few cognitive demands on the individual. Mastery of the academic functions of language (academic registers or Quadrant D), on the other hand, is a more formidable task because such uses require high levels of cognitive involvement and are only minimally supported by contextual or interpersonal cues. Under conditions of high cognitive demand, it is necessary for students to stretch their linguistic resources to the limit to function successfully. In short, the essential aspect of academic language proficiency is the ability to make complex meanings explicit in either oral or written modalities by means of language *itself* rather than by means of contextual or paralinguistic cues (e.g. gestures, intonation etc.).

As students progress through the grades, they are increasingly required to manipulate language in cognitively demanding and context-reduced situations that

Text B2.3
J. Cummins

differ significantly from everyday conversational interactions. In writing, for example, as Bereiter and Scardamalia (1981) point out, students must learn to continue to produce language without the prompting that comes from a conversational partner and they must plan large units of discourse, and organize them coherently, rather than planning only what will be said next.

 Task B2.3.2

> Take the list of tasks you developed in Task B2.3.1. Try to classify each of these tasks into one of the quadrants in the figure. Put the age group the task is for in brackets after the task (e.g. copying sentences (5); composition about recent holiday (9); written science report (14). How well do you find the tasks fit neatly into the quadrants? What, if any, difficulties do you encounter in trying to allocate the tasks to the different quadrants? To what extent do the tasks change with age from context embedded to context reduced, and cognitively undemanding to cognitively demanding?

Text B2.3
J. Cummins

Evidence for the relevance and usefulness of the conversational/academic language distinction comes from observations made by Carolyn Vincent in an ethnographic study of a program serving second generation Salvadorean students in Washington DC:

> All of the children in this study began school in an English-speaking environment and within their first two or three years attained conversational ability in English that teachers would regard as native-like. This is largely deceptive. The children seem to have much greater English proficiency than they actually do because their spoken English has no accent and they are able to converse on a few everyday, frequently discussed subjects. Academic language is frequently lacking. Teachers actually spend very little time talking with individual children and tend to interpret a small sample of speech as evidence of full English proficiency. However, as the children themselves look back on their language development they see how the language used in the classroom was difficult for them, and how long it took them to acquire English. (1996:195)

In this respect, Vincent notes on the basis of her classroom observations: 'It is clear that student achievement is promoted by instructional practices such as cooperative learning, the use of manipulatives, and project-based lessons' (1996: 201). These are activities that place a significant emphasis on Quadrant B insofar as they tend to be cognitively demanding but contextually supported.

Pauline Gibbons has similarly expressed the difference between the everyday language of face-to-face interaction and the language of schooling in outlining the distinction between what she terms *playground language* and *classroom language*:

> This playground language includes the language which enables children to make friends, join in games and take part in a variety of day-to-day activities that develop and maintain social contacts. It usually occurs in face-to-face contact, and is thus highly dependent on the physical and visual context, and on gesture

Text B2.3
J. Cummins

and body language. Fluency with this kind of language is an important part of language development; without it a child is isolated from the normal social life of the playground . . .

But playground language is very different from the language that teachers use in the classroom, and from the language that we expect children to learn to use.

The language of the playground is not the language associated with learning in mathematics, or social studies, or science. The playground situation does not normally offer children the opportunity to use such language as: *if we increase the angle by five degrees, we could cut the circumference into equal parts.* Nor does it normally require the language associated with the higher order thinking skills, such as hypothesizing, evaluating, inferring, generalizing, predicting or classifying. Yet these are the language functions which are related to learning and the development of cognition; they occur in all areas of the curriculum, and without them a child's potential in academic areas cannot be realized. (1991: 3)

Thus, the context-embedded/context-reduced distinction is not one between oral and written language. Within the framework, the dimensions of contextual embeddedness and cognitive demand are distinguished because some context-embedded activities are clearly just as cognitively demanding as context-reduced activities. For example, an intense intellectual discussion with one or two other people is likely to require at least as much cognitive processing as writing an essay on the same topic. Similarly, writing an e-mail message to a close friend is, in many respects, more context-embedded than giving a lecture to a large group of people.

It follows that cognitive academic language proficiency is not synonymous with literacy. It is manifested as much in oral interactions in academic contexts as in written interactions. For example, a classroom or small group discussion of the social consequences of industrial pollution will draw on participants' familiarity with features of academic registers (e.g. how to express cause–effect relationships linguistically) and will reveal the depth and richness of their understanding of words and concepts. In Aitchison's (1994) terms, the extent to which students have built extensive semantic networks will be evident in the way they use and relate words and concepts in such discussions. Thus, words are not just known or unknown; there is a continuum with respect to depth of vocabulary/concept knowledge (Paribakht & Wesche, 1997; Verhallen & Schoonen, 1998). One of the major functions of schooling is to deepen and broaden students' knowledge of words and their meanings and to develop what Norah McWilliam (1998) calls *semantic agility*. Oral classroom discussions do not involve reading and writing directly, but they do reflect the degree of students' access to and command of literate or academic registers of language. This is why CALP can be defined as *expertise in understanding and using literacy-related aspects of language*.

Skourtou has provided a particularly clear description of how the processing of experience through language transforms experience itself and forms the basis of literacy:

It seems to me that the entire process of language development both starts and ends with experience. This implies that we start with a concrete experience, process it through language and arrive at a new experience. In such a manner, we develop the main features of literacy, namely the ability to reconstruct the world through symbols, thus creating new experiences. Creating experiences through language, using the logic of literacy, whether speaking or writing, means that once we are confronted with a real context, we are able to add our own contexts, our own images of the world. (1995: 27)

Highlighted here is the fact that *context* is both internal and external, representing two sides of the same experiential coin; furthermore, the development of literate modes of thought cannot be separated from these experiential contexts.

It should now be clear that this model Cummins presented has major implications for pedagogy as well as for the assessment of language ability in the school context. Its value, as Cummins points out, lies in showing how learners can move from context-embedded and cognitively undemanding tasks to more cognitively demanding tasks, which remain none the less context-embedded. From this point learners can move into more context-reduced tasks, which may vary between those which are more cognitively demanding and those which are less cognitively demanding. He provides an example, taken from the work of Gibbons (1995), in which a science class began with the students working in small groups. In this context they were able to use context-embedded language. They then moved to a context where the teacher was standing in front of the class and required the children to describe and explain the activities they had been carrying out in their small groups. This allowed the children to be led into the use of more decontextualized language, but with material with which they were very familiar from working in groups. After this, the children were asked to write up their reports, using some of the language which had earlier been introduced by the teacher in a discussion which led up to the written work. Cummins uses the example of the teacher introducing the word 'repel' to replace the children's more familiar 'push away' (2000: 71).

The model presented by Cummins provides us with a useful tool both to understand the range of language children need for effective schooling and also to evaluate the extent to which children are able to manipulate different aspects of this language, as well as to manage the pedagogical content of the classroom.

As we have seen in this unit, the measurement of language is never easy. As it is a latent (or invisible) trait, we need firstly to define exactly what language is so that we are able to know what to measure. In addition to this, the complexities of defining bilingualism itself (see Unit A1) mean that this will always be a difficult task. There is an increasing awareness in the measurement literature of the problems of bias with respect to the testing of bilingual children who come from linguistically and culturally diverse populations (see Unit A4). Yet for children to be able to participate fully in both education and later in the workforce, it is crucial to be able to identify potential developmental delays in language accurately, and to be able to assess children in the educational system in as fair and unbiased a way as we can.

Unit B3
Bilingual acquisition extended

In this unit, we will focus more explicitly on two issues: the role of language input, and aspects of the child's language development. Firstly, we will look at an article which examines in more detail the issues related to input and the kinds of strategies caregivers use with the children they are raising bilingually. Following this, we will return to the child's development and look at an article focusing on the early language choices of children, beginning with lexical choices. Finally, we will look at an article which examines phonological development in bilingual children. This latter focus relates to the problem we discussed in Unit A3 in relation to whether the bilingual child begins with one system or two. It is now clear from the research that by relatively early in their second year, children have functionally differentiated their languages. As a result, one of the aspects of bilingual acquisition which is now being focused on is whether children differentiate their two languages very early on, and at the phonological level.

THE IMPORTANCE OF THE SOCIOLINGUISTIC CONTEXT

We will begin by exploring further the relationship between caregiver strategies in speaking to their children, and the child's bilingual development. As we saw in Unit A3, Lanza (1992) has argued that certain behaviours on the part of the parents encourage children to code-mix while others discourage it. However, Lanza's study was conducted in Norway, through a detailed case study of the language acquisition of a single child growing up with a Norwegian father and an English-speaking mother. In the article by Nicoladis and Genesee (1998) from which we provide an extract, the researchers adopted the same methodology as used by Lanza to examine the language practices and the language production of parents and children in bilingual Canadian families in Montreal between the ages of two and two and a half. The sociolinguistic context in which these children were being raised was quite different from that of the child reported on by Lanza, since the children in Montreal were being raised in the multilingual environment of Quebec. The study was designed to investigate empirically what has been termed the Parental Discourse hypothesis (PDH). This hypothesis

> suggests that children's patterns of language use grow out of the essentially interactive or communicative nature of parent–child language use ... More specifically, according to the PDH, certain speech acts encourage

monolingual conversations because they indicate parental lack of acceptance and/or comprehension of a child's codemixing. In other words, they implicitly indicate that the child's language choice (and, in particular, their use of both languages) is unacceptable or incomprehensible.

(Nicoladis and Genesee 1998: 86–87)

In the extract below, two types of analysis were conducted. The first examined the rates of code mixing which were used overall by the parents and children.

Task B3.1.1

➤ Imagine that you had collected samples of bilingual parents interacting with their bilingual children and you wanted to identify how much code mixing was taking place in these conversations. Can you think of any hypotheses you might come up with in relation to which parents might code-switch more than others? What would you need to do first in order to begin this type of analysis? How do you think you might approach the analysis of the data?

Text B3.1
E. Nicoladis
and F. Genesee

E. Nicoladis and F. Genesee (1998) Parental discourse and code-mixing in bilingual children. *International Journal of Bilingualism*, 2 (1): 85–99.

In Analysis 1, we examine the relationship between the parental discourse strategies and children's overall rates of codemixing and lexical rates of mixing on the assumption that children interacting with parents with relatively more bilingual discourse style would codemix more than children interacting with parents with relatively monolingual discourse styles. Alternatively, the effects of parental strategies might be seen on children's choice of language in the conversation turn immediately following the parental response; this possibility is examined in Analysis 2.

Parental strategy scores were calculated by assigning a weight from 1 to 5 to each response type on the continuum – a weight of 1 was given to the most monolingual strategy type ('minimal grasp') and a weight of 5 to the most bilingual strategy type ('code-switching'); weights of 2 to 4 were assigned to the intervening strategy types . . .

The weighted total of all strategy types was divided by the total number of parental response in order to adjust for differences in frequency of child-initiated codemixed utterances. The above formula yields scores that increase as the parents' use of bilingual strategies increases and decrease as parents' use of monolingual strategies increases.

We then calculated correlations between the parental strategy scores and their respective children's rates of codemixing. It was expected that as parental scores increased (i.e., indicating use of more bilingual strategies), the children's rates of codemixing would also increase, yielding positive correlations. Conversely, as parental scores decreased, children's rates of codemixing would also decrease, also yielding positive correlations.

In fact, what was found was that there were negative correlations between the parental strategy scores in response to their children's lexical mixing and that these were significant, indicating that as the parents' scores *increased* (that is, as they used more bilingual, as opposed to monolingual, strategies) the children code-switched less, rather than more. When both parents were present, the correlations were positive, but not significant, as was the case when all sessions (i.e. both parents present, and a single parent present) were included together. The second analysis investigated:

Text B3.1
E. Nicoladis
and F. Genesee

. . . the effect of each type of parental speech act on the children's codemixing in the next conversational turn, on the assumption that the effects of parental discourse styles might be most evident immediately following the relevant speech acts. More specifically, these analyses sought to examine if the children continued to codemix more after relatively bilingual parental strategies in comparison with relatively monolingual strategies.

All episodes in which the children initiated a lexical codemix were identified and analyzed further; there were 199 such episodes. As noted earlier, in 51 of these cases, the parents did not respond verbally to the children's codemixing. These 51 sequences were dropped from all subsequent analyses because it was impossible in these cases to examine the impact of parental strategy on the children's language choices in the next turns. For the remaining 148 sequences, the children made no rejoinder to 75 parental responses to their lexical mixing. The children's responses in the remaining 73 episodes were classified as either: 1) continued codemixing (i.e., an utterance in the non-native language of the addressee or a mixed utterance) or 2) no codemixing (i.e., an utterance in the parent's language or a both-language utterance). The relative rates of children's codemixing in response to the five parental response types were aggregated across the sessions for all the children because the token number of some strategy types for some parents was very small and, thus, analyses by individual children or families were likely to yield unreliable patterns.

Figure B3.1.1 shows the percentage of children's utterance types that were codemixed immediately following each parental strategy. The PDH predicts that the children would codemix more in response to the bilingual strategies (at the top of Figure B3.1.1) and less to the monolingual strategies (at the bottom of Figure B3.1.1).

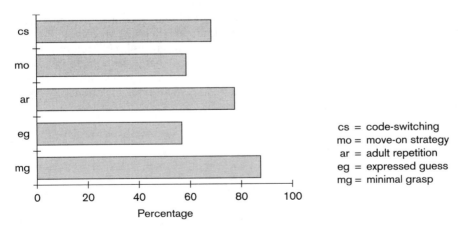

Figure B3.1.1 Percentage of children's utterances that were codemixed following each parental strategy

Text B3.1
E. Nicoladis
and F. Genesee

The parents' responses to the children's mixing did not show the pattern expected by the PDH. The most marked exception to the PDH is the minimal grasp strategy. Lanza (1992) considered this the most monolingual of parental strategies and yet the children in this study continued to codemix almost 90% of the time. Also, it is important to note that the children's preferred response was to codemix no matter what the parents' strategy; on average, the children codemixed 70% of the time in response to their parents' strategies.

In order to see how generalizable the results were, we also looked at the children's rates of codemixing following a parental strategy in response to their grammatical mixing and their overall rates of mixing. The results of these analyses did not differ remarkably from the children's rates of codemixing following a parental strategy in response to their lexical mixing alone.

Discussion

The results of this study did not directly support the PDH, either in terms of children's overall rates of codemixing or in terms of their codemixing in the conversational turn following a parental strategy. In the first analysis, we found significant negative correlations (when the PDH had predicted positive correlations) between parental discourse styles and their children's rates of codemixing within a single observation session. This result could be interpreted to mean that parents are responding to children's high rates of codemixing by using monolingual strategies in an effort to reduce their codemixing. If this were the case, the result would be negative correlations and the effects of the parental strategies might not be seen until later. This interpretation is, however, doubtful because . . . the parents in this study used a preponderance of the more bilingual strategies. Thus, a more accurate interpretation would be that as the parents used more bilingual strategies, the children in this study codemixed less! In the second analysis, we failed to find the predicted relationship between kind of parental response and the children's codemixing in the next conversational turn.

One possible reason that the results of the present study differed from those of Lanza's (1992) was the difference in sociolinguistic contexts between the two studies. Thus, it is possible that Siri's English-speaking mother may have worried that her child's English proficiency was at risk in Norway and thus encouraged more monolingual ways of communication; in contrast, Montreal is a bilingual community and so the parents in this study may not have worried about their children eventually learning French and English. If this is indeed the case, then it remains to be shown how parents convey their worry of a language-at-risk to their two-year-old children. Clearly, a study looking at the same language pairs in a bilingual community and a monolingual community might shed light on this matter.

Task B3.1.2

➤ Think about how you might design a study which would examine this question about whether parents convey their 'worry of a language-at-risk to their two-year-old children'. Where might you find appropriate participants for both the monolingual and the bilingual communities? What factors would you need to take into account to ensure comparability of the two groups?

Another possible reason for the negative results is that the children in this study may not have understood the subtle implicatures involved in the parental strategies targeting the children's language choice. For example, the children repeated what they said originally 88% of the time in response to a parental minimal grasp after all the children's codemixed utterances, compared to 38% after codeswitching, 17% after move-on, 33% after adult repetition, 57% after expressed guess, and 43% when the parents did not respond at all. It would appear from this that the children most often interpreted their parents' minimal grasp of their message not as a request for reformulation of their utterance in the parent's language, but as a request for repetition. In other words, the children did not target the language as the source of the problem. While Lanza (1992) pointed out that minimal grasps could be used to request repetition, it is not clear how children would learn to tell the difference between a minimal grasp that targets the language choice and a minimal grasp that targets pronunciation, semantic coherence or mumbling. On this note, we would like to point out that different kinds of knowledge are required to respond to the different parental strategies. For example, children might respond monolingually to an adult repetition simply because the parent has supplied a word in the 'correct' language while they might respond bilingually to an adult codeswitch simply because words were available in the other language. In both these scenarios, it is not necessary for the children to understand that their language choice was ever at issue. In any case, the findings from the present study replicate other research showing that bilingual children do not target language as a source of communication breakdown even when interacting with monolingual strangers at least up to the age of three years (Comeau, Genesee, Nicoladis, & Vrakas, 1997).

The results of this study do not negate the evidence showing that bilingual children show pragmatic differentiation at or around the age of two years (de Houwer, 1990; Döpke, 1992; Genesee, Nicoladis, & Paradis, 1995; Köppe & Meisel, 1995; Nicoladis & Genesee, 1996; Quay, 1992). If children are sensitive to the one person–one language rule, then the question arises as to why the children in this study did not switch languages when the parents' discourse strategy may have indicated that they should. We mentioned above that cognitive abilities may play a role in children's ability to respond to subtle implicatures of discourse strategies. Another possible factor is their relative proficiency in their two languages. Some studies have shown that bilingual children are sometimes limited in their ability to show their pragmatic sensitivity by their unequal proficiency in their two languages. Thus, it is possible that the kind of bilingual awareness displayed by the child in Lanza (1992) may require a certain threshold of proficiency in one or both languages. Future studies of how linguistic proficiency interacts with children's ability to respond to the implicatures of parental discourse strategies will be revealing.

While the present study did not support the PDH, it is undoubtedly true in the limit that parental speech acts affect children's codemixing. A case in point is that children raised in different sociolinguistic communities come to use codemixing in different ways (e.g., Poplack, 1988). The present study addressed one specific version of this general hypothesis with one age group. Alternative versions remain to be explicated and explored before we can clarify precisely what aspects of parental language use are influential and how and when they are influential. If future studies show that parents can affect their bilingual children's language choice, the implications are far-reaching and might indicate greater pragmatic sensitivity on the part of young children than has previously been thought (e.g., Volterra & Taeschner, 1978; compare, Genesee, Boivin, & Nicoladis, 1996; Wellman & Lempers, 1977). For example, such results would indicate that parents can shape some surface features of their children's language from a very early age (see also Newport, Gleitman, & Gleitman, 1977, for a similar suggestion with monolingual children). Furthermore, bilingual children would be seen as sensitive to subtle implicatures in parental speech acts (e.g., bilingual children must have a complex understanding of pragmatics in order to switch language in response to a minimal grasp strategy). How children's understanding of speech acts in their input develops would receive some deserved attention (Ninio & Snow, 1996).

This extract emphasizes once more the importance of the sociolinguistic context when appraising bilingual language acquisition. As we indicated above, this study was specifically designed to replicate Lanza's (1992, 1997) detailed investigation of a single child, Siri, growing up in Norway (a monolingual community) in a bilingual Norwegian/English family. While Lanza's findings in relation to Siri supported her Parental Discourse hypothesis, Nicoladis and Genesee did not find support for this, in fact finding that, following the parent's use of the most 'monolingual' of the strategies, the children continued to code-mix almost 90 per cent of the time. They argue that a possible explanation for these contrary results may be related to the sociolinguistic context. In Montreal, a bilingual community, the parents may have felt quite confident that the child would grow up speaking both languages. In Siri's case, her mother was the minority-language speaker, and she may have adopted more monolingual strategies with her child which were a reflection of her concern that her child might not acquire English.

 Task B3.1.3

➤ How much more difficult do you think it would be to raise a child bilingually in a monolingual community than in a bilingual one? If one parent speaks the same language as that of the community, what kinds of additional activities do you think would be important for the other parent to involve the child in to encourage him/her to actively engage with the non-dominant language? Do you think there would be particular ages at which the child's linguistic proficiency in this language might be more at risk than at others?

LEXICAL ACQUISITION IN TWO LANGUAGES

Much of the research into lexical acquisition of two languages has focused on the question of whether the acquisitional strategies of the child demonstrate early separation of the two languages or not. We alluded earlier to the idea that one of the problems in measuring bilingual competence is whether we should compare bilingual acquisition to monolingual acquisition. If we are to compare the lexicon of the bilingual child to that of monolingual children, then it may be that our expectations are too high. We also need to take into account such issues as cognates between the two languages (i.e. where languages have closely related words for the same object), as well as issues related to translation equivalents (where the child has two words for the same object – one in each language). Further, as we saw in Unit 3A, bilinguals, whether children or adults, will not use both their languages in exactly the same ways across different domains (see Meisel 2004).

There is now a considerable body of detailed individual case studies which have examined the issue of lexical acquisition in bilingual children. However, the study of bilingual acquisition is extremely complex, and there are several factors which impact on it: the great variation in the environment, differences in access to the two or more linguistic codes, as well as the differences and similarities in language typologies – in other words, how alike or not the languages are (for example, English and German are more similar to each other than English and Japanese are). Given the variables which can impact on bilingual acquisition, the importance of highly detailed, careful studies cannot be overestimated. Deuchar and Quay (2000), in a detailed case study of a single child acquiring Spanish and English, argue not only that the different aspects of what is studied may variously support the existence of one or two systems but also that the one system/two system dichotomy is itself an oversimplification. In the following extract, Deuchar and Quay consider the stage at which early bilingual children are able to differentiate their languages by a detailed examination of the lexical production of an English–Spanish bilingual child. They focus on the impact of the context of language use, and on the other factors which might influence the child's language choice. This case study illustrates the importance of paying very close attention to the kind of input the child receives and to methodological concerns with how the data are collected.

Task B3.2.1

➤ Think about ways in which you might investigate the language context of a bilingual child. Clearly, it would not be possible to record, either by video or by audio, the environment 24 hours a day. What other methods might you use? What would be the advantages and disadvantages of each? How might you redress some of the disadvantages of each?

M. Deuchar and S. Quay (1999) Language choice in the earliest utterances: a case study with methodological implications. *Journal of Child Language*, 26: 461–475.

Text B3.2
M. Deuchar
and S. Quay

Explanations for asymmetry in language choice

It is possible that this asymmetry we have found in language choice could in part be explained by aspects of our methodology. Whereas the diary data were collected mostly in two situations defined according to location (inside the home versus on the university campus), the audiovideo data were collected, for convenience, at home. But as far as the input to the child in everyday life was concerned, the main determining factor for the language addressed to the child was the situation. The mother, who was the child's main interlocutor in terms of number of hours per day, addressed the child in Spanish while at home and in English when on the university campus, where English was the language of the environment and other English speakers were often present. The child was also addressed in English on the university campus, mostly by caregivers in the crèche, including her grandmother who helped in the crèche one afternoon per week. At home, the child was addressed in Spanish by her father. The only situation at home in which the child would be addressed in English was when there were monolingual English-speaking visitors present, such as her grandmother. The grandmother in fact visited the home once a week for half a day, the other half of the day being spent with the child in the crèche. While the grandmother was visiting the home, she addressed the child in English, and the mother also addressed the child in English in the presence of the grandmother. In our analysis of the recordings made in the home, the assumption was made that the language used in addressing the child was the main factor determining the language context as English or Spanish. However, the fact that the audiovideo recordings (on which the quantitative analysis is based) were made at home, the normal location for Spanish being spoken, may have influenced the child's production in the direction of Spanish. We know from the sociolinguistic literature that the factors determining language choice are complex, and may include, for example, interlocutor, location, topic etc. (Ferguson, 1959; Fishman, 1965; Grosjean, 1982). In our study it is possible that in the so-called 'English context' of the audiovideo recordings, the language of the interlocutor influenced the child towards choosing English, but that the location at home, with its Spanish-speaking associations (the grandmother only spent time there half a day per week), provided a counter-influence towards English. In the Spanish context, however, both the language used by the interlocutor and the location would have pointed in the same direction, towards Spanish.

Additional data from English language context outside the home

To check the possibility that the location or setting was more important than we had anticipated in influencing the child's language choice, we needed to analyse data collected in an English language context OUTSIDE the home. For the period on which we are focusing (age 1;7–1;8), such data were available in diary records kept by the mother while with the child on the university campus, and in one audiovideo recording made in the university crèche when the child was 1;7.24. This recording had been made in addition to the normal schedule for recordings made in the home, and had been excluded from our original analysis. In this recording (made with the mother absent), the child produced 15 clearly identifiable English word types, and three Spanish word types. Of the Spanish words produced, none had equivalents in the child's vocabulary. These data turned out to pattern in a similar way to those collected in diary records: during the period covered by the audio videotapes (from the ages of 1;7.5 to 1;8.18 inclusive), thirteen one-word utterances were noted in the diary as being produced in the context of the university campus. (Two-word utterances were excluded at this stage, as in the audiovideo recordings.) Of the 13 word types produced, 11 were English and two were Spanish. Neither of the Spanish words had English equivalents in the child's vocabulary at the stage at which they were produced. Both these small sources of English context data, then, seem to pattern differently from data collected in the English context at home in that the child uses Spanish much less in English-context situations OUTSIDE the home than within it.

Deuchar and Quay go on to discuss the factors which might have influenced the child's language choice in relation to Lanza's parental discourse strategies (discussed in Unit 3A and above), but found that without

a more detailed analysis of the adult interlocutors' communication strategies, it cannot be said that there is a clear difference between the strategies used in the English and the Spanish contexts. If anything, it is likely that a more monolingual context was negotiated by the grandmother in the English-speaking context, and yet this is the context where the child produced more words in the inappropriate language. This tendency, however, disappeared when the child was in an English-speaking environment OUTSIDE the home, whether or not her mother was present.

Text B3.2
M. Deuchar
and S. Quay

Task B3.2.2

➤ Consider the importance of the way in which the person the child was talking to used language. To what extent do you think that the behaviour of the child's different interlocutors might have influenced the choices the child made with respect to language?

➤ Do you think that other factors, such as location, may have had an effect on the child's language choice?

This study illustrates how careful we need to be to document clearly the entire environment in which the child is being raised. It also points to the importance of maintaining detailed records of the type of input the child receives, but also of all other aspects of the child's life. This is because these may well affect both the manner in which the child becomes bilingual and the outcome of the child's bilingualism.

PHONOLOGICAL DEVELOPMENT IN A BILINGUAL ENVIRONMENT

Children born into bilingual situations will, from the time of their birth, hear different languages spoken around them. For example, a child born into a family adopting the 'one parent one language' approach (Döpke 1992) may hear her mother speaking in one language, while her father speaks in another. Research into the ability of infants to discriminate between sound contrasts suggests that even children as young as one month of age can perceive differences in voicing contrasts (such as /p/ as in 'pat', which is unvoiced, and /b/ as in 'bat', which is voiced) (Eimas et al. 1971).

Presumably, infants are born with the ability to hear all the different phonetic sound contrasts they may come across in any of the languages to which they may be exposed. However, there is experimental evidence that suggests they rapidly lose this ability if a particular contrast does not occur in the language(s) they are exposed to:

It appears, then, that infants start out the language-acquisition process with the capacity to discriminate the phonetic contrasts of any of the world's languages. With exposure to their own language, they begin to focus on those contrasts that are relevant for that particular language. However, this does not mean that infants (or adults) fail to distinguish among all nonnative contrasts; . . . the decline in discrimination abilities affects primarily those foreign sounds that are phonetically similar, though not identical, to sounds of the native language.

(Stoel-Gammon and Menn 1997: 83)

Any phonological system consists of a number of phonemes, with a range of associated allophones. In other words, any individual phoneme may be realized slightly differently in different phonemic environments because phonemes are conditioned by the sounds that occur next to them. For example, in English, the /p/ in 'spit' is not aspirated, but the /p/ in 'pit' is. If you hold a finger in front of your mouth as you say these words, you will find a puff of air follows the /p/ in 'pit', but not in 'spit'. In English, this difference never makes a difference to meaning because the sounds are in *complementary distribution*. In other words, when /p/ occurs at the beginning of a word (i.e. in word-initial position), it is always aspirated. Conversely, unaspirated [p] never occurs at the beginning of a word. However, this is not always the case. In other languages, both aspirated [pʰ] and unaspirated [p] occur in word-initial position and make a difference to meaning. Even in the same language, the same lexical item can be pronounced quite differently depending on the dialect, or regional accent.

 Task B3.2.3

> Think about some people you know who come either from different countries where the same language is spoken (e.g. the US and Australia, France and Belgium) or from different regions of the same country (e.g. Yorkshire and Hampshire in the UK, or Texas and Boston in the US). What kinds of differences can you identify in the ways in which they pronounce different words?

Watson (1991) stresses that with bilingual children it is essential to an understanding of children's phonological development to recognize that a phonological element can be achieved in one language without necessarily being achieved in the other. He also proposes that although bilinguals are required to adopt different strategies during the process of phonological development, this does not necessarily mean that they must use different processes once development is complete. In fact, he argues that there are three possibilities with respect to the language processing systems of balanced bilinguals:

▪ Bilinguals may develop completely independent phonological and phonetic systems, each of which is identical to those of monolinguals.

■ There may be some degree of integration between the two systems.
■ The bilingual may have two separate systems, but these systems may vary in some way from those of monolinguals.

Although bilinguals may have different systems in this way, the reality is that such differences in the phonological and phonetic systems of bilinguals may well be indistinguishable from the systems monolinguals have, except by precise instrumental measurement. However, as Watson (1991: 45) argues, 'such an economy does not threaten either the satisfactory realization of the two different systems or the identification of the bilingual with either of the language communities'. In other words, if the bilingual is able to sound like a native speaker in either community, the fact that their phonetic production is not perfectly matched to that of monolingual speakers may not matter, since to the untrained ear the bilingual speaker sounds native-like.

Investigation of the bilingual child's acquisition of the phonological system involves highly detailed and painstakingly accurate recording and transcription of the words the child uses. A brief examination of a few of the studies which have examined phonological development suggests that, on the whole, bilingual children have well-differentiated phonologies. For example, Deuchar and Clark (1996) studied a single English–Spanish-speaking child over a period of time between the ages of 1;7 and 2;3, who was growing up in an environment in which she received approximately half of her input in each language. (It may be worth noting that the quality of the input may have differed (for example, in intensity, attention etc.) since the English input came from the crèche she attended and her monolingual grandmother (specifics regarding frequency of contact not provided), while her Spanish input came from the home environment, where Spanish was spoken by her native-speaker father and non-native-speaker mother.) The development of voicing contrasts (e.g. /p/ is voiceless, /b/ is voiced, and /t/ which is voiceless versus /d/ which is voiced) in the two languages the child was learning were specifically examined through regular recordings with the child in naturalistic situations, which were functionally separated for language – in other words, the situations were clearly differentiated in terms of which language was being used. Picture prompts were used to elicit the relevant voicing contrasts in each language (in this case, words beginning with voiced and voiceless stops). The voicing contrast data were then subjected to acoustic analysis. The data were supplemented by additional analyses of the Spanish input (from the mother and father) since this input was limited to two people, whereas the English input came from a variety of different sources. Deuchar and Clark argue:

> The sequence of acquisition of the two voicing contrasts is particularly clear in the present study because the data come from a bilingual child being exposed to both languages simultaneously. Because the child is bilingual, these results also have implications for the question of whether there are two voicing systems in a developing bilingual from the very beginning. The authors have shown, at least, that there is not a single, unified English/ Spanish system. What has been seen is a progression from a lack of system

in either language at 1;11 (though there are indications of a system beginning to be established in English) to the establishment of a clear voicing system in English at age 2;3, and the beginning of a distinct system in Spanish.

(1996: 363)

In summarizing their findings, Deuchar and Clark point out the importance of studying a single bilingual child because this is the only way in which age and cognitive stage of development can be held constant. They argue that their findings indicate that there is a move from a lack of a formal system to a dual system, but that at no stage is there any evidence to suggest there is an initial unified system.

Johnson and Lancaster (1998), in their detailed study of a child acquiring Norwegian and English, address a number of important issues about the simultaneous acquisition of the two phonological systems. The authors provide a detailed outline of the input the child received during the first two years from birth. Data were collected through diaries kept by the parents, audio recordings which were made at regular intervals between the ages of 1;2 and 1;8, and the use of the MacArthur–Bates Communicative Development Inventory (CDI) (Fenson et al. 1993). The CDI allows parents to report on their child's language(s) development by completing an inventory in a 'tick the box' format. Parents are asked to report on words the child understands and produces using an inventory provided. The inventory has been translated into several languages, and in the case of bilingual children, each parent is asked to report on the language they speak with the child. Thus, for this study there were three sources of data: the diaries, the CDI and the audio recordings. Clearly, the audio recordings need to be transcribed, and this is a painstaking undertaking, since the transcriptions must be both very detailed and very accurate in order for the analyses to be reliable. In other words, for the purposes of this research, *fine transcriptions* were required.

Task B3.3.1

➤ Consider the kind of detail you would require in a transcription in order to be able to draw conclusions about the phonological development of a child. Read the paragraph below and note down the various checks the authors carried out in order to be able to rely on this transcription. How long do you think it might take to transcribe five minutes of a recording like this?

Text B3.3
C.E. Johnson
and
P. Lancaster

C.E. Johnson and P. Lancaster (1998) The development of more than one phonology: a case study of a Norwegian–English bilingual child. *International Journal of Bilingualism*, 2 (3): 265–300.

Both authors independently transcribed Andreas's words from one English session and one Norwegian session using the International Phonetic Alphabet (IPA; International Phonetic Association, 1990) supplemented by symbols created to describe young children's speech (Bush, Edwards, Luckau, Stoel, Macken, & Petersen,

Text B3.3
C.E. Johnson
and
P. Lancaster

1973) to produce a fine transcription. Utterances that were overlapped or too faint were not transcribed. Disagreements on segments and diacritics were discussed, and the affected segments were independently transcribed a second time; these clustered around fricatives and affricates that were close to [ʃ, ç, s], or [ʤ, ʧ, tç] and a low unrounded vowel that could not be accurately described as [ʌ], [ɑ], or [ɐ] (cf., Hildegard in Leopold, 1947). The final reliability between the transcribers was 95%, based on phone by phone comparison. Following this procedure, the second author transcribed the remaining utterances.

The study of the acquisition of the phonological system is complex, requiring analysis at a number of levels. These include not only a phonetic analysis of the child's phonetic inventories in both languages, and an analysis of the child's seg-mental abilities in terms of sounds and syllables, but also an analysis of the prosodic structures, or stress and intonation patterns, the child uses in both languages. As Johnson and Lancaster (1998: 288) point out, it is often difficult to examine the phonological aspects of the acquisition of two languages when the languages have very similar sets of sounds. This is particularly the case where there are only limited data available on how monolinguals acquire those languages, and this is often the case. Traditionally, English has received a disproportionate share of research investigation time, and this is particularly the case where first-language acquisition is concerned. The vast majority of studies of bilingual acquisition have also tended to compare the acquisition of two European languages, rather than comparing languages which come from different roots (for example, there are only limited studies of the bilingual acquisition of a European language and an Asian language). In particular, the limited nature of long-term acquisition studies conducted on languages other than English means that it is difficult to determine how much children vary in normal, monolingual acquisition. In other words, we do not at present know enough about the range of variation which might normally be expected within any particular language across a variety of individual children.

In the extract below, Johnson and Lancaster summarize Andreas's phonological acquisition and compare it with that of monolinguals, before discussing in more depth some of the theoretical considerations:

Text B3.3
C.E. Johnson
and
P. Lancaster

In sum, Andreas demonstrated a number of similarities with both English and Norwegian monolinguals, which we would expect, given universal constraints on children's early speech sounds. Andreas's recordings also revealed differences between his productions and those of each monolingual group; in some cases the differences made him more like the speakers of the other language and in some cases they did not. For example, Andreas shared nine word-initial consonants with the English-language 2-year-olds and eight with the Norwegian 2-year-olds; the English and Norwegian 2-year-olds shared eight (of 11 and 10, respectively) word-initial conso-nants. Andreas's [ɟ] was not produced by either group of monolinguals; his [k, w] compared with the English but not the Norwegian 2-year-olds, and his [v] compared with the Norwegian but not the English children. His [ʧ, ʤ, ɹ, j] are typical of English but were not produced by the 2-year-olds; /j/ is also Norwegian but was produced by

Text B3.3
C.E. Johnson
and
P. Lancaster

only two of four Norwegian 2-year-olds. Both Norwegian and English monolinguals produced word-initial [s], but Andreas did not. Andreas's consonant inventory was larger than the inventory of either monolingual 2-year-old group, and much larger than the English-speaking children's inventory at 1;9. However, it did not include the English monolinguals' word-final [ɹ] or the Norwegian children's retroflexed [ʂ] or [ɭ].

Andreas's variable vowel production does not match the English group data in either accuracy or order of acquisition (comparing his production frequency with the group accuracy data), although characteristics of his production are similar to the data for one child reported by Davis and MacNeilage (1990). His use of front round vowels compares with the Norwegian monolinguals', though there is no evidence that he produced [ʉ], which the monolinguals frequently did. The Norwegian monolinguals used many more long vowels but fewer diphthongs than Andreas did.

Combining these comparison data with the results we summarized earlier, we conclude that, at 1;9, Andreas did not match either English or Norwegian monolingual 2-year-olds' speech-sound production data. Neither were his productions (and especially constraints on them) dramatically different from those of monolingual children in either language. Although his phone productions were highly variable, they included sounds from both languages not used by monolingual children several months older. It is possible that his attention to distinguishing his languages – as demonstrated by his translation equivalents and appropriate preferential use of words belonging to each language – led him to attempt phones unique to each language.

The extent of variability in Andreas's productions compares with that of individual monolingual children but is not seen in the group data. There are enough reports of individual English-speaking children to show that there is a wide range of individual differences within this monolingual community and to find a match for Andreas on specific parameters, such as preference for fricatives and affricates and coda consonants. We have no comparable data from Norwegian children under age two, which seriously limits our analysis.

One system or two?

A question motivating this research was whether Andreas's productions would provide evidence for two phonological systems or a single unified system. The answer to this question depends crucially on assumptions about how phonological productions are related to phonological perceptions and to the lexicon. For the purposes of this discussion we will assume, based on the results presented above, that Andreas distinguishes Norwegian speakers from English speakers and is in some sense aware that a given concept can be related to a distinct phonetic form in each language environment.

Within the field of child phonology, there is no consensus on whether (monolingual) children have a single lexicon that serves both production and perception (Macken, 1980; Smith, 1973; Stampe, 1969, 1973) or separate lexicons (both referring to the same semantic/conceptual information) for perceiving input and producing output (Ingram, 1974; Kiparsky & Menn, 1977; Menn, 1983; Menn & Matthei, 1992). (See Bernhardt & Stemberger, 1998, pp. 43–55, for a succinct discussion of the arguments for and against single-lexicon and two-lexicon representation models.) Both of these models assume that an abstract phonological representation based on perception of the adult form is part of the lexical entry. If this is the case, then we can argue that Andreas has differentiated lexical entries for Norwegian and English words

Text B3.3
C.E. Johnson
and
P. Lancaster

that differ phonetically. That is, since he can distinguish Norwegian and English language environments (demonstrated by his preferential use of Norwegian and English words in those environments, respectively), and given infants' perception abilities in general, he perceives the distinctions between even highly similar Norwegian and English words (we did not test this directly); to the extent that the underlying phonological representations of these words respect the perceived phonetic distinctions, the lexical entries are distinct in each language.

. . .

Conclusion

Andreas's lexical productions provide evidence that he did not treat English and Norwegian as a unified language system. His translation equivalents and preference for using English words with English speakers and Norwegian words with Norwegian speakers show that he was attempting to distinguish his languages. He maintained this distinction in aspects of his sound production at 1;9, including (1) the size and some distributional characteristics of his phonetic inventory in each language environment, (2) differential accuracy by word position in matching adult phonemes in the two languages, and (3) relative preference for monosyllables and coda consonants in English.

Whether Andreas had two distinct phonological systems is a much more difficult question to answer . . . Andreas's word pronunciation variability, phonotactic constraints on segment production, and low match rates for adult phonemes in the recorded data indicate a highly constrained sound production system with few resources to maintain adult contrasts. The claim that Andreas provided evidence for distinguishing English and Norwegian is different from the claim that he had two separate systems, at least for production (cf., Wode, 1990, p. 43). How many levels of the phonology must be in place before a system exists? Is it necessary to include prosody and features and segments, or is systemic quality at one level enough?

Andreas's phonological development does not match either English or Norwegian monolingual children's, although it shows considerable overlap with both. His production of phones that are characteristic of each language in the words and/or environment of that language, but not typical of 2-year-olds' productions, indicates a heightened attention to the phonemes that contrast his languages. This conclusion is consistent with observations of other bilingualism researchers that bilingual children are early to focus on formal properties of their languages and develop linguistic awareness (see De Houwer, 1995, pp. 220–221, for a summary). Andreas's own metalinguistic comment at age two is further evidence of this early awareness.

Production evidence of Andreas's distinctions between English and Norwegian and differences between him and both English and Norwegian monolingual peers led us to conclude that Andreas was able to perceptually distinguish his two languages and even focus on the phonological distinctions between them, even though we did not test this directly. This highlights the consequences of the methodological choice to analyze the production data by both target language and language environment. What are the consequences for language separation of a large number of lexical items shared between the two languages (those categorized Both)? Might a high proportion of incoming words judged to be the 'same' across language environments lead a child to disregard phonetic differences between speakers of the two languages as normal interspeaker differences that should be ignored (perceptual constancy; Kuhl, 1980)? Or, rather, is it likely that such a judgment of 'same' would not be made because the adult Norwegian and English pronunciations of words like 'bunny,' 'papa,' and *tittei* sound as phonetically different to the child as the pronunciations of cognates such as 'milk' and *melk* or 'bread' and *brød*? If this is the case, it is more valid to look for evidence of language differentiation in the results presented by recording environment than by target language. If children preferentially use lexical items from one of their languages when interacting with speakers of that language (as shown by Genesee et al. (1995), Lanza (1992, 1997) and Quay (1995) and in our study), then – to the degree they are able to differentiate their languages at the sound production level at all – they should analogously use the characteristics of one language's sound system preferentially in all productions in that language environment.

Data collection in separate language environments is relevant to the issue of what Grosjean (1985, 1997) calls bilinguals' 'language modes.' Mode refers to the 'state of activation of the bilingual's languages and language processing mechanisms' (1997, p. 7). Modes range along a continuum from monolingual in L_A to bilingual to monolingual in L_B. In each mode, each language is activated or deactivated to a degree dependent on contextual features such as the monolingual or bilingual abilities of the coparticipant(s) and the purpose, content, and situation of the discourse. Grosjean does not specify the age at which this model becomes relevant; assuming it applies to bilingual children, to sample a bilingual child's speech in a prototypically monolingual context, the researcher should ensure that the child's conversational partner is monolingual and known by the child to be so. With respect to Andreas, it would not be possible to test a pure monolingual Norwegian mode because virtually all the Norwegian speakers he knows speak English fluently, and he has heard them switch codes.

The notion of modes leads in turn to a more general consideration of language production. Just as conclusions from BFLA research ultimately must be compatible with and inform theories of language acquisition and sociolinguistics, they must be compatible with and inform models of speech production. Grosjean (1998) made it clear that there is much work to be done to develop a model adequate to represent adult bilinguals' speech production and processing. The work has not even begun with respect to children's speech production (but see Bernhardt & Johnson, 1996, for explication of how an adult speech production model can be used to account for the difference between one monolingual child's linguistic knowledge and productions). In bilingual phonological acquisition, addressing the issue of single versus two-lexicon models of phonological representation is a possible starting point for constructing a relevant production model.

 Task B3.3.2

➤ Imagine you are going to undertake a study examining the phonological development of a bilingual child. Make a list of the most important factors you would need to take account of in order to complete the study.

➤ Think about how the factors would change in different environments and with different participants.

As can be seen from the above extract, the investigation of the child's phonological system requires data to be collected from a very early age. Ideally this should involve documentation of the amount of input provided to the child in each of the two languages. The questions are complex, and the transcription and analyses required to answer these questions must be reliable and detailed. None the less, such studies are crucial if we are to move forward in our understanding of how bilingual children develop their linguistic skills.

Summary

These extracts have provided an indication of the complexity that surrounds both the acquisitional processes and the methodological complexities of children's bilingual acquisition. They also present very clear examples of the kind of detailed analyses which need to be undertaken in this kind of work with bilingual children. It is only through this type of detailed study that we will come to understand the processes at play when children are exposed to two languages from early on in life. We still have a lot to learn about how children learn two languages, and about the effect the social environment may have on their success.

Unit B4
Bilingualism and cognitive ability extended

In this unit, we will read extracts which shaped the research on the relationship between cognitive ability and bilingualism. The focus in the reading will be on the methodology and conclusions drawn by the researchers and the ramifications of this research on current practices.

As discussed in Unit A4, the research in this area can be categorized into the period before and after 1962. Before the publication of Peal and Lambert's 1962 study, bilingualism was predominantly associated with negative effects, but after 1962, researchers paid more attention to the issues of methodology and the ways in which poor control of variables could compromise the outcome.

METHODOLOGICAL CONCERNS

In Unit A4, we discussed how methodological concerns plagued the studies which reported detrimental effects of bilingualism. Major methodological errors included the poor identification of bilingual samples and, often, the lack of rigorous justifications in the choice of tasks.

One of the most challenging factors which researchers into bilingualism have to deal with is the issue of sample selection. For example, Torrance et al. (1970) found that bilingual children in Singapore performed poorly in tests of creative flexibility. However, this study was compromised by the authors' poor understanding of the sociolinguistic situation in Singapore. Children who attended bilingual schools were classified as bilingual despite the fact that most of them were functionally learning two new school languages. Most Chinese children spoke a different Chinese language at home, and at school learned Mandarin and English, both of which were second languages. Thus, sample selection is a critical issue and without careful sampling, most results can be interpreted only with caution. In the first extract, we will examine how this problem of sampling was overcome in Peal and Lambert's (1962) study (briefly discussed in Unit A4).

PEAL AND LAMBERT (1962): THE PIONEER STUDY

Peal and Lambert's research was considered a watershed as it reoriented the way researchers approached the issue of bilingualism. By carefully reviewing the major shortcomings of the previous studies, they pointed out that bilinguals were defined at best inadequately and at worst totally haphazardly and arbitrarily. As indicated in Unit A1, bilingualism as a concept is notoriously difficult to capture. Parentage, range of usage or competence alone cannot fully describe a bilingual population, and not only did early studies not pay sufficient attention to the issue of sampling, they also failed to control adequately for socio-economic status (SES). Therefore, there was a tendency for bilingual groups to be conflated with lower SES.

After carefully reviewing the literature, Peal and Lambert hypothesized that in a comparison of the French–English bilingual and English monolingual population:

- There should be no difference in non-verbal IQ for bilinguals and monolinguals.
- Monolinguals were expected to be superior to bilinguals in verbal IQ tests.

The study also explored the relationship between bilingualism and school grades as Morrison (1958) had found bilinguals to lag 1.5 years behind their monolingual counterparts in school grade. Attitudinal aspects were also included, but this was discussed in Unit A7.

The participants in the study were 364 ten-year-old schoolchildren from six French schools in Montreal. All the schools were classified as middle-class schools by the School Commission and the children were carefully matched on SES, sex and age. They were tested on language, intelligence and attitude. We begin by looking at some of the key methodological concerns Peal and Lambert raised before examining how they selected their samples and tasks.

E. Peal and W.E. Lambert (1962) The relation of bilingualism to intelligence. *Psychological Monographs*, 76 (27): 1–23.

Text B4.1
E. Peal and
W.E. Lambert

Psychologists and linguists have wondered whether bilingualism affects intellectual functioning since as early as the 1920s when Saer (1923) and Smith (1923) reported research on the topic. Numerous studies since then have attempted to determine whether monolingual and bilingual young people differ in intelligence as measured by standard tests. A large proportion of investigators have concluded from their studies that bilingualism has a detrimental effect on intellectual functioning. The bilingual child is described as being hampered in his performance on intelligence tests in comparison with the monolingual child. A smaller proportion of the investigations have found little or no influence of bilingualism on intelligence, in that no significant difference between bilinguals and monolinguals on tests of intelligence was apparent. Only two empirical studies were encountered which suggest that bilingualism may have favorable intellectual consequences. An attempt will be made to understand these seemingly contradictory findings by critically reviewing representative studies reporting each type of effect. The studies will be evaluated mainly in terms of how well other relevant variables were controlled, particularly certain personal characteristics which are known to be related to intelligence and which should be taken into account when the effect of bilingualism on intelligence is examined.

In the design typically used, where two groups of subjects are being compared on intelligence, it is necessary to match the groups on as many features known or suspected to correlate with intelligence as possible so that the difference between the groups, if any, may be attributed to linguality itself. This model requires a clear definition of monolingualism and bilingualism in order that the two can be objectively determined without risk of overlap or confusion. Socioeconomic status has been repeatedly found to be related to intelligence and linguistic development (Jones, 1960; McCarthy, 1954). McCarthy states that 'there is considerable evidence in the literature to indicate that there exists a marked relationship between socioeconomic status of the family and the child's linguistic development' (p. 586). From past research it is well established that girls are more advanced than boys in language development, especially in the early years. They have a larger vocabulary and are more skilled in the use of words. Since most intelligence tests draw heavily on verbal skills, it would be advisable to have approximately equal numbers of boys and girls in the groups to be compared. Furthermore, groups should also be matched for age. The educational background of children may also affect their performance on standardized tests of intelligence. This variable could be approximately controlled by using subjects from the same schools or school system. The intelligence tests should be constructed and standardized on a population similar to the one being tested, especially with respect to language. A translation of a test from one language to another, without standardization, might bias the results for or against one group. Also, the tests should be given in the language in which the bilinguals are most proficient.

. . .

Theoretical considerations

Theoretically, what would be the expected effects of bilingualism on intelligence or mental development? Few of the psychologists who have studied this problem have attempted any explanation beyond rather vague references to a 'language handicap' or 'mental confusion.'

An inquiry into the effects of the learning of two languages on mental development demands a serious consideration of the broader question of the relation between language and thought, and modern psychology has generally eschewed this question. The apparent belief of many is that at least partial answers to the broad question may appear from the study of the interrelation of language and intelligence. Arsenian (1937), after examining various theories of language and thought, hypothesized that language and intelligence are not identical. In line with this hypothesis, he maintained that:

> the influence of bilingualism, whatever for the moment we may suppose it to be, does not extend to the whole area of thinking or intelligence, but to that particular section where linguistic symbolism and schemata are involved in the thinking process.

Susanne Langer (1942) made a distinction between speech and thought. She argued that: 'It [speech] is the normal terminus of thought. But in fact, speech is the natural

Text B4.1
E. Peal and
W.E. Lambert

outcome of only one kind of symbolic process'. Assuming then, that language and thought are not isomorphic, how would the learning of two languages influence scores on intelligence tests, which obviously require thought?

Several writers, assuming a lack of identity between language and thought, suggest that the learning of two languages from childhood has favorable effects on the thinking process. Two writers in particular have made this point. Leopold (1949a), after extensive observations of the mental development of his own child, felt that the bilingual child learns early to separate the sound of a word from its referent. He writes:

> I attribute this attitude of detachment from words confidently to the bilingualism. Constantly hearing the same things referred to by different words from two languages, she had her attention drawn to essentials, to content instead of form (p. 188).

S. J. Evans of Wales (1953) also argues that the:

> teaching of Welsh along with English does what the efficient study of any two languages must do: it frees the mind from the tyranny of words. It is extremely difficult for a monoglot to dissociate thought from words, but he who can express his ideas in two languages is emancipated (p. 43).

These arguments, suggesting that a bilingual has an intellectual advantage over a monolingual because his thinking is not restricted by language, give support to those few studies which found favorable effects of bilingualism on intelligence and mental development. In view of these arguments, it also seems possible that the type of benefit that comes from bilingualism might not become apparent on standard intelligence tests. It could be argued that the studies finding no difference or a deficit for bilinguals were simply using inappropriate measures.

O'Doherty (1958) suggests that it is necessary in any consideration of the influence of bilingualism on intelligence to distinguish between two types of bilinguals for whom the effects may differentiate the pseudo-bilingual and the genuine bilingual. The pseudo-bilingual knows one language much better than the other and does not use his second language in communication. The true bilingual masters both at an early age and has facility with both as means of communication. O'Doherty states that there can be no question that bilingualism of the genuine kind is an intellectual advantage. 'The pseudo-bilingual is the real problem, since very often he fails to master either language, while the bilingual by definition has mastered both' (p. 285), Thus, O'Doherty's writings lend additional support to the notion that 'genuine' bilingualism may be an asset.

Can we find any theoretical support for the detrimental effects of bilingualism on intelligence? Weinreich (1953) makes the point that any individual who speaks two or more languages will experience interference due to the contact between them. That is, a bilingual's speech in each language will be different than it would have been had he only learned one language. The extent of the interference in any particular case will depend in part on certain linguistic differences between the two language systems.

The more numerous the mutually exclusive forms and patterns in each, the greater is the learning problem and the potential area of interference. But the mechanisms of interference would appear to be the same whether the contact is between Chinese and French or between two subvarieties of English (pp. 1–2).

The language handicap reported for bilinguals could thus be attributed to interlingual interference. The effect of this interference would show up on verbal tests, but could be expected to influence performance on non-verbal tests only in so far as these depend on verbal skills.

It could be hypothesized that bilingualism might affect the very structure of intellect. Such a hypothesis could be developed from a current conceptualization of intellect as consisting of factors. Guilford (1956) and others propose that intelligence is composed of a general factor and many different specific factors, each of which may be isolated by factor analytic methods. Ferguson (1954) has put forth the thesis that human abilities are learned. Stated another way, a large proportion of an individual's intellectual ability is acquired through experience and its transfer from one situation to another. The 'factors of intellect' are gradually developed through a series of learning situations. This learning process may proceed in different ways for different individuals depending on their experiences. Thus the structure of intellect will very likely vary from one individual to another. The developmental process for monolinguals and bilinguals is certainly different in respect to language, and the learning of abilities depends greatly on language. Bilinguals could have different and more complex contexts for learning than monolinguals. Arsenian (1937) states that, 'The two different words in two different language systems for the same referent may carry different connotations and put the bilingual person in contact with two worlds of experience.' We could, therefore, hypothesize that the structure of the intellect of monolinguals and bilinguals might differ in various aspects. Guilford (1956) states: 'to the extent that factors [of intellect] are developed by experience, they would appear at such ages as the effects of experience have sufficiently crystallized' (p. 287). That is, the emergence of an intellectual factor is dependent on the accumulation of experiences. From this notion, it seems reasonable to propose that such factors would appear at different ages in monolinguals and bilinguals, since their linguistic and cultural experiences are quite different. It may therefore be important to discover the nature of the effects of bilingualism on intellectual functioning.

. . .

Task B4.1.1

➤ What is Peal and Lambert's view about the relationship between language and intelligence?

General methodological framework of Peal and Lambert's study

Peal and Lambert used tests such as the Word association test, Word detection test and Peabody Vocabulary tests to gauge the level of bilingualism of each child. The tests were administered in both French and English, and the purpose was to evaluate the level of language dominance in each child. In addition, the children were also asked to rate themselves on a set of self-evaluation scales. On the basis of these tests, the sample of 364 subjects was divided into three groups:

■ clearly monolingual
■ clearly bilingual

a third group which could not be unambiguously classified as monolingual or bilingual.

The third group was excluded from the next stage of testing. After this initial stage of screening, they were left with 164 children: 75 were monolinguals and 89 were bilinguals (96 males, 68 females). The screening was carefully monitored to ensure that only those with extremely high bilingual skills were included in the group of bilinguals. The children were also administered three types of intelligence tests as well as a series of complex attitudinal measures. The intelligence tests include cognitive tests for both verbal and non-verbal intelligence.

Method

Text B4.1
E. Peal and
W.E. Lambert

Subjects

The subjects were 10-year-old school children from six French schools under the jurisdiction of the Catholic School Commission of Montreal. Three of these schools were located in the western region of Montreal, and the remainder in the extreme eastern region of the island. All were roughly classified as middle class schools by the School Commission. In each school all the 10-year-olds available were tested, regardless of school grade.

Procedure

The testing took place in the classroom and was divided into five sessions of 1 hour each, spaced about a week apart. All instructions to the children were given in French by native speakers of French, except for the test of English vocabulary which was administered by a native speaker of English.

In the first session, all the 10-year-olds were administered a questionnaire and several tests to determine degree of bilingualism. The questionnaire sought general information about the child and his family, specific information about his language history, and details about his father's occupation. Three tests were used to determine whether the child was a *balanced bilingual*, that is, equally skilled in French and English, or whether he was a monolingual. His own self-ratings of his ability in English were also taken into account.

Criteria for Selection of Subjects

Word Association Test. The first test of bilingualism was based on an association fluency technique developed by Lambert (1956). Modifications were introduced to make the technique appropriate for use with children in a group setting. French and English words were presented alternately and the children were asked to write down as many words as they could think of in the same language as the stimulus which seemed to 'go with' or 'belong with' that word. An interval of 60 seconds was allowed for association to each word. For each subject the sum of the associations to all the French words was calculated (NF). The same was done for the associations to the English words (NE). These two sums were used to form a balance score:

$$\text{Balance} = \frac{NF - NE}{NF + NE} \times 100$$

A zero score indicates perfect balance between the two languages, a plus score means French dominance, and a minus score English dominance.

Word Detection Test. This test was also a modification of one developed by Lambert, Havelka, and Gardner (1959). It was postulated that bilingualism would express itself in the facility of finding short embedded English and French words in a series of letters such as DANSONODEND. The subjects were given four such series and allowed 1½ minutes to work on each. Approximately equal numbers of English and French words were embedded in each group of letters. A balance score was obtained here, similar to the one described above.

Peabody Picture Vocabulary Test. This test, derived from Dunn (1959), was used because it made possible a distinction between oral and graphic language skills. It was thought that there might be bilinguals who were not able to read or write English, but who would nevertheless be balanced bilinguals in the oral sense. Such bilinguals might be at a disadvantage on the two previous tests which required some knowledge of written English. The test consists of a series of plates, each of which has four pictures of objects or actions numbered 1–4. The examiner says one English word aloud and the subject has to point to the picture corresponding to the word. To adapt this for use with a group, we flashed each plate on a screen by means of an epidiascope, and an examiner pronounced the word in English. The children wrote down the number of the picture which corresponded to the English word pronounced. In this way, no graphic skills in English were required of the subjects. Twenty-one plates of increasing difficulty were presented. A score of the number of correct responses out of 21 was obtained for each child.

Subjective Self-Rating Score. The subjects were asked to rate their ability to speak, read, write, and understand English on 4-point scales ranging from 'not at all' (scored 1) to 'very fluently' (scored 4). For each subject an oral self-rating score was obtained by summing his weights on 'speak' and 'understand,' and a graphic score by doing the same on 'read' and 'write.' The maximum possible score was 8 on each (oral and graphic scores).

On the basis of these tests, the entire sample of 364 subjects originally contacted was divided into three groups: one group composed of monolinguals, a second group of bilinguals, and a third group which could not be unambiguously classified as either monolingual or bilingual. Only the first two of these groups were further tested. The third group was not used again.

The criteria used in the classification of subjects were as follows: (*a*) Monolinguals – Word Association Test, a balance score of at least +75; Word Detection Test, a balance score of at least +75; Peabody Picture Vocabulary, a score of not more than 6; Subjective Self-Rating, a score of not more than 7 in oral and graphic skill in English (combined). (*b*) Bilinguals – Word Association Test, a balance score of 0 ± 30; Word Detection Test, a balance score of 0 ± 30; Peabody Vocabulary, a score of at least 15 out of 21; Subjective Self-Rating, a score of at least 13 out of a possible 16 in oral and graphic English (combined).

Two judges consulted on the classification of each subject. In some cases where the different criteria were in disagreement, more weight was given to the Vocabulary score than to the others.

Our selected sample was composed of 164 subjects: 75 monolinguals and 89 bilinguals; 96 boys and 68 girls. These subjects were tested four additional times.

Measures of Intelligence

Text B4.1
E. Peal and
W.E. Lambert

Lavoie–Laurendeau (1960) *Group Test of General Intelligence* (*Variables* 6–9; *Variables* 16–23). Previous studies pointed to the importance of using a test of intelligence standardized in the native language of the subject and preferably prepared for use in that language community. The Lavoie–Laurendeau test, standardized by psychologists at the University of Montreal on a Montreal French-speaking school population, seemed to meet these requirements. It is based on several other well-developed tests (Wechsler–Bellevue, WISC, Barbeau–Pinard) using those sections which could best be adapted for group testing. The nonverbal and verbal sections of this test were administered to each group. Nonverbal, verbal, and total IQ scores were calculated for each subject. A ratio score was obtained by dividing the verbal IQ by the nonverbal IQ and multiplying by 100.

Raven (1956) *Progressive Matrices Test* (*Variable* 10). The colored form of this (Sets A, Ab, and B) was administered as a group test. This was included as a measure of basic intelligence (pure 'g'). A total raw score was obtained for each subject (maximum 36).

Thurstone (1954) *Primary Mental Abilities* (*Variables* 11–15). An attempt was made to select those subtests from the Primary Mental Abilities which draw least directly on verbal skills. The following five were chosen and administered in French: Space, Figure-Grouping, Perception, Number, and Verbal Meaning. This test was translated by a linguist at McGill.

. . .

Task B4.1.2

> As is evident, Peal and Lambert were very careful in screening the bilingual proficiency of the bilinguals. Consider the three language tests the children took and comment on the type of linguistic ability each one measures. Do you think they are representative of general language proficiency skills? What are some concerns you may have with using such tasks for measuring language proficiency?

Achievement measures

Text B4.1
E. Peal and
W.E. Lambert

From the teachers, ratings were obtained of how well each child did in school in relation to the others in his class. The teacher rated each child along a five-point scale in terms of his achievement in general (Variable 24), in French (Variable 25), and in English (Variable 26) if this happened to be one of his subjects. We also obtained the marks in French that each subject received in *dictée* (Variable 27), *lecture* (Variable 28), and *composition* (Variable 29) at midterm.

The following measures were based on information from the original questionnaire filled out by each subject.

Sex (*Variable* 1); *School Grade* (*Variable* 4); *Number of Years Speaking English* (*Variable* 5); *French Skills of Parents* (*Variable* 30). Each subject rated the ability of his father and mother to speak, read, write, and understand French. These were scored in the same manner as his self-ratings of his English ability. The scores for mother and father were summed.

English Skill of Parents (*Variable* 31). This variable was derived in the same way as above, using the items about English in place of those about French.

Balance between English and French Skills of Parents (*Variable* 32). The score on Variable 30 was subtracted from the score on Variable 31 and a constant of 100 added. A score of 100 on this variable indicates that the parents are equally skilled in French and English. A score of less than 100 means that the parents are more skilled in English than in French, and vice versa.

Socioeconomic Class (Variable 3). Realizing the relevance of socioeconomic class to language learning, we decided to investigate its role in detail. On the basis of information received from the child, the school records, the school principal, and the parents themselves when necessary, we placed each child into one of the seven categories outlined by Warner, Meeker, and Eelis (1949). A small sample of 110 children was selected from the large sample so that there were equal numbers of bilinguals and monolinguals in each of the seven classes.

Task B4.1.3

➤ Why do you think Peal and Lambert were interested in the children's English and French achievement scores?

➤ Similarly, what information can we gather from the parents' skills in both French and English?

➤ What are some of the common ways of measuring SES?

Generally, the findings indicate that the bilingual group performed significantly better than the monolingual group on most non-verbal tasks. Contrary to the hypothesis, the bilinguals performed better than the monolinguals in verbal IQ tasks as well, and, overall, bilinguals were found to be cognitively more flexible than monolinguals. Peal and Lambert's study was significant because it highlighted the importance of paying careful attention to sampling issues for results to be interpretable.

BIALYSTOK'S CONTROL AND ANALYSIS HYPOTHESIS (2001)

Following Peal and Lambert, several studies explored the relationship between various levels of metalinguistic awareness and bilingualism. In Unit A4, we noted that positive effects were not consistently reported across all samples and all tasks even in the cases where careful attention had been paid to controlling sample selection. Bialystok (2001b) explained that these differences were due to the different cognitive demands of the tasks. In the next extract, we will read more about Bialystok's hypothesis about the cognitive processes underlying different metalinguistic tasks.

In Unit B2, we discussed the need to differentiate between different types of bilingual proficiencies. The Analysis and Control framework can be used to explain the cognitive processes underlying different task demands. In general terms, metalinguistic tasks require us to pay explicit attention to form. Bialystok identified metalinguistic tasks which require children to ignore distracting information and pay attention to relevant information. Recall that in the symbol substitution task, children were asked to replace 'the boy' with 'pencils' when given the sentence 'The boy sings loudly'. For this task, the children have to pay attention to the correct substitution even though the substitution itself may violate grammatical rules in the language. Here, the violation of the rule is a misleading factor which the children have to ignore. These tasks are categorized by Bialystok as being 'high in control'.

Tasks which are 'high in analysis' are tasks which require children to have detailed knowledge about the language data around them and to be able to develop mental representations of this knowledge. Tasks that involve explanations (e.g. asking children to explain why particular sentences are ungrammatical) are 'high in analysis'. In the following extract, Bialystok looks at how these differences in cognitive demands influence a range of metalinguistic tasks.

E. Bialystok (2001) Metalinguistic aspects of bilingual processing. *Annual Review of Applied Linguistics*, 21: 169–181.

Text B4.2
E. Bialystok

Extracting the pattern

The group comparisons provided little ground for claiming a consistent core to the tasks described as metalinguistic. Bilingual and monolingual children acquired aspects of these concepts on different schedules, even undermining any consistency in the subcategories of linguistic competence. Therefore, instead of defining 'metalinguistic' in structural terms by pointing to a set of tasks that indicate the ability, it will be considered in processing terms, identifying the cognitive components that are implicated in the solution to specific metalinguistic tasks.

The processing description, elaborated elsewhere (Bialystok, 1993, 2001a), is based on two cognitive processes that are implicated in language acquisition and other cognitive developments. These processes are called analysis of representational structures and control of selective attention. Greater involvement of each makes tasks more difficult, and this difficulty results in behavior appearing to be increasingly metalinguistic. However, no specific boundary in the development of either process signals a category shift into metalinguistic performance; it is a gradual transition into a continuously evolving domain.

The first process, analysis of representational structures, is children's ability to construct mental representations with more detail and structure than was part of their initially implicit knowledge. Representations that are more explicit are more amenable to conscious access and to intentional manipulation. Karmiloff-Smith (1992) articulates a theory in which representational redescription is the central mechanism for cognitive development. Although not identical to the process of analysis, there is much common ground in the two descriptions. This processing component captures the need for metalinguistic behavior to be based on knowledge that is more explicit or more formal than that needed for more ordinary linguistic performance.

The second process, control of attention, is responsible for directing attention to specific aspects of either a stimulus field or a mental representation as problems are solved in real time. The need for control is most apparent when a problem contains conflict or ambiguity and the correct solution requires attending to one of two plausible representations and inhibiting or resisting attention to the other. Tipper and McLaren (1990) have identified this development of inhibition as one of the crucial advances in attention. Problems that present greater degrees of conflict require higher levels of control of attention. These problems also elicit performance that is more metalinguistic.

Defined in terms of underlying processes, any task that places high demands on these processes is metalinguistic. This processing criterion allows different meta-linguistic tasks to be compared in more detail. A selection of some metalinguistic tasks with their processing demands is illustrated in Figure B4.2.1.

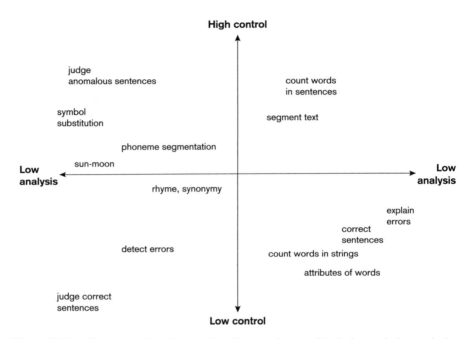

Figure B4.2.1 Some metalinguistic tasks with an estimate of their demands for analysis and control

Task B4.2.1

> The central idea in Bialystok's argument is the different demands made by two cognitive processes: 'analysis of representational structures' and 'control of selective attention'. Tasks which produced a bilingual advantage are considered to be high in control and tasks which did not produce a bilingual advantage are considered to be high in analysis. Look at the two metalinguistic tasks (Table B4.2.1). Discuss how these tasks differ in their demand for control and analysis.

Table B4.2.1 Two metalinguistic tasks

Tasks which produced a bilingual advantage	Tasks which did not produce a bilingual advantage	Explanation of task
count words in sentences	count words in strings	Words were presented either in meaningful sentences 'I love eating ice-cream' or in a scrambled string, e.g. 'love I ice-cream eating.'
phoneme segmentation	phoneme substitution	In phoneme segmentation, the children were asked to determine the number of phonemes in each word. In phoneme substitution, they were instead asked to replace one phoneme in a word with another, e.g. 'Take away the first sound from cat and put in the first sound from mop. What do you get?'

This processing framework provides a means for re-interpreting the results of mono-lingual and bilingual comparisons of metalinguistic development. Simply put, tasks that are high in their demands for control of attention are solved better by bilinguals than monolinguals; tasks that are high in their demands for analysis of representations are not necessarily solved better by either group. The bilingual advantage, therefore, is in the ability to control attention when there is misleading information.

Consider some of the tasks used in the research described in this review. The following tasks produced an advantage for bilingual children: count words in sentences, symbol substitution, sun–moon problem, use novel names in sentences, word-referent problem ('giraffes'), judge grammaticality of anomalous sentences, and phoneme segmentation. The following tasks did not produce a bilingual advantage: count words in strings, describe attributes of words, determine ambiguity, explain grammatical errors, judge grammaticality of incorrect (but meaningful) sentences, understand count–mass distinction, and phoneme substitution. The difference is in the primary demands imposed by each set of tasks. The tasks in the former group include mis-leading information, making them high in their demand for control of attention. The tasks in the latter group require detailed knowledge, making them high in their demand for analysis of representations. The effect of bilingualism on children's development is that it enhances their ability to attend to relevant information in the presence of misleading distractions. There is no domain description that defines this bilingual advantage: some metalinguistic tasks are solved better by bilinguals and others are not. Even the subcategories of word awareness, syntactic awareness, and phonological awareness do not capture what is unique about the access to these problems by bilingual children. It is only at the level of underlying processing that the pattern becomes clear.

The conclusion from this interpretation is that bilingual children do not have different control over a domain of knowledge than monolinguals. Specifically, there is no evidence that metalinguistic ability per se is developed more easily or more quickly in bilingual children. It is the case, nonetheless, that bilingual children consistently outperform monolinguals on some metalinguistic tasks. Rather than

Text B4.2
E. Bialystok

Text B4.2
E. Bialystok

attributing this advantage to privileged access to a domain of knowledge, however, the benefit is traced to a specific cognitive process that develops more readily in bilingual children. This process, control of attention, is central to certain metalinguistic problems, and it is in solving these problems that bilingual children excel. Although this analysis leaves little ground for claiming a bilingual superiority in an important developmental ability, it isolates nonetheless a formidable advantage in cognitive processing. The potential impact of this cognitive process goes well beyond the domain of metalinguistic, or even linguistic competence.

Bialystok argues that mental activity is distributed across the brain and cannot be decomposed, even abstractly, into independent units. That is, if bilingualism has a positive effect, the positive effect should be seen across all domains and should not just manifest itself in a specific domain like metalinguistic awareness. In her framework, bilingualism affects mental functioning by influencing the way information is processed, rather than by qualitatively affecting a part of the mind. As she indicated in the extract, in many ways this claim has far-reaching implications for the different ways in which bilingualism can enhance our life.

Summary

In Unit B4, we read two extracts; one focused on the way the researchers conduct the sampling of the bilinguals and the tasks used to measure 'cognitive functioning', and the other examined the specific cognitive process which is enhanced by exposure to two languages. The research questions asked in these two studies are indicative of the development in this field of research. Beginning with the broad question of whether bilingualism has positive or negative effects on cognition, the question has now evolved to more refined investigation into the specific types of influence bilingualism has on underlying cognitive processes.

Unit B5
Language attrition in bilinguals extended

In this unit, we are going to examine in some more depth some of the issues we discussed in Unit A5. From the research we examined in Unit A5, some clear patterns have emerged with respect to the kinds of factors which impact on language attrition. The younger children are when they no longer have access to the language, the more likely they are to lose the language and the more quickly this is likely to occur. This appears to be a relatively robust finding. Literacy appears to interact with attrition, reducing the impact of the attrition, and the greater an individual's proficiency the less likely it seems they are to lose that language. Comprehension often remains even though production has been affected.

In this unit, we will read an extract from an empirical study of language attrition which examines the later stages of attrition in the language of a bilingual child who lived for several years in a second-language environment before returning to his first-language environment. This extract illustrates the process of attrition, but also introduces the concept of relearning. The second extract picks upon on the issue of what happens to second-language knowledge once it is apparently lost. In the extract, we examine what happens when two learners of Dutch who have not had contact with the language for thirty years are tested on various aspects of the language, and we see that perhaps more remains than we might intuitively expect to be the case. This reflects an increasing interest in focusing on the psycholinguistic processes which are at work in language attrition, and this has led to the development of the Savings Paradigm from cognitive psychology to examine the processes of relearning (Hansen 2001) despite apparent attrition.

A CHILD'S SECOND-LANGUAGE ATTRITION

The study of Japanese children who have returned to Japan after a period living abroad has been, as discussed in Unit A5, the source of considerable attention in the attrition literature. The first extract is a report of a longitudinal study of one of these children, 'Ken', whose first language was Japanese and whose second language was English. He had learned English during the period that he lived with his parents in the United States, from the age of 1;3 to 8;0. The study is unusual in that it examined language attrition over a much longer period of time than most of the studies. The study focused on Ken's language skills in English at 20 months and 33 months following his return to Japan. The study adopted a qualitative approach to the data, with the intention of providing as full a description as possible of the processes of the child's second language. In particular, the focus was on ways in which the attrition of the child's morphology, lexicon and syntax were affected, how his fluency was affected and whether his productive skills were more affected than his receptive skills (Tomiyama 2000: 307).

Ken moved to the US owing to his father's job commitments. The result of this was that Ken attended pre-school in the United States, and attended elementary school up to second grade. Japanese was spoken only at home but his friends were English-speaking and English became his dominant language in the final year of his stay in the United States. Once he returned to Japan, he attended a local Japanese school and had only very limited access to English.

Data were collected in monthly visits to the child's Japanese home for the first part of the study (up to 19 months) and then once every two months after that. A variety of different instruments were used, and the data were video- and audio-recorded. The following types of data were collected:

- free conversation about everyday topics
- the Peabody Picture Vocabulary Test, which measures vocabulary using pictures
- the bilingual syntax measure (BSM), used to evaluate oral proficiency, and sub-sequently his morphological skills
- two picture books, used to elicit longer spans of discourse and storytelling language: *A Boy, a Dog, a Frog and a Friend* (Mayer and Mayer, 1971) and *Wacky Wednesday* (LeSieg, 1974).

This second book involves a variety of strange objects and phenomena which appear in the book, and Ken was asked to describe these.

In the following extract, we begin with a brief overview of the data analysis procedures, and then discuss the baseline data (at 2 months after return), and the findings from both Stage I (19 months after return) and Stage II (33 months after return).

 Task B5.1.1

➤ Think about a language you have learned and no longer have contact with. Do you feel you have lost some aspects of the language more than others? For example, do you have trouble remembering specific vocabulary items? How easy or difficult is it to remember the way in which sentences are structured, i.e. the grammar of the language?

M. Tomiyama (2000) Child second language attrition: a longitudinal case study. *Applied Linguistics*, 21 (3): 304–332.

Text B5.1
M. Tomiyama

Data analysis procedures

The free conversation, storytelling, and W*acky Wednesday* portions of the audio-taped materials were later transcribed for analysis. To obtain quantitative data of selected features, the following procedures were performed. For fluency measurement in the storytelling data, the total number of tokens, the total seconds of unfilled pauses, the total occasions of self-repetitions and self-repairs were tallied. Accuracy rates of the grammatical morphemes targeted for the study (*plural, third person singular, progressive, auxiliary, copula, regular past* and *irregular past*) were calculated based on the spontaneous speech, BSM, and storytelling data. The accuracy rate was expressed as the number of correct morphemes supplied divided by the total number of obligatory occasions. For the accuracy rate of preposition use, the storytelling data were employed.

Baseline data

At the first session (2 months after returning), Ken showed no signs of difficulty in expressing himself and sustaining a conversation with the researcher for a con-siderable length of time, approximately 20 minutes. He would volunteer a topic and would not only answer the researcher's questions but expand on the topic being brought up. He would respond to the researcher's English in English right from the beginning of the session and would continue to do so throughout. His non-verbal behavior and pronunciation were native-like.

In the formal assessments, he scored a raw score of 101 on the PPVT, an age equivalent of 9;3, when his chronological age was 8;2. He measured Level 4 – intermediate English – on the BSM. The main reason he did not measure Level 5 – proficient – was because he had not acquired the conditionals.

Task B5.1.2

➤ For the analysis of the accuracy rate, the correct number of morphemes supplied was divided by the total number of obligatory occasions. An obligatory occasion is one in which the morpheme must occur (e.g. in the expression 'the two dogs ran into the park' an 's' is obligatory, but in the sentence 'the dogs ran into the park' the plural 's' is not obligatory without additional information about the context). Why is the concept of obligatory occasion important?

. . .

Text B5.1
M. Tomiyama

Findings

Summary of Stage I

The overall attrition pattern up to 19 months after returning will be briefly recapitu-lated below so that the change observed in Stage II can be illustrated . . . First, code-switching to L1 started to appear at around eight months after his return. The instances of code-switching were concentrated on interjections and emotional utterances such as expressing frustration and excitement . . .

At the same time, Ken started to experience lexical retrieval difficulty . . . He used a number of strategies including *code-switching, paraphrasing, avoidance*, and *approximation* in order to compensate for his deficiency . . . Loss of fluency caused primarily by difficulty in lexical retrieval also became evident.

On the other hand, Ken's morphological attrition was less observable. A slight decline in his accuracy for supplying the past irregular morpheme and the plural morpheme was observed, but none of the morphemes targeted for examination was seriously affected or lost. There was virtually no change in receptive vocabulary showing the gap between his productive and receptive skills . . . Syntax also remained quite robust throughout the period . . .

. . .

Stage II

Stage II, the subsequent months covering from 20 months to 33 months after his return to Japan, can be characterized as the phase of change in syntax and morphology, and stability in fluency and productive lexicon. In general, affected areas in Stage I were stabilized in Stage II, and unaffected areas in Stage I underwent some observable change.

Change

Noun modification

In Stage II, there was a structural change in the modification of nouns, from post-noun modification to pre-noun modification. While Ken predominantly employed post-noun modification patterns in Stage I, his use of pre-noun modification structures became conspicuous in the corpus of Stage II data. Table B5.1.1 shows actual examples of the pre-noun modification patterns that appeared in the *Wacky Wednesday* data and

Table B5.1.1 Typical pre-noun modification examples from *Wacky Wednesday* data

Pre-noun modification	(Analogous post-noun modification)
By nouns a tiger mom a giraffe head	(a mom who is a tiger) (a head of a giraffe)
By -s genitives the window's place *for sale*'s spelling	(the place of the window) (the spelling for *for sale*)
Multiple modification a no neck student	(a student with no neck) (a student who does not have a neck)
a one tire baby car [= stroller]	(a baby car with one tire) (a baby car which has one tire)
By -ing participles the sitting place	(the place for sitting) (the place where you sit)

the analogous post-noun modifications. The first pattern is pre-modification of head nouns by nouns, such as *a tiger mom*. Pre-modification of nouns by -*s* genitives is also frequent, for example *the window's place*. Multiple pre-modification of nouns such as *a one tire baby car* [= stroller] is present as well. Finally, although not frequently, he sometimes used the pattern: pre-noun modification by -*ing* participles, such as *the sitting place*.

The following data shown in (1) and (2)[1] capture the change from post-noun modification to pre-noun modification. These come from the *Wacky Wednesday* data where the change over time in a particular structure, vocabulary, and morpheme use can be observed under a controlled environment [although . . .] caution must be taken in claiming the loss of a particular item in L2 attrition research. To do so, the fact that the item indeed existed in the corpus of the baseline data must first be established; unlike acquisition research . . . attrition cannot safely be discussed alone without confirming acquisition. Evidence of attrition may be examined by looking at a change only after establishing the fact of acquisition. (1) and (2) provide two examples of this type of evidence: the change in Ken's use of noun modification from post-nominal to pre-nominal can he observed.

(1) Stage I–Session 3 [hereafter I–3] (6 mos) not elicited

	I–8	(12 mos)	post	*There's a p-pig with a feet for chicken*
	I–12	(17 mos)		not elicited
	II–16	(24 mos)	pre	*And there's a (1 sec) chicken foot pig*
	II–18	(31 mos)	pre	*There's a (pause) chicken f-feet pig*
	II–19	(33 mos)	pre	*There's a (1 sec) chicken leg leg (pause) pig*

(2) I–3 (6 mos) not elicited

	I–8	(12 mos)	post	*There's a shoe walking*
	I–12	(17 mos)	pre	*There's a um walking shoes*
	I–16	(24 mos)	pre	There's *a walking shoe?*
	II–18	(31 mos)	pre	*There's a walking (pause) shoes*
	II–19	(33 mos)	pre	There's *a w-walking shoe*

---

1 The following symbols are used in the transcription.

.	downward intonation
?	upward intonation
–	cut off
:	lengthening
(x sec)	pause in seconds
(pause)	pause less than one second
< >	explanation of situation
[=]	English translation
UPPER CASE	Japanese utterance
{--}	featured examples

Text B5.1
M. Tomiyama

To refer to the wackiness of the pig in one of the pictures . . . , in Session 8, which is 12 months after his return in Stage I, Ken said, *There's a pig with a feet for chicken*, using post-noun modification. From Session 16 on, which are all in Stage II, he used pre-noun modification: *a chicken foot pig*, and *a chicken leg pig*. Also, to refer to a pair of shoes on the street . . . , Ken used post-noun modification in 1–8 but used pre-noun modification in II–12 through 19.

Spontaneous speech data from free conversation also revealed Ken's increasing use of the pre-noun modification pattern . . .

In sum, a switch in the noun modification pattern, from post-noun modification to pre-noun modification, was observed during Stage II.

Relativization

During this stage Ken started to show some difficulty in relativization as well. The following utterances are taken from the storytelling data.

(3)	1–6	(9 mos)	*the boy* (1 sec) *um* (5 sec) *went where the children was he went* (4 sec) *back where he was*
	1–9	(13 mos)	*he* (pause) *went to the place where the fishing pole was*
	1–13	(19 mos)	*so he* (pause) *take the dog to where he was fishing*
	II–16	(24 mos)	*the* (pause) *dog* (pause) *went* (pause) *to the place* (pause) *where* (pause) *they* (1 sec) *fish fish they were fishing*
	II–17	(27 mos)	*he was going to* (pause) *the place fis- he was fishing*
			the dog and a frog (2 sec) *got to the* (1 sec) *place* (1 sec) *fished* (pause) *that they were fishing*
	II–18	(31 mos)	*he was going to the place where* (first start) *first fishing*
	II–19	(33 mos)	*they* (pause) *were* (1 sec) *going backs* (1 sec) *the place first fishing*

As can be seen above, Ken handled the structure without any problem up until Session 13. However, from Session 16 on, which are all in Stage II, he started to show some dysfluency in producing the structure. He paused (Sessions 16, 17, 19), hesitated, and self-repaired (Session 17), all of which are signs of difficulty. In Sessions 18 and 19, he was finally unable to produce the correct structure.

. . .

Prepositions

Another area in which Ken began to show difficulty was prepositions. Table B5.1.2 reveals quantitatively his accuracy in the use of prepositions taken from the storytelling data. The total number of preposition uses and the number of incorrect uses were tallied. Incorrect use includes missing prepositions and wrong prepositions. Accuracy is given in percentage figures. The figures show that Ken handles them well up to Session 13, but not so after that.

Text B5.1
M. Tomiyama

Table B5.1.2 Accuracy of preposition use from storytelling data

	Stage I			Stage II			
Session	#6	#9	#13	#16	#17	#18	#19
Months	9	12	19	24	27	31	33
Accuracy %	100	100	100	80	78	85	77
	(11/11)	(18/18)	(16/16)	(16/20)	(14/18)	(17/20)	(10/13)

The following data in (4), all depicting the same scene in the story, illustrate his change in preposition use from Stage I to II.

(4) I–19 (13 mos) *And one day he was fishing at a lake?*

II–16 (24 mos) *One day* (pause) *they went <u>to</u> fishing* (pause) <u>*to*</u> *a lake*

II–17 (27 mos) *And one day they* (1 sec) *went <u>to</u> fishing at a lake.*

II–18 (31 mos) *One day they went <u>to</u> fishing.*

This tendency is also supported by the *Wacky Wednesday* and spontaneous speech data.
. . .

Morphology

The grammatical morphemes that were focused on for the investigation were: *plural, third person singular, progressive, auxiliary, copula, regular past,* and *irregular past.* Overall, not much attrition in morpheme use was observed during Stage I.

The BSM data in Stage II did not yield much change . . . [table removed]. Most morphemes remained stable at the 100 per cent accuracy level except for *plural* at Session 17 (27 months) and *third person singular* for Session 18 (31 months) . . .

On the other hand, the spontaneous speech data, where obligatory occasions for *plural* were larger than the BSM data, revealed a more pronounced degree of attrition [. . . and] the accuracy rate for *plural* dropped to as low as 65 per cent . . .

. . . The storytelling data, where obligatory occasions for *irregular past* were larger than those of the BSM data, again showed less than perfect accuracy hovering at around 90 per cent. Regular past showed a gradual decline as well.

Stability

Fluency

Recall that one of the more salient signs of attrition in Stage I was fluency. However, in Stage II, fluency as measured by pauses, repetitions, and self-repairs stabilized. Table B5.1.3 lists the total length of pauses in seconds and the number of occurrences of repetitions and self-repairs based on the figures taken from the storytelling data. Since the total number of words for each storytelling was of course not equal for each session, the total length of pauses and the number of occurrences were converted into percentage figures (showing how many seconds or how many times he had paused, made repetitions, or repaired himself per 100 words). As the table shows, his overall fluency was the worst in Session 13, the tail end of Stage I, but since then it improved and stabilized throughout Stage II.

Table B5.1.3 Fluency from storytelling data

	Stage I			Stage II			
Session	#6	#9	#13	#16	#17	#18	#19
Months	9	13	19	24	27	31	33
Pauses %	23	24	40	29	18	29	22
	(58/256)	(109/451)	(119/334)	(116/399)	(58/331)	(92/314)	(59/268)
Repetition %	1.6	2.9	3.0	1.5	1.2	1.6	0.4
	(4/256)	(13/451)	(10/334)	(6/399)	(4/331)	(5/314)	(1/268)
Self-repairs %	1.6	2.7	2.4	2.0	2.1	2.2	1.5
	(4/256)	(12/451)	(8/334)	(8/399)	(7/331)	(7/314)	(4/268)

Lexicon

Ken's productive vocabulary also stabilized in Stage II. Stage I was a period which could be characterized by his difficulty in lexical retrieval. In Stage II, however, not much decline in productive vocabulary was observed. Rather, he retained what he had by the end of Stage I, and surprisingly, he recovered some of the items that were seemingly lost in Stage I.

. . .

Some of these items in the 'lost' category were recovered by the end of Stage II: five items out of 13, or 38 per cent. (6) shows his forgetting (Session 12) and subsequent recovery of the item *smoke* (Session 16). Note the phenomena of code-switching, abandonment, fillers, talking to himself in Japanese, and pauses; they are all considered to be signs of struggle.

(6) I–3 (6 mos)   *There's not supposed to be a shoe there*

  I–8 (12 mos) *Uh, there's a shoe on the EETO [= um] <whispers> KEMURI [= smoke] smoke?*

  I–12 (17 mos) *There's a shoe on the um (2 sec) the (2 sec) the shoe ha- (3 sec) the shoe has to be (3 sec) on somebody's foot but not <abandoned>*

  II–16 (24 mos) *And there's a shoe on the uh: uh:: <whispers> NAN DA [= What is it?] (12 sec) smoke*

  II–18 (31 mos) *There's a (pause) shoe on the smoke.*

  II–19 (33 mos) *There's a (pause) shoe on the (2 sec) shoe (pause) on (pause) the (1 sec) smoke*

(7) demonstrates Ken's use of the vocabulary item *chase* over time. This is another example that illustrates his forgetting in Stage I and recovery in Stage II.

(7) I–3   (6 mos)   *Um the worm um <u>chasing</u> the bird.*

I–8   (12 mos)   *And the worm's* (pause) *wor-worm is* (1 sec) *um* (16 sec) <sighs> (7 sec) <The researcher prompts: The worm's what.> *It should be the bird trying <u>to get</u> the worm but the worm trying <u>to get</u> the bird.*

I–12   (17 mos)   not elicited

II–16 (24 mos)   *And the it should be* (2 sec) *the bird* (2 sec) *will um* <whispers> EETO ARE [= um what] (7 sec) *the worm is um* (8 sec) *trying to <u>catch</u> the bird.*

II–18 (31 mos)   *The* (2 sec) *worm is um fish-<u>chasing</u> the bird.*

II–19 (33 mos)   *And the* (pause) *worm is* (1 sec) *the worm is* (2 sec) *the bird and the worm is* (2 sec) */apsayt/.*

In Session 3, he did possess the word *chase*. He used the more general term *get* in Session 8, thereby giving an observer the impression that *chase* was lost. However, after using a paraphrase, *catch*, in Session 16, he recovered *chase* in Session 18, which is well into Stage II. However, he seemed to be unable to use *chase* in Session 19 and uttered */apsayt/* meaning *opposite*.

. . .

His receptive vocabulary was one of the areas that was not affected by attrition in Stage I. This was also true in Stage II as can be seen in Table B5.1.4. His raw score on the PPVT remains stable except for the last session where there is a drop.

Table B5.1.4 Receptive vocabulary – PPVT scores

	Stage I			Stage II			
Session	#1	#8	#12	#16	#17	#18	#19
Months	2	12	17	24	27	31	33
Raw Score	101	101	105	102	101	103	96

Discussion

Compared to Stage I, the development of attrition in syntax became evident in Stage II, the noun modification pattern, in particular. Some signs of morphological attrition were also present at this stage. On the other hand, the subject's productive lexicon stabilized, parallel with his fluency. His receptive lexicon remained constant throughout Stages I and II. Thus, exploration into the subject's attrition beyond 20 months extending to 33 months after returning showed overall that his L2 skills attrited differentially but that he was still capable of producing speech spontaneously.

Task B5.1.3

➤ After not using a language for a long time, most people notice a substantial decrease in fluency in the initial stages. What are some linguistic and non-linguistic factors that can affect fluency? In this study, Ken's fluency decreased toward the end of Stage I but improved and became more stable by Stage II. What are some possible reasons for this improvement?

Text B5.1
M. Tomiyama

. . .

Conclusion

By tracking the subject's L2 linguistic behavior in the L1 environment longitudinally, it was possible to observe differential attrition in his linguistic subsystems (lexicon, morphology, syntax) as well as the gradual and fluctuating nature of the process. His attained proficiency level, age of return, and acquired literacy skill seem to have contributed to his prolonged retention of L2 ability. Both his attrition curve and differential attrition pattern in vocabulary and grammar show what are characteristic of high-proficiency subjects reaching the critical threshold. His receptive vocabulary remained intact in contrast to his productive vocabulary indicating a gap between the two skills.

Abundance of the pre-noun modification pattern in the data at Stage II was interpreted as the result of his employment of compensatory strategies such as syntactic reduction and interlingual transfer. The subject appeared to be avoiding the two problematic areas, relativization and prepositional phrases, simplifying the noun-modification structure, and also relying on the pattern which is congruent to the L1 structure. Viewed in this light, this study disclosed that eliciting a variety of linguistic elements longitudinally will enable the researcher to integrate isolated phenomena to grasp a more general picture of the process.

The study also revealed the fluctuating nature of attrition in productive vocabulary and in morphology. Some items seemed to be lost at one point but recovered at a later point only to be lost or seemingly lost once again. This suggests that acquired L2 knowledge is not permanently lost, but that its access is in trouble. It also demonstrates that the L2 attrition process shares 'the peaks and valleys' pattern with L1 and L2 acquisition. It can also be seen as variability found in learner/attriter language. Moreover, it points out the significance of examining data longitudinally since with the peaks and valleys, a short-term observation can often lead to an erroneous portrayal of the overall process of attrition.

Because the antecedent state of attrition can be well established, longitudinal studies of this sort make it possible to assess attrition in a relatively accurate manner. Certainly, disadvantages of case studies should be recognized, but by collecting various types of data and a variety of linguistic elements they can be a viable tool for capturing a macroscopic view of the attrition process.

Task B5.1.4

➤ If you were interested in looking at how word frequency affects attrition, how would you achieve this? What other questions do you have about Ken's attrition pattern in English? Are English speakers Ken's only possible source of contact with English? In the absence of an English-speaking community, what other sources of contact may be beneficial to Ken's maintenance of English?

As this extract demonstrates, the process of attrition is not necessarily a straightforward one of increased attrition across all domains. As we see with Ken, although he lost some elements of his language in the second stage, other elements actually appeared to return. As Tomiyama pointed out, it is possible to speculate as to the factors which may have contributed to the pattern of attrition found in Ken's language. When he left the United States, Ken was a very proficient speaker and his vocabulary knowledge measured higher than that of his average English-speaking peers; he had lived there for several years, and his literacy skills were assessed by his teachers as excellent. Tomiyama discussed the fact that the literature indicates that the generally high level of Ken's proficiency upon leaving the US is consistent with the patterns of attrition demonstrated by his data.

To this point we have talked about attrition as a process which occurs, and is measured in terms of what is lost, because generally when we discuss attrition we focus on what is lost, rather than on what is not lost or what remains. Yet, of course, when we think we are losing a language, we probably don't really lose the language entirely – what is more likely is that we lose our ability to activate it. This is consistent with Cohen's (1989) findings, discussed in Unit A5, that production was more affected than comprehension. Thus, in some ways, lack of practice means that we find it more difficult to access the language – just as a sport which one once played well becomes more difficult without practice.

Task B5.1.5

➤ Think of a sport or skill you had as a child or teenager, which you no longer play or practise. Think about how it used to feel when you played or practised well.

➤ Try to find a situation in which you can play the sport or practise the skill again now. How does it feel?

- comfortable or uncomfortable?
- co-ordinated or uncoordinated?
- pleasant or unpleasant?

If you continue with this activity, do you begin to feel the level of skill returning? Work by Kees de Bot and Lynne Hansen (e.g. Hansen et al. 2002; De Bot and Hansen 2001), adopting a model from cognitive psychology known as the Savings Paradigm, approached these issues from a different perspective which suggests that all is not lost when we cease to have contact with languages we have learned in the past. As we will see in the extract from the following article, even thirty years on there appears to be an advantage in having previously learned a language.

The authors tested two German speakers who learned Dutch as children for their knowledge of Dutch despite the fact that they had had no contact with the language for thirty years. The study was designed to evaluate the 'Savings' approach. It is interesting to speculate that the findings from this study may well have relevance to Ken at some later stage in his life since the results suggest that some residual language knowledge is retained despite lack of contact with the second language over long periods. This also has relevance, of course, to those of us who learned a language in childhood and feel we have forgotten it all! The second extract investigated the question of whether language knowledge acquired early in life is lost or overridden by languages acquired later, or to what extent it is maintained despite the lack of use.

The study reports on a brother (A) and sister (S) from a German-speaking family who lived in Holland for four years. S lived in Holland from the age of three until she was seven, while A was there from the age of seven to the age of eleven. The family subsequently moved to Finland, where A spent six years and S spent eight years, before moving back to Germany. As an adult, S married an American and moved to the US, where she completed a PhD, and A also moved to America. Neither has had much contact with Dutch, the focus of the paper, since their primary school years.

 Task B5.2.1

> Ideally, in such studies, the researcher would like to have access to a databank of A and S's language skills at the time they left Holland as this would provide them with the 'baseline data' – the data with which they could compare A and S's language competence at the time of study. However, this is often not possible. To draw conclusions about attrition patterns, researchers do need to compare the participants' performance with a 'model' of their competence before attrition sets in. In the absence of baseline data, how can researchers make comparisons? To what extent would you rely on self-report data? Apart from self-report data, what other methods are available?

> Given the various factors we know that have an impact on attrition patterns, what are your predictions for A and S's competence in Dutch after a gap of thirty years?

There are a number of points that need to be taken into consideration when reading the extract below from the study by De Bot and Stoessel. Firstly, because no data were available from the participants' primary years, there is no baseline data which can be used for comparative purposes, and this is explicitly acknowledged by the authors. At the same time, it is clear from the grades the participants were receiving at school that their Dutch knowledge was good. Secondly, Dutch, German and English are all related languages and share many cognates. In the following extract, the authors discuss their findings following a brief discussion of the testing procedures.

K. de Bot and S. Stoessel (2000) In search of yesterday's words: reactivating a long-forgotten language. *Applied Linguistics*, 21 (3): 333–353.

Text B5.2
K. de Bot and
S. Stoessel

In this article we present data on two subjects who acquired a second language (Dutch) at a very early age and who have never used the language subsequently. Various tests were used to assess different levels of knowing. To assess word recognition, a translation task (Dutch–English (for S), Dutch–German (for A)) and a Dutch picture–word matching task were used. To assess word recall, a picture-naming task was used. By means of a relearning task based on the savings approach, an attempt was made to assess lexical knowledge not detected through recognition and recall tasks. The question was whether or not, through some elaborate tests assessing linguistic knowledge at a level lower than regular recall or recognition, vocabulary knowledge could resurface after some initial reactivation. It was expected that words that are cognates in two or more languages would be easier to retrieve than non-cognates.

In addition to the assessment of lexical knowledge at a given point in time, the aim of the study was also to look at changes over time, in particular in relation to the part-set hypothesis of memory performance. We looked at the percentages for words translated correctly in subsequent sessions. If the part-set hypothesis is correct, we expected to find lower error scores over time.

Recognition tasks (L2 to L1 translation, picture–word matching)

In the recognition tasks, as mentioned above, there is a clear effect for cognateness, but there is considerable variation between sessions and also between subjects . . . The first observation is, as we expected, that both A and S have the best scores for the words which are cognates in both languages (A-category). For the B-category words, it seems that A profits more from English cognateness, while S profits more from German cognateness (A shows a mean of 18.5 per cent errors for English cognates vs. 25.3 per cent errors for German cognates; S has 24.6 per cent errors for the German cognates and 43.5 per cent errors for English cognates). This is interesting in the light of the fact that A's test was conducted in German, while S's test was conducted in English. It suggests that the cognates in the language in which the test was conducted were rejected more strongly. Despite this seeming conformity between the subjects, cognateness was not always perceived in the same way, however, something which most strongly came up in the picture-naming test which will be discussed further below. During the testing sessions, S indicated that she prefers to keep her languages separate and rather refrains from assuming cognateness. For A, it seems that he possibly makes use of cognateness more freely.

Highly important for this study is the finding that both A and S showed an error rate lower than 50 per cent for the non-cognate words . . . For these words they could only rely on their residual Dutch knowledge, and for this reason we can here make the claim that both A and S have indeed retained a considerable part of their Dutch

Text B5.2
K. de Bot and
S. Stoessel

vocabulary even over a 30-year period, at least on a recognition level. What is surprising in this finding is that there is no real difference between S and A, although A was somewhat older than S, was more exposed to Dutch due to his longer attendance at the Dutch school, and possibly also encountered more varied vocabulary during those years than S.

For the picture–word matching task, the other recognition task, very high correct scores were found, again supporting the above finding that there is residual and retrievable lexical knowledge of Dutch in the two subjects. Also in this group of words, there were multiple instances of C-category words (non-cognates), so that the subjects could not simply rely on cognateness.

Recall task (picture-naming)

The recall task (picture-naming) rendered a slightly different picture, in particular when the two subjects are compared. We were able to observe two things: First, the two subjects differed remarkably in their readiness to offer suggestions for the picture naming. While the recall task seemed rather difficult for S and she accordingly did not produce very many answers, A seemed more at ease and offered solutions readily.

Secondly, it seemed that S, although she gave fewer responses, was surer about her answers than A. This can be demonstrated in particular with the non-cognate words: S gave correct answers for over 50 per cent of the non-cognate words. A, in contrast, would not hesitate to offer supposed cognates like 'umbrella' (supposedly English cognate for Dutch parapluie) or 'naashorn' (supposedly German cognate 'Nashorn' for Dutch neushoorn) to denote the respective pictures of an umbrella or a rhino. For him only 38 per cent of the non-cognate words were correct . . .

The ease/non-ease with which the subjects responded correlates with the subjects' own estimates of their proficiency in Dutch: while S did not claim any remaining knowledge of Dutch, A still listed Dutch as one of the languages in which he was somewhat proficient. So it seems that this confidence contributes to the feeling of comfort when giving answers, but the correctness of the answers cannot necessarily be trusted. (A had 30 per cent wrong answers, whereas of the few answers S gave, only 14 per cent were incorrect.)

For S, then, recognition is clearly an easier task than recall. After the tests, S remarked that, even with the above-mentioned shyness about using cognateness of words as a help, she did to some degree use her other languages in recognizing words. For the recall task, she was not able to do this, however, and she did not feel any 'competition' from other languages. There thus seems to be a real gap between recall and recognition, at least for S. From her experience it looks as if in recognition, information from the other languages was helpful in finding the translation when making use of similarities between languages, but at the same time disruptive, because it was never clear whether the meanings/translations popping up were actually Dutch-based. In production there was less cross-linguistic interference, and cognateness accordingly played less of a role. We did not obtain qualitative remarks of this kind from A.

Task B5.2.2

➤ Although S and A were sister and brother, there were clearly differences in the way in which they approached these activities. Consider the extent to which individual differences might be important not only in the way we approach learning a second language, but in the ways in which we might lose it. Could individual differences account for different rates of attrition in any way?

The part-set hypothesis

Text B5.2
K. de Bot and
S. Stoessel

In the recognition/translation task no clear part-set effect was found. We had hypo-thesized that there might be an increase of correct forms over time due to an activation of the total set of previously known Dutch lexical items through reactivation of a part. There was, however, little retrieval of previously tested items in the long term. The words not recognized in one session were retested the following session, but this led to very few words that were remembered between sessions. S made remarks like 'I've been thinking about this word all week, but I still don't know what it means.'

This suggests that finding those words is not like the normal 'tip-of-the-tongue' (TOT) phenomenon, in which known words cannot be found in time. Research on TOT-states in a second language shows that most words looked for are found after some time, though that may be a few days (cf. Ecke 1997). Apparently the feeling that this might be a word that was known at some point is different from the normal TOT-state in which there is no doubt that the word is there, but for some reason it cannot be retrieved right away.

While the above might suggest that knowing or not knowing words is quite stable, this study also demonstrates that the subjects were engaging in a fair amount of linguistic game-playing and guessing while giving the meanings of lexical items. The status of a cognate was often just assumed rather than firmly known. This shows how unstable this knowledge is, in the end, and while a considerable number of the translations given were correct, we can only to a certain degree make the claim that this represents true residual knowledge. Only the C-category words really allow for this conclusion.

Another point of evidence for the instability of the lexical knowledge is the fact that some words were recognized (or perhaps better: correctly guessed) in one session, but in the next session the subject failed to reuse the previous guess, and indeed failed to provide any meaning at all for the item.

Savings task

For the savings approach, evidence of residual lexical knowledge was found using two versions of the learning task. In the first version of the task, there were clear differences between the scores of the subjects and the mean scores of the control groups. While the control groups showed little increase in number of words remembered over time, there was a noticeable increase of remembered words for both A and S . . . This suggests a savings effect, but we should add that there was considerable variation within the control groups, and some individuals in those groups actually had a higher relearning score than our subjects. This shows that learning this type of savings list may be a question of learning strategy rather than a sign of residual lexical knowledge. In particular, the data on the pseudo-word task show that S is an extremely efficient word learner, so she might have outscored the control groups on any language, not just Dutch. S, as a matter of fact, remarked after the savings tests that she did change her learning strategies after having done the pseudo-words. Since in this test cognateness or intuition did not help, she had to use other strategies such as visual cues, length of words, letter combinations, etc. to learn the words. She then also started using these strategies for the following Dutch savings tests.

It is thus questionable how far the savings test in the first format we used is really a worthwhile test to conduct, at least for foreign language purposes, as it is almost impossible to distinguish between learning strategy and previously acquired knowledge. Given the fact, however, that for both A and S the scores for Dutch are much higher than for the control groups in session 2 and 3, there does seem to be a savings effect which is not only due to improved strategy use.

The existence of residual lexical knowledge is more evident in the alternative version of the test we used in which A and S had to relearn a list of words consisting of both 'old' and 'new' words which they had not been able to translate in the pretest. The data show that in all instances the 'old' words were recalled better than the 'new' ones.

Presentation of words with or without a context?

In rethinking the tests used for this study, one concern was the effect of presenting words in isolation. One could argue that our subjects might do better at recalling/recognizing words presented in a semantically embedded structure. This is probably true, but we would claim that since it is more difficult to recall or recognize words in isolation, this approach gives a better picture of what is really still there. If words had been presented in a context, it would have been very difficult to assess to what extent success depends on word knowledge or effective use of the context or an interaction between those two. So, while our findings on relearning may be an underestimation of the full lexical knowledge, a contextualized test might have resulted in an overestimation of that knowledge. Meanwhile, the differences between the subjects and the control groups in the savings experiment do suggest differences in lexical knowledge.

Considering further the issue of presenting lexical information in context, one can look at the compound nouns presented to the subjects (words like *buitendeur* 'front door' and *tandarts* 'dentist'). Many of these were, in fact, more easily recognized and then gave away some other, previously not recognized, single noun. Two examples from S's data for this are *visserboot* – 'fishing boat', which made her then recognize *vis* as 'fish'; and *poppenwagen* – 'doll carriage', which then made her recognize *pop* as 'doll', or *tandarts* – 'dentist', which made her recognize *tand* 'tooth'. Another interesting occurrence was the term *beschuit* – 'rusk': S said: 'The stuff you put on bread, little things like hagelsalg ("chocolate sprinkles") but with sugar, they are red and white or blue.' Here S is referring to the other component of a phrase in which *beschuit* is usually used: When a baby is born in the Netherlands, the parents will present 'Beschuit met muisjes' (Rusk with coloured sugar sprinkles in red for a girl and in blue for a boy) to visitors. So during the session, S mixed up the two parts of the concept, rusk and sugar sprinkles, and referred to the wrong part of the expression, although it had not even been mentioned. This shows the power of association when a part of a compound is used. Interestingly, A made the same error but corrected himself a day later.

Conclusions

Text B5.2
K. de Bot and
S. Stoessel

The general conclusion from this study is that even for a language that was learned in childhood for a limited number of years, quite a lot of knowledge is still available after 30 years of non-use. This is in line with other research on foreign/second language attrition, in particular with the data from Bahrick (1984) on the retention of Spanish learned at school/college, which showed that part of the knowledge of Spanish is still intact after more than 25 years. Practically speaking, this also means that people who acquired a language at an early age can be at an advantage, both time and cognition-wise, in relearning that language compared with people who have never been in touch with the language before.

The data presented here open up a new line of research on language acquisition and language retention. There clearly is retention of linguistic knowledge over a long period of time for languages learned in childhood, but how we can best reactivate them is still unclear. The savings paradigm may be a promising approach to testing such reactivation, but our data shows that it is clearly not without problems. The savings paradigm needs to be tested further for its applicability in long-term attrition research and special attention should be paid to controlling the point of reference, i.e. the more exact nature of previously learned material. Further work on the savings paradigm in foreign language learning can be found in de Bot and Stoessel (1999).

As in SLA-research, the effect of individual differences has to be taken into account: even between the two family members in this study we can see differences in learning strategies, aptitude, and response strategies. Larger group studies may enable us to test the effect of age, time elapsed since learning, and other variables. Finally, research should be extended to other early acquirers with different first languages and language histories.

Task B5.2.3

➤ Have you had the experience of:

- ▨ learning a language and not using it for some time?
- ▨ returning to the place where it is spoken, or having access to it again?

➤ When you had access to the language again, to what extent did you feel you had regained some level of knowledge of the language? Did this vary across different aspects of the language (e.g. consider pronunciation, vocabulary, syntax, discourse structure)?

Language attrition, as we have seen with language acquisition, is a complex process which is affected by a variety of factors. These include the age at which access to the language is no longer available, the degree of language knowledge obtained in the first place, and the individual's motivation to maintain their language knowledge once regular contact with the language is lost. We must also expect, of course, that, quite apart from these factors, individual differences are likely to have a considerable

Summary

role to play. For some people, language attrition, once contact with the language is no longer available, will be a slower or faster process than it is for others, because of the range of factors which we know to play a role. It is also apparent that the advantages of learning a language at any time in life are pervasive, and that lack of contact with the language does not mean that nothing is retained.

Unit B6
Education and literacy in bilingual settings extended

In Unit A6, we discussed a range of different approaches to bilingual education, often motivated by very different needs. We also examined the development of biliteracy in children, focusing on the cognitive issues facing bilingual children when they start school. In this unit, we will look at the outcomes of both immersion and submersion programmes. The first extract will present the study of immigrant children in immersion programmes in Canada and the second extract will outline the literacy challenges facing children of Turkish migrants in the Netherlands.

IMMERSION EDUCATION

While the aim of many bilingual programmes is to develop children's linguistic skills to the level that they can manage in the mainstream classroom, these programmes vary enormously in how they do this. In Unit A6, we reviewed various models of immersion programme and discussed how they have been beneficial for the participants. With changing demography, the participants of immersion programmes have also been transformed. In the next section, we will read an extract from an article by Swain and Lapkin (2005) in which they discuss the ways in which children from much more linguistically diverse backgrounds are now participating in the immersion programmes in Canada, and consider the implications of these socio-political changes for language policy.

M. Swain and S. Lapkin (2005) The evolving sociopolitical context of immersion education in Canada: some implications for program development. *International Journal of Applied Linguistics*, **15** (2): **169–186.**

Text B6.1
M. Swain and
S. Lapkin

Introduction

Some years after its inception in 1965, the immersion model developed in Canada began to be exported (Lambert and Tucker 1972). Immersion programs emphasize developing fluency in an initially unknown language through content-based teaching in the second/foreign language, at no expense to the home/first language of the students. In 1965 in Canada, the home language in question was English and the second language French; the central premise of immersion education was additive bilingualism, adding the second language without detriment to the development of the first. The first programs were early immersion, beginning in kindergarten or grade 1 with 100% of the day devoted to instruction in French. Other models followed, with starting points at age 10, 12 or even 14.

In an attempt to sort out what differentiated immersion education from other forms of bilingual education, Swain and Johnson (1997) developed a set of criteria to define a prototypical immersion program. One of the purposes of this article is to review the core features they identified in order to explore their applicability in 2005. Changes in Canadian demographics do not necessarily herald changes elsewhere, but they encourage us to re-examine the immersion 'scene', searching for insights that might benefit the design of immersion programs both in Canada and elsewhere.

 Task B6.1.1

➤ As Swain and Lapkin indicate, the fact that demographic patterns have changed in Canada does not necessarily mean that they have changed elsewhere. On the other hand, they may have. Consider your own community. To what extent would you say that the language demography of your local area has changed in the last ten to twenty years? (You might want to talk to someone who has lived in your area for a long time if you haven't.) How has this affected the linguistic diversity of the area?

The central claim of this article is that if the core features of immersion are to retain their integrity, changes in pedagogy need to be made to reflect the evolving socio-political context of immersion education in Canada and possibly elsewhere.

That evolving context is characterized by the rapid growth of highly diverse populations in large Canadian urban centres. Immigrant parents who speak languages other than English or French at home are sending their children to French immersion classes. If, for example, overt support for the home language is to continue to be a defining characteristic of immersion education, then immersion programming needs to change to recognize home languages other than English.

. . .

Core features of immersion programs

What features define immersion as a category within bilingual education? Have these features changed since Swain and Johnson identified them in 1997? These core features are listed in Table B6.1.1. On the left, the first core feature specifies that, in immersion programs, the second language (L2) is a medium of instruction. In the Canadian context, historically the L2 has been French, and the original participants in immersion were anglophones. As specified in the middle column, however, today many students who enrol in immersion, especially in Canada's urban centres, speak home languages other than English. French, for them, is a third or fourth language; therefore, French is better characterized as the immersion language (as shown in column 3 of the table). However, as we will see, relabelling the L2 as the 'immersion language' has important consequences for most of the other core features.

The second feature of prototypical immersion programs refers to the principle that the immersion curriculum parallels that of the local curriculum. This principle still

Text B6.1
M. Swain and
S. Lapkin

Table B6.1.1 Revisiting core features of immersion as identified by Swain and Johnson (1997)

Core features of prototypical immersion programs (Swain and Johnson 1997)	Observations made in 2005	Core features restated to reflect new realities
1. The L2 is a medium of instruction.	The L2 is not always the L2 any more; for many young immigrants, if they choose immersion, it's L3 learning.	1. The immersion language is the medium of instruction.
2. The immersion curriculum parallels the local L1 curriculum.	This is still true in principle.	2. No change.
3. Overt support exists for the L1.	This has changed dramatically with the influx of immigrants, some of whom enrol in immersion. This is a point of focus for us in this article.	3. Overt support needs to be given to all home languages.
4. The program aims for additive bilingualism.	In subtractive bilingualism, L2 proficiency develops at the expense of the L1. We need to avoid this in the face of the influx of immigrants into immersion.	4. No change.
5. Exposure to L2 is largely confined to the classroom.	Still true.	5. Exposure to the immersion language is largely confined to the classroom.
6. Students enter with similar (and limited) levels of L2 proficiency.	Usually the immersion language, French in this case, is new to all students.	6. Students enter with similar levels of proficiency in the immersion language.
7. The teachers are bilingual.	Teachers are not inevitably multilingual and cannot speak all the minority languages represented in the classroom.	7. No change.
8. The classroom culture is that of the local L1 community.	In urban centres we are dealing with multiple and diverse communities.	8. The classroom culture needs to recognize the cultures of the multiple immigrant communities to which the students belong.

holds. A question that arises in the face of the more ethnically diverse student body in immersion today is whether these immigrant children have difficulty mastering the regular school curriculum. One study of French immersion students that separated out results of 'mainstream' from immigrant students was a curriculum-based, province-wide testing program in Ontario. It found that immigrant students in grades 3 and 6 enrolled in immersion did, in fact, perform at levels in mathematics and English literacy comparable to those of mainstream students (e.g. Turnbull, Lapkin and Hart 2003). Thus, as indicated in the middle and left-hand columns of B6.1.1, this principle remains applicable.

The third feature invokes overt support for the L1. Swain and Johnson (1997: 7) explained: 'At a minimum, the students' L1 is taught as a subject in the curriculum at some stage and to advanced levels.' Today, with a more linguistically diverse student body in many urban areas, the need to support a variety of home languages has asserted itself. However, according to Cummins (personal communication, August 2004), although there are exceptions,

in most immersion programs diverse students' first languages are invisible and inaudible in the classroom. Unfortunately, teachers are typically not at all proactive in searching for ways to use students' first languages as a resource, either in immersion or English programs.

In order to maintain the integrity of the core features of immersion in column 1, finding ways to support the diverse first languages in immersion is essential, as indicated under point 3 in column 3.

Using the L1 as a resource for academic learning occurs explicitly in two-way immersion programs in the United States where half the students are anglophones and half are minority language speakers. In such programs, the minority language speakers are the language experts, for example in Spanish, as are the American anglophones in English. For both language groups the objective of the two-way program is to acquire the other classroom language while maintaining and developing literacy in the home language. Such programs are not yet found in Canada. A key feature of successful two-way immersion programs is that they provide overt, sustained first language (L1) support for the minority language and culture. In this case, students as well as teachers provide models of the target language.

The fourth feature is perhaps the most defining feature of immersion: it speaks to the additive nature of the program. Unlike subtractive bilingualism where L2 proficiency develops at the expense of the L1 or home language, immersion education is intended to teach the target language while providing for the full development of the home language. Where the home language is English, full support is ensured in the school setting as well. Where the home language is an immigrant language, that support has not been built in so far. We will look at some of the relevant research on this aspect below.

The fifth feature involves the principle that exposure to the L2 is largely confined to the classroom. This is still the case, but we must now refer to the target language as the immersion language.

The sixth core feature of immersion programs specifies that students enter the program with similar (and limited) levels of target-language proficiency. This feature still characterizes immersion education in Canada today and again makes it different from two-way immersion programs in the US. In Canadian classrooms, there may be multiple immigrant languages represented, but none of them is used as a medium

Text B6.1
M. Swain and
S. Lapkin

of instruction. All students are seeking to acquire a high level of proficiency in the immersion language, French.

The seventh core feature refers to the languages spoken by the teachers. Teachers are characteristically bilingual in English and French but are rarely multilingual.

The eighth core feature is of particular interest. Swain and Johnson articulated it as follows: 'The classroom culture is that of the local L1 community.' In Canada's large urban centres today, however, the local community may often be a highly hetero-geneous multilingual group. The challenge in Canada is to celebrate this rich diversity while teaching through the medium of the second official language.

Increasing diversity in the Canadian immersion population

In major cities in Canada (Toronto, Vancouver, Edmonton, Montreal) approximately 20–40% of the population speaks a language other than French or English at home. Across Canada nearly 20% of census respondents in 2001 were recent immigrants. A recent UN report finds that Toronto has the second largest proportion of foreign-born residents of any city in the world (Federation for American Immigration Reform 2004), with almost half its residents born outside of Canada. In the last decade we have had to let go of the assumption that early immersion classes would be full of homogeneous young anglophones and begin to think about how we can apply the principles of multilingual education not only to regular classrooms but also in the immersion setting: 'Multicultural education provides an alternative vision for organizing teaching and learning in contemporary schools, one that contrasts with the largely ethnocentric models that exist at present in Canada, the United States, and elsewhere' (Genesee and Gándara 1999: 670). Genesee and Gándara construe multi-lingual education as a philosophy of education, emphasizing the value of what children bring to school with them in terms of language, cultural and community resources.

Task B6.1.2

In the following section, Swain and Lapkin discuss the reading, writing and speaking outcomes in French for a group of immigrant children living in Canada from a variety of different language backgrounds who were enrolled in a French immersion programme from Grade 5. They were tested in Grade 8.

➤ What would you expect the outcomes to be for these children in comparison to the 'mainstream' children (i.e. children who did not come from immigrant backgrounds)? Some of them were literate in their first language as well as English (and French). What difference might you expect this to make?

What does the Canadian research on immigrant children enrolled in immersion tell us about their relative success? Three key studies speak to this issue. The first is a large-scale study focusing on the achievement in French of students enrolled in immersion who spoke an immigrant language at home. The second is a case study of three immigrant children enrolled in early French immersion in Vancouver. The third study is also situated in Vancouver and focuses on Asian parents who enrol their children in early immersion. We discuss each of these studies before turning to a US-based study of a two-way immersion program.

Text B6.1
M. Swain and
S. Lapkin

Text B6.1
M. Swain and
S. Lapkin

In 1990, immigrant children in Toronto tended to enrol in immersion programs with a later start. Parents reasoned that it was important for their children to establish skills in the dominant language of the community, English, before tackling French (their third language). Swain et al. (1990) studied close to 200 such students at the grade 8 level (approximately 13 years old) who had begun immersion in grade 5. The language backgrounds represented included both Romance (Italian, Spanish, Portuguese) and non Romance (German, Polish, Hebrew, Tagalog, Chinese, Greek and Korean) languages. When the researchers compared the achievement of these students in French writing, reading, speaking and listening to that of mainstream anglophone students enrolled in French immersion, they found that the immigrant students performed as well as or better than anglophones in French. The subset who performed even better were those immigrant students who had developed literacy skills in their home languages. From this study it was concluded that literacy in the immigrant language 'contributed to a generalized higher level of proficiency in the third (immersion) language' (Swain et al. 1990: 120).

At the time Swain et al. were conducting the above study, they were also evaluating the French skills of early immersion students. But they could not identify a sufficiently large number of immigrant children in the program with the early start to conduct similar analyses. Since that time, other Canadian researchers have conducted small-scale studies that have yielded rich descriptive information on the progress of immigrant students in early French immersion.

In a qualitative case study of three immigrant children in grades 3, 4 and 6, Dagenais and Day (1998) studied three school communities. Two of the schools had populations in excess of 500, representing 21–23 language groups. The other school was more suburban, serving primarily children of English and Asian-speaking families.

The three children in question came from upper middle-class families that chose to maintain the home language and foster trilingualism through French immersion at school. The families were tied to their cultural communities and intent on preserving their cultural identity. They also had had some experience of bilingualism themselves and believed that trilingualism for their children would confer social and economic advantages. Cathryn's mother reported:

> The benefit is when we go back to Vietnam, people say that she has no problem communicating and I told them that she can't read [in Vietnamese]. I also told them that she also studies in English and French. They were very impressed. My cousin was unable to speak Vietnamese to my grandma but she [my daughter] could. So to me it was a compliment. (Dagenais and Day 1998: 113)

Immersion teachers generally echoed the positive attitudes of parents and children. One of them commented:

> And all those pupils who speak a language other than English at home, they aren't afraid . . . to make attempts; to make predictions, to take risks . . . They seem more comfortable with uncertainty. (Dagenais and Day 1998: 389; our translation)

In sum, for the most part, immersion and regular English teachers interviewed in this study viewed trilingualism as a resource, not 'a handicap' (Dagenais and Day 1998: 388).

Task B6.1.3

➤ Consider the finding that immigrant children who developed literacy in the home language performed better than mainstream anglophone children. What type of home conditions do you think would be necessary for the support of literacy development and literacy skills? What other external factors do you think may explain the better performance of this subset of immigrant children?

In another related ethnographic study, Dagenais and Berron documented 'language practices, educational strategies and representations of self in South Asian families of diverse language backgrounds' (2001: 145) living in the greater Vancouver area. These parents were well educated and moved between their family languages (including Punjabi, Hindi, Gujarati, Urdu, and English) with ease. The researchers noted that, based on the parents' 'own multilingual practices in their country of origin . . . and their continuing multilingual interactions in their country of adoption' (Dagenais and Berron 2001: 149), they supported and encouraged multilingualism in their children. Here are two of the reasons provided in the parental interviews:

Text B6.1
M. Swain and
S. Lapkin

> (1) . . . They learn [English] from their friends. French is more difficult and to get the accent and those sort of things, we could not be helpful to them. So, that was our priority.
> (2) And we chose French, okay, English, we knew she would be able to pick up easily, right. And we chose French. We did that because it is Canada's second official language. (Dagenais and Berron 2001: 150)

Other reasons included the importance of French as a world language, the association of a command of several languages with tolerance, and the fact that enrolment in immersion presents a challenging school experience. According to the researchers, for these immigrants' children 'the coexistence of languages is a reality not only at home, but at school as well, where French is added to their daily linguistic repertoire' (Dagenais and Berron 2001: 152). The researchers undertook to follow these families and document how such children construct their multilingual identities.

Task B6.1.4

➤ Consider the implications of parental attitudes to and support for immigrant children enrolled in these programmes. Do you think these are important considerations?

In the next section of this extract, Swain and Lapkin (2005) discuss in more detail the study we introduced briefly in Unit A6 which focused on a two-way Korean–English immersion programme in Los Angeles.

The last study we will discuss is a two-way Korean/English immersion program in Los Angeles. Rolstad (1997) focused on several speakers of Tagalog and Spanish enrolled in the program and its impact on their academic achievement, language development and ethnic identity. The study is unique in investigating how minority language

Text B6.1
M. Swain and
S. Lapkin

children fare in an immersion program involving a second minority language. In contextualizing her study, Rolstad (1997: 48) states:

> while in the U.S. bilingualism among ethnic minorities is often viewed as threatening to political and cultural unity, in the European context, multilingualism is frequently seen as a solution to the problem of easing ethnic conflict and increasing solidarity among various groups.

Rolstad explained that in some highly diverse areas of large cities, there may be too few majority (English) language speakers to achieve the optimal balance of students for a two-way immersion program, where half the students should be from one language group and the other half from the second. Such was the case in the Korean/English two-way program in Los Angeles, where half the children spoke Korean at home and developed both Korean and English at school. The other half were Spanish or Tagalog speakers, who learned Korean and English at school; thus for them, Korean was a third language.

The researcher followed nine students, five from kindergarten through grade 5 and four from kindergarten through grade 4. The comparison students were matched for ethnicity and came either from a Spanish bilingual class or the English mainstream class in the same school. The comparison students from the Spanish program all spoke Spanish as an L1, and those from the English class also spoke Spanish, Korean or Tagalog. The findings of the study indicated that the third-language minority students (Spanish and Tagalog speakers) in the Korean/English bilingual program

> experienced no detrimental effects in terms of their ethnic identification, academic achievement or linguistic development [in English and Korean] in comparison with language minority children in other programs, with the exception that they have not developed, or in some cases may have lost, their first language proficiency. (Rolstad 1997: 59)

The importance of the study lies in its finding that such children flourished in the two-way immersion program, with no apparent loss of ethnic identification. Indeed, it is possible that the two-way program constitutes a better alternative for them than mainstream schooling. In the immersion classroom, they gained another language and developed their English in a climate where each language was valued. This stands in contrast to what might otherwise happen to the language minority students in mainstream English classes; there they might have a *sub*mersion experience. In both settings they could be in danger of losing their home language, but in the two-way immersion setting, they gained another minority language, and they studied in an atmosphere that was supportive of minority languages and cultures.

In summary, we have shown that a number of the core features of immersion education as stated by Swain and Johnson in 1997 need to be revised in order to maintain the main goal of additive bilingualism. This is because the population of immersion students – in large urban cities in Canada, at least – has diversified, linguistically and ethnically. This has meant that for many immersion students the immersion language is really an L3 or L4; and the L1 is not just English but could be one of many other languages.

. . .

In the next section, the authors discuss the importance of L1 as a mediating learning tool in the context of immersion education. This socio-cultural approach means that even if the first language is being used, it is being used as a tool for learning, and such activity contributes towards mental activity, and may allow students to work at a higher level than that which can be achieved in a second or third language. Swain and Lapkin argue that:

> collaborative dialogue, in the L1 or L2, mediates L2 learning. Collaborative dialogue is dialogue in which speakers are engaged in problem solving and knowledge building (Swain 2000: 102). The data presented in these studies show that through collaborative dialogue students engage, often in the L1, in co-constructing their L2 and in building knowledge about it. From their collective behavior, individual mental resources develop: that is, 'the knowledge building that learners have collectively accomplished becomes a tool for the further individual use of their second language' (Swain and Lapkin 2000: 252).

Text B6.1
M. Swain and S. Lapkin

In the next section, they provide empirical support from a variety of studies about the benefits of using L1 to support learning in cognitively demanding contexts. Given that many immigrant children's L1 is not English, this creates a challenge to practitioners as traditional immersion programmes assume that the students' L1 is English. With immigrant children, this is further complicated by the presence of many different first languages. How, then, can traditional approaches to immersion education integrate this new cohort of children?

Summary and implications for program development

Text B6.1
M. Swain and S. Lapkin

This article began with a review of the core features of immersion programs identified in 1997 by Swain and Johnson. We have seen that some of the eight core features have remained the same while others need to change to reflect the changing demographic of large cities in North America and the multilingual, multiethnic nature of many immersion programs.

We discussed several studies focusing on the participation of immigrant children in immersion programs in Canada. One showed that immigrant children with literacy in their home language outperformed mainstream anglophone immersion students in French, the L2 of the anglophone students and the L3 of the immigrant students. Two qualitative studies suggested that where families choose to maintain the home language and culture and value multilingualism, their children thrive in immersion; they transfer reading skills across languages, tolerate ambiguity well, and succeed academically.

In a US-based study of two-way immersion, the researchers had little information about language practices in the minority language homes. But those minority language students filling the places of anglophone students in a Korean/English two-way program also fared well in terms of academic achievement, linguistic development and ethnic identification. Even though their own home languages (Tagalog and Spanish in this case) received no support in the immersion program, the climate was supportive of minority languages and affirming of the children's ethnic identity.

How does one establish such a climate? It is important to allow for the use of multiple L1s in the classroom and celebrate the diverse cultures represented. In this way additive bilingualism/multilingualism is made possible. In the previous section, we discussed a perspective on the first language provided by a sociocultural theory of mind. Regardless of what language is used, speaking and writing are cognitive tools that mediate learning. Learning the immersion language is mainly done through the immersion language, of course; but some of that learning, specifically solving language problems or building new knowledge, can occur in language production in the L1 or the immersion language.

We reviewed several studies that identified functions of the L1, including:

- developing strategies to manage the task
- helping learners to scaffold each other
- maintaining intersubjectivity/negotiating one's way through the task
- externalizing inner speech during cognitively demanding activities
- releasing tension/socializing.

These functions act to support immersion language learning and learning during the 'mainstream' (in the Canadian case, English) portion of the school day. How can multiple L1s be brought into classrooms that allocate half the day or more to teaching and learning in the immersion language? Here we turn to insights from regular classes with high concentrations of immigrant students. These insights are garnered from the work of researchers like Cummins. In a chapter written by Cummins and Chow, a grade 1 teacher from a progressive, innovative school in the greater Toronto area, the authors explain how students' home languages and cultures can been seen as 'potential resources for learning' (Chow and Cummins 2003: 33). In a school where English was the only language of instruction for a student body representing over 40 languages, the staff engaged in brainstorming about how to make those languages central to the learning process, based on a view of literacy as 'multidimensional and integrated with all aspects of students' lives inside and outside the school' (ibid.). They drew on Edwards' (1998) book, *The Power of Babel*, citing the following excerpt:

> While it is clearly very difficult for language learners to write in English in the early stages, there is no reason why they cannot draft, revise and edit in their first language. This approach allows them to develop their skills while joining in the same activity as their peers. It can also enhance their status in the class. Instead of emphasizing what they cannot do, the focus shifts to their achievements. (Edwards 1998: 67)

One way Chow and her colleagues decided to implement this approach was through dual-language books which the children carried between home and school. These books were accompanied by audio-cassettes for recording the stories both in English and the home language. They exposed students and their parents to English texts while permitting students to access prior knowledge through their L1. They enabled the school to let parents and students know that minority languages and cultures were valued and were seen as resources for the classroom and school. The dual-language book project affirmed the value of the L1 in both oral and written communication and helped to minimize the frustration that comes with an inability to express one's ideas or feelings adequately in the mainstream language. In order to be better informed about the students' homes, the teachers developed a questionnaire focusing on home literacy practices and recruited parents to help out in classrooms by telling some of their favorite stories in the home language or English in the class. Some families had L1 books that they were willing to share. These supplemented the multilingual books the school could acquire from publishers, books which were selected because of their repetitive language, colorful illustrations, and embedded academic concepts (related to science or math). The grade 1 students also wrote their own stories that were translated by older students in the school or by parents. The books were displayed outside the school office, helping to show new families registering their children for the next academic year that the school valued immigrant languages and cultures. The dual-language book project (and the story-telling events related to it) prompted students to transfer literacy skills from their home language to the school language, connect meanings across languages, create their own literature and art in two languages and publish their stories. Can the philosophy and values that underlie such a project prove applicable to the immersion context? We think that they can. Immersion education encourages concept development across two languages and literacy/language development across the curriculum; adding other home languages to the mix is consistent with these principles. Projects such as the one described above (see also Skourtou, Kourtis-Kazoullis and Cummins 2006) have affective as well as academic value and point the way to effective immersion practices in the twenty-first century.

Text B6.1
M. Swain and
S. Lapkin

Task B6.1.5

➤ See if you can think of some ways in which teachers can support the use of the home language in the classroom even though they themselves may not be speakers of that language. Consider in particular the primary or elementary school.

➤ Also, you might like to think about the demands which collaborations between the school and home may place on the resources and time of the parents. What are the implications of this level of home involvement for children from more disadvantaged backgrounds?

We have seen that immersion programmes can bring great benefits to both monolingual and bilingual children. Swain and Lapkin (2005) began with a review of the eight core features of immersion programmes initially identified by Swain and Johnson (1997). In doing this they pointed out different ways in which these core principles must now be interpreted, and explained how they need to change in order to remain faithful to their original goal of additive bilingualism if they are to take into account the increasingly diversified student population. They also summarized ways in which immersion programmes and multilingualism are compatible. In particular, there is now a considerable body of evidence to support the view that children who have developed literacy skills in more than one language will not be disadvantaged when learning another language. However, as we saw in Unit A6, many children do not have the advantage of participating in a programme that supports their bilingualism equally in both languages. In stark contrast, the following extract will explore literacy attrition in L1 of children in a submersion programme.

SOCIO-CULTURAL VARIABLES IN THE DEVELOPMENT OF BILITERACY

In Text B6.2, we will look at a community which constitutes a significant presence in Western Europe. Owing to the population explosion and high unemployment in Turkey, a large number of migrants left Turkey for different parts of the world (Middle East, Australia, Germany, the Netherlands) in the 1960s and 1970s (Backus 2004). This diaspora comprises mainly migrant workers from rural areas in Turkey such as central Anatolia, south-western Anatolia and the Black Sea. The early waves of migrants were mainly men and unskilled, while subsequent migration involved more women, who were recruited to work in factories. By 1994, there were close to 2.76 million Turkish people living in Europe, half of whom settled in Germany. Such a huge displacement of population is bound to have significant implications for society, both for the migrants and for the host country. One of the most immediate problems to confront these communities is schooling. What types of schools are available and are these schools able to cater to the newcomers?

In Text B6.2, we look at the children of these Turkish migrants who ended up living in the Netherlands and being submersed in majority schools learning L2, with minimal L1 support from home. In this extract, the authors Aarts and Verhoeven (1999) assessed the literacy skills of these children after full submersion in the elementary years. They tracked 222 Turkish students enrolled in 45 primary schools in the Netherlands. All the children were in Grade 8 of primary school and aged between 11 and 14. They were compared to 140 Dutch monolinguals matched for SES, age and sex. Another control group was 276 students from a primary school in Turkey. The objectives of the study were to:

- compare the literacy level of the children in L1 and L2 with the two control groups
- examine the relationship between school and functional literacy
- explore individual variation in the biliteracy levels of the Turkish children with regard to pupil, family and school characteristics.

Text B6.2
R. Aarts and
L. Verhoeven

R. Aarts and L. Verhoeven (1999) Literacy attainment in a second language submersion context. *Applied Psycholinguistics*, **20: 377–393.**

. . .

The present study offers a descriptive account of the levels of literacy attainment of Turkish children in the Netherlands by the end of primary school. The goals of the study were threefold. First, we wished to assess the school and functional biliteracy level of Turkish children in the Netherlands. We set out to compare the literacy level of these children, both in their L1 and L2, with the literacy levels of monolingual peers in Turkey and the Netherlands. Second, we wanted to discover if there were interrelationships between school and functional literacy in L1 and L2. Third, we wished to explore individual variation in the biliteracy levels of Turkish children in the Netherlands with regard to pupil, family, and school characteristics.

Design of the study

Text B6.2
R. Aarts and
L. Verhoeven

Subjects

In the Netherlands, 222 Turkish pupils enrolled in 45 primary schools participated in the research. They were randomly selected from primary schools throughout the country. All were in the final grade (grade 8) of primary school. Their ages varied between 11 and 14 years; the mean age was 12;7. Of the pupils, 54% were boys. The number of siblings varied between 0 and 9, the mean number of siblings was 3. The socioeconomic status of the children was generally low. One-third of the fathers and two-thirds of the mothers had not completed primary education: 20% of the mothers and 2.5% of the fathers were illiterate. Most (83%) of the mothers and 23% of the fathers did not work; 50% of the fathers and 13% of the mothers performed unschooled labor (i.e., they worked in factories or ran small shops). All the pupils had entered primary school in the Netherlands. Although a number of them were born in Turkey, they did not enter school there; they came to the Netherlands at a young age.

In addition to the group of Turkish pupils, a randomly selected group of 140 Dutch pupils participated in the research. The aim was to compare the level of functional literacy in Dutch as an L1 and as an L2. These children came from the same classrooms as the Turkish children. They were matched for socioeconomic background, age, and sex.

We also established a control group in Turkey comprised of 276 pupils at the end of primary school. The Turkish authorities allowed us to perform our investigation in six primary schools in Central Anatolia, the region where most of the Turkish immigrants in the Netherlands came from. The schools were located in a big city in the south and in a provincial town in the middle of Turkey. Schools in the center of town as well as schools in the poorer suburbs (*gecekondu*) were selected. In the control group, 52% were boys. The number of siblings varied between 0 and 8; the mean number of siblings was 3. The age of the pupils varied between 10 and 12 years; the mean age was 10;6.

The younger age of the Turkish control group has to do with two factors. The first factor is that Turkish primary school only includes five grades. Another option would have been to select students from secondary school. We decided against this because a large proportion of children in Turkey leave the school system after finishing primary school. According to figures of the OECD (1989) for the 1985/1986 school year, 98% of the children attended primary school, but only 54% of the children attended secondary school. The second reason for the age difference is that a large number of Turkish pupils in the Netherlands had to repeat a grade in primary school.

Task B6.2.1

> Aarts and Verhoeven's decision to use the younger Turkish cohort was unavoidable but, given the big age gap (ten to twelve and eleven to fourteen) between the Turkish control group and the Turkish–Dutch group, what methodological concerns might you have? (The difference in mean age is 25 months.)

Extension

Instruments

School literacy proficiency. To measure school literacy in Turkish we used the Turkish School Literacy Test; this test consists of five different tasks which assess various linguistic levels. At the grapheme level, a Word Decoding task was constructed in which a word was spoken as the child was shown four written word representations, one of which corresponded with the correct representation of the word. The child was asked to mark the correct representation. The task included a total of 35 items. At the word level, two tasks were constructed. The Word Spelling task, consisting of 35 items, required the child to mark an incorrect spelling out of four alternatives. In the Reading Vocabulary task, 36 items were offered in which a word was presented along with four definitions of the word, one of which was correct. At the sentence level, a Syntax task was developed, consisting of 31 items. In each item, four syntactic constructions were offered, one of which was correct. The child was asked to mark the incorrect constructions. Finally, at the textual level, a Reading Comprehension task was constructed which consisted of four text fragments and 19 multiple choice questions. For a detailed overview of this test, see Aarts, De Ruiter, and Verhoeven (1993). Table B6.2.1 presents a summary of the tasks and the Cronbach's alphas that were established after the administration of the tests in the Netherlands and in Turkey.

Table B6.2.1 Overview of the tasks of the Turkish School Literacy Test and Cronbach's alphas for the tasks as established after administration in the Netherlands and Turkey

Level	Task	n of items	Netherlands	Turkey
Grapheme	Word decoding	35	.73	.91
Word	Spelling	35	.86	.88
Word	Reading vocabulary	36	.79	.83
Sentence	Syntax	31	.78	.82
Text	Reading comprehension	19	.64	.78

To assess school literacy in Dutch, we obtained the results for the Turkish pupils on the Eindtoets Basisonderwijs [Final Assessment of Primary School], a standardized test which is administered to pupils at the end of primary school (see Uiterwijk, 1994). The results of two subtasks were used, one measuring grammatical abilities and the other measuring discourse abilities in written Dutch. The Grammatical Abilities task consisted of 60 multiple-choice items in the areas of vocabulary, spelling, and syntax. The Discourse Abilities task involved 60 multiple-choice reading comprehension items.

Functional literacy. The Functional Literacy Test was designed to measure the abilities and knowledge required to perform literacy tasks in everyday life. It has become evident that the literacy skills taught in schools may not be relevant to everyday literacy tasks. Spratt et al. (1991) developed the Household Literacy Assessment, an instrument composed of a series of tasks representing the sorts of literacy activities that arise in Moroccan households. The Household Literacy Assessment measured the children's ability to make sense of the written features of four items: a letter, a newspaper, an electricity bill, and a box of medicine.

Taking this test as an example, we developed our own functional Literacy Test. For our test we used items that are commonly found in Turkey and in the Netherlands; these included a letter, a page of a TV guide, the front page of a newspaper, an application form, and a map. Children encounter these items in everyday life; therefore the literacy activities these items require are functional activities. We gathered authentic material in Turkey and in the Netherlands. The tasks were constructed in a parallel fashion for the two languages. The 31 questions concerned, for example, the addressee and the sender, the time a certain program starts, the data of the newspaper, the place to sign the form, etc. The reliability of these tasks was established using Cronbach's alphas. Cronbach's alpha for the Functional Literacy Test in Turkish was .71 for the children in the Netherlands and .74 for the children in Turkey. Cronbach's alpha for the functional Literacy Test in Dutch was .70.

. . .

Text B6.2
R. Aarts and
L. Verhoeven

Task B6.2.2

➤ How are the functional literacy measurements different from the school-based literacy tasks? Do you think one is more difficult than the other?

Conclusions and discussion

Text B6.2
R. Aarts and
L. Verhoeven

The comparison of the acquisition of literacy by Turkish children in a L1 and L2 environment yields some interesting conclusions. Presenting these conclusions, we have to keep in mind that, although we tried to match the research and comparison groups as closely as possible with regard to region of origin, educational experience, and socioeconomic background, there were some significant differences between the groups. First of all, due to differences in the educational systems of Turkey and the Netherlands, our sample of Turkish children in the Netherlands was compared with a younger group of children in Turkey. Furthermore, there were undoubtedly differences regarding the social class of the family, the literacy level of the parents (e.g., more mothers in the Netherlands were illiterate), the quality of schooling, and pedagogical approaches. These differences should be kept in mind as we discuss our conclusions.

In general, the Turkish children in the Netherlands did not arrive at native like literacy proficiency levels in both Turkish and Dutch. They were two to three years behind in their literacy skills in Turkish when compared to Turkish children in Turkey. At the same time, they were substantially behind monolingual Dutch children on measures of literacy and school achievement in Dutch. In other words, the Turkish children in the Netherlands were incapable of competing with the monolinguals in either country.

Task B6.2.3

➤ In Unit A2, we discussed the problem of treating a bilingual like two separate monolinguals (Grosjean 1989). Think back to the issues we covered in Unit A2: what are some factors in this study which make such comparisons inappropriate?

With respect to the attainment of Turkish literacy, it should be taken into account that the children in the Netherlands had received only a limited amount of home language instruction in the Dutch schools. In general, word decoding did not seem to be a problem for the Turkish pupils in the Netherlands. Their scores on this task were as high as those of the pupils in Turkey. This may be due to the fact that word decoding is a basic skill, which is mastered by the children at the end of primary school, regardless of the language environment in which the children grow up. Also, it is true that learning to read Turkish is relatively simple, because of the shallowness of the Turkish orthography (cf. Oney & Goldman, 1984); once the basic system of phoneme–grapheme correspondence is mastered, one can read. Also, given the fact that both Turkish and Dutch make use of the Latin alphabet, it seems that decoding skills can be easily transferred from one language to the other (cf. Verhoeven, 1994). However, a word of caution should be offered, given the fact that our decoding measure reflected accuracy and not speed. Speed of word reading is a better predictor of reading comprehension; it is an achievement that requires practice and relates to the amount of time spent reading in the target language (cf. Stanovich, 1986). Therefore, it is entirely possible that the expatriate Turkish children could read Turkish words quite well but had limited comprehension because of effortful processing and therefore would not make continued progress in comprehension. On the reading comprehension task, the Turkish pupils in the Netherlands obtained similar scores as their younger peers in Turkey. Their current parity with the Turkish comparison group might reflect the fact that, since they are attending relatively poor schools, the children in Turkey in their fifth year of schooling are just emerging into the stage of fluent reading. It is also the case that the children in Turkey have more opportunities to read Turkish and thus develop fluency and comprehension-opportunities which inevitably are more limited in the Netherlands. On spelling, reading vocabulary, and syntax, the children in the Netherlands obtained reasonable scores, but their scores were substantially lower than those of their peers in Turkey. These tasks refer to typical school literacy skills, which are somewhat less fully mastered in a L2 submersion environment, in which only a limited amount of home language instruction is given. Turkish children in the Netherlands also obtained lower scores on functional literacy tasks than the children in Turkey. On these measures they also seemed to lag two to three years behind.

With respect to the development of literacy in Dutch as a L2, it is clear that Turkish children generally lagged behind their monolingual Dutch peers. On school literacy tasks, the differences were quite substantial. This finding conforms to the results of earlier studies (see Uiterwijk, 1994; Verhoeven, 1990; Verhoeven & Vermeer, 1985). On functional literacy tasks, however, the children in the Netherlands attained almost native-like performance. This finding shows that, although Turkish children lag behind in the acquisition of the Dutch language, Dutch schools succeed in teaching functional language skills in that language.

The study on individual variation points to some interesting findings. Home stimulation, parents' motivation for schooling, and children's self-esteem were the factors that most strongly related to the children's literacy level in both Turkish and Dutch. Home stimulation in particular appears to be a crucial factor. This result is consistent with the outcome of earlier studies that examined the relationship between the involvement of parents and the language and academic performance of their children (see Snow et al., 1991; Stevenson & Baker, 1987).

Another finding is that Turkish language instruction in the Netherlands turned out to be effective in enhancing the children's school literacy in the L1. The number

Text B6.2
R. Aarts and
L. Verhoeven

of Turkish books read by the child was also positively related to the acquisition of literacy in the L1. It is clear that sufficient support helps children maintain their L1. Furthermore, the children's school literacy in Dutch turned out to be related to their sociocultural orientation. This finding lends support to the claim that the degree of identification of minority children with the majority culture is a crucial factor for L2 development (see Lambert, 1967, 1978; McNamara, 1996). Furthermore, both the children's L1 and L2 literacy levels appeared to be negatively related to their age level. This finding shows that there are children in the Netherlands who continue school without being very successful over the years.

The present study also found that the children's school and functional literacy levels in Turkish and Dutch were interrelated. As such, empirical evidence for Cummins' interdependency hypothesis is found. It could be hypothesized that sufficient support to literacy in the L1 may enhance children's literacy skills in that language, which in turn may have a positive effect on their literacy skills in the L2. However, given that in this study we were dealing with cross-sectional data, we should be extremely cautious with causal reasoning (see also Verhoeven 1994).

Finally, our study made clear that children's functional literacy level in both the L1 and L2 was moderately related to their level of school literacy. School achievement in the Netherlands seems to share some important features with functional competence but does not necessarily include it. There is the risk that school practices make the beginning of literacy more difficult, especially for children with a low socioeconomic background. Because these children generally lack the full participation in literacy events in the home, they start primary school with little understanding of the meaning and purposes of written language. In most contemporary primary schools in the Netherlands, the social purposes of reading and writing remain outside the school setting. As a result, disadvantaged children learn that literacy is a function of an exclusive school activity. Repetition of classes and school drop-out may be the consequences of such a narrow scope of literacy. In order to overcome such problems, we recommend that children participate in small-group activities related to literacy experiences in which the (re)creation of written language is considered meaningful (cf. Verhoeven, 1996).

Naturalistic studies like the present one may be the first step towards answering questions about the attainment of literacy in a L2 environment. To arrive at a more complete understanding, we need longitudinal studies in which literacy data as well as detailed observations concerning the sociocultural and linguistic background of minority children are collected. In that case, causal explanations between background characteristics and differential patterns of L1 and L2 literacy under the conditions of submersion in a L2 environment can be uncovered.

Task B6.2.4

➤ In Text B6.1, we read about how teachers utilized the immigrant children's L1 as a resource and incorporated several tasks into the curriculum which involved them using their L1 skills. What are some ideas the school can adopt to provide support for these Turkish L1 children without major disruption to the other students?

Overall, it is not surprising to see poorer literacy attainment in the Turkish–Dutch group. This result is more or less representative for children of Turkish migrants across Europe. Backus (2004) reported that the educational profiles of Turkish children are generally not very good, with very few students moving on to higher education. He further observed that all over the Western world, low levels of proficiency in the majority language have been given as the main reason for this poor performance. In the case of the Turkish children, this poor proficiency cannot be attributed to negative attitudes as the same children actually preferred the majority language over Turkish. However, in spite of this very positive orientation to their new language, their language skills in Dutch remained poor. This led Backus to suggest that language proficiency is perhaps a red herring and that the more sinister and difficult problem is that of marginalization and inequality. He surmised that sociocultural structures in society, rather than language factors, are the more likely cause of the poor proficiency reported. As evidence for this, Backus pointed out how the low status of Turkish in the school curriculum extended to the attitudes of school teachers and the students who took the course. Such attitudes may also be reflected at the government level, as Backus (2004: 691) points out:

> It has been observed that, while many Western European governments express great interest in promoting multilingualism among their inhabitants, stimulating children to learn foreign languages such as English, German, and French, the official attitude towards the maintenance of immigrant languages is hostile, as it is commonly viewed as an obstacle to full integration.

Generally, the association of any language with low status and prestige does not help the cause of language maintenance for that language in the long run. As we saw in Unit A7, attitudes of the community and institutional support are both critical for the retention of minority languages. In the case of the Turkish children in the Netherlands, eroding literacy standards and the negative attitude of the wider community work together to accelerate the shift away from the minority language. However, Clyne (2006) identifies literacy as one of the factors which promotes language maintenance as it allows the speakers to increase their opportunities to use the language. Being able to read enables them to have access to the Internet and to read current discussions and books, and it also allows them to use the language in both formal and informal domains. Apart from this, being literate also enables them to keep in touch with the heartland and emigrant communities worldwide. Hence, the loss of literacy in one of the bilinguals' linguistic repertoire represents a significant loss in terms of opportunities and access to a different world.

Summary

There is no greater endorsement for bilingual communities than a bilingual education programme that is positively oriented to building up and maintaining bilingual proficiency as well as biliteracy skills across the school grades. However, for this to happen on a widespread basis, many societies would need to have policy changes at the official level that might well involve questioning our assumptions and attitudes at various points. We will explore these issues in Unit B7 when we look at the role that attitudes and beliefs play in shaping bilingual communication and bilingual identity.

Unit B7
Attitudes and bilingualism extended

In Unit A7, we explored various attitudinal factors which affect bilingual speakers. In particular, we examined how bilinguals may have different attitudes towards the different languages they speak, how being bilingual can transform attitudes and perceptions of society, and, more importantly, how society at large views bilingual communities. In this unit, we will read two extracts which expand on the themes we have already covered. The discussion in Unit A7 centred on attitude as a variable, and we considered various factors which impacted on it. Here, we will look at two concepts that are indirectly linked to attitude. The first extract, on accommodation theory, examines how language choice is both influenced by the interlocutor and moderated by the situation in which the conversation is taking place. The second, on language and identity, looks at how these symbols take on personal values we then use to define who we are.

ACCOMMODATION THEORY

We briefly introduced the application of Giles's Accommodation theory to the study of bilinguals in Unit A7. Our first extract represents one of the early attempts at bridging sociolinguistic research on language attitudes with Giles's (1973) socio-psychological approach to the study of language choice in bilinguals. Genesee and Bourhis (1988) integrated sociolinguistic approaches to making observations about language use (based on topic, setting, purpose, social and cultural background of the speakers) with the social psychological approach of examining speakers' motivations, cognition and feelings of group loyalty.

In this study, Genesee and Bourhis examined French Canadians' (FC), English Canadians' (EC) and French–English bilinguals' (FE) ratings of a dialogue in Quebec City. Using a modified matched-guise test (see Unit A7), they controlled the study strictly to focus only on four exchanges between either a French-speaking salesman and an English-speaking customer or an English-speaking salesman and a French-speaking customer. The dialogue was manipulated to reveal either accommodation or 'maintenance' at each turn of the conversation. In this context, maintenance refers to the speaker maintaining the use of the original language; that is, the speaker does not converge. This 'segmented dialogue' was then played to three groups of participants, namely FC, EC and FE, who were then asked to rate the speaker after each turn of the conversation on six person perception scales: *friendly*, *kind, considerate, competent, intelligent* and *honest*. This clever technique allowed the researchers to gauge and monitor change in the evaluation of the guises at every turn.

The extract presented here is a summary of the findings of an earlier study by Genesee and Bourhis (1982) conducted in Montreal. The study in Text B7.1 (Genesee and Bourhis 1988) sought to compare Quebec City (a largely francophone city) with this earlier study in Montreal, a more bilingual city with a different demographic and sociolinguistic profile. Situational factors were found to be very important in Montreal, but Genesee and Bourhis (1982) hypothesized that, given the different socio-structural make-up of Quebec City, the findings with respect to accommodation patterns might well be different. They argue that, given the stronger vitality of FCs in Quebec, there may be greater use of accommodation factors. Genesee and Bourhis's studies demonstrate how both sociolinguistic analysis and social psychological approaches explain the process of speech accommodation.

Task B7.1.1

Recall that adapting or accommodating speech towards that of the interlocutors is known as convergence and the reverse is known as divergence.

➤ Think about occasions in which you speak to people who have different language mannerisms to your own (e.g. in terms of accent, the vocabulary they use, their level of formality etc.). Do you ever find that you adapt your own speech to be more like theirs, or try, on the contrary, not to adapt?

F. Genesee and R. Bourhis (1988) Evaluative reactions to language choice strategies: The role of sociostructural factors. *Language and Communication*, 8 (3/4): 229–233.

Text B7.1
F. Genesee and
R. Bourhis

. . . In multilingual settings, convergence to an outgroup language may be an effective strategy for promoting interpersonal liking and for enhancing the climate of cross-cultural encounters where linguistic dissimilarities may otherwise be a serious stumbling block to intergroup harmony. This was demonstrated empirically in a study carried out in Montreal by Giles *et al.* (1973). In this study, it was found that bilingual English Canadian students perceived French Canadian bilinguals more favourably when the latter converged to English than when they maintained French. Moreover, the EC students were more likely to communicate in *French* with their FC interlocutor if the latter had previously converged to *English* than if he had maintained his communications only in French. Since both the EC and FC interlocutors communicated in each other's weaker language (the EC used French while the FC used English), this study showed that mutual language convergence could be used as a strategy to promote ethnic harmony even at the possible cost of communicative effectiveness.

Although speakers from different ethnolinguistic groups may wish to converge linguistically towards each other at times, there may be circumstances where speakers wish to *maintain* their own language or *diverge* linguistically from their interlocutor (Bourhis, 1979). Speakers may use speech maintenance and divergence because they dislike their interlocutors as individuals or because they wish to assert their group identity vis-a-vis outgroup interlocutors. Experimental evidence depicting language divergence and language maintenance has been obtained in bilingual settings such as Belgium (Bourhis et al., 1979) and Quebec (Bourhis, 1984a). In the Quebec setting, language maintenance was demonstrated in a series of field studies in Montreal in which it was found that overall 30% of the EC pedestrians sampled maintained English in response to a plea for directions made in French by an FC interlocutor (Bourhis, 1984a). Language maintenance was obtained even though the EC respondents had sufficient linguistic skills to utter a few words of French, as was made evident to the experimenter in follow-up interviews. Given the anonymity of these casual encounters indications were that English language maintenance was used by the ECs as a dissociative response to an interlocutor who was categorized as an outgroup member.

 Task B7.1.2

➤ Convergence and divergence is something we do subconsciously. Think about the people you interact with daily. Do you maintain the same style of communication with everyone in the same setting? Observe the way people communicate around you and identify instances of convergence and divergence.

There are limitations to studying the dynamics of language use from only one of the above perspectives at a time. By focusing on social norms and rules, the traditional sociolinguistic approach has tended to downplay or ignore the importance of social psychological factors such as the interlocutor's motives and cognitions. In turn, most of the empirical work using the social psychological approach has studied language strategies in settings which lack clear situational norms that could interact with the process of interpersonal accommodation (e.g. Giles et al., 1973; Bourhis, 1984a). An integration of the social psychological and sociolinguistic approaches would be concerned with how sociolinguistic norms are obeyed or broken as a function of speaker's motives, cognitions and feelings. For instance, in a cross-cultural encounter, speakers may converge not only because they personally like their interlocutor but also because they believe they should do so by virtue of their role positions, and perhaps also because as subordinate-group members they feel they should switch to the language of their dominant-group interlocutor.

. . .

 Task B7.1.3

➤ Consider the following situations:

- ■ an interaction between a patient and a doctor during a medical consultation
- ■ a chat between two colleagues.

What are some factors that may affect the type of convergence or divergence that may take place? Can you think of any other situations where it is clear that one party has to do the converging?

Text B7.1
F. Genesee and
R. Bourhis

Accordingly, we developed a segmented dialogue technique in which listeners give their impressions of each of two speakers after each speech turn in a conversational sequence heard on a tape recording. The assumption of this procedure is that listeners form impressions of speakers based on what they say, how they speak, and which language they use during the course of a conversation. Other experimental procedures elicit holistic perceptions of speakers after a sequence of speech turns. We have argued that the segmented dialogue procedure can be akin to real-life situations in which we overhear speakers engaged in conversations that consist of sequences of speech turns (Genesee and Bourhis, 1982). It follows, furthermore, that impressions of a speaker or speakers in real conversations can change as the conversation proceeds. Holistic procedures give the impression that perceptions and evaluations of others are holistic and static across speech turns. At the same time, the segmented dialogue procedure cannot claim to reveal the impressions of speakers actually engaged in face-to-face encounters. As Street (1985) points out there are reasons to believe that participants' (speakers') and observers' (listeners') impressions of the same speech behaviours are likely to differ because they attend to different aspects of the encounter. This must be borne in mind when interpreting the present results.

One aim of the present study was to replicate the major findings obtained by Genesee and Bourhis (1982). However, for reasons that will be made clearer later, the present research was conducted not in the bilingual setting of Montreal, as was the original study, but in the monolingual French setting of Quebec City. Consequently, it was possible to examine the importance of sociostructural differences in these two settings on the listeners' evaluative reactions to the language switching depicted in the stimulus dialogues. It is worthwhile to discuss the major findings from the Montreal research since these results will be used as a baseline for interpreting the empirical and conceptual contributions of the Quebec City results.

The conversational setting chosen by Genesee and Bourhis was that of a salesman/ customer encounter in a downtown Montreal retail store. The traditional residential, social and economic segregation of FCs and ECs in Montreal has meant that such encounters in downtown Montreal are perhaps the most likely casual setting in which they have a chance to interact in everyday life. In one of the Montreal studies, an FC salesman was portrayed serving an EC customer while in another study, an EC salesman was portrayed serving a FC customer. As controls, the verbal content of the dialogues was always the same and the salesman/customer roles were played by the same two bilingual actors in both studies. The dialogue sequences consisted of up to four speaker turns which evolved as follows: turn 1 = salesman speaks; turn 2 = customer speaks; turn 3 = salesman speaks; turn 4 = customer speaks. The salesman always began the conversation in his native language. Subsequent replies by the customer and salesman were systematically varied combinations of French and English language switches reflecting common patterns of language use heard in Montreal.

Task B7.1.4

➤ Think about some typical salesperson and customer encounters that you are familiar with. What are some of the routine interaction patterns that occur? Who does the greeting first? What are some predictable turns? Are these routines likely to be different for different settings (e.g. interchanges in departmental stores, markets or privately owned shops)?

Text B7.1
F. Genesee and
R. Bourhis

The results showed that listeners' reactions to the French/English language choices in the scenarios depended on a complex interaction of four factors: (1) situational language norms, (2) speech accommodation, (3) ingroup favouritism, and (4) sociostructural factors. Each of these factors will be discussed briefly in turn.

(1) Situational language norms

It was shown in a number of studies conducted in Quebec in the 1970s that anglophones usually maintained English in the work place when interacting with francophone co-workers, while the latter usually switched to English when interacting with anglophones (Quebec, 1972). Likewise, attitudes toward the English and French languages typically favoured English over French even among French-speaking Montrealers (Genesee and Holobow, 1989). However, in public encounters, such as salesman/customer transactions, norms which hold that the 'customer is always right' imply that salespersons should switch to the native language of their client (Scotton and Ury, 1977). Field observations carried out in Montreal as well as surveys and experimental studies have shown that indeed FCs and ECs expect salespersons to use English with EC customers and French with FC customers (Bourhis, 1983; Domingue, 1978; Sandilands and Fleury, 1979). In line with this situational norm, Genesee and Bourhis (1982) found that FC and EC subjects downgraded the salesman (depicted as an EC or FC) who violated the situational norm by failing to switch to the language of his customer. At the same time, the FC salesman was not upgraded by either the EC or FC listeners when he switched to the language of his EC customer as this was expected according to the situational norm. However, when the salesman was depicted as an EC, he was upgraded if he switched to the language of his FC customer. It seems that as a member of a traditionally high status group the EC salesman in Montreal was rewarded for converging linguistically to the traditionally low status FC speaker. Taken together, the subjects' reactions could be interpreted in terms of both situational norms and sociostructural factors.

Task B7.1.5

➤ As the extract is densely packed with findings, it may be useful to review some of the key results in Montreal by considering the following questions:

▪ In the salesman–customer interaction, what are the expected norms for both FC and EC? What are the consequences should the norms be violated?
▪ Is the FC upgraded when he switches to the language of the EC customer? Why?

■ Is the EC upgraded when he switches to the language of the FC customer?
Why?

(2) Speech accommodation

Text B7.1
F. Genesee and
R. Bourhis

Research on speech accommodation suggests that language convergence between the salesman and the customer would be evaluated positively in comparison to language maintenance, regardless of whether the convergence was in favour of French or English (Giles et al., 1987). Indeed, results obtained by Genesee and Bourhis revealed that language choices in turn 4 were rated mainly in terms of speech accommodation even though language choices in turns 2 and 3 had been evaluated mostly in terms of situational norms. When both the salesman and the customer had maintained their respective ingroup languages at the beginning of the dialogue (turns 1–3), subsequent language choices of the customer in turn 4 were evaluated differentially. The listeners perceived the customer (EC and FC) negatively when he maintained his ingroup language in turn 4, but he was perceived relatively favourably when he converged to the outgroup language of the salesman. In contrast, when the salesman and customer had previously demonstrated mutual language convergence (the EC and FC each converged to the other's language), subsequent language choices by the customer in either language during turn 4 seemed emptied of their divisive ideological content and had no differential impact on EC and FC listeners' evaluations. Thus, mutual language convergence at the onset of the dialogue seemed to foster a climate of mutual good will and respect between the interlocutors.

Task B7.1.6

➤ What is the difference in significance for situational norms between turn 1 and turn 4?

➤ What are the listeners' responses to the EC and FC customer who maintained ingroup language in turn 4?

➤ What is the effect of mutual convergence at the onset on ratings in turn 4?

(3) Ingroup favouritism

Text B7.1
F. Genesee and
R. Bourhis

Intergroup research conducted by Tajfel and Turner (1979) has shown that the mere act of categorizing people into 'us' and 'them' is sufficient to trigger prejudice and discrimination against outgroup members and favouritism towards ingroup members. In the Montreal setting, language not only serves as an important cue for categorizing FCs and ECs as ingroup or outgroup members, but is also a salient badge of ethnic identity and group pride (Bourhis, 1984b). On the basis of ingroup favouritism, Genesee and Bourhis (1982) expected both FC and EC respondents not only to favour representative speakers of their own group but also to favour the use of their ingroup language over the outgroup language. Their results showed that when the customer was depicted as an EC and the salesman as an FC, both FC and EC listeners rated speakers of their own group more favourably than outgroup speakers. Moreover, when the customer was depicted as an FC and the salesman as an EC, EC listeners showed a strong preference in favour of English language usage. These latter results suggest that rather than responding to the situational norm alone, the EC listeners also displayed ingroup favouritism in their evaluations of the speakers. This was not the case for FC listeners whose evaluative reactions mostly reflected concern with the speaker's adherence to the situational norm.

⭐ **Task B7.1.7**

When the salesman was a FC, both EC and FC listeners rated speakers of their own group more favourably – that is, FC listeners rated the FC salesman more positively and EC rated the EC customer more favourably.

➤ Which language was preferred by EC listeners when the salesperson was EC?

➤ Which language was preferred by FC listeners when the salesperson was EC?

(4) Sociostructural factors

The relative position of language groups in the social structure may affect the use and evaluation of language choices in cross-cultural encounters. In this regard, Giles et al. (1977) have proposed a framework for assessing the strength and vigour of language groups in multilingual settings in terms of three different characteristics: demographic strength, institutional support, and the social status ascribed to each group. Using such a framework, language groups can be classified roughly as low, medium or high in ethnolinguistic vitality. It has been suggested that the language choices made by speakers from different language groups may differ according to the vitality of their respective groups (Bourhis and Sachdev, 1984). In particular, the language of the high vitality group is likely to be dominant in cross-cultural encounters involving members of high and low vitality groups.

As regards the ethnolinguistic situation in Quebec [province], the FC majority (83% of the 6 million population) has long been the economic 'underdog' relative to the EC minority (10% of the population). Consequently, the English language has dominated the French language in status value and as the primary language of business and economic advancement in Quebec (d'Anglejan, 1984). The predominance of English has been especially evident in the bilingual city of Montreal (population: 2.5 million) where anglophones form 20% of the city's population; francophones make up 60%; and allophones, whose mother tongue is neither French nor English, make up the remainder. Thus, despite their minority demographic position, Montreal ECs have traditionally enjoyed a higher ethnolinguistic vitality than the FC majority in Montreal.

However, discontent among majority group francophones led to forceful demands for linguistic and political changes in Quebec during the 1960s and 1970s. This led to the election of the pro-independence Parti Quebecois in 1976 and the passage of Law 101 in 1977 making French the only official language in Quebec (d'Anglejan, 1984). Anglophone minority opposition to the passage of Law 101 was centred in Montreal and was influential in changing aspects of the law (Coleman, 1984). It was in the after-math of this tense, unstable intergroup situation that the original Genesee and Bourhis (1982) study was conducted.

Although the sociostructural context in which the Genesee and Bourhis research was conducted most likely played an important role in determining the outcome of the study, a proper assessment of the importance of sociostructural factors requires

Text B7.1
F. Genesee and
R. Bourhis

investigations in contexts with different sociostructural characteristics. Therefore, a replication of the Montreal study in Quebec City provided an ideal opportunity to more clearly assess the relative importance of sociostructural factors in determining evaluative reactions to the dialogues in both intergroup settings.

In contrast to Montreal, Quebec City (population: ½ million) has a very small anglophone population, making up only 3% of the population, while francophones form the overwhelming majority (96% of the city's population), As such, Quebec City is the most homogeneous francophone city in North America. Social contact between francophones and anglophones is infrequent and French is the customary lingua franca of casual public encounters involving members of the two language groups, However, despite its minority language position, English has long enjoyed much status as a language of work and upward mobility owing to the traditionally high economic status of anglophones in Quebec City. According to a recent sociolinguistic survey conducted among FCs in Quebec City, French has only recently supplanted English as the language of work in the higher echelons of industry (Hardt-Dhatt, 1982). Results from this survey also showed that FCs had positive attitudes towards the use of both French and English, though they felt that French was a more important language than English. Finally, the FC respondents surveyed in the Hardt-Dhatt study reported that they felt that language conflict was more acute in Montreal than in Quebec City. Overall, it is reasonable to conclude that FCs enjoy a much stronger ethnolinguistic vitality than ECs in Quebec City and that the patterns of intergroup relations between francophones and anglophones have been much more stable and harmonious in Quebec City than in Montreal.

. . .

Task B7.1.8

➤ What is the difference in the demographic composition of Quebec City and Montreal?

➤ How does the demographic difference affect the language vitality in both cities?

➤ Do you see a relationship between demographic composition and language vitality in your own context?

Text B7.1
F. Genesee and
R. Bourhis

Two complementary studies were conducted to address the above issues. In Study 1, the salesman was depicted as an FC while the customer was portrayed as an EC. In Study 2, the salesman was depicted as an EC and the customer as an FC. The present studies were conducted during 1980–82, two years after the Montreal studies. The time period during which both sets of studies were conducted can be characterized as the aftermath of Bill 101. During this time, the French language gained relative ascendancy in the province while the implementation of Bill 101 was adjusted somewhat to better accommodate concerns voiced by the anglophone community (Gagnon, 1988). Given the bilingual nature of Montreal where anglophones are most concentrated in the province, it remains that linguistic tensions are always felt more sharply there than in Quebec City (d'Anglejan, 1984).

The same study went on to discuss the findings for Quebec City, where two studies were conducted. In study one, an FC played the role of the salesperson, and in study two, an EC played the role of the salesperson. Each listener rated one dialogue and there were six possible sequences in each study. In the first study, the FC salesman always spoke first and always used French in the first turn and the EC salesman did likewise in the second study.

 Task B7.1.9

➤ What other situational norms can you think of which would be suitable for such a study in specific multilingual communities? Here, it may be useful to think about situations where it is likely for participants in the speech event to use more than one language.

The Quebec City study also found that situational norms were significant in predicting the ratings of the listeners. Regardless of language background, both FC and EC salesmen were downgraded if they failed to converge to the native language of the customer. Language convergence was seen by the listeners as an effective way of promoting positive interpersonal relationships between ethnic groups. However, unlike in the Montreal study, where there is a preference for English when the salesperson was EC, in Quebec City there tended to be an overall trend to favour French.

The Montreal bilinguals (native in English, fluent in French) also responded differently when compared to the Quebec City bilinguals (native in French, fluent in English). (Recall that these groups are different from the FCs and ECs as they are completely fluent in both languages.) In the Montreal study, the bilinguals reacted negatively to the French salesperson who continued using French with the English customer but in the Quebec City study, the bilinguals did not show this negativity towards the English salesperson for maintaining English with the French customer. In both studies, the EC groups were more likely to show ingroup bias by rating EC speakers higher. Genesee and Bourhis argued that the perceived threat to group identity and the overall nature of relations between English and French Canadians in the province of Quebec may be the reason for ingroup display in ECs. The FCs' tolerance for English may be due to the fact that francophones are less threatened or English still enjoys a form of covert prestige in Quebec. The response of the Montreal bilinguals is interesting as it seems to indicate that bilingualism on its own may not foster more tolerance to the outgroup as we discussed in Unit A7. Other socio-cultural factors, such as the perceived threat of an ethnic majority, may contribute to feelings of alienation and insecurity. As pointed out by Genesee and Bourhis (1988: 247):

In any event, it would seem that bilingualism *per se* does not necessarily foster more tolerant views towards outgroup language use in bilingual settings as initially proposed in the literature (Lambert 1977). Rather, the present results suggest that both the sociostructural position of the ingroup along with individual feelings of threat among group members may be important determinants of bilingual speakers' attitudes towards use of an outgroup language.

Studies on Accommodation theory indicate that we use language as a symbol to channel and guide our attitudes both to members of our communities and to those from without. Sometimes, the outcomes may be trivial but often they can have severe consequences. For example, Altarriba and Morier (2004) reported that bilinguals presented themselves in different ways depending on the language used and they often use their second language to serve as a distancing function in psychological assessment and diagnosis. Given the tendencies for psychological consultations and practices to be conducted in the language of the majority, are minority speakers able to have access to good psychological treatment in their second languages?

In a more dramatic example, Dixon et al. (1994) reported on how a Black Afrikaans-speaking criminal suspect in South Africa was more likely to be judged not guilty by students listening to the audiotape if the suspect converged in English to his white interrogator. However, if he diverged away in Afrikaans, the opposite effect resulted. This clearly has implications in a court setting where jurors make decisions about innocence or guilt.

Generally, studies on Accommodation theory show repeatedly that the way we use language to accommodate to people around us provides us with a mirror to gauge the status, function and vitality of a language in any given society. In the next extract, we will turn to look at how language is often used as a symbol to communicate an individual's identity.

LANGUAGE, CULTURE AND IDENTITY

Over the last few decades, there has been much debate about the relationship between language and identity and there is some consensus that language is a marker of ethnic identity (Giles et al. 1977). Researchers who support this hypothesis also argue that speakers who have strong group identification are likely to consider language to be an important symbol of their identity, and this identification may translate into greater use of the language itself. Thus, language identity has often been viewed as an important gauge of language vitality in any given community (Giles and Johnson 1987).

Apart from the significance it has for the community, living with two languages and cultural worlds means that, to a large extent, being bilingual means being bicultural, and several studies have explored the impact of this on the formation of identity in bilinguals. Though the process of being bilingual does not necessarily lead to biculturalism, it is commonly accepted that such a process does require a synthesis of the cultural systems the bilingual is exposed to. This has been known to have varying effects ranging from a sense of anomie, of not fitting in anywhere, to a successful creation of a blended culture. In the next extract, we will read about the role language plays in the life of ten third-generation Punjabi children living in England. Despite their diminishing proficiency in Punjabi or Mirpuri (spoken in the Mirpur region of northern Pakistan), the languages still carry for them a special significance. The methodology adopted in this study is markedly different from the more quantitative approach in Extract B7.1 as Mills (2001) adopted a more ethnographic framework using qualitative analysis based on a semi-structured interview.

Background of the study

The participants of the study were ten third-generation Punjabi children who were fluent in English and also spoke, to varying degrees, Punjabi or Mirpuri and Urdu (the official language of Pakistan). They also knew some Arabic, used in reading the Qur'an from their religious classes. The children interviewed were Amina (age five), Naseem, Shaida (both aged eight), Arafa (nine), Ahmed (twelve), Safina (thirteen), Abida, Zahid (both fourteen), Hanif (eighteen) and Uzma (nineteen). They were all born and educated in England.

Mills used a semi-structured interview methodology as she was particularly interested in promoting reflection on language use. She used the following questions to guide the interview (2001: 385):

- What term do the participants use to describe their languages other than English?
- What are the participants' attitudes and feelings towards the different languages in their repertoire?
- What expectations have been placed upon them, by themselves and others, in maintaining their cultural heritage languages?
- What specific language maintenance strategies have come about as a result of these attitudes and how do they operate?
- What are the opinions of other members of the family in relation to language maintenance?

The interview session was tape-recorded, and since this study was part of a larger ongoing project which involved the mothers of the ten children, the researcher was a familiar figure in the children's lives.

The children were all asked for their proficiency and competence in the different languages, and all except for one (Hanif) noted their lack of fluency in both Punjabi and Urdu. All the children cited English to be the language they were most at ease in and all had parents who strongly encouraged them to maintain their proficiency in their other languages.

Task B7.2.1

➤ In multilingual settings, bilinguals often have to negotiate many identities and many languages. Some manage to integrate both these distinct worlds successfully but some may go through a temporary phase of feeling 'conflicted'. What do you think are some issues of identity that they may face?

Jean Mills (2001) Being bilingual: Perspectives of third generation Asian children on language, culture and identity. *International Journal of Bilingual Education and Bilingualism*, **4 (6): 396–399.**

Text B7.2
J. Mills

Language and identity

Four children – Zahid, Ahmed, Hanif and Uzma – indicated a much wider awareness of the potential of their languages and the functions of languages generally and conceptualised their views in different ways. For Zahid, as noted previously, these were the attitudes that Punjabi was a signal of being Pakistani and that retaining it could lead to a career:

> We've got to speak it sometimes in our life like Christians speak English most of the time so Pakistani people they speak Punjabi most of the time . . . like I said extra GCSE in Urdu and maybe, like, my mom's got a friend and she is an interpreter and you know she goes down to the police stations and she interprets . . . an extra like on the CV.

Ahmed, too, cited an instrumental reason, but couched this in affective terms not as a career aspiration like Zahid:

> Well, if you can speak more than one language you can help other people who are stuck for languages, like they only know the one, and you can, if you want to work around the world you want to help other people like, if you say, 'Are you alright?' instead of watching them suffer.

He also allied himself with the desire to maintain Pakistani culture and used a humanistic metaphor:

> It's important to keep your culture going and not leaving it dying in the past. Sort of like, if you carry on with the language and teach your children the language then it will just carry on.

It is not questioned here that one might abandon this culture for another (British?). It is axiomatic that the way to do this is to pass the language on to one's children.

The children, then, reflect the notion that culture, language and heritage are mutually interdependent and relate to an individual's identity. As Zahid put it:

> Most of my family members know English, although a little bit of it, but it's just like a part of your life not being there.

This was further explored by Uzma in again introducing the notion of multiple identities, which in this explanation extends to the community as well:

> I think being able to speak more than one language is a skill and maybe to an extent like a part of who we are because the fact that we are able to speak other languages is part of our identity as individuals and maybe as a society and that I think is important to achieve . . .

There are two aspects for which language is an identifier for an individual and for a local community, and a further reminder to the person of their 'pastpresent' (Bhabha, 1994: 7), that is how one makes sense of the present by looking to the past. Here, too, the emphasis was on being able to help others:

> I think the fact that you can speak other languages helps you to interact with other people and just get points across to them. Maybe just help them as well. Maybe advancing their achievements or whatever they want to do and just help them.

Hanif explained the cultural link in linguistic terms in an acute appreciation of the total context:

> In Urdu and Punjabi one word can mean ten different things . . . with Punjabi or Urdu you have to look at the whole sentence, you have to look at the circumstances, you have to look at the person saying it to you and then you understand exactly what's been said. But with English it's just a language . . . Punjabi and Urdu are part of the culture. You can't have the language on its own, you have to have the culture behind it.

It is intriguing that for this young man his awareness of the linguistic context of an utterance appears only to come into play with his Asian languages, not with English which is just a language. Thus, although he is fluent in English and born in this country it is these languages that speak most powerfully of a particular culture and, in turn, of a country:

> When you go to Pakistan or you go to India . . . it's like you feel you can see the language in what they've done, in the people, in the buildings . . . You can see the culture behind the language and the language behind the culture. When we're here they are two separate things . . . if you speak Urdu here it's not the same as speaking it back home . . . with Urdu, Punjabi, with any language, if you take it away from the country, you take the bit away from the language.

Potent as it remains in Hanif's terms it is as if the power of the language–culture relationship is diluted once the language is removed from its territory, that culture has much broader associations than being located in individuals' ethnicity.

Consequently, when the children were asked what term they used to describe their languages and why, their answers reflected some of the positions mentioned above. At the same time, there was no unanimity in readily accepting the term 'mother tongue' nor in specifying which language had primacy in their lives. Abida, for example, refused to specify a term and then cited English as her first language, while Hanif also would not be precise and he had particular reasons:

I count them all the same. A language is a language . . . If someone says, 'What is your language?' I don't say 'English', I say, 'I can speak Urdu, I can speak Punjabi and English . . . Take which one you want'.

In excluding the feeling of ownership of a language Hanif seems also to have excluded tensions and conflicts which were a feature of the mothers' transcripts. In his explanation there is the sense that all his languages are part of him in an undemanding way. Uzma, in contrast, preferred Urdu although she recognised that the family spoke Punjabi more. Urdu was chosen:

Because that's the language of Pakistan and that's what, if you're living in Pakistan, that's the language you study in and that is predominantly the language that you are taught at home.

Thus, as with Hanif, the language confirms one in maintaining those links with Pakistan, not just at regional level, which would be the effect of Punjabi, but at national and academic level through the country's official language, Urdu, which is also its literary language.

Ahmed chose the term 'home language' and for him 'home' meant two things:

Because Pakistan, even though I was born here, I class Pakistan as my home country. That's where the language originates from so I call it my home language. We speak it at home and like with my family and friends, well some friends. So, I call it my home language because that's one of the languages that I like to express things. In Pakistan you get much more people speaking Mirpuri right, so my dad came from there he bought it with him and then we started speaking here. So it's from my dad's home country as well. I like to class [it] as my home country and therefore my home language.

Here, once more, is the pastpresent 'woven into the text of everyday living. Finding a "home" within an adopted country then becomes a journey of learning to understand past experiences in order to clarify the present' (Rassool, 1997: 190).

Thus, although Ahmed had never been there, he saw his languages as affiliating him in terms of belonging to a country, to Pakistan:

I'd say I come from England but I like to, I say I was born in England but that I come from Pakistan because that's where my family originates from.

There is an intriguing ability of managing two ideas, recognising two affiliations without the sense of anguish and struggle evident in the testimony of some of the mothers. Similarly, for Uzma, Urdu was a crucial signal:

It tells me where we originate from.
JM: Where then in fact do you feel you belong?
U: I would say here because I was born here and the way I've been brought up is very much different to if I was born in Pakistan . . . I wouldn't say westernised because I don't think I am and I don't think that's the right word to use either but it is different from being brought up in Pakistan. But at the same time, if somebody was to ask me who I am my first response would be Muslim because that is my religion and that is what I believe I

am, my religion comes first and then it would be British and then Pakistani after that because it is my ethnic origin. And because of that, because I do feel that, because of my ethnicity I feel that is where the language comes in[;] to maintain the ethnicity you have to have the language. And if you haven't got the language then basically you've lost that identity, the origin.

There is for Uzma a gradation, with religion (personal belief, values) taking precedence over citizenship, which, in turn, comes before ethnicity. However, what is interesting is that this young woman can define herself in three different but coexisting ways.

Hanif finally gave a very similar answer after searching through his responses and his ambivalent feelings to the associations of the word 'home'. In this response there was very much the sense that learning was achieved by having to articulate a previously unacknowledged stance:

> I don't really know because here's family, there's less family here though. In Pakistan I feel closer there because there's more family. If I went to another country . . . I'd miss home, what I call home would be Pakistan. I class this as home and I class Pakistan as home . . . I don't feel close to any country really. It's like England is England, Pakistan is Pakistan, my family live here, my family live there . . . If somebody said to me, 'Who are you?' I'd say I'm a Muslim, I believe in God. I don't say I'm Pakistani.

Task B7.2.2

> ➤ Hanif (eighteen) and Uzma (nineteen) are both much older than Ahmed (twelve) and Zahid (fourteen). What developmental trends can you see in the way they describe their relationship with the languages they speak?

In their own ways, all the children explained the indispensable role that their other languages play in their lives despite the fact that they were functionally not proficient in these languages. However, this judgement is based on self-report data and, as we saw in Unit A7, self-report data can be unreliable, especially when bilinguals view language mixing negatively, as was the case for this group of children. We also saw in their own moving accounts how important the languages were to them in interpreting their heritage, in understanding the context of their family, and in their relationships with the community. In the words of Uzma, who was nineteen:

> And because of that, because I do feel that, because of my ethnicity I feel that is where the language comes in[;] to maintain the ethnicity you have to have the language. And if you haven't got the language then basically you've lost that identity, the origin.

More significantly, Hanif's resistance in prioritizing one language as a primary language indicates clearly how all the languages are integrated in his identity. This echoes Ghuman's (1994) findings that second-generation British Asian adolescents possess what he calls a 'hyphenated identity', a blend of both British and Asian cultural ways.

Summary

In this unit, we read two very different extracts. The first extract was a quantitative study looking at integrating sociolinguistics and social psychological frameworks. The study by Genesee and Bourhis (1988) attempted to generalize the findings from a very controlled and defined setting to a wider context. In contrast, Mills (2001) took a different approach. In Mills's study, we heard multilingual children between the ages of five and nineteen articulating their feelings and thoughts about the significance of speaking their parents' languages. In spite of the fact that they were third-generation children facing the pressure of language shift, they attributed strong and positive emotional roles to the languages of their parents. The contexts of the two studies are very different. Quebec City and Montreal both represent communities where, although there may be tension between the French- and English-speaking communities, neither of the languages is seriously threatened. In the case of the third-generation children in Mills's study, the chances of Punjabi, Mirpuri, Urdu or written Arabic being transmitted to the fourth generation are limited. What the study brings home is that achieving language maintenance requires more than simply the positive attitude of the individual or the will of the parents. Without adequate socio-structural support, it is likely that we will continue to see children such as those in Mills's study slowly move towards passive bilingualism and, subsequently, to monolingualism.

SECTION C
Exploration

Preface
Guidelines for collecting data
and writing up reports

In Part C of this book, there are a number of activities and tasks which involve collecting data or making observations with human participants. In some cases, you are then asked to write up your findings in the form of a report. In this preface, we firstly discuss the ethical considerations that must be taken into account when undertaking empirical research, and secondly we discuss the standard formats of report writing which are observed in the social sciences.

ETHICAL CONSIDERATIONS WHEN CONDUCTING RESEARCH

In any study which involves asking people for information, or collecting other kinds of data from them, you need to consider the ethical implications of what you are doing. Many institutions in the world today have very strict guidelines about the conduct of ethical research. Because these tend to come out of the medical model of research, they may initially appear unnecessary for social science research. However, the principles that underlie all ethical guidelines are very important to understand, and apply equally in social science research. The single most crucial principle is that the people you are involving in your research should understand what you are going to do, and any possible implications of this. This concept is generally known as *informed consent*.

You will find that you need to approach speakers (adults or children) for a lot of the studies suggested in this section. You need to bear in mind that all your participants, whether adults or children, are not obliged to help you and they participate in the study on a purely voluntary basis. Hence, it is very important that all the usual rules of consideration and politeness are observed when interacting with your participants. The first thing you need to do is to check whether the educational institution you are enrolled in has its own procedures and proformas which need to be followed or used. If this is the case, then you should discuss these with your lecturer and follow them as appropriate. However, if your institution does not have its own ethical guidelines, or you are planning to conduct this research for your own interests, and not as part of a course, you should follow the guidelines outlined below.

OBTAINING INFORMED CONSENT

Obtaining informed consent for child participants

Most higher education and other research and education institutions require anyone who is conducting research to obtain informed consent from their participants. This is particularly important with children, in which case you need to obtain the parents' consent. You need to assure the parents of the child that you are not going to exploit the child, or use the data in any way that is inappropriate. It is also very important to ensure that the parent does not in any way feel forced into agreeing to participate. This participation should be entirely voluntary, and if they do not want their child to participate, you should immediately accept their decision and not try to change their mind.

In addition to obtaining permission from the parent, it is important to obtain permission from the child also. This becomes increasingly important as children get older as they must be willing to take part in your study if it is to be successful. Ideally, therefore, depending on the age of the child, informed consent should be obtained from both the parent and the child.

Once the parent and child have agreed in conversation, we suggest that you provide them with a letter along the following lines asking them to agree to the activities you are going to undertake with the child. This must be done in advance of the actual recording. An example is given below, although you may need to change this letter to suit your purposes, and depending upon whether you know the parents and children involved well or not. If the participants do not speak English you will need to provide a translation of this letter in a language that they understand.

A very important aspect of informed consent is that the participants must feel able to withdraw both themselves and their data from the study at any time, without prejudice. If this happens, you must not make any attempt to coerce your participant into continuing, or make them feel uncomfortable, and you must, if they request it, return to them any data you have collected, and not use those data in any way.

Sample letter

Dear (name of parent/s),

My name is (**your name**) and I am currently learning about bilingualism and how children become bilingual. I am interested in (**specify what you want to do with the participant**). I would be most grateful if you would allow me to (**record/observe/interview**) your child (**interacting either with yourself, or with me, for this purpose**).

I would like to assure you that the recording will be used solely for the purposes of my own research, and no one else will have access to the recording or to the transcription. I would be happy to provide you with a copy of the recording and/or the transcription if that would be of interest to you.

Yours sincerely,
(Your name)

I agree to (**your name**) recording my child and understand that this will be used solely for the purposes of his/her research. I understand that I may withdraw consent at any time without any adverse consequences.

Signed   _____   (parent)

Signed   _____   (you)

You should take two copies of the letter with you, one to give to the family, and one for you to keep.

With older children (over about the age of ten or eleven) you should prepare a simplified version of this letter for the child to sign.

Obtaining informed consent from adults

Obtaining informed consent is also necessary when your participants are adults, and where you are interviewing them or recording them, or observing them for a period of time. In general, no one should be coerced into participating in any study. Always seek permission!

You can use a modified version of the letter above for your adult participants.

In some cases, you may not wish to divulge precisely what you intend to do with your participants if this may influence their language behaviour. In these cases, you do not need to give your precise objectives, but ideally you should explain, after you have completed the data collection, what it is you are interested in.

MAINTAINING ANONYMITY

It is important in research to maintain the anonymity of participants, so you should not write the name of the child or family on the tape, but rather assign some kind of code to it so that the participants are not identifiable. This is important also when you transcribe your data – do not use the participants' names or, in the case of children, the names of their parents. Always use a pseudonym or a code. You should state that you are using such a pseudonym or code in any written material which derives from the interviews or recordings, and it is crucial that you do so.

If you are using questionnaires, you have to make sure that unnecessary information that can identify the participants is omitted.

MAINTAINING CONFIDENTIALITY

All materials and the contents of the recordings or interviews should remain confidential. Although the findings can be shared, you should take care that the identity of the participants is protected at all times, especially if the discussion is of a sensitive nature.

MAINTAINING GOODWILL

In all interactions, note that you are leaving an impression of language researchers in general. A positive experience with you will mean it is likely that other researchers will be received well, while a negative experience may cause your participants to distrust other researchers. Hence, it is important that you maintain good relationships with your participants at all times, acknowledge their help and provide follow-up explanations, all of which are an important part of building up goodwill in the community. A follow-up thank-you letter will never go amiss.

GUIDELINES FOR WRITING UP THE REPORT

The following are some brief guidelines which you can consider when writing up your project. There are several texts available if you need a detailed guide on how to write each section of the report. A very useful text that provides practical tips on organization and language use in research report writing is Weissberg, R. and Buker, S. (1990) *Writing up research* (Englewood Cliffs, NJ: Prentice Hall), but there are numerous texts on linguistics, social science and educational research which provide guidelines about this.

Step-by-step guide to writing a report

There are five main sections to a report:

Abstract – This is approximately 150–200 words long. It states the rationale for the project and gives a brief idea as to the nature of the project, the findings and the implications. It is a summary to orient your reader before the main report. (This appears first in the report but it is usually written last.)

Literature review – The related research (literature) is introduced so that the motivation for the study can be discussed. You need to identify the issues which are directly relevant to the aim(s) of your study and the rationale for why you are conducting the study. Tight, concise writing is needed here as you usually have to complete your discussion in 1000 to 1500 words.

The first thing to do is to carry out a search for relevant research in the specific area of your interest. The easiest way to do this to use databases in the library. The most productive database for linguistics research is the LLBA (Linguistics and Language Behavioural Abstracts) database. Try to read at least six to ten articles which are relevant to the study.

Method – This is a brief discussion of the methodology you used – that is, who your participants are, how the study was conducted and the materials used. Again, clear and concise writing is very important. Usually, a methodology section follows the following format:

- participants
- materials used
- procedures.

Results and discussion – Here, you comment on the results obtained and, if necessary, explain how figures are arrived at. Note that tables and figures help in presenting the information but do not take the place of prose. (They do not explain themselves!) Number and label all tables and figures. In discussing the results, it is important to do three things:

- Identify where the results are obtained from (e.g. 'As can be seen from Table 2 . . .').
- Identify the findings ('Figure 2 indicates that six-year-olds are more likely to . . .').
- Comment on the findings – here, you go through the results pointing out the generalizations and the implications.

Relate the discussion back to the research introduced in the literature review. Are your findings the same as or different from other claims? If there are differences, can you explain why? It is customary to suggest directions for future research in the conclusion (1000 words).

References and appendices (these are not included in the word count) – Check with your institution or lecturer the preferred method of referencing. You might want to append a copy of the questionnaire or interview schedule you used, or perhaps an anonymized copy of the transcripts.

Unit C1
Describing bilingualism explored

In Unit A1, we examined five key descriptors relevant to bilingual studies. In Unit B1, we looked at an extract from Hoffmann (1991) which discussed real-life bilingual experiences, and we tried to work out whether the descriptors were adequate to capture all the different instances of bilingualism. We also studied in detail Mackey's description of bilingualism and examined some of his ideas, looking at how we can relate them to our knowledge of the bilingual world around us. In this unit, we will build on this knowledge by systematically testing out some of the concepts we have discussed. We will do this by analysing published studies and available data as well as proposing some topics for conducting your own investigations.

An important aspect of undertaking research with human participants is to ensure that they are aware of what they are doing and why, and that ethical considerations have been appropriately taken account of. The preface to this section provides some guidance about ethical consideration when working with human participants, and about some methodological issues. It is important that you read this before embarking on the tasks in the section C units.

Task C1.1 – How do non-experts describe bilingualism?

In Unit A1 and B1, we examined mainly experts' views of bilingualism. Generally, we know very little about the views of the general public towards bilingualism. In daily life, bilinguals are more likely to interact with people who are not trained in linguistics, and these people (parents, relatives, teachers, doctors etc.) are more likely to have an immediate influence in their lives. For example, parents and teachers may have unrealistically high expectations from a child if they expect balanced bilingualism. For this reason, it is important to find out how people in general perceive the status of bilingualism. The objective of this activity is for you to survey or interview members of the general public in order to gauge their perceptions of bilingualism. You can approach the task in a number of different ways and we've made some suggestions about your options.

PARTICIPANTS

You should select between five and ten people you know to do the following task with.

TASK

We have given a choice of two activities to do below. You can choose to do either Option 1 or Option 2, but you should do the same task with each participant. The second task involves the scenarios used by Hoffmann, and this should be easier to manage. You need always to bear in mind with data collection that you are using people's time, and so you should plan to be relatively brief. The first activity should take only about ten minutes, and the second activity not much more. Remember that you will need either to take notes during the interview or to tape-record your interviews so you can remember the responses.

When you have done the tasks, collect some personal data from each of your respondents.

COLLECTING BACKGROUND INFORMATION

You will find it helpful to collect some personal details from your participants if you do not already know this information. You might ask:

- their age
- their occupation
- what they do professionally
- how many languages they speak
- how many languages they read and write
- the extent to which they use other languages in their daily lives
- the extent to which they come into contact with other languages.

We normally do this when we have finished the task so as not to alert people to the type of information we are interested in. While it may not matter in this case, it is generally a good habit to get into. If you are collecting your data remotely (i.e. if you are mailing the questionnaire in option 2), you will need to put this into question format and send it along with the questionnaire.

OPTION 1: OPEN-ENDED QUESTIONS

This option is a brief interview with open-ended questions. The advantage of asking open-ended questions is that you are tapping into what participants really think without influencing them with your own ideas. However, you may find that most participants find this task difficult and they will ask you for more information. You will have to be careful to provide similar information to all participants so that your results are comparable.

Ask about five questions to find out what each speaker thinks about bilingualism. Here are some examples, but you may change them if you wish:

➤   *What does it mean to you to be bilingual?*

➤   *Do you consider yourself bilingual?*

➤   *Do you know people whom you would consider to be bilingual?*

➤   *Do people generally consider you to be a bilingual?*

➤   *Do you think of yourself as a native speaker in both languages?*

For this task, you may choose to take notes during the interview or to tape-record the interview session. When you have spoken to all your participants, summarize the data you have. Listen to your tapes, and note under each question the responses of each individual, as briefly as you can without losing the gist of the comment. When you have done this, write a paragraph about each question, summarizing the general views.

OPTION 2: CLOSED QUESTIONS

The scenarios in the extract from Hoffmann (1991: 17) that you read in Unit B2 present a range of degrees of bilingualism which fall along the minimalist to maximalist continuum. Using the 15 situations presented by Hoffmann (you can modify them if you like) as stimuli, ask participants to rate each case from (1) 'definitely not bilingual' to (5) 'definitely bilingual'. This kind of scale is called a Likert scale, and looks like this:

Definitely not bilingual   *Definitely bilingual*

1 ——————2———————3———————4 ——————5

The scenarios are reiterated below (Hoffmann 1991: 17):

(1)   the two-year-old who is beginning to talk, speaking English to one parent and Welsh to the other

(2)   the four-year-old whose home language is Bengali and who has been attending an English playgroup for some time

(3)   the schoolchild from an Italian immigrant family living in the United States who increasingly uses English both at home and outside but whose older relatives address him in Italian only

(4)   the Canadian child from Montreal who comes from an English-speaking background and attends an immersion programme which consists of virtually all school subjects being taught through the medium of French

(5)   the young graduate who has studied French for eleven years

(6)   the sixty-year-old scholar who has spent a considerable part of her life working with manuscripts and documents written in Latin

(7)   the technical translator

(8)   the personal interpreter of an important public figure

(9)   the Portuguese chemist who can read specialist literature in his subject written in English

(10)   the Japanese airline pilot who uses English for most of his professional communication

(11)   the Turkish immigrant worker in . . . Germany who speaks Turkish at home and with his friends and work colleagues, but who can communicate in German, in both the written and the oral forms, with his superiors and the authorities

(12)   the wife of the latter, who is able to get by in spoken German but cannot read or write it

(13)   the Danish immigrant in New Zealand who has had no contact with Danish for the last forty years

(14)   the Belgian government employee who lives in bilingual Brussels, whose friends and relatives are mainly Flemish speakers but who works in an entirely French-speaking environment and whose colleagues in the office (whether they are Flemish or not) use French as well

(15)   the fervent Catalanist who at home and at work uses Catalan only, but who is exposed to Castilian Spanish from the media and in the street and has no linguistic difficulty in the latter language

It is always best to collect these data from participants while you wait, but you can send this questionnaire out and ask the participants to return it to you at a later date. If you do this, be sure to specify a date by which you would like it back (not too far in the future or it will get forgotten!), and to remember to include a stamped self-addressed envelope so that it will cause them as little trouble as possible. Your return rates will be much higher if you can stay and wait for your participants to finish filling in the questionnaire. Once you get the questionnaires back, go through the items question by question and note the answers. If you have ten questionnaires, you should have ten answers for each item. If you know how to use a spreadsheet program, you can enter your data into the program, which should be able to generate graphs and provide summary data for you. When you have done this, work out what the average is for each response, and see which scenario your participants find is the 'most bilingual' and the 'least bilingual'. Do you agree? Which responses did you find had the most variable answers? Why do you think this was?

OTHER SUGGESTIONS

Using the same task as set in Option 2 above, you can work with different groups of participants. This will of course depend on the availability of participants in your vicinity. In general, trying to find participants from particular professions can be very challenging. However, if participants are available, you will be able to answer some interesting questions. For example, teachers who are bilingual themselves may have different perceptions and expectations of bilinguals as compared with their monolingual counterparts because of their personal experience with being bilingual. The views of teachers and healthcare providers are important as often they are the main official point of contact for bilingual children. Teachers, in particular, are very influential in children's lives. The views of parents are also important as their perceptions may be related to their expectations of their children's bilingual abilities. Age could be a variable if older members of your community are less likely to have contact with languages other than the dominant variety.

It is generally a good idea to spend some time thinking about who you will use as your participants as you are likely to be able to gather more interesting data if you choose your participants carefully. Here are some suggestions, though you are not limited to the options listed here, as you may find other questions which are more pertinent in your local setting. For each scenario you should select between five and ten people for your groups (the more you have, the more reliable your results will be).

➤ Compare bilinguals with monolinguals.

➤ Compare high-proficiency bilinguals with bilinguals of lower proficiency.

➤ Compare young monolinguals with older monolinguals.

➤ Survey the views of parents.

➤ Survey the views of teachers.

➤ Survey the views of health providers (e.g. speech therapists and doctors).

Generally, the findings should give you an idea of the discrepancy between the views of experts and non-experts and alert you to how this could affect the experience of bilingual individuals. In explaining your findings, you should also try to relate them to relevant areas in the field.

Task C1.2 – Bilingual samples used in research

In Unit A1, we discussed the importance of understanding the profiles of bilinguals as their experiences can be extremely diverse. These differences may have an impact on their degree of bilingualism as well as their language choice. Let's look at the brief extract below and examine the methodology which was used in the research by referring to the descriptors we explored in Unit A1.

The extract is from Saer (1923). In this study, Saer compared monolingual English-speaking children with bilingual Welsh–English children on a range of tasks. Two of the language-related tasks required the children to have competence in vocabulary in both languages equivalent to monolingual norms. On the basis of the excerpt provided below, comment on the author's selection and perception of bilinguals.

> The investigation was conducted in seven districts in Carmarthenshire, Cardiganshire and Montgomeryshire. In six of these districts the mother tongue of the majority was Welsh, but the children of the rural districts learn English at the school and those of the urban districts have learnt English both in school and from playmates.[1] The seventh was a rural district with English as the mother tongue. In rural districts a few children whose mother tongue was English had learnt Welsh, but the number of such cases was negligible . . . Five of the districts were rural where the social conditions and habits of the people were very nearly alike. The other two districts were urban and industrial. With very few exceptions the whole child population from 7 to 12 years of age was tested . . . Nearly 1400 children were examined individually, and as the examinations were all conducted personally, the standard of estimation was uniform throughout.
>
> Every child was tested by means of his mother tongue, as I found, by an experiment on 148 boys who were retested after an interval of more than a year, that even when Welsh speaking boys are able to speak English fluently and prefer it to Welsh, since they use it in their play, their mother tongue is the best oral medium by which we can gain a just estimate of their mental capacity. In rural Welsh speaking districts, when the children were addressed in Welsh, their shyness disappeared, they immediately became interested, natural in attitude and responsive, their best effort being thus readily secured.
>
> (Saer 1923: 26)

The bilinguals in this study came from rural and urban districts. Bilinguals in the rural districts were exposed to English in school and bilinguals in the urban districts were exposed to English in both play and school settings. In the results, urban

---

1   Some of the districts were rural and some were urban, and though the majority spoke Welsh as a mother tongue, some were English mother tongue speakers. [Editors' note]

monolinguals were compared with both rural and urban bilinguals. These participants were administered five tests, two of which were language-based tests: *vocabulary* and *composition*. Both tests compared the bilinguals' performance to monolingual norms. The test on composition required the children to, firstly, provide a vivid account of a dream they had had, and, secondly, to write about the things they like. Children who were identified as having Welsh as their mother tongue (meaning they came from those districts identified as Welsh) were tested in Welsh (i.e. they were not given an option).

GENERAL COMMENTS

In your evaluation of the methodology of the study, you may want to focus on the following points:

- problems with comparing urban and rural populations
- concerns about doing the test in Welsh
- equivalence in vocabulary in both languages.

Task C1.3 – Alternative ways of determining degree of bilingualism?

In Unit A1, we raised the problem of the difficulty we face in measuring bilingual language proficiency. The most direct method is to apply objective language measures, as has been done in various studies. In the study quoted below, Gutierrez-Clellen and Kreiter (2003: 269–270) administered questionnaires to parents as well as teachers and found that the results were highly correlated with other studies using objective measures. Read the following extract, which should provide you with some basic idea of what the researchers did. Using the ideas presented in the extract, design a very simple questionnaire (no more than ten questions) for parents to assess the bilingual proficiency of their bilingual child. If you are able to, see if you can find a family or two who are raising their child bilingually to respond to your questionnaire.

Parent and teacher questionnaires
Both parent and teacher questionnaires were adapted from Restrepo's (1998) research with Spanish-speaking children. The parent questionnaire was designed to determine the child's years of exposure to the language(s) with regard to the Spanish-speaking country of origin, language(s) spoken in the home, and language(s) spoken in other settings such as day care, preschool, and elementary school, as well as to obtain a measure of language input at home. Because bilinguals may not always be aware of the language being spoken, parents were asked to list all members of the household with whom the child had the opportunity to interact, indicate the number of hours that the child spent with each member, and report each person's language abilities (either Spanish only, English only, or both),

based on Pearson, Fernandez, Lewedeg, and Oller's (1997) procedures. In the present study, the number of hours of exposure to each language was computed and then converted to percentages. Whenever input was reported in both languages, one-half of the time was allocated to English and one-half to Spanish. In addition, parents were asked to rate the proficiency of each language spoken by each member of the household with whom the child had the opportunity to interact and the child's language proficiency and use, using a 5-point rating scale for each measure (0 = *no use or proficiency*, 4 = *use all the time and native like proficiency*). Finally, an estimate of the time spent in other language activities was obtained by asking the parent to estimate the number of hours per day the child participated in independent reading of books or magazines, using the computer for writing, watching television or movies, and participating in extracurricular activities. The teacher questionnaire contained four questions to obtain an estimate of the child's language use and proficiency for each language using a 5-point rating scale for each measure (0 = *no use or proficiency*, 4 = *use all the time and native like proficiency*). In addition, teachers were asked to estimate the percentage of time that the child was exposed to each language as a measure of language input at school.

GENERAL COMMENTS

➤ What problems do you think might arise in gathering the data?

If you were able to ask a family to respond to this questionnaire:

➤ Were parents able to comment adequately on the competence of the child's two languages?

➤ Were parents able to comment on the competence of the child's interlocutors' language proficiency?

Also consider the following:

➤ Do you think most teachers have the ability to comment on the child's bilingual proficiency?

 Task C1.4 – Investigating language use in the home domain

In some census data, there may be a question about 'languages spoken at home'. Given our understanding of the many factors at play within the home domain from Unit A1 and B1, we know that the census data cannot provide a complete picture. How else could we gather more detailed information? The best way is, of course, to follow a family around with a tape recorder! These kinds of ethnolinguistic studies, in which people spend a lot of time with the family or community, and record extensively, have been done but are extremely time-consuming. A less arduous method is the use of a questionnaire to elicit self-report data.

See if you are able to find five to ten people who speak two languages from the same language group in your community and design a questionnaire to find out patterns of language use. The following is an adaptation of a questionnaire used to explore language input patterns in Singapore, a multilingual community (Ng, in press). The participants were lower-middle-class Chinese parents and Chinese students between nineteen and twenty-four years of age. The questionnaire was designed for a multilingual community, therefore not all the questions will be relevant to your study, so you will need to modify the questionnaire for your own use.

Questionnaire for Students –
Circle the most appropriate answer

Male

Female

Mother's highest education attained: Primary, O-level, A-level/diploma, University

Father's highest education attained: Primary, O-level, A-level/diploma, University

1. **What language(s) do you use to speak to your mother?**

   Mandarin   *all the time – most of the time – sometimes – rarely – not at all*

   English   *all the time – most of the time – sometimes – rarely – not at all*

2. **What language(s) do you use to speak to your father?**

   Mandarin   *all the time – most of the time – sometimes – rarely – not at all*

   English   *all the time – most of the time – sometimes – rarely – not at all*

3. **What language(s) do you use to speak to your siblings?**

   Mandarin   *all the time – most of the time – sometimes – rarely – not at all*

   English   *all the time – most of the time – sometimes – rarely – not at all*

---

continued

4. **What languages do you use to speak to your grandparents?**

   Mandarin   *all the time – most of the time – sometimes – rarely – not at all*

   English   *all the time – most of the time – sometimes – rarely – not at all*

5. **What language(s) did your mother use to speak to you when you were little? (before 12)**

   Mandarin   *all the time – most of the time – sometimes – rarely – not at all*

   English   *all the time – most of the time – sometimes – rarely – not at all*

6. **What language(s) did your father use to speak to you when you were little? (before 12)**

   Mandarin   *all the time – most of the time – sometimes – rarely – not at all*

   English   *all the time – most of the time – sometimes – rarely – not at all*

7. **What language(s) do you use with your close friends?**

   Mandarin   *all the time – most of the time – sometimes – rarely – not at all*

   English   *all the time – most of the time – sometimes – rarely – not at all*

8. **Mandarin**

i. Do you read Mandarin?

   all the time – most of the time – sometimes – rarely – not at all

   (This includes books, newspapers and magazines)

If applicable, please indicate the typical types of materials you read in Mandarin.

ii. Do you write Mandarin?

   all the time – most of the time – sometimes – rarely – not at all

If applicable, please indicate the situation(s) when you are likely to write in Mandarin.

9. **English**

i. Do you read English?

   all the time – most of the time – sometimes – rarely – not at all

If applicable, please indicate the typical types of materials you read in English.

ii. Do you write English?

  all the time – most of the time – sometimes – rarely – not at all

If applicable, please indicate the situation(s) when you are likely to write in English.

10. Spoken language (circle the relevant answer)

i.   Which language are you more comfortable in when you are socializing with your friends?

  English   Mandarin   Equally comfortable

  Why?

ii. Which language do you think you are better in?

  English   Mandarin   Equally good

11. Written language

i.   Which language are you more comfortable with on a daily basis?

  English   Mandarin   Equally comfortable

  Why?

ii. Which language are you more comfortable with for academic purposes?

  English   Mandarin   Equally comfortable

iii. Which language do you think you are better in?

  English   Mandarin   Equally good

12. When you have children, which language(s) are you likely to use to speak to them?

  English   Mandarin   Both

13. Which language do you think is less important for the future generation? If you had to sacrifice one, which one would it be?

  Mandarin   English

Some points to think about in relation to the questionnaire:

➤ What are some of the problems with comparing frequency ratings of this type?

➤ What problems do you think there might be with asking participants to remember a communication routine many years back in time?

➤ What do you think are some of the problems associated with self-report data in general?

➤ What do you think are some of the problems associated with comparing this type of data across subjects?

➤ Other technical questions you may want to consider include ones about the presentation, the layout of the questionnaire, the wording of the questions and the sequencing of the information.

 Task C1.5 – Attitude and identity of bilinguals

Being bilingual is more than the ability to speak two languages. For most bilinguals, the issue of bilingualism goes beyond language proficiency. For this task, find three to five bilingual speakers from different language groups and interview them about their bilingual experience. Here, you may have to use a 'loose' definition of bilingualism to find your bilingual participants. You can ask them general questions surrounding these issues:

■ whether they identify more strongly with one language group and why
■ whether they feel their two languages are valued equally by the wider society
■ whether their parents or relatives encourage them to be bilingual
■ whether they think their bilingual skills are needed for their professional life and their personal life
■ whether they are likely to use both languages with future generations.

In general, probe your participants for reasons for using both languages. The findings should tell you something about the role the two languages play in your interviewees' life.

Unit C2
Measuring bilingualism explored

The assessment of bilingual skill, as we have seen, is very important for a number of reasons. For elective bilinguals, assessments are often required for the purposes of further study or vocational ambitions. The major high-stakes tests, such as the Test of English as a Foreign Language (TOEFL), or the International English Language Testing System (IELTS), are well known and the confidentiality of such tests is strictly maintained. There are, however, a variety of tests available on the Internet which are not high-stakes, but which can give you an idea of the different ways in which tests can be constructed. The exercises below are designed to allow you to explore the issues we have so far discussed in further detail and to think about the implications of these different aspects of assessment for both elective and circumstantial bilingual populations.

Task C2.1 – Assessing bilinguals in the classroom

Teachers in schools are inevitably involved in the process of assessing their students. The types of assessment they administer will vary from one place to another and may include, among others:

- standardized assessments (produced by educational authorities)
- achievement tests related to content areas of the curriculum
- teacher observation and evaluation of student performance
- teacher-prepared in-class tests
- end of year or semester exams
- ongoing continuous assessment through essays, reports, homework exercises etc.

It is also true to say that there are a large number of school teachers in many countries across the world who have a number of children in their classes who come from different language backgrounds, and who may not speak the classroom language when they first come to school. In this task, we ask you to develop an interview schedule which will address the following points:

➤ What kinds of assessments do teachers use routinely in the classroom? This may include standardized types of assessments which are required by their educational authorities, or their schools, as well as assessments related to the curriculum.

> Whether, and if so how, they accommodate children from non-English-speaking backgrounds when they are required to do the various different forms of assessment?

> How effective do the teachers find these kinds of assessment and which do they consider work best?

When you have prepared your questions, try to find about five teachers to interview. As teachers tend to be very busy people, you should try not to take more than ten to fifteen minutes for each interview.

When you have completed your interviews, you might like to try to write a report outlining what you have discovered from the teachers' views, taking into account both the language backgrounds of the children and their ages.

 Task C2.2 – Evaluating language tests

There are numerous language tests now freely available on the Internet, and we are going to ask you to look at some of these and evaluate them. You can decide whether you would like to evaluate a test of English, or whether you would like to evaluate a test in another language of which you have some knowledge, or even a good knowledge.

You might access these tests by typing 'language tests' into a search engine, or alternatively you might begin by looking at the following websites:

http://www.allthetests.com/language.php3

http://www.transparent.com/tlquiz/proftest/

http://www.world-english.org/tests.htm

http://www.sprachcaffe.com/english/study_abroad/language_test/language _test.htm

For this activity you should try to examine at least two of the tests that you find. The first thing to do is to actually take the tests, even if they are in your native language, as this gives you a much better idea of what they are about. If there are tests available on the same website in two languages you know, then you could do them both.

As you work your way through the tests, make notes about the following:

> How many parts does each test have (e.g. vocabulary, grammar, reading comprehension)?

➤ How many items are there within each part?

➤ What form do the items take (e.g. multiple choice, insert correct word)?

➤ Do the items vary in difficulty (i.e. are some much easier than others)?

➤ Did you find the layout of the test encouraged you to participate?

➤ Is there a score which is automatically generated?

➤ Are you able to access some sort of standardized scores? Is there an explanation of how the standardized score is reached?

➤ To what extent do any of the items test broader 'world knowledge' rather than just language knowledge?

When you have done this, answer the following questions:

➤ How good a test of language knowledge do you think the test is (how valid was the test)?

➤ How reliable was the scoring method used in the test? Were there any responses that you disagreed with?

➤ Are there other aspects of language knowledge which could be assessed via a freely available computer-based test? What are these and how would you assess them?

If you would like to learn more about these concepts, which are central to testing, we recommend Fulcher and Davidson (2007).

There are obviously clear limitations on the kinds of knowledge that freely available computer-based tests can tap. But consider the following:

➤ Did you enjoy doing the test?

➤ If you are not a fluent speaker, did you feel it gave you a realistic evaluation of your language ability in the language?

➤ What are some of the reasons individuals might choose to do these tests?

Compare your two tests on the following dimensions. You can respond to the same questions regardless of whether you compared two tests of the same language or two tests of different languages.

➤ Did you think one was a better measure of your language ability than the other? If so, in what ways?

➤ What was it about the test that you felt was better able to tap your language knowledge?

➤ Did you feel that they were both equal in terms of difficulty? If not, in what ways did they differ?

➤ Were they roughly equal in terms of the length of time they took? If one was longer than the other, how did this impact on your view of the test?

 Task C2.3 – Translating tests: why it can't be done

There are numerous reasons why standardized (or other) tests both cannot and should not be translated into another language. In the following extract from Pert and Letts (2003: 270), the authors discuss the problems which arise when speech pathologists (clinicians) translate language assessments for a population whose language is different from that for which the assessment was originally intended:

> Sometimes clinicians have responded to the need for assessment materials in different languages by translating standardized tests that have been shown to be valid and reliable in English. This is not acceptable for two reasons. Firstly, the population on which the test was originally standardized will be different from the target clinical population (if only because they speak a different language), so any test norms or standardized scores will be invalid. This difficulty can be overcome by re-standardizing the test in the target language. More serious is the fact that differences between languages will mean that, when considering development, translated test items will not be equivalent in terms of either level of difficulty or order of emergence in development. Put simply, a meaning that may be expressed with a straightforward structure in one language may be expressed through a much more complex structure in another language. Some structures important in the target language may not appear at all if translations are adopted. For example, in Mirpuri there are gender markers appearing as inflections on verbs that show 'agreement' with the gender of the agent or experiencer (or grammatical 'subject') of the sentence. Since this is not a feature of English, no translated version of an English test will attempt to measure this. Tests may be adapted rather than translated into other languages, but this pre-supposes knowledge about both the grammar of the target language and the order in which specific structures are acquired.

Kester and Peña (2002) also point to problems inherent in test translation, arguing that linguistic items have different developmental patterns in different languages (see also Unit A3). This means that, when translated, the difficulty level of the items may not reflect the same developmental difficulty in the language into which the item is being translated. In other words, children learning different languages do not necessarily acquire words and structures in the same order in their two different languages. Kester and Peña (2002: 2) cite the findings of a study by Restrepo and

Silverman (2001), designed to investigate the validity of the Spanish version of the Preschool Language Scale-3 to illustrate this, pointing out that the researchers

> found several item difficulty discrepancies between the original English and the translated Spanish version when tested with predominately Spanish-speaking preschoolers. For example, items related to prepositions, which were relatively easy for English speakers, were more difficult for Spanish speakers. On the other hand, the 'function' items requiring students to point out objects based on a description of their use (something like 'Show me what people use for cooking' or 'What do you sweep with?') were easier for the Spanish speakers than the English speakers. Figueroa (1989) noted that words may generally represent the same concept but have variations and different levels of difficulty across languages. An illustration of this is found in a study of vocabulary test translations (Tamayo, 1987). When test items were translated from English to Spanish, they differed in frequency of occurrence in each language. Because the Spanish translations were of lower frequency within Spanish, test scores obtained from Spanish speakers were lower compared to scores obtained from the original English version. However, when the vocabulary items were matched for their frequency of occurrence in the original and target language and matched for meaning, test scores obtained from Spanish and English speakers were equivalent. Similarly, across different languages, the same general category may have different prototypical members, and different words may be associated with each language for the same situation. These contextual variations make translated vocabulary tests particularly vulnerable to imbalance. When Peña et al. (2002) asked bilingual four- to six-year-olds to give examples of animals, the children's three most frequent English responses were 'elephant,' 'lion,' and 'dog,' while in Spanish they used 'caballo' (horse), 'elefante' (elephant), and 'tigre' (tiger) in these orders. In addition to vocabulary differences, grammatical structure also affects the validity of test translation practices. For example, nouns are marked by gender in Spanish, but not English. An English test translated to Spanish will miss aspects of Spanish, such as gender marking, that are not present in the English language. Furthermore, in Spanish, subject information is frequently carried in the verb, resulting in more complex verbs and less salient pronouns as compared to English. In English language assessment, pronoun omission is a hallmark of language impairment, yet this would not be true for Spanish. Thus, translated language tests may target inappropriate features for the target language, resulting in inaccurate assessment of language ability.

Using one of the tests you found in Task C2.2 (you may use the same one or a different one):

➤ Try translating a number of items in the test into another language which you know well.

➤ Did you encounter any of the problems discussed above in your translation, e.g. gender or articles? frequency with which a word may occur in each language? differences in difficulty or frequency of grammatical structures?

➤ What other problems did you encounter in this translation exercise?

Unit C3
Bilingual acquisition explored

In Unit A3, we defined bilingual first-language acquisition as the learning of two languages simultaneously from birth and we discussed a range of factors which impact on the child's successful acquisition of two languages, including the type of input the child receives, various sociolinguistic factors in the child's home and community environment, and the ways in which all of these factors interact. In Unit B3, we read three extracts. The first extract explored the results of empirical data on the kind of language input the parents were providing to their children, using Lanza's (1997) taxonomy of parental strategies. The next article raised the importance of detailing the child's linguistic surroundings, showing how important these are in identifying factors which will contribute to successful bilingualism in children. The final article examined the issue of differentiation of languages, looking at phonological development in a bilingual child. What must be clear from these readings is the importance of detail. We need detailed notes about both the linguistic environment of the child and the types of strategies that are used, and we need to be able to make recordings of both the child and the input the child receives which we can use for further analysis. In this unit, we guide you through exploring further some of the points we have raised and give you some tasks so that you can get a glimpse first-hand of the types of issues that face researchers in this field.

It will be helpful if you know a family whose members speak more than one language at home, especially if you yourself know both the languages. However, we appreciate that this may not always be possible and so with each task we have provided options for those who may not have access to such a bilingual environment.

Task C3.1 – How do parents approach the task of raising a child bilingually?

In this research task, we are going to ask you to design a series of questions, or an interview schedule, which you could use to find out from parents how they approach the task of raising their child in a bilingual environment.

The kinds of question you ask in your interview are going to vary to some degree depending upon the bilingual circumstances under which the child is growing up. You need to begin by thinking about which variables are going to apply for the interviews you are going to conduct. This will probably depend on the situation you yourself live in, because ideally we would like you to be able at least to trial your schedule on three or four families so that you can see how well it works, and whether you are able to elicit the kind of information you want.

The kinds of variables you will need to consider are the following:

➤ Is the community in which the child is being raised multilingual (i.e. Is more than one language spoken routinely in the community)?

➤ Do the parents speak the same language or different languages?

➤ Do either of the parents speak the language of the community?

When you have made a decision about which variables are likely to apply to your participants, design an interview schedule that you could use to ask the parents of the child being raised bilingually about their language use at home, and the child's language development. The interview should not take more than fifteen to twenty minutes altogether.

Consider how you might use the questionnaire:

➤ Would you use this with both parents together, or would you interview each parent individually?

➤ How important do you think it would be to observe the parents interacting with their child if this were possible?

If you know a family (or even two) who are raising their children bilingually, you could try your questionnaire out on them. This may indicate that you need to make some changes to it (for example, if they don't understand, or can't answer, a question). It may also show you how adequate it was to get a first indication of the types of strategies parents use with their children when raising them bilingually.

 Task C3.2 – Patterns of bilingual acquisition

As we have seen in our discussion of bilingualism in general, each bilingual is an individual who will have come to his or her bilingualism by a different route. Romaine (1995) distinguishes six different routes to bilingual first-language acquisition, each of which varies along three dimensions. The first dimension is the parents, and whether they speak the same language or different languages from each other, whether they are themselves bilingual and the extent to which they share each other's native language. The second dimension is that of the community and whether or not either of the parents' languages is that of the community in which the family is residing, or whether the community itself is bilingual. The third dimension is the strategy used by the parents in terms of which language each of them speaks to the child.

Romaine's (1995) different types of bilingual acquisition

Type 1: 'One person – one language'

Parents:	The parents have different native languages with each having some degree of competence in the other's language.
Community:	The language of one of the parents is the dominant language of the community.
Strategy:	The parents each speak their own language to the child from birth.

Type 2: 'Non-dominant home language'

Parents:	The parents have different native languages.
Community:	The language of one of the parents is the dominant language of the community.
Strategy:	Both parents speak the non-dominant language to the child, who is fully exposed to the dominant language only when outside the home, and in particular in nursery school.

Type 3: 'Non-dominant home language without community support'

Parents:	The parents share the same native language.
Community:	The dominant language is not that of the parents.
Strategy:	The parents both speak their own language to the child from birth.

Type 4: 'Double non-dominant home language without community support'

Parents:	The parents have different native languages.
Community:	The dominant language is different from either of the parents' languages.
Strategy:	The parents each speak their own language to the child from birth.

Type 5: 'Non-native parents'

Parents:	The parents share the same native language.
Community:	The dominant language is the same as that of the parents.
Strategy:	One of the parents always addresses the child in a language which is not his or her native language.

Type 6: 'Mixed languages'

Parents: The parents are bilingual.

Community: Sectors of the community may also be bilingual.

Strategy: Parents code-switch and mix languages.

➤ Consider each of the six alternatives outlined above. Think about:

- ■ Which of the above types would you expect to lead to more, and which to less, successful bilingualism in the child?
- ■ Provide reasons as to why you make your choices.
- ■ What do you see as essential for successful bilingualism?

In Text B3.2, you read an extract from Deuchar and Quay (1999) in which a child growing up bilingually in Spanish and English was discussed. Which of the types suggested by Romaine would that child fit into, if any?

When you have addressed this question, see if you can identify some children you know, or know of, who are being raised bilingually. See to what extent you can categorize them into one of the environmental types outlined by Romaine. Do you have examples of children being raised bilingually who do not fit into one of these types?

 Task C3.3 – Recording and transcribing bilingual language data

All of the extracts we read in Unit B3 involved detailed transcriptions of the utterances of one or more bilingual children and their caregivers. As you read through more of the research literature on raising children bilingually, you will find that most researchers make use of these techniques. As you can see from the extracts in Unit B3, such detailed information is important if we are to move ahead and understand more about bilingual development.

In this task we are going to ask you to record and transcribe a small amount of child language data. If you have access to a child who is being raised bilingually, and you speak both the languages, you may be able to record some data in both languages. If you do not have access to a child who is being raised bilingually, try the exercise with a child who is being raised monolingually. While this is not ideal, it will allow you to experience undertaking a transcription exercise. While phonetic transcription is often preferable, in this case an orthographic transcription will be adequate.

DOING THE RECORDING

With small children it is always easiest, if possible, to record them with a digital video camera, since it can often be difficult to understand what they are saying without the context. However, there are disadvantages to this because it requires more equipment (e.g. a tripod) and often makes the participants more uncomfortable than a tape recorder does. We will leave this decision to you. If you do choose to video-record the child then you should also have an audio recorder (e.g. an MP3 player which records, or a small cassette recorder) to ensure the best possible quality.

Either take some age-appropriate toys or find out from the parents in advance what the child enjoys, and set up a situation in which you or the parent/s play with the child. Try to record about twenty minutes of play, which hopefully will include a reasonable amount of language.

Remember that you might want to take a box of chocolates or a bunch of flowers to thank the family for their time!

DOING THE TRANSCRIPTION

Listen to the recording and try to transcribe it as accurately as you can. This will probably take quite a bit of time and you will find you have to listen to the recording several times. You should put each utterance on a different line, indicating who said it. You might find it helpful to use the following transcription conventions as you do your transcription:

Transcription conventions

Normal font:	The caregiver's utterances
Bold print:	**The child's utterances**
[word]	The word provided is what was probably said, but it is not clearly audible on the tape
XXXX	a word or phrase is unintelligible
{ }	contextual notes
. . .	indicates a pause with no speaking

Here is a small example of a piece of transcript:

Mother:	what's this? {holding up toy kitten}
Child:	. . . **XXXX** {pointing at toy kitten}
Mother:	what did you say?
Child:	**[cat]**
Mother:	cat, yes it's a cat

ANALYSING YOUR DATA

The analysis will be more interesting if you have managed to collect data in both of the child's languages. The MacArthur–Bates CDI (Fenson et al. 1993) was used in the Deuchar and Quay (1999) study. Information about these can be found at http://www.sci.sdsu.edu/cdi/cdiwelcome.htm. These are inventories of words used by young children at different ages. The words are sorted into the following categories:

> Action words (e.g. bump, cry, draw, fall, get, help, wash)
> Animals (real or toy)
> Body parts
> Clothing
> Descriptive words (e.g. all gone, asleep, blue, cold, dirty, fine, happy, hungry, naughty, old, tired, thirsty)
> Food and drink
> Furniture and rooms
> Games and routines (e.g. peekaboo, thank you, please, night night, nap)
> Outside things and places to go (e.g. backyard, moon, pool, shovel, water, beach, park, house)
> People (mummy, daddy, grandpa, proper names)
> Pronouns (e.g. I, it, me, mine, this, your)
> Quantifiers (e.g. all, another, more, not, none, other, same, some)
> Question words (e.g. how, what, when, why)
> Small household items (e.g. bowl, clock, comb, hammer, keys, plant)
> Sound effects and animal sounds (baa baa, miaow)
> Toys (ball, balloon, doll, book)
> Vehicles (real or toy)
> Words about time (e.g. later, morning, tomorrow)

Look at your transcription and try to fit the words your child uses into these different catetegories. If your child is under two and a half (thirty months) and you are looking at English (or Spanish, which is also provided on the website), you can then look at the website and see how your child compares to other children of this age because the tables will indicate what proportion of children understand or produce each word at different ages. Note that you may find some words that are not in the inventory.

 Task C3.4 – Strategies for raising children bilingually

> Imagine that you have been asked to prepare a document of approximately five hundred words which is designed to encourage new parents to raise their children bilingually. You should include the following types of advice in the document:

- at what stage the parents should begin speaking to the child in both languages
- what kinds of strategies should be used when speaking with their child; you might want to provide a range of strategy types which may depend to some extent on location, language of community, degree to which the extended family is involved with the child
- whether and how the strategies they use might change at different ages and if so how
- what strategies the parents could include to ensure that the child has adequate access to the minority language.

Remember that this document is being written for parents with no background in linguistics and therefore it should not be academic in nature, but rather discursive and encouraging. A very good example of this type of accessible writing can be found in Harding-Esch and Riley (2003), which provides a detailed and authoritative guide for parents interested in raising their children bilingually.

Unit C4
Bilingualism and cognitive ability explored

In Unit A4, we traced the research on the relationship between bilingualism and cognition, and examined several studies spanning a few decades which reported both negative and positive effects of bilingualism. By comparing different studies, it is apparent that the differences in findings can be explained by the difference in choice of subjects and tasks used. Our aim was to highlight methodological concerns to do with sampling and instrumentation and discuss how these factors impact on research findings and interpretations. In Unit B4, we continued to examine this issue of methodology in two different studies. In this unit, you will have the opportunity to explore some of the concepts you have been introduced to and to test them out by conducting and designing your own study. As most standard psychological tests (e.g. the Peabody Vocabulary Test, Raven Progressive Matrices) are not available to the public, and some may even require special licences or permits before you can use them, we will not be using them in these tasks.

 Task C4.1 – Perceptions of bilinguals

Given that publications about the benefits of bilingualism have dominated the literature on cognitive effects in the last forty years, one would expect some of these opinions to have filtered into public knowledge. Here, we suggest how you can conduct a small-scale study to find out if lay people do indeed have a favourable view of bilingualism.

DESIGN A QUESTIONNAIRE TO CONTAIN QUESTIONS USING A VARIETY OF FORMATS

- open-ended questions, e.g. 'How do you think learning or using another language can affect the way we think?'
- closed questions, e.g. 'Monolinguals speak better because they don't get confused by another language – do you agree?' The responses can be rated on a Likert scale (this was discussed earlier – see Unit C1).
- indirect questions, e.g. 'If you had a son or daughter who had a hearing impairment, would you encourage him or her to learn a second language?'

LENGTH OF QUESTIONNAIRE

Limit your questionnaire to 15 questions.

SELECTION OF PARTICIPANTS

Find ten to twelve adult monolinguals or bilinguals (or both, if you can work with someone else as a team). The usual guidelines set out for selection of participants in Unit C1 apply here. You may want to include questions to investigate the friendship circle of your participants. For example, monolinguals who have a wide circle of bilingual friends may be more likely to be aware of issues related to bilingualism. Try to avoid using linguistics students, who may have already been primed about the debate.

Task C4.2 – Torrance test of creativity

This is a divergent thinking task which has been used to measure cognitive flexibility in many studies. Find five bilingual and five monolingual children. Form two groups, one monolingual and the other bilingual. (You can choose children between five and eight years of age but children in each group have to be in the same age group.)

➤ Do this task in one language only.

➤ Ask your participants how many uses they can think of for a *shoebox*.

➤ Record the answers in writing.

➤ What types of skills do you think are required for this type of task?

➤ Analyse your findings and then summarize them.

➤ Can you think of other ways in which you could have done the analysis?

Task C4.3 – Semantic and phonetic preference study (data collection)

This is a simple replication of the semantic and phonetic preference study by Ben-Zeev (1977). Choose one of the three objectives below. Your choice of participants will depend on which objective you have chosen. As the types of task involved are very easy, you will need to start with participants younger than eight years of age.

OBJECTIVES OF THE STUDY

■ to examine whether different age groups differ in their responses
■ to examine whether bilinguals differ from monolinguals in their responses
■ to see whether onset of literacy has an impact on the responses of both monolinguals and bilinguals.

TARGET PARTICIPANTS

1   Preliterate five-year-old bilinguals and preliterate five-year-old monolinguals
2   Seven-year-old bilinguals and seven-year-old monolinguals

➤   Try to have at least eight to ten participants in each age group. The bigger the
number of participants you have in each group, the more reliable your findings
will be.

➤   All participants should be carefully screened following the guidelines discussed
in Unit C1. The questionnaire should be modified for the children and it should
be administered orally.

STIMULI AND INSTRUCTIONS FOR SEMANTIC-PHONETIC
PREFERENCE TASK

The list (Table C4.1) contains eight sets of words. In each set, one word is phonetically similar to the target and one word is semantically similar to the target. For
example, for the first set, *Can* is phonetically similar to the target, *Cap*, but *Hat* is
semantically closer to the target, *Cap*. The first four sets of words (cap/can, book/
boot, lamp/lamb, bag/bat) are minimal pairs. That is, they are phonetically similar
except for the last phoneme. Similarly, the last four set of words (mouse/house,
mug/bug, dish/fish, hen/pen) are phonetically similar except for the first phoneme.

Table C4.1 List of stimuli

Target	Phonetically similar	Semantically similar
Cap	Can	Hat
Boot	Book	Shoe
Lamp	Lamb	Light
Bag	Bat	Purse
Mouse	House	Rat
Mug	Bug	Cup
Dish	Fish	Plate
Hen	Pen	Chick

METHOD

The task should be administered individually to all the participants and the instructions read out clearly and in the same way for each of the participants. The instructions should be modelled on the following pattern:

I have three words *Cap, Can* and *Hat.* Which is more like *Cap – Can* or *Hat*?

Make sure that you randomize the presentation of the phonetically similar and semantically similar words. That is, do not present the phonetically similar words first in all trials. The trials should also be randomized. (Suggestion: write each set of words on a separate card and shuffle the card for each child to randomize the presentation.)

If you are working with a partner in the data collection, it is better to pre-record the word list and the instructions to ensure that they are consistently presented.

You can either have a score sheet (see Table C4.2) ready to note down the responses or tape the session and transcribe the answers later.

Table C4.2 Sample score sheet for semantic and phonetic preference test

Participant	1	2	3	4	5	6	7	8	9	10	Total number of semantic responses
Trials											
1											
2											
3											
4											
5											
6											
7											
8											

RESULTS

Add up the number of semantic and phonetic responses for each participant using a spreadsheet. This should generate frequency counts for you to compare the percentage of phonetic and semantic preferences across all the groups.

Can you see any trend in the response pattern or is the response pattern random?

DISCUSSION

As discussed in Unit A4, semantic preference is not necessarily a good indicator of metalinguistic awareness. Looking at your own results, can you see whether semantic preference is clearly associated with any particular group? What inferences might you draw for a group that has higher phonetic preference responses?

WRITE-UP REPORT

Write up the study in the form of a research report by following the sections of report writing indicated in the preface to section C.

Task C4.4 – The Wug Test

The Wug Test, designed by Berko (1958), is used to test simple morphological productive rules in English. Information and jpeg versions of the Wug Test can be downloaded from *Wugs-Online* on http://childes.psy.cmu.edu/topics/. The simple Wug Test is an engaging task, well liked by children and, therefore, a good way to get the feel of how children extend morphological rules to novel instances.

STEP 1

Compare the abilities of (two to three) four-year-old bilingual children and monolingual children in their performance in the Wug test in English designed by Berko (1958).

STEP 2

Can you design a similar task for the other language of your bilingual sample?

➤ What conclusions can you draw about the language competence of bilinguals compared to monolinguals?

➤ What conclusions can you draw about the language competence of bilinguals in each of their two languages?

Task C4.5 – Metalinguistic awareness

A number of phonological awareness tests are available on the Internet which can be found by typing 'phonological awareness test' into a search engine. http://www.elr.com.au/apar/index.htm and http://ca.geocities.com/phonological/childtest.htm are two examples. Have a look at the tests you find (you can even take some of them yourself, and submit them on-line and you will be sent your results!) so that you get an impression of the types of items these tests include. What are the skills these items test? What aspect of language knowledge do they relate to?

Alternatively, you can use some of the tasks discussed in Unit A4 on phoneme awareness, word awareness or sentence awareness. Some of the tasks on counting phonemes and syllables are fairly simple to design, as is the task involving counting words in a meaningful or non-meaningful string. Here is an example of a more complicated word awareness task used in Yelland et al. (1993).

WORD AWARENESS: THE BIG WORD–SMALL WORD TASK

In this task, the children were asked to make judgements on word size. In this rather charming task, the children were asked to indicate the bigger word in word pairs of two types:

■ the bigger word referred to the bigger object (e.g. *hippopotamus/skunk*)
■ the bigger word referred to the smaller object (e.g. *train/caterpillar*)

Making correct judgements on the incongruent (*train/caterpillar*) pairs requires considerable word awareness. The child has to deliberately attend to the size of the word and not the object. In other words, the child has to separate word attributes from object attributes. Little words were monosyllabic and big words were multi-syllabic. There were four stimuli types. They were:

■ little objects whose name is a little word (e.g. *ant, pin*)
■ little objects whose name is a big word (*caterpillar, thermometer*)
■ big objects whose name is a big word (e.g. *hippopotamus, aeroplane*)
■ big objects whose name is a little word (*whale, car*)

For this task, you will need to prepare pictures to use as stimuli. Ensure that stimuli are all the same size. Table C4.3 is a complete list of words you can use in this task (adapted from Yelland et al. 1993: 441). You do not have to use the entire list. Instead, you can choose to do four 'little words' and four 'big words' instead of the entire list.

Table C4.3 Items for the big word/little word test

Little word		Big word	
Little object	*Big object*	*Little object*	*Big object*
Ant	Bed	Butterfly	Aeroplane
Bee	Car	Button	Crocodile
Frog	Horse	Caterpillar	Elephant
Keys	Sun	Cigarette	Giraffe
Leaf	Train	Envelope	Hippopotamus
Mouse	Tree	Mushroom	Policeman
Pin	Truck	Strawberry	Skeleton
Snail	Whale	Thermometer	Stegosaurus

PARTICIPANTS

Ten to twelve six- to seven-year-old bilinguals and monolinguals who all speak English.

METHOD

1   Familiarize the children with the idea of word size by explaining that big words take a 'long time to say' (for example *hurricane*) and little words take 'very little time' (for example *cat*).
2   Administer the task to each child individually. Present the stimuli (randomized) for each child and ask the child to name each object to make sure that the child knows the object. After the child has successfully named the object, ask the child 'Is this a big word or a little word?'
3   Record the answer on a score sheet.
4   In your analysis, focus on the responses to congruent and incongruent pairs. High scores on incongruent pairs are indicative of word awareness.

Unit C5
Language attrition in bilinguals explored

Language attrition in bilinguals is closely related to language acquisition in bilinguals, and, as we have seen, one affects the other. Although there are four different types of language attrition (L1 in an L1 environment, L1 in an L2 environment, L2 in an L1 environment, and L2 in an L2 environment), we have explored only two of these – the two most common types of attrition. In the first case we looked at issues related to the attrition of the first language in a second-language environment. As we saw, this is not a very unusual situation – children are moved overseas or adopted overseas and removed from regular access to their first language, and it atrophies. In the second case we looked at the attrition of a second language in the first-language environment. We noted that there was a higher likelihood of attrition in children than was the case with adults.

In this section, we will consider some of these issues in more depth. In some ways, attrition is quite difficult to investigate empirically because by its nature it involves longitudinal investigation, and this can be difficult to organize. In doing these types of tasks, therefore, it is important that you ensure that your participants know in advance if they are going to be required to come back a second or a third time, because you will not be able to complete the tasks if they don't. It will waste everyone's time to do the first part of the task and then find out that they will be away on holiday when you come to doing the second part of the task! Once again, because you are undertaking studies here which involve human participants, you should refer to the notes at the beginning of this section on undertaking empirical activities with people, and the importance of obtaining from them informed consent.

Task C5.1 – L1 attrition in an L2 environment

The study by De Bot and Clyne (1994), discussed in Unit A5, looked at the extent to which the first language (Dutch) of a group of immigrants to Australia had been lost over a long period of 17 years. This study compared the data to an earlier study, reported in the literature as De Bot and Clyne (1989). In the 1989 study, De Bot and Clyne outline the way in which they collected the data. Most of the interview was in Dutch (including some of the talking about pictures), and some was in English (including the rest of the talking about pictures).

All informants were interviewed in their own homes. They were asked to talk about their life in Australia, their children, the Dutch community, and whatever else might come up during the conversation. After some time had elapsed and the informants no longer paid much attention to the tape recorder, a more guided interview was administered. In this interview, data were gathered about such matters as age, age on arrival, education in the Netherlands and Australia, language use in the last few years in different domains, and attitudes toward maintenance of Dutch by them and by their children; finally they were asked about changes in use and proficiency in both Dutch and English in the last 10 years. Accordingly, a number of formal language tests were administered, and at the end of the session informants had to describe two pictures – one depicting a typical Dutch scene and one a typical Australian scene – in Dutch, and describe one picture in English.

(De Bot and Clyne 1989: 170)

The methodological design of this study allowed the researchers initially to collect naturalistic data in casual conversation which allowed the participants to get used to the tape recorder. Having collected more informal conversation, the researchers used the same interview to collect more specific data about the backgrounds of their participants, and the factors which might have impacted on any potential language attrition, such as age, age on arrival, educational background etc. They were also asked about attitudes and changes they might have noticed in their own proficiency, which provides a measure of self-assessment of language skills. The final contribution came from the language tests. In this way, the different types of data collected were triangulated. This means that different perspectives are taken on the same phenomenon – in this case their language use. So in this case, there was casual conversation which could be transcribed and analysed, personal details which provided information about potential background variables, self-report data about their own language, and information about their attitudes towards their languages. The language tests provided a more objective measure of their language.

Although in this study data were collected from 40 participants, it is possible to do a case study of a single person, although we will limit the data collection to the interview in this case, since it will probably not be possible for you to obtain appropriate language tests.

IDENTIFYING YOUR CASE STUDY PARTICIPANT

Your participant in this activity should preferably be an adult who has been living in your country of residence for several years, and who arrived in the country as an adult. Ideally you should choose someone who is a member of a community in which their first language is spoken. While it would be helpful if you also spoke their first language, this is not a requirement for this activity.

When you approach your participant, it is important that you explain what you are going to do, but try not to tell them what you are going to focus on. So you can say you are going to do an interview, but not what it is about specifically (but don't lie!). They need to be told how long this will take so that they do not get impatient towards the end. If it is acceptable to the person, it is probably easiest to go to their house, where they will be more relaxed. If you do not know them, they might prefer to meet in a café, where you might buy them a cup of coffee. It is never a bad idea to take a small gift (e.g. a bunch of flowers, a small plant, a small box of chocolates) to give your participant as a thank-you for taking part.

Remember that you need to tell your participant that you are going to record the interview.

PREPARING THE INTERVIEW

Interview preparation is very important. For the purposes of this interview, you need to prepare three sets of questions. You may not need to ask all these questions, but it is important to have them prepared in case the conversation flags.

Part 1: Prepare some questions about:

- their life in _____ (insert the name of the country you live in)
- their family/children
- their local community
- any other issues you think they may like to chat about.

Part 2: You could prepare this in the form of a questionnaire which you could complete as they talk; ask about:

- their age
- when they arrived to live in the country
- their education before they arrived
- any further education after arrival
- their work life.

Part 3: Talk to them about their language use; you might want to use some parts of the questionnaire in Task C1.4 (but be careful not to ask all of it, or it will take too long). Find out about:

- how much they use their first language
- how much they use their second language
- what language(s) their children speak
- their perceptions of how their first language has changed.

You may want to add your own ideas to any of these question parts.

When you have completed your interview, listen to the recording and make some notes about each of these points. In particular, look at what they have had to say about the ways in which their language use has changed, and their language proficiency has changed. Write up your case study.

Task C5.2 – Comparing monolinguals' and bilinguals' language attrition

In Unit A4, we looked at some research which suggested that bilinguals would learn their third language better than monolinguals would learn their second language. One aspect of this could be hypothesized to be the fact that bilinguals would have better retention of a new language than monolinguals.

In this task, you are going to teach a language you know well, but your participants don't, to two different groups: one monolingual, for whom this will be a second-language experience; and one bilingual, for whom this will be a third-language experience. We will hypothesize that the bilingual group will retain the new language better than the monolingual group.

You will need to identify two groups of people, one of them monolingual, the other bilingual. Obviously it is important that none of them knows the language you intend to teach them.

Prepare a short lesson (no more than one hour) in the language you know. You need to be quite clear about exactly what you are teaching your participants, because you will have to test them on the same language items later. Make sure you teach both classes exactly the same language in exactly the same way. At the end of the class, thank them, ask them to return the next day or two days later or a week later – really, whatever is most convenient, as long as it is the same for all. Let them know that they need to do nothing between now and then.

For your second meeting you will need to prepare a short test of the items you taught them. Administer the test to both groups, and see whether one group does better than the other. Remember that the test will need to be very simple, and must test only items you taught them:

➤ Was the hypothesis upheld?

➤ Can you identify any differences between the two groups?

Task C5.3 – L2 attrition in an L1 environment

In this task you are going to need to identify a group of second-language speakers who have had roughly equivalent periods of formal or instructed language learning, followed by roughly equivalent periods of non-learning. An ideal group might be a group of late teenagers or people in their early twenties who learned a language in high school but have not used it since.

As you did for Task C5.1, design an interview schedule which asks them questions about their language learning experience:

➤ How long did they learn the language for?

➤ How often were their classes and for how long (e.g. hours per week)?

➤ How proficient were they by the end of the period?

➤ Did they spend time in the country? If so, for how long? How long ago?

Next, ask them about their current lifestyle and the extent to which this exposes them to the language:

■ through friends
■ newspapers
■ movies
■ holiday in the country
■ television, radio
■ clubs, etc.

If possible, and if the language is one of those for which you can find a language test on the Internet (see Unit C2), when you have done this, administer the language test and see if the results correlate to any of the 'exposure' variables. In other words, do those people who have had greater exposure to the language since learning it do better than those who have not?

Task C5.4 – Preventing attrition

Imagine you know a family who are about to move to another country in which the language spoken is not the same as the language they speak. They want to ensure that the children in the family remain fluent in their first language, but they are also aware of the fact that the children's education will be in their second language. They are planning to live in this other country permanently.

On the basis of what you have learned in this unit, and in the acquisition unit, what information and advice would you give them in relation to the development and maintenance of their children's first language? How would your advice vary in relation to:

■ their pre-school child?
■ their primary school child?
■ their secondary school child?

Investigating language attrition empirically is not easy because of the longitudinal nature of such investigations. However, if you are able to do the activities listed above, you will get a real sense of both the challenges, and the rewards, of undertaking an extended piece of empirical research.

Attrition is, of course, closely related in many ways to acquisition, and for this reason both these issues are addressed in the units on dynamic aspects of second-language acquisition in another book in this series – De Bot, Lowie and Verspoor (2005). You will find further insights and activities in that volume.

Unit C6
Education and literacy in bilingual settings explored

In Units A6 and B6, we reviewed a range of bilingual programmes, noting their strengths and weaknesses. In this unit, you will be able to explore different educational practices in your community and evaluate how they provide (or fail to provide) support for the development of bilingualism and multilingualism. You may find that some of the educational programmes in practice vary from those that have been described in Units A6 and B6. This is not unusual, as available resources and the cultural and linguistic make-up of particular communities will to a great extent determine the type of programmes adopted. It is important to note the differences and be aware of the objectives of the programmes that are being studied.

Task C6.1 – Attitudes towards immersion education for majority-language children

Bilingual immersion programmes for majority-language students can be developed in almost any situation, provided there is an adequate supply of bilingual teachers, and the support of the surrounding community from which such a programme will draw its students. In the first task, we ask you to investigate the attitudes of some majority-language speakers in your community towards bilingual immersion programmes, and to discuss with your participants whether they would choose to send their child to an immersion school if they had the opportunity.

PART 1

Briefly describe the community you live in, particularly in terms of its linguistic resources. For example, are there speakers of many languages? Is there a majority (prestige) language? Is the community bilingual or multilingual? What are the languages spoken?

To some extent, the answers to Part 1 will guide the questions you ask in Part 2.

PART 2

Design a brief interview schedule based on the following template that would be appropriate to use in the community situation you have described above. Depending on the language demography of your community, choose an immersion language. For example, if there is a large Italian population in your community, you may want to propose Italian as the immersion language.

Sample template interview schedule

I would like to explore with you your attitudes towards bilingual immersion education. In Canada, immersion schools are now quite widespread and can be found in most provinces. These schools are largely designed for English-speaking children. While there are various models, for many children this means that when they first go to school their entire school day is in French. For the first few years they may learn entirely in French, with the exception of literacy skills, which is taught in English and French.

POSSIBLE QUESTIONS TO ASK TO ELICIT DISCUSSION

➤ What can you see as being the main advantages of sending monolingual children to a bilingual setting of this type for their education?

➤ Do you think that parents should perhaps make some attempt to learn the language too (if they are not already familiar with it)?

➤ What do you think might be the potential disadvantages (if any) of this type of education?

➤ If you had the opportunity to send your five-year-old to a bilingual immersion school, would you be interested in taking up this option?

➤ Do you think your reactions would be influenced by a particular immersion language?

PARTICIPANTS

This brief interview should take you no more than ten to fifteen minutes. Try to interview about ten individuals, preferably those who come from a monolingual background. Are their attitudes what you expected?

Task C6.2 – Exploring bilingual immersion education in your community or country (Part 1)

As we all know, the Internet is a major source of information about many different things. Using the Internet resources you have available to you, find out, firstly, whether there are any bilingual immersion programmes (for majority children, two-way, or indigenous) available in the community or the country in which you live. If there are none, you may need to search further afield and find some information about an immersion programme somewhere else. Try to find information on an actual school website, rather than second-hand through a journal article or chapter. Explore the site, and see if you can find the answers to the following questions:

➤ Do all children enrolled in the school attend the bilingual programme, or can parents choose to have their children educated in the mainstream majority language?

➤ What language is the majority language, and what is the immersion language?

➤ What ages does the programme cater for?

➤ How much immersion is there in the children's second language (e.g. is it 90/10, 60/40, 50/50 etc.)?

➤ Does the proportion of immersion change over time, and if so, how?

➤ What subjects are taught in the child's second language?

➤ What subjects are taught in the child's first language?

➤ Is there any indication of the extent to which parents are involved in the school's activities?

➤ What kinds of arguments are made as to the advantages of bilingual schooling on the school's website?

➤ Are you told on the website about children's ability to join the bilingual programme in later years?

➤ Is there any information for families of children for whom the immersion language will be a third or fourth language?

➤ Are there any aspects of the immersion programme you examined, specifically in relation to immersion education, which you think could have been better covered in the website?

Task C6.3 – Exploring bilingual immersion education in your community or country (Part 2)

Using the library facilities of your university or college (or using Internet resources if you are not enrolled or do not have access to a university or college library), find a published article about an immersion education programme (there is a vast amount of literature on this, and you should have no trouble finding quite a number of articles). Choose one article and read it carefully. When you have done this, prepare a presentation on the particular programme you found to your class or a group of friends. Make sure you cover the following areas:

- country the programme was found in
- type of programme (what kind of immersion)
- what languages are included
- what type of immersion (partial, full, late, early)
- how immersion works through the school levels
- number of children enrolled in the school.

Now, using Swain and Johnson's (1997) list of core features of immersion programmes (outlined in Unit 6B and reiterated here), work out the degree to which these core features are represented in the programme you are reading about. Swain and Lapkin's (2005) core features are listed here:

1   L2 is the medium of instruction.
2   The immersion curriculum parallels the local L1 curriculum.
3   Overt support exists for the L1.
4   The programme aims for additive bilingualism.
5   Exposure to L2 is largely confined to the classroom.
6   Students enter with similar (and limited) levels of L2 proficiency.
7   The teachers are bilingual.
8   The classroom culture is that of the local L1 community.

 Task C6.4 – Examining the support for biliteracy in the home environment

Aarts and Verhoeven (1999) identified the home environment as a crucial support for developing literacy skills in very young children. One very easy way to see if biliteracy is supported in the home environment is to note the presence of literacy materials in the household. Reporting on an ethnographic study of literacy practice in a Lancaster community, Barton (2001) drew attention to the fact that much literacy learning takes place outside the school, and this is evidenced in the literacy encountered in daily life, for example noticeboards containing details of appointments or social activities, the use of calendars and appointment diaries, address books, lists of phone numbers, handwritten notes, shopping lists, lists of things to do, cards written, collections of books, classification of books etc. Barton observes that such adults' practices provide a crucial point of reference for young children as these contexts are usually their first encounter with literacy.

For the purpose of this task, you will need to visit the home of a bilingual child or teenager, so it might be easier to choose someone you know rather than a stranger.

For this study, try to choose a bilingual child or teenager you know who is between four and fifteen years old. This study can take the style of a semi-structured interview.

➤   First, design a questionnaire to find out about your participant's literacy practices. You may want to ask questions which will lead you to have an understanding of how and when both languages are used.

➤   With the permission of your participant and your participant's parents, do a quick survey of printed materials (e.g. reference books, novels, magazines, newsprint, brochures, posters) in each language available in the home.

➤   Are there age-appropriate materials for your participant in both languages?

➤   Are the child's or teenager's personal literacy practices similar to those of other members of the household?

➤   Look out for temporary notes or lists around the house. For example, do they have a noticeboard? Or invitation cards posted on the fridge? Do parents and children communicate with notes? What languages are used in these notes?

➤   You may want to ask for permission to take pictures of some of these instances of literacy practices.

➤   Finally, collate the information and discuss whether the environment at home is one that encourages literacy practice in both languages.

The main purpose is for you to have a chance to focus on how biliteracy is maintained in a home environment. For the study to be more representative, try interviewing a few more bilinguals of the same age group and from the same language background if possible. However, be aware that this will involve a lot more time in terms of data collection and analysis. For a study of this scale, the data collection for each participant may take up to at least three hours (including travel time), and the analysis may take an additional hour or so. Another approach to interviewing more participants would be to work as a group or a pair.

Task C6.5 – Exploring the extent of biliteracy in bilingual programmes

This task focuses on the extent to which biliteracy is developed in bilingual programmes. You will need to find a bilingual programme in your community to do the study. Note that you will need to get permission from relevant authorities. Some questions which you might want to consider include:

➤   Do the two languages use different scripts?

➤   Are both languages represented in the written communication (notes to parents, pamphlets, announcements)?

➤ Do children perceive themselves to be equally biliterate or do they perceive themselves to be stronger in one language?

➤ Do they read books of the same level in both languages?

➤ Do the schools have any explicit policies on literacy practices? For example, what are some of the school's public statements about multilingualism?

Note that you may have to derive some of these answers through careful questioning and some via observation and that you need to comply with ethical considerations discussed in the preface to this section.

 Task C6.6 – Emergent Literacy Task

As the term suggests, emergent literacy refers to the child's emerging awareness of literacy. Naturally, this happens at different points in time for different children. But generally children take a huge interest in print just before or after their fourth birthday. These three tasks were adapted from Dickinson et al. (2004: 341–342). You can either choose one or two of these tasks to try out with four to five bilingual children of the same language background, or design an equivalent task in another language and try both tasks with four to five bilinguals.

ENVIRONMENTAL PRINT

For this task, you need to collect logos or signs which children are likely to see in your specific environment. You can take pictures of shop signs, trademarks, road signs etc. and use them as stimuli. Show the children the logo or sign and say, 'Tell me what this says.' You can prompt the child if needed with 'Can you guess what it says? What might it say?'

These stimuli are suggested by Dickinson et al. (2004) but you should modify this list and use items that are culturally relevant:

- milk carton
- stop sign
- popcorn
- bread
- McDonald's logo

SENSE OF PRINTED LANGUAGE

The objective of this task is to evaluate children's awareness and sense of printed language. We are going to ask you to show the children word and non-word strings as well as pictures. They will be asked to identify whether each stimulus is a word.

Table C6.1 Stimuli for sense of printed language test

	Word	*Non-word*	*Non-word*
Set 1	BABY	Picture of a baby	Picture of a toy
Set 2	MILK	W3#NJ	NNNT
Set 3	*Mommy*	qfby[	W!a$
Set 4	BIG	🐚☺👕☞😕🍩 ⚡👐	Picture of a tall tree

Present each stimulus on an A4 card. Some examples are shown in Table C6.1. The following is the instruction: 'Now I am going to show you some cards. I want you to show me things that are words. Look at these.' Present the cards from Set 1. Then, say, 'Which one is a word? Point to the word.' Again, when necessary, prompt the child with 'Make a guess. Which one do you think looks most like a word?'

EARLY WRITING

The purpose of this task is to examine children's early writing attempts. For this task, children are given a piece of paper and asked to write their names on it.

Observe what they do and ask, 'Now I would like you to talk about your writing. Can you tell me what you wrote?' A follow-up prompt is asked ('Can you show me how you wrote that?') to determine the children's intentions. In your observation, pay attention to the following:

- directionality (does the child work across the page from left to right, and from top to bottom?)
- intentionality (using a sign to indicate a sound is an example of intentionality)
- conventionality (developmental spelling) (using a sign to regularly indicate a sound is an example of knowing the conventions of how sounds are represented)

Directionality, intentionality and conventionality are all emergent signs of spelling. (For further reference on emergent literacy see Dickinson and Chaney 1997.) When you have finished with the data collection, analyse the responses for each group of children and write up your findings as a report in the format suggested in the preface to this section.

Unit C7
Attitudes and bilingualism explored

In Unit A7, we explored the role language attitudes play in moderating communication in bilingual contexts. We examined the impact of attitudes on proficiency, language choice and identity as well the methodology used in these studies. In Unit B7, we focused on two methodologically different studies. The first is an experimental study which examined how speakers accommodate to each other in a sales context and the other is an ethnographic study which documents the relationship between language and identity as expressed by four English–Punjabi children and teenagers. In both Units A7 and B7, we discussed the methodology used in language-attitudes research.

In this unit, we will ask you to reflect further on the many ways in which bilinguals evaluate and react to the environment in which they live. By replicating some straightforward research methodologies, you will be able to examine some of the tasks we discussed in Unit A7. By replicating these tasks, you will explore at first hand something of the thorny issues that researchers talk about when critiquing data collected from language-attitude research. However, this will also help you appreciate the complexity of measuring a concept like 'attitude'.

Task C7.1 – Attitudes to a minority language: direct questions

Design a questionnaire (see below for possible participants) using some of the questions developed by Hakuta and D'Andrea (1992: 80).

SAMPLE QUESTIONS

Note: all ratings are done on a seven-point Likert scale; the first two are done for you.

Questions indicating maintenance orientation

1   Knowing how to speak language X (indicate the language you are studying) is important to a person's family history.

Strongly disagree   *Strongly agree*

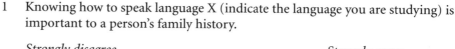

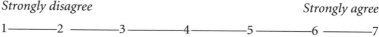

2   How important is it for you to know Language X well?

Not at all important   *Very important*

1 ———2———3———4———5———6———7

3   Using Language X allows a person to feel good about him- or herself.

(strongly disagree/strongly agree)

4   People who know Language X should use it daily, especially at home,

(strongly disagree/strongly agree)

5   It's OK if a person grows up speaking Language X and later forgets it.

(strongly disagree/strongly agree)

Questions indicating subtractive orientation

1   Two Language X-speaking people who also know Language Y should speak Language Y together when they are in public.

(strongly disagree/strongly agree)

2   Two Language X-speaking people who also know Language Y should speak Language Y together even when they are alone.

(strongly disagree/strongly agree)

3   It's possible to speak Language X better without losing the ability to use Language Y.

(strongly disagree/strongly agree)

4   In this country, it is all right for people of Language X descent to not know Language X well because Language X is not this country's main language.

(strongly disagree/strongly agree)

5   It's possible to learn Language Y well without forgetting Language X.

(strongly disagree/strongly agree)

PARTICIPANTS

In relation to participants, there are many variables you can explore, but you may want to start by thinking about aspects of bilingualism that you are interested in, or to come up with some real questions drawn from your own experiences to which you would like to find some answers. As a suggestion, consider the following options for your groups of participants:

- Study one group of bilinguals.
- Study one group of monolinguals.
- Study gender differences in bilinguals.
- Compare bilinguals with monolinguals.
- Compare young bilinguals with elderly bilinguals.
- Compare bilingual children with bilingual adults.
- Compare two groups of bilinguals from different speech communities.

You may also do a methodological study by comparing data collected from one-on-one interviews with data from pen and paper questionnaires using the same questions. For each group, choose eight to ten bilinguals from the same language background and preferably around the same age.

METHOD

As indicated above, you could distribute the questionnaire and get respondents to rate each of the statements along a 1–7 Likert scale, or you could interview them and note the responses down yourself, or you could ask open questions and get respondents to answer each question in writing.

Optional study: If you are working together with someone else, you may also want to collect self-report data on language proficiency. You can develop a simple questionnaire with four questions requiring your participants to rate themselves on the four macro skills (reading, writing, speaking, listening) from 1 to 7. These additional data will enable you to cross-check attitude data against self-report proficiency data.

RESULTS

Do a simple frequency count and discuss the findings in relation to the issues discussed in Unit A7. You may also want to comment on the advantages and disadvantages of using this method to study language attitudes. Can you determine the extent to which one variable may have a greater impact than another? Is it possible to order variables in terms of impact?

Task C7.2 – Perceptions of language groups: semantic differential scale

Using the semantic differential scale (see Unit A7), ask ten bilinguals from the same language background to rate the following languages on a 1–5 Likert scale. Some languages you might consider working on (but you could use others, of course) are:

- Mandarin
- German
- Arabic.

You can provide a simple instruction such as: 'Rate the following languages using the scale provided.'

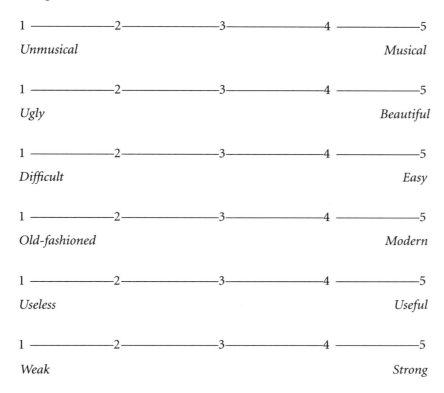

```
1 ——————2————————3————————4 ——————5

Unmusical                                    Musical


1 ——————2————————3————————4 ——————5

Ugly                                        Beautiful


1 ——————2————————3————————4 ——————5

Difficult                                         Easy


1 ——————2————————3————————4 ——————5

Old-fashioned                                  Modern


1 ——————2————————3————————4 ——————5

Useless                                        Useful


1 ——————2————————3————————4 ——————5

Weak                                           Strong
```

As in Task C7.1, you can either just work with bilinguals or monolinguals or you can explore some of the other variables listed in Task C7.1.

Exploration

 Task C7.3 – Code switching (CS) and code mixing (CM): case study

Read this anecdote taken from Ritchie and Bhatia (2004: 338), which demonstrates very well some of the pragmatic constraints on code switching. Pragmatic constraints refer to language-external constraints such as whom someone code-switches with, or aspects of the situational context which triggers code switching.

> The intelligence officer was quite distressed about the trustworthiness of one of the agency's moles. The intelligence agency had made a good decision by hiring a bilingual mole who spoke the language of the target community in addition to English. However, since the agency and its members could not speak the ethnic language of the mole, they felt totally in the dark and were hopelessly dependent on the mole and began to doubt his/her intentions.
>
> At one point, the decision was made that during a major upcoming interaction between the mole and a suspect, the mole would use English so that an officer of the agency could determine his/her loyalty . . . The day came, and when the mole telephoned the suspect in the presence of the officer, (s)he started the conversation with the suspect in their shared ethnic language. However, something remarkable then happened: because of the tacit pragmatic conventions of LMS [language mixing/switching], the violation of which would have tipped the suspect off (with possible dire consequences for the mole), (s)he could not switch to English in spite of his/her explicit assurance to the agency in general and the officer in particular that (s)he would do so. Feeling betrayed, the agency lost its faith in the mole and sought expert advice from the second author. After playing a couple of tape recordings between the mole and the suspect in their native language, the officer asked: Is the mole trustworthy? Is (s)he trying to hide something from the agency? Why didn't (s)he switch to English in accordance with the agency's explicit directive and the mutual agreement?

As we can see from the extract, bilinguals do observe some form of systematic conventions when it comes to code switching. In this case, reverting to the use of English for the mole would have seriously violated the pragmatic constraints of that specific exchange and the mole's relationship with the interlocutor. Can you think of other pragmatic constraints which may govern code switching?

 Task C7.4 – Code switching: observational study

As an exploratory study into code switching, spend a day, or at least a few hours, with a bilingual in their bilingual community (or you can study yourself if you are a bilingual). If you can afford to spend only a few hours, it is best to choose a time when your bilingual friend is surrounded by family members, so mealtimes are often a good occasion for language study. You may want to tell your friend's family to behave as normally as possible, even though it will be hard for them!

METHOD

You will need to use *one* of the following methods for data collection.

➤ Observe your participant and take detailed notes about their language use in a notebook; you will need to identify whom they are talking to, the topic, the language they are using, and whether or not they code-switch. When you have done this, you will need to look through your notes, and make sure that they are legible and understandable, and preferably type them up.

➤ Using a small tape recorder or digital recorder, preferably with a lapel microphone, record your participant interacting with a variety of people during the day. When you have done this, you will need to listen to the recording and transcribe it.

Remember to be careful about obtaining informed consent (see notes in the preface to section C).

RESULTS

If you tape the interactions, you will need to transcribe the recording. It is best to do the transcription as soon as you can so that you can annotate the transcripts with contextual details while they are still fresh in your mind. Transcription is time-consuming, and often can take between five and ten times the time of the original recording, depending on the quality of the tape, and the difficulty level of the original recording.

ANALYSING YOUR DATA

Using your typed transcript of your notes or recording, identify incidents of code switching by either highlighting or marking them in some other way.

In your analysis, you may want to answer the following questions:

➤ Which language does your informant speak the most?

➤ Whom do they speak to in each language?

➤ To what extent do they code-switch when speaking Language A and Language B?

➤ Do their patterns of code switching vary depending on:
  ■ age of interlocutor?
  ■ language of interlocutor?
  ■ the topic or theme of the talk at various moments?
  ■ any other criteria you can identify?

After you have answered all the questions, check to see if you can draw any generalizations about when and why code switching takes place. Remember that this is a case study only and your bilingual friend may or may not conform to the findings that have been reported in the literature. The general idea is for you to have a feel for how natural code switching is for bilingual speakers. You may ask your friend to try hard not to mix languages with a person they normally code-switch with for one day. After that, ask them if they were successful in doing so and get them to talk about the process of trying to change such a pragmatic routine.

 Task C7.5 – Attitude to code switching

If you have completed Task C7.4, you may want to isolate a two-minute segment of the tape, if you have a recording. If not, find a bilingual who can give you a one- to two-minute recording of a speech sample which includes some code switching. This will provide you with material for the study.

PARTICIPANTS

The choice of participants may remain similar to those listed in Task C7.1.

METHOD

Play the tape or the MP3 recording to the participant either individually or in a group and ask them to rate the speaker on a semantic-differential scale. Which adjectives would you use for such a scale in this context?

RESULTS

Summarize and discuss the attitudes to code switching of your participants. If you have access to speech pathologists or teachers, you could also try using them as your participants.

 Task C7.6 – Matched-guise (MG) tests

Matched-guise tests are not too difficult to design and implement. The hardest part is to find a bilingual who can perform the guises naturally. The next difficulty is to find a scripted scenario for the bilingual where the content is neutral in each language. For example, the script could be an answer to the question 'What do you do every morning?' To preserve neutrality, most researchers choose topics such as 'What do you do every morning?' or 'What do you like about the zoo?' Naturally, the samples have to be controlled in such a way that the two versions do not incorporate clues about social status. So, for example, 'Most mornings I start the day with a swim in our pool' contains a clue that the speaker has an affluent lifestyle. Similarly, 'I normally wake up with a hangover' also provides a clue to the speaker's socially active lifestyle. All these could affect the response of the participants. The following is a possible script:

> My alarm usually goes off at 7.30. The first thing I do is to let the cat out. By the time I am showered and dressed, it is usually 8. I normally have the radio on so that I get to hear the morning news. Breakfast is a simple affair of coffee and toast but on days when I have a bit more time, I may make myself a sandwich. I like to take my time over breakfast and read the newspaper. Just before leaving for work, I water the plants and leave some food and water out for the cat. I normally leave for work at 8.45. Since I don't work too far away, I am usually in my office by 9.20.

If you are surveying the attitudes to English compared with those to French, you will need to script the same speech in French, and then ask your English–French bilingual to record the two guises. It is also important to make the two recordings as natural as possible and it is always advisable to separate the two guises with another recording. This could be a recording of another speaker, answering either the same question or a different question. The main purpose is to separate the two matched-guise recordings.

For the procedure, you just have to ask the participants (either singly or in a group) to rate the speakers on a set of semantic-differential scales. For this study to be really meaningful, it is ideal to find at least twenty participants. This may not be too onerous if you can do the study in batches or in a group.

Further reading

UNIT A1 DESCRIBING BILINGUALISM

Grosjean, F. (1998). An important paper which highlights the methodological pitfalls in bilingual studies in both normal and special populations. Another writer who discusses this issue clearly is Li Wei (2000).

Fishman, J. (1965). A significant paper 'Who speaks what language to whom and when?' which discusses the importance of *domain* when discussing language use in bilingual contexts.

Myers-Scotton (2006). Chapter 2 provides a good description of the distinction between 'dialects' and 'language' and Chapter 3 presents bilingual situations around the world and discusses the factors that create bilingualism.

UNIT A2 MEASURING BILINGUALISM

McNamara (2000) is an accessible introduction to language testing and assessment. The book includes a survey of each area discussed followed by some brief but pertinent readings, and an annotated bibliography and a glossary.

Driessen et al. (2002) reports on the results of a large-scale longitudinal study focusing on the language proficiency of primary school children in the Netherlands who come from different language backgrounds. The study examines the impact of these different backgrounds on the children developing proficiency in Dutch.

UNIT A3 BILINGUAL ACQUISITION

Cenoz and Genesee (2001) is an edited volume which consists of ten papers by well-known authors which present detailed studies of topic issues in bilingual (and trilingual) acquisition.

De Houwer (1999) discusses the impact that parental attitudes and beliefs can have on children's bilingual language development and examines some of the sociolinguistic factors which can impact upon the extent to which children maintain their two languages over time.

Zentella (1997) details an in-depth account of Puerto Ricans growing up in New York in a bilingual environment and raises a range of fascinating insights into the complexities of living in culturally diverse multilingual settings.

UNIT A4 BILINGUALISM AND COGNITIVE ABILITY

Bialystok et al. (2005). The paper discusses the performance of bilinguals compared to monolinguals on tasks requiring controlled attention across the lifespan. With the exception of young adulthood, bilinguals performed better than monolinguals in early childhood, adulthood and older adulthood on such tasks. This paper is important when considering earlier papers which argue that bilingual advantage is shortlived.

The following studies explore how bilingualism enhances third-language acquisition. The paper by Clyne et al. (2004) discusses how learning a third language can in fact strengthen the home language.

Cenoz (2003)
Clyne et al. (2004)
Sanz, C. (2000)
Huber and Lasagabaster (2000)
Swain et al. (1990)

UNIT A5 LANGUAGE ATTRITION IN BILINGUALS

Hansen et al. (2002) focuses on vocabulary relearning and examines how length of time and level of proficiency impact on learning and relearning of vocabulary items from previously learned languages (Japanese and Korean).

Schmid et al. (2004) is an edited volume which examines both theoretical and methodological issues in relation to language attrition, and includes several empirical studies, as well as an annotated bibliography. This is a very useful book for anyone interested in pursuing their interests in language attrition.

UNIT A6 EDUCATION AND LITERACY IN BILINGUAL SETTINGS

Brisk (2006) provides detailed insights into the range and variety of bilingual programmes available with a focus on the features which contribute to successful bilingual outcomes.

Rickard-Liow and Lee (2004). Investigates spelling errors by Malay children and demonstrates that their spelling development is influenced by their knowledge of syllables and morphemes, unlike English-speaking children.

Wang et al. (2006). A study on biliteracy transfer in Korean–English bilinguals.

UNIT A7 ATTITUDES AND BILINGUALISM

Pakir, A. (1994) and Wee, L. (2003) present two contrasting perspectives on the development of bilingualism in Singapore. Also see Li and Milroy (2003).

Shohamy, E. (2006). A succinct and insightful discussion of how language policies and other agencies such as language tests work to uphold particular ideology and belief systems.

Pavlenko, A. (2004). This study looks at how emotions affect the parent–child relationship and language choice. This author has also written two books on bilingualism and emotions (see, for example, Pavlenko, A. (2006) *Emotions and multilingualism* (Cambridge: Cambridge University Press).

References

Aarts, R., De Ruiter, P., and Verhoeven, L. 1993. *Tweetaligheid en schoolsucces* [Bilingualism and school success]. Tilburg: Tilburg University Press

Aarts, R. and Verhoeven, L. 1999. Literacy attainment in a second language submersion context. *Applied Psycholinguistics*, 20: 377–393

Abu-Rabia, Salim. 2001. Testing the Interdependence Hypothesis among native adult bilingual Russian–English students. *Journal of Psycholinguistic Research*, 30 (4): 437–455

Adams, M.J. 1990. *Beginning to read: Thinking and learning about print.* Cambridge, MA: MIT Press

Adegbija, E. 2000. Language attitudes in West Africa. *International Journal of the Sociology of Language*, 141: 75–100

Agheyisi, R. and Fishman, J. 1970. Language attitudes: a brief survey of methodological approaches. *Anthropological Linguistics*, 12 (5): 137–157

Aiken, L.R. and Groth-Marnat, G. (2006) *Psychological testing and assessment* (12th ed.). Boston: Allyn and Bacon

Aikenvald, A. 2003. Multilingualism and ethnic stereotype: The Tariana of north-west Amazonia. *Language in Society*, 32: 1–22

Aitchison, J. 1994. *Words in the mind: An introduction to the mental lexicon* (2nd ed.). Oxford: Blackwell

Allen, M. 2004. Reading achievement of students in French immersion programs. *Education Quarterly Review*, 9 (4): 25–48

Altarriba, J. and Morier, R.G. 2004. Bilingualism: language, emotion, and mental health. In Bhatia, T.K. and Ritchie, W.C. (eds) *The handbook of bilingualism.* Malden, MA, and Oxford: Blackwell, pp. 250–281

Anderson, R. 2001. Lexical morphology and verb use in child first language loss: A preliminary case study investigation. *International Journal of Bilingualism*, 5 (4): 377–401

Arsenian, S. 1937. *Bilingualism and mental development.* New York: Teachers College Press

Arthur, G. 1937. The predictive value of the Kuhlmann–Binet Scale for a partially Americanized school population. *Journal of Applied Psychology*, 21: 359–364

Bachman, L. 1990. *Fundamental considerations in language testing.* Oxford: Oxford University Press

Bachman, L.F. and Cohen, A.D. 1998. Appendix: Language testing–SLA interfaces: An update. In Bachman, L.F. and Cohen, A.D. (eds) *Interfaces between second language acquisition and language testing research.* Cambridge: Cambridge University Press, pp. 1–31

Bachman, L. and Palmer, A. 1996. *Language testing in practice.* Oxford: Oxford University Press

Backus, A. 2004. Turkish as an immigrant language in Europe. In Bhatia, T.K. and Ritchie, W.C. (eds) *The handbook of bilingualism.* Malden, MA, and Oxford: Blackwell, pp. 689–724

Baetens Beardsmore, H. 1982. *Bilingualism: Basic principles.* Clevedon: Multilingual Matters

Baetens Beardsmore, H. and Swain, M. 1985. Designing bilingual education: aspects of immersion and European school models. *Journal of Multilingual and Multicultural Development*, 6 (1): 1–15

Bahrick, H. 1984. Fifty years of second language attrition: implications for programmatic research. *Modern Language Journal*, 68: 105–118

Bain, B. and Olswang, I. 1995. Examining readiness for learning two-word utterances by children with specific expressive language impairment: dynamic assessment validation. *American Journal of Speech-Language Pathology*, 4: 81–91

Baker, C. 1992. *Attitudes and language.* Clevedon: Multilingual Matters

Baker, C. 2006. *Foundation of bilingual education and bilingualism* (4th ed.) Clevedon: Multilingual Matters

Baker, S. and MacIntyre, P. 2003. The role of gender and immersion in communication and second language orientations. *Language Learning*, 53 (1): 65–96

Baker, C., Placensia-Pienado, J., and Lezcano-Lytle, V. 1998. The use of curriculum-based measurement with language-minority students. In Shinn, M. (ed.) *Advanced applications of curriculum based assessment.* New York: Guilford Press, pp. 174–213

Balkan, L. 1970. *Les effets du bilinguisme français–anglais sur les aptitudes intellectuelles.* Brussels: Aimav

Baron, R.A. and Byrne, D. 1997. *Social psychology.* Boston, MA: Allyn and Bacon

Barreña, A. 2001. Grammar differentiation in early bilingual acquisition: subordination structures in Spanish and Basque. In Almgren, M., Barreña, A., Ezeizabarrena, M.-J., Idiazabal, I., and MacWhinney, B. (eds) *Research on child language acquisition: Proceedings of the Eighth Conference of the International Association for the Study of Child Language.* Somerville, MA: Cascadilla Press

Barton, D. 2001. Literacy in everyday contexts. In Verhoeven, L. and Snow, C. (eds) *Literacy and motivation: Ready engagement in individuals and groups.* London: Lawrence Erlbaum, pp. 23–38

Batalova, J. 2006. Spotlight on limited English proficient students in the United States. *Migration Information Source*, accessed at http://www.migrationinformation.org/USfocus/display.cfm?ID=373 on 3 May 2006

Ben-Zeev, S. 1977. The influence of bilingualism on cognitive strategy and cognitive development. *Child Development*, 48: 1009–1018

Bentahila, A. 1983. *Language attitudes among Arabic–French bilinguals in Morocco.* Clevedon: Multilingual Matters

Bere, M. 1924. *A comparative study of the mental capacity of children of foreign parentage.* New York: Teaching College, University of Columbia

Bereiter, C. and Scardamalia, M. 1981. From conversation to composition: the role of instruction in a developmental process. In Glaser, R. (ed.) *Advances in Instructional Psychology*, vol. 2. Hillsdale, NJ: Lawrence Erlbaum, Unit B2

Berko, J. 1958. The child's learning of English morphology. *Word*, 14: 150–177

Bernhardt, B. and Johnson, C.E. 1996. Sentence production models: explaining children's filler syllables. In Johnson, C.E. and Gilbert, J.H.V. (eds) *Children's language*, vol. 9. Mahwah, NJ: Lawrence Erlbaum, pp. 253–281

Bernhardt, B.H. and Stemberger, J.P. 1998. *Handbook of phonological development from the perspective of constraint-based nonlinear phonology.* San Diego: Academic Press

Bettoni, C. 1985. Italian language attrition: a Sydney case study. In Clyne, M. (ed.) *Australia, meeting places of languages.* Pacific Linguistics C92. Canberra: Department of Linguistics, Research School of Pacific Studies, pp. 63–79

Bhabha, H. 1994. *The location of culture.* London: Routledge

Bhatia, T.K. and Ritchie, W.C. 2004. Bilingualism in the global media and advertising. In Bhatia, T.K. and Ritchie, W.C. (eds) *The handbook of bilingualism*. Malden, MA, and Oxford: Blackwell, pp. 513–546

Bialystok, E. 1986a. Children's concept of word. *Journal of Psycholinguistic Research*, 15: 13–31

Bialystok, E. 1986b. Factors in the growth of linguistic awareness. *Child Development*, 57: 489–510

Bialystok, E. 1987a. Influences of bilingualism on metalinguistic development. *Second Language Research*, 3 (2): 112–125

Bialystok, E. 1987b. Words as things: development of word concept by bilingual children. *Second Language Learning*, 9: 133–140

Bialystok, E. 1988. Levels of bilingualism and levels of linguistic awareness. *Developmental Psychology*, 24: 560–567

Bialystok, E. 1993. Metalinguistic awareness: the development of children's representations of language. In Pratt, C. and Garton, A. (eds) *Systems of representation in children: development and use*. London: Wiley, pp. 211–233

Bialystok, E. 1997a. The structure of age: in search of barriers to second language acquisition. *Second Language Research*, 132: 116–137

Bialystok, E. 1997b. Effect of bilingualism and biliteracy on children's emerging concepts of print. *Developmental Psychology*, 33: 429–440

Bialystok, E. 2001a. *Bilingualism and development: Language, literacy, and cognition*. Cambridge: Cambridge University Press

Bialystok, E. 2001b. Metalinguistic aspects of bilingual processing. *Annual Review of Applied Linguistics*, 21: 169–181

Bialystock, E. 2004. The impact of bilingualism on language and literacy development. In Bhatia, T.K. and Ritchie, W.C. (eds) *The handbook of bilingualism*. Malden and Oxford: Blackwell, pp. 577–601

Bialystock, E., Luk, G., and Kwan, E. 2005. Bilingualism, biliteracy, and learning to read: interactions among languages and writing systems. *Scientific Studies of Reading*, 9 (1): 43–61

Bialystok, E., Martin, M., and Viswanathan, M. 2005. Bilingualism across the lifespan: the rise and fall of inhibitory control. *International Journal of Bilingualism*, 9 (1): 103–119

Bild, E.-R. and Swain, M. 1989. Minority language students in a French immersion programme: their French proficiency. *Journal of Multilingual and Multicultural Development*, 10 (3): 255–274

Birdsong, D. 1992. Ultimate attainment in second language acquisition. *Language*, 684: 706–755

Birdsong, D. 2005. Interpreting age effects in second language acquisition. In Kroll, J. and De Groot, A. (eds) *Handbook of bilingualism: Psycholinguistic approaches*. New York: Oxford University Press, pp. 109–127

Birdsong, D. and Molis, M. 2001. On the evidence for maturational constraints in second-language acquisition. *Journal of Memory and Language*, 44: 235–249

Bloomfield, L. 1933. *Language*. New York: Holt, Rinehart and Winston

Bokamba, E.G. 1988. Code-mixing, language variation and linguistic theory. *Lingua*, 76: 21–62

Bortoni-Ricardo, S.M. (1985) *The urbanization of rural dialect speakers*, Boston, MA: Allyn and Bacon

Bostwick, M. 2001. English immersion in a Japanese school. In Christian, D. and Genesee, F. (eds) *Bilingual education*. Arlington, VA: TESOL

Bourhis, R.Y. 1979. Language in ethnic interaction: a social psychology approach. In Giles,

J. and Saint Jacques, B. (eds) *Language and ethnic relations*. Oxford: Pergamon Press, pp. 117–142

Bourhis, R.Y. 1983. Language attitudes and self reports of French–English language usage in Quebec. *Journal of Multilingual and Multicultural Development*, 4: 163–179

Bourhis, R.Y. 1984a. Cross cultural communication in Montreal: two field studies since Bill 101. *International Journal of the Sociology of Language*, 46: 33–47

Bourhis, R.Y. 1984b. The charter of the French language and cross-cultural communication in Montreal. In Bourhis, R.Y. (ed.) *Conflict and language planning in Quebec*. Clevedon: Multilingual Matters, pp. 174–204

Bourhis, R.Y., Giles, H., Leyens, J., and Tajfel, H. 1979. Psycholinguistic distinctiveness: language divergence in Belgium. In Giles, H., and St Clair, R. (eds) *Language and social psychology*. Oxford: Blackwell, pp. 158–185

Bourhis, R.Y. and Sachdev, 1. 1984. Subjective vitality perceptions and language attitudes. *Journal of Language and Social Psychology*, 3: 97–126

Bowey, J.A. and Tunmer, W.E. 1984. Word awareness in children. In Tunmer, W., Pratt, C., and Herriman, M. (eds) *Metalinguistic awareness in children: Theory, research, and implications*. Berlin: Springer, pp. 73–91

Brice, A.E. 2002. *The Hispanic child: Speech, language, culture and education*. Boston: Allyn and Bacon

Brisk, M.E. 2006. *Bilingual education: From compensatory schooling to quality schooling*. Mahwah, NJ: Lawrence Erlbaum

Brisk, M.E. and Harrington, M.M. 2000. *Literacy and bilingaulism: A handbook for all teachers*. Mahwah, NJ: Lawrence Erlbaum

Brown, H.D. 2004. *Language assessment: Principles and classroom practices*. New York: Longman

Bruck, M. and Genesee, F. 1995. Phonological awareness in young second language learners. *Journal of Child Language*, 22: 307–324

Bush, C., Edwards, M.L., Luckau, J., Stoel, C., Macken, M. and Petersen, J. 1973. *On specifying a system for transcribing consonants in child language: A working paper with examples from American English and Mexican Spanish*. Stanford, CA: Stanford University, Committee on Linguistics, Child Phonology Project

Calderón, M. and Slavin, R. 2001. Success for all in a two-way immersion school. In Christian, D. and Genesee, F. (eds) *Bilingual education*. Arlington, VA: TESOL

Campbell, R. and Sais, E. 1995. Accelerated metalinguistic phonological awareness in bilingual children. *British Journal of Developmental Psychology*, 13: 61–68

Cargile, A.C., Giles, H., Ryan, E.B., and Bradac, J. 1994. Language attitudes as a social process: a conceptual model and new directions. *Language and Communication*, 14 (3): 211–236

Carranza, M.A. and Ryan, E.B. 1975. Evaluative reactions of bilingual Anglo and Mexican adolescents toward speakers of English and Spanish. *International Journal of the Sociology of Language*, 6: 83–104

Cavallaro, F.P. 1998. Language dynamics of the Italian community in Australia. Unpublished Ph.D. thesis, Monash University

Cenoz, J. 2003. The additive effect of bilingualism on third language acquisition. *International Journal of Bilingualism*, 7: 71–87

Cenoz, J. and Genesee, F. (eds) 2001. *Trends in bilingual acquisition*. Amsterdam and Philadelphia: John Benjamins

Chapelle, C.A. 1998. Construct definition and validity inquiry in SLA research. In Bachman, L.F. and Cohen, A.D. (eds) *Interfaces between second language acquisition and language testing research*. Cambridge: Cambridge University Press, pp. 32–70

Cheng, L.-I. 1991. *Assessing Asian language performance: Guidelines for evaluating Limited-*

English-Proficient students (2nd edn). Oceanside, CA: Academic Communication Associates

Chiung, Wi-vun Taiffalo 2001. Language attitudes towards written Taiwanese. *Journal of Multilingual and Multicultural Development*, 22 (6): 502–523

Choi, J. 2003. Language attitudes and the future of of bilingualism: the case of Paraguay. *International Journal of Bilingual Education and Bilingualism*, 6 (2): 81–94

Chow, P. and Cummins, J. 2003. Valuing multilingual and multicultural approaches to learning. In Schecter, S.R. and Cummins, J. (eds) *Multilingual education in practice*. Portsmouth, NH: Heinemann, pp. 32–61

Clark, E. 2003. Critical periods, time and practice. *University of Pennsylvania Working Papers in Linguistics*, 92: 39–48

Clarkson, P.C. and Galbraith, P. 1992. Bilingualism and mathematics learning: another perspective. *Journal for Research in Mathematics Education*, 23 (1): 34–44

Cline, T. 1998. The assessment of special educational needs for bilingual children. *British Journal of Special Education*, 25 (4): 159–163

Clyne, M. 1991. *Community languages: The Australian experience*. Cambridge: Cambridge University Press

Clyne, M. 1996. Multilingualism. In Coulmas, F. (ed.) *Handbook of sociolinguistics*. London: Basil Blackwell, pp. 301–314

Clyne, M. 2003. *Dynamics of language contact: English and immigrant languages*. Cambridge: Cambridge University Press

Clyne, M. 2005. *Australia's language potential*. Sydney: University of New South Wales Press

Clyne, M. 2006. Some exploratory comments relating sociolinguistic typology to language shift. In Thornburg, L. and Fuller, J.M. (eds) *Studies in contact linguistics: Essays in honor of Glenn G. Gilbert*. New York: Peter Lang, pp. 207–230

Clyne, M., Hunt, C., Rossi, C., and Isaakidis, T. 2004. Learning a community language as a third language. *International Journal of Multilingualism*, 11: 33–52

Cohen, A. 1986. Forgetting foreign-language vocabulary. In Weltens, B. De Bot, K., and Van Els, T. (eds) *Language attrition in progress*. Dordrecht: Foris Publications

Cohen, A. 1989. Attrition in the productive lexicon of two Portuguese third language speakers. *Studies in Second Language Acquisition*, 11 (2) (June): 135–149

Coleman, W. 1984. Social class and language polices in Quebec. In Bourhis, R.Y. (ed.) *Conflict and language planning in Quebec*. Clevedon: Multilingual Matters, pp. 130–147

Comeau, L., Genesee, F., Nicoladis, E., and Vrakas, G., 1997. Can young bilingual children identify their language choice as a cause of breakdown in communication? In Hughes, E.., Hughes, M., and Greenhill, A. (eds) *Proceedings of the Twenty-first Annual Boston University Conference on Language Development*. Somerville, MA: Cascadilla Press, pp. 79–90

Cotacachi, M. 1996. Attitudes of teachers, children and parents toward bilingual intercultural education. In Hornberger, N.H. (ed.) *Indigenous language literacies in the Americas: Language planning from the bottom up*. Berlin: Mouton de Gruyter, pp. 285–298

Cromdal, J., 1999. Childhood bilingualism and metalinguistic skills: analysis and control in young Swedish–English bilinguals. *Applied Psycholinguistics*, 20: 1–20

Crutchley, A. 1999. Professional attitudes and experience in relation to bilingual children attending language units. *British Educational Research Journal*, 25 (3): 371–387

Crutchley, A., Conti-Ramsden, G., and Botting, N. 1997. Bilingual children with SLI and standard assessments: preliminary findings from a study of children in language units. *International Journal of Bilingualism*, 1 (2): 117–134

Cruz-Ferreira, M. 2006. *Three is a crowd? Acquiring Portuguese in a trilingual environment.* Clevedon: Multilingual Matters

Cummins, J. 1976. The influence of bilingualism on cognitive growth: a synthesis of research findings and explanatory hypotheses. *Working Papers on Bilingualism*, 9: 1–43

Cummins, J. 1977. Delaying native language reading instruction in immersion programs: a cautionary note. *Canadian Modern Language Review*, 34: 46–49

Cummins, J. 1978. Immersion programs: the Irish experience. *International Review of Education*, 24: 273–282

Cummins, J. 1979. Linguistic interdependence and the educational development of bilingual children. *Review of Educational Research*, 49: 221–251

Cummins, J. 1981. Empirical and theoretical underpinnings of bilingual education. *Journal of Education*, 163 (1): 16–29

Cummins, J. 1984. *Bilingualism and special education: Issues in assessment and pedagogy.* Clevedon: Multilingual Matters

Cummins, J. 1991. Interdependence of first- and second-language proficiency in bilingual children. In Bialystok, E. (ed.) *Language processing in the bilingual child.* Cambridge: Cambridge University Press

Cummins, J. 1994. Semilingualism. In *Encyclopedia of language and linguistics* (2nd ed.). Oxford: Elsevier Science, pp. 3812–3814

Cummins, J. 2000. *Language, power and pedagogy: Bilingual children in the crossfire.* Clevedon: Multilingual Matters

Cummins, J. and Gulutsan, M. 1973. Some effects of bilingualism on cognitive functioning. Mimeo. Edmonton, Alberta: University of Alberta

Dagenais, D. and Berron, C. 2001. Promoting multilingualism through French immersion and language maintenance in three immigrant families. *Language, Culture and Curriculum*, 14: 142–155

Dagenais, D. and Day, E. 1998. Classroom language experiences of trilingual children in French immersion. *Canadian Modern Language Review*, 54: 376–393

D'Anglejan, A. 1984. Language planning in Quebec: an historical overview and future trends. In Bourhis, R.Y. (ed.) *Conflict and language planning in Quebec.* Clevedon: Multilingual Matters, pp. 29–52

Darcy, N.T. 1953. A review of the literature on the effects of bilingualism upon the measurement of intelligence. *Journal of Genetic Psychology*, 82: 21–57

Darling-Hammond, L. 1994. Performance-based assessment and educational equity. *Harvard Educational Review*, 64 (1): 5–30

Davies, A. 1991a. *The native speaker in applied linguistics.* Edinburgh: Edinburgh University Press

Davies, A. 1991b. The notion of native speaker. *Journal of Intercultural Studies*, 122: 35–45

Davies, A., Brown, A., Elder, C., Hill, K., Lumley, T., and McNamara, T. 1999. *Dictionary of language testing.* Cambridge: Cambridge University Press

Davine, M., Tucker, G.R., and Lambert, W.E. 1971. The perception of phoneme sequences by monolingual and bilingual elementary school children. *Canadian Journal of Behavioral Science*, 3 (1): 72–76

Davis, B. and MacNeilage, P. 1990. Acquisition of correct vowel production: a quantitative study. *Journal of Speech and Hearing Research*, 33, 12–27

Dawe, L. 1983. Bilingualism and mathematical reasoning in English as a second language. *Educational Studies in Mathematics*, 14: 325–353

De Bot, K. 2001. Language use as an interface between sociolinguistic and psycholinguistic processes in language attrition and shift. In Klatter-Folmer, J. and Van Avermaet, P. (eds)

Theories on maintenance and loss of minority languages: Towards a more integrated explanatory framework. Münster: Waxman

De Bot, K. and Clyne, M. 1989. Language reversion revisited. *Studies in Second Language Acquisition,* 11: 167–177

De Bot, K. and Clyne, M. 1994. A 16 year longitudinal study of language attrition in Dutch immigrants in Australia. *Journal of Multilingual and Multicultural Development,* 15 (1): 17–28

De Bot, K. and Hansen, L. 2001. Reactivating a 'forgotten' language: the Savings-paradigm applied. Symposium presented at AAAL, St Louis, MI, 26 February

De Bot, K., Lowie, W., and Verspoor, M. 2005. *Second language acquisition: An advanced resource book.* London: Routledge

De Bot, K. and Stoessel, S. 1999. Finding residual lexical knowledge: the 'savings' approach to testing vocabulary. Paper presented at the American Association for Applied Linguistics Conference, Seattle, March

De Bot, K. and Stoessel, S. 2000. In search of yesterday's words: reactivating a long-forgotten language. *Applied Linguistics,* 21 (3): 333–353

De Bot, K. and Weltens, B. 1991. Recapitulation, regression and language loss. In Seliger, H.W. and Vago, R.M. (eds) *First language attrition.* Cambridge: Cambridge University Press, pp. 31–51

De Bot, K. and Weltens, B. 1995. Foreign language attrition. *Annual Review of Applied Linguistics,* 15: 151–164

De Groot, A. and Kroll, J. 1997. *Tutorials in bilingualism: Psycholinguistic perspectives.* Mahwah, NJ: Lawrence Erlbaum

De Houwer, A. 1990. *The acquisition of two languages from birth: A case study.* Cambridge: Cambridge University Press

De Houwer, A. 1995. Bilingual language acquisition. In Fletcher, P. and MacWhinney, B. (eds) *The handbook of child language.* Oxford: Blackwell

De Houwer, A. 1999. Environmental factors in early bilingual development: the role of parental beliefs and attitudes. In Extra, G. and Verhoeven, L. (eds) *Bilingualism and migration.* Berlin and New York: Mouton de Gruyter

De Klerk, V. 2000. To be Xhosa or not to be Xhosa . . . That is the Question. *Journal of Multilingual and Multicultural Development,* 21 (3), 198–215.

D'Entremont, Y. and Garneau, A. 2003. French immersion in Alberta: are the Sciences being taught in French at the secondary level? *Journal of Educational Thought,* 37 (3): 329–347

Deuchar, M. and Clark, A. 1996. Early bilingual acquisition of the voicing contrast in English and Spanish. *Journal of Phonetics,* 24: 351–365

Deuchar, M. and Quay, S. 1999. Language choice in the earliest utterances: a case study with methodological implications. *Journal of Child Language,* 26: 461–475

Deuchar, M. and Quay, S. 2000. *Bilingual acquisition: Theoretical implications of a case study.* Oxford: Oxford University Press

Diaz Rico, L. and Weed, K. 1995. *The crosscultural, language and academic development handbook.* Needham Heights, MA: Allyn and Bacon

Dickinson, D.K. and Chaney, C. 1997. *Emergent literacy profile.* Newton, MA: Education Development Center

Dickinson, D., McCabe, A., Clark-Chiarelli, N., and Wolf, A. 2004. Cross-language transfer of phonological awareness in low-income Spanish and English bilingual preschool children. *Applied Psycholinguistics,* 35: 323–347

Disbray, S. and Wigglesworth, G. In press. Variability in children's language input in three communities in Aboriginal Australia. In Robinson, G., Goodnow, J., Katz, I., and

Eickelkamp, U. (eds) *Contexts of child development: Culture policy and intervention*. Alice Springs: Charles Darwin University Press

Dixon, J.A., Tredoux, C.G., Durrheim, K., and Foster, D.H. 1994. The role of speech accommodation and crime type in attribution of guilt. *Journal of Social Psychology*, 134: 465–473

Domingue, N. 1978. L'usage bilingue dans le centre de Montréal. In Paradis, M. (ed.) *Aspects of bilingualism*. Columbia, SC: Hornbeam Press

Döpke, S. 1992. *One parent, one language: An interactional approach*. Amsterdam: John Benjamins

Döpke, S. 2003. Theoretical and practical issues in the language assessment of culturally and linguistically diverse children. MA coursework thesis, Faculty of Health Sciences, School of Human Communication Sciences, La Trobe University, Australia

Dorian, N. 1978. The dying dialect and the role of the schools: East Sutherland Gaelic and Pennsylvania Dutch. In Alatis, J.E. (ed.) *International dimension of bilingual education*. Washington, DC: Georgetown University Press, pp. 646–656

Dorian, N. 2004. Minority and endangered languages. In Bhatia, T.K. and Ritchie, W.C. (eds) *The handbook of bilingualism*. Malden, MA, and Oxford: Blackwell, pp. 437–459

Dörnyei, Z. and Clément, R. 2001. Motivational characteristics of learning different target languages. In Dörnyei, Z. and Schmidt, R. (eds) *Motivation and second language acquisition*. Honolulu: University of Hawai'i Press, pp. 399–432

Downes, Simon. 2001. Sense of Japanese cultural identity within an English partial immersion programme: should parents worry? *International Journal of Bilingual Education and Bilingualism*, 4 (3): 165–180

Driessen, G., Van der Slik, F., and De Bot, K. 2002. Home language and language proficiency: a large-scale longitudinal study in Dutch primary schools. *Journal of Multilingual and Multicultural Development*, 23 (3): 175–194

Dunn, L.M. 1959. *Peabody picture vocabulary test*. Nashville, TN: American Guidance Service.

Ecke, P. 1997. Foreign language learners' retrieval strategies for words that are on the tip of the tongue. Paper presented at AAAL Annual Conference, Orlando, FL, 9 March

Edelsky, C., Hudelson, S., Flores, B., Barkin, F., Altweger, J., and Jilbert, K. 1983. Semilingualism and language deficit. *Applied Linguistics*, 4: 1–22

Edwards, V. 1998. *The power of Babel: teaching and learning in multilingual classrooms*. Reading: Trentham Books

Eimas, P.D., Siqueland, E.R., Jusczyk, P., and Vigorito, J. 1971. Speech perception in infants. *Science*, 171: 303–306

Erickson, J. and Iglesias, A. 1986. Assessment of communication disorders in non-English proficient children. In Taylor, O. (ed) *Nature of communication disorders in culturally and linguistically diverse populations*. San Diego, CA: College-Hill Press, pp. 181–217

Evans, S.J. 1953. Address of the Conference of Headmasters of Grammar Schools, Wales, 1906. In Central Advisory Council for Education (Wales) *The place of Welsh and English in the schools of Wales*, London: Her Majesty's Stationery Office

Fasold, R. 1984. *The sociolinguistics of society*. Oxford: Basil Blackwell

Federation for American Immigration Reform (2004) *The Stein report*. Retrieved 18 January 2005 from: http://www.steinreport.com/archives/004022.html

Feldman, C. and Shen, M. 1971. Some language-related cognitive advantages of bilingual five-year-olds. *Journal of Genetic Psychology*, 118: 234–235

Fenson, L., Dale, P.S., Reznick, J.S., Thal, D., Bates, E., Hartung, J.P., Pethick, S., and Reilly, J.S. 1993. *MacArthur communicative development inventories*. San Diego, CA: Singular Publishing Group

Ferguson, C.A. 1959. Diglossia. *Word*, 15: 325–340

Ferguson, G.A. 1954. On learning and human ability. *Canadian Journal of Psychology*, 8: 95–112

Figueroa, R. 1989. Psychological testing of linguistic-minority students: knowledge gaps and regulations. *Exceptional Children*, 56: 145–148

Fishman, J.A. 1965. Who speaks what language to whom and when? *La Linguistique*, 2: 67–88

Fishman, J. 1972. Varieties of ethnicity and varieties of language conciousness. In Dil, A.S. (ed.) *Language and socio-cultural change: Essays by J. Fishman*. Stanford: Stanford University Press, pp. 179–191

Frederickson, N. and Cline, T. 1990. *Curriculum related assessment with bilingual children: A set of working papers*. London: University College London

Fulcher, G. and Davidson, F. 2007. *Language testing and assessment: An advanced resource book*. London: Routledge

Gagnon, A.G. 1988. Intercommunal relations and language policy in Quebec, 1960–1986. In Forcese, D. and Her, S. (eds) *Social issues: Sociological views of Canada*. Ontario: Prentice Hall

Galambos, S. and Goldin-Meadow, S. 1983. Metalinguistic awareness and learning a second language. *Papers from the Chicago Linguistic Society*, 19: 117–133

Galambos, S.J. and Goldin-Meadow, S. 1990. The effects of learning two languages on levels of metalinguistic awareness. *Cognition*, 34: 1–56

Galambos, S.J. and Hakuta, K. 1988. Subject-specific and task-specific characteristics of metalinguistic awareness in bilingual children. *Applied Psycholinguistics*, 9 (2): 141–162

Garcia, A.G. 2001. Attitudinal differences among elementary teachers toward the use of the native language. *Dissertation Abstracts International, A: The Humanities and Social Sciences*, 62 (1): 55-A

Garcia, G.E. 2003. The reading comprehension development and instruction of English-language learners. In Sweet, A.P. and Snow, C.E. (eds) *Rethinking reading comprehension*. New York: Guilford Press, pp. 30–50

Gardner, M.F. 1979. *Expressive one-word picture vocabulary test* (rev ed.). Novato, CA: Academic Therapy Publications

Gardner, R. 1985. *Social psychology and second language learning: The role of attitudes and motivation*. London: Edward Arnold

Gardner, R. 2001. Integrative motivation and second language. In Dörnyei, Z. and Schmidt, R. (eds) *Motivation and second language acquisition*. Honolulu: University of Hawai'i Press, pp. 1–20

Gardner, R.C., Lalonde, R.N., Moorcroft, R., and Evers, F.T. 1987. Second language attrition: the role of motivation and use. *Journal of Language and Social Psychology*, 6: 29–47

Gardner, R.C. and Lambert, W.E. 1959. Motivational variables in second-language acquisition. *Canadian Journal of Psychology*, 13: 266–272

Garret, P., Williams, A., and Evans, B. 2005. Attitudinal data from New Zealand, Australia, the USA and UK about each other's Englishes. Recent changes or consequences of methodologies? *Multilingua*, 24: 211–235

Genesee, F. 1984. On Cummins' theoretical framework. In Rivera, C. (ed.) *Language proficiency and academic achievement*. Clevedon: Multilingual Matters, pp. 20–27

Genesee, F. 1989. Early bilingual development: one language or two? *Journal of Child Language*, 16: 161–179

Genesee, F. 1995. The Canada second language immersion program. In Garcia, O. and Baker, C. (eds) *Policy and practice in bilingual education*. Clevedon: Multilingual Matters, pp. 118–133

Genesee, F., Boivin, I., and Nicoladis, E. 1996. Bilingual children talking with monolingual adults: a study of bilingual communicative competence. *Applied Psycholinguistics*, 17: 427–442

Genesee, F. and Bourhis, R.Y. 1982. The social psychological significance of code switching in cross-cultural communication. *Journal of Language and Social Psychology*, 1: 1–27

Genesee, F. and Bourhis, R. 1988. Evaluative reactions to language choice strategies: the role of sociostructural factors. *Language and Communication*, 8 (3/4): 229–250

Genesee, F. and Gándara, P. 1999. Bilingual education programs: a cross-national perspective. *Journal of Social Issues*, 55: 665–685

Genesee, F. and Holobow, N. 1989. Change and stability intergroup perceptions. *Journal of Language and Social Psychology*, 8: 17–38

Genesee, F., Nicoladis, E., and Paradis, J. 1995. Language differentiation in early bilingual development. *Journal of Child Language*, 22: 611–631

Genesee, F. and Upshur, J. 1996. *Classroom-based evaluation in second language education*. New York: Cambridge University Press

Genishi, C. and Brainard, M.B. 1995. Assessment of bilingual children: a dilemma seeking solutions. In Garcia, E.E. and McLaughlin, B. (eds) *Meeting the challenge of linguistic and cultural diversity in early childhood education*. New York, NY: Teachers College Press, pp. 49–63

Geva, E. 2000. Issues in the assessment of reading disabilities in L2 children: beliefs and research evidence. *Dyslexia*, 6: 13–18

Geva, E. and Siegel, L. 2000. Orthographic and cognitive factors in the concurrent development of basic reading in two languages. *Reading and Writing: An Interdisciplinary Journal*, 12: 1–30

Geva, E. and Wang, Min 2001. The development of basic reading skills in children: a cross-language perspective. *Annual Review of Applied Linguistics*, 21: 182–204

Gholamain, E. and Geva, E. 1999. Orthographic and cognitive factors in the concurrent development of basic reading in English and Persian. *Language Learning*, 49: 183–217

Ghuman, P. 1994. *Coping with two cultures: British Asian and Indo-Canadian adolescents*. Clevedon: Multilingual Matters

Gibbons, J. 1987. *Codemixing and code choice: A Hong Kong case study*. Clevedon, PA: Multilingual Matters

Gibbons, J. and Ramirez, E. 2004. Different beliefs: beliefs and the maintenance of a minority language. *Journal of Language and Social Psychology*, 23 (1): 99–117

Gibbons, P. 1991. *Learning to learn in a second language*. Newtown, NSW: Primary English Teaching Association

Giles, H. 1970. Evaluative reactions to accents. *Educational Review*, 22: 211–227

Giles, H. 1971. Patterns of evaluation in reactions to RP, South Welsh and Somerset accented speech. *British Journal of Social and Clinical Psychology*, 10: 280–281

Giles, H. 1973. Accent mobility: a model and some data. *Anthropological Linguistics*, 15: 87–105

Giles, H. 1977. Social psychology and applied linguistics: towards an integrative approach. *ITL, Review of Applied Linguistics*, 35: 27–42

Giles, H., Bourhis, R.Y., and Taylor, D. 1977. Towards a theory of language in ethnic group relations. In Giles, H. (ed.) *Language, ethnicity and intergroup relations*. London: Academic Press, pp. 307–348

Giles, H. and Johnson, P. 1987. Ethnolinguistic identity theory: a social psychological approach to language maintenance. *International Journal of the Sociology of Language*, 68: 69–99

Giles, H., Mulac, A., Bradac, J., and Johnson, P. 1987. Speech accommodation theory: the first decade and beyond. *Communication Yearbook*, 10: 8–34

Giles, H., Taylor, D.M., and Bourhis, R.Y. 1973. Towards a theory of interpersonal accommodation through language: some Canadian data. *Language in Society*, 2: 77–192

Giles, H., Taylor, D.M., and Bourhis, R.Y. 1977. Dimensions of Welsh identity. *European Journal of Social Psychology*, 7: 165–174

Ginsberg, E. 1996. Bilingual language acquisition: A case study. Master's in Applied Linguistics dissertation, Department of Linguistics, La Trobe University

Glynn, T., Berryman, M., Loader, K., and Cavanagh, T. 2005. From literacy in Maori to biliteracy in Maori and English: a community and school transition programme. *International Journal of Bilingual Education and Bilingualism*, 8 (5): 433–454

Goetz, P. 2003. The effects of bilingualism on Theory of Mind development. *Bilingualism: Language and Cognition*, 6 (1): 1–15

Goldstein, B. 2000. *Cultural and linguistic diversity resource guide for speech-language pathologists*. San Diego, CA: Singular

Goncz, L. and Kodžopelijć, J. 1991. Exposure to two languages in the pre-school period: metalinguistic development in the acquisition of reading. *Journal of Multilingual and Multicultural Development*, 12 (3): 137–163

Goodz, N. 1989. Parental language mixing in bilingual families. *Infant Mental Health Journal*, 10: 25–44

Goodz, N. 1994. Interactions between parents and children in bilingual families. In Genesee, F. (ed.) *Educating second language children: The whole child, the whole curriculum, the whole community*. Cambridge: Cambridge University Press

Goral, M. 2004. First language decline in healthy aging: implications for attrition in bilingualism. *Journal of Neurolinguistics*, 17: 31–52

Grammont, M. 1902. *Observations sur le langage des enfants*. Paris: Mélanges Maillet

Grosjean, F. 1982. *Life with two languages: An introduction to bilingualism*. Cambridge, MA: Harvard University Press

Grosjean, F. 1985. The bilingual as a competent but specific speaker-hearer. *Journal of Multilingual and Multicultural Development*, 6: 467–477

Grosjean, F. 1989. Neurolinguists, beware! The bilingual is not two monolinguals in one person. *Brain and Language*, 36 (1): 3–15

Grosjean, F. 1998. Studying bilinguals: methodological and conceptual issues. *Bilingualism: Language and Cognition*, 1 (2): 131–149

Guardado, M. 2002. Loss and maintenance of first language skills: case studies of Hispanic families in Vancouver. *The Canadian Modern Language Review*, 58 (3): 341–363

Guilford, J.P. 1956. The structure of intellect. *Psychological Bulletin*, 53: 267–293

Gürel, A. 2004. Selectivity in L2-induced L1 attrition: a psycholinguistic account. *Journal of Neurolinguistics*, 17: 53–78

Gutierrez-Clennen, V. 1996. Language diversity: implications for assessment. In Cole, K., Dale, P., and Thal, D. (eds) *Assessment of communication and language*. Baltimore: Paul H. Brookes, pp. 29–56

Gutierrez-Clennen, V. 1998. Syntactic skills of Spanish-speaking children with low school achievement. *Language, Speech, and Hearing Services in Schools*, 29: 207–215

Gutierrez-Clennen, V. and Kreiter, J. 2003. Understanding child bilingual acquisition using parent and teacher reports. *Applied Psycholinguistics*, 24: 267–288

Hakuta, K. 1987. Degree of bilingualism and cognitive ability in mainland Puerto Rican children. *Child Development*, 58: 1372–1388

Hakuta, K. 1999. A critical period for second language acquisition? A status review. Paper written for the National Center for Early Development and Learning (University of North Carolina, Chapel Hill). To be published in proceedings. On-line draft available at http://www.stanford.edu/hakuta/docs/CriticalPeriod.PDF

Hakuta, K., Butler, Y.G. and Witt, D., 2000. *How long does it take English learners to attain proficiency?* The University of California Linguistic Minority Research Institute, policy report 2000–1

Hakuta, Kenji and D'Andrea, Daniel 1992. Some properties of bilingual maintenance and loss in Mexican background high-school students. *Applied Linguistics*, 13 (1): 72–99

Hakuta, K. and Diaz, R.M. 1985. The relationship between degree of bilingualism and cognitive ability: a critical discussion and some new longitudinal data. In Nelson, K.E. (ed.) *Children's language*, vol. V. Hillsdale, NJ: Lawrence Erlbaum, pp. 319–344

Hamers, J.F. 1994. The role of social networks in maintaining the native tongue, in the development of bilingualism, and in the development of literacy. *Bulletin Suisse de Linguistique Appliquée*, 59: 85–102

Hamers, J. and Blanc, M.H.A. 2000. *Bilinguality and bilingualism* (2nd ed.). Cambridge: Cambridge University Press

Hammer, C.S. 1998. Toward a 'thick description' of families: using ethnography to overcome the obstacles to providing family-centered early intervention services. *American Journal of Speech-Language Pathology*, 7: 5–22

Hand, L. 2001. Setting the tone: interview between speech pathologists and parents of children from non-dominant cultural groups. In Wilson, L. and Hewat, S. (eds) *Evidence and innovation: Proceedings of the 2001 Speech Pathology Australia National Conference*. Melbourne: Speech Pathology Australia, pp. 299–306

Hansen, L. (ed.) 1999. *Second language attrition in Japanese contexts*. New York: Oxford University Press

Hansen, L. 2001. Language attrition: the fate of the start. *Annual Review of Applied Linguistics*, 21: 60–73

Hansen, L., Umeda, Y., and McKinney, M. 2002. Savings in the relearning of second language vocabulary: the effects of time and proficiency. *Language Learning*, 52 (4): 653–678

Harding-Esch, E. and Riley, P. 2003. *The bilingual family: A handbook for parents* (2nd edn.). Cambridge: Cambridge University Press

Hardt-Dhatt, K. 1982. *Les attitudes face à l'utilisation de l'anglais et du français chez les travailleurs francophones dans trois enterprises de production au Québec*. Québec: Office de la langue française

Harley, B., Allen, P., Cummins, J., and Swain, M. 1990. *The development of second language proficiency*. Cambridge: Cambridge University Press

Hasselgreen, A. 2005. Assessing the language of young learners. *Language Testing*, 22, 3: 337–354

Haugen, E. 1953. *The Norwegian language in America: A study in bilingual behavior*. Philadelphia: University of Pennsylvania Press (2nd ed.). Bloomington: Indiana University Press, 1964)

Henning, G. 1987. *A guide to language testing: Development, evaluation, research*. Cambridge: Newbury House

Hickey, T. 1999. Parents and early immersion: reciprocity between home and immersion pre-school. *International Journal of Bilingual Education and Bilingualism*, 2 (2): 94–113

Hiraga, Y. 2005. British attitudes towards six varieties of English in the USA and Britain. *World Englishes*, 24 (3): 289–308

Hoffmann, C. 1985. Language acquisition in two trilingual children. *Journal of Multilingual and Multicultural Development*, 6: 479–495

Hoffmann, C. 1991. *An introduction to bilingualism*. New York: Longman

Holm, A., Dodd, B., Stow, C., and Pert, S. 1999. Identification and differential diagnosis of phonological disorder in bilingual children. *Language Testing*, 16 (3): 271–292

Hornberger, N.H. 2004. The continua of biliteracy and the bilingual educator: educational linguistics in practice. *Bilingual Education and Bilingualism,* 7 (2–3): 155–171

Hornby, P. 1979. *Bilingualism: Psychological, social and educational implications.* New York: Academic Press

Huber, E. and Lasagabaster, D. 2000. The cognitive effects of bilingualism. *ITL, Review of Applied Linguistics,* 129–130

Hudson, A. 2002. Outline of a theory of diglossia. *International Journal of the Sociology of Language,* 157: 1–48

Hughes, A. 1989. *Testing for language teachers.* Cambridge: Cambridge University Press

Huguet, A. and Llurda, E. 2001. Language attitudes of school children in two Catalan/ Spanish bilingual communities. *International Journal of Bilingual Education and Bilingualism,* 4: 267–282

Huguet, A., Vila, I., and Llurda, E. 2000. Minority language education in unbalanced bilingual situations: a case for the linguistic interdependence hypothesis. *Journal of Psycholinguistic Research,* 29 (3): 313–333

Hunt, K. 1966. Recent measures in syntactic development. *Elementary English,* 43: 732–739

Ianco-Worrall, A. 1972. Bilingualism and cognitive development. *Child Development,* 43: 1390–1400

Imhasly, B. 1977. A sociolinguistic approach to bilingual education. *Bulletin CILA,* 25: 52–56

Ingram, D. 1974. Fronting in child phonology. *Journal of Child Language,* 1: 49–64

Ingram, D.E. 1980. Aspects of personality development for bilingualism. In Afendras, E.A. (ed.) *Patterns of bilingualism.* Singapore: RELC, pp. 25–42

Isaac, K. 2001. What about linguistic diversity? A different look at multicultural health care. *Communication Disorders Quarterly,* 22 (2): 110–113

Isaac, K. 2005. Managing linguistic diversity in the clinic: interpreters in speech-language pathology. In Ball, M. (ed.) *Clinical sociolinguistics.* Oxford: Blackwell, pp. 265–280

Isurin, L. 2000. Deserted island or a child's first language forgetting? *Bilingualism Language and Cognition,* 3 (2): 151–166

Jacobs, E. 2001. The effects of adding dynamic assessment components to a computerized preschool language screening test. *Commmunication Disorders Quarterly,* 22: 217–226

Jakobson, R. 1941. *Kindersprache, Aphasie, und allgemeine Lautgesetze.* Uppsala: Almqvist & Wiksell

James, C.B.E. 1960. Bilingualism in Wales: an aspect of semantic organization. *Educational Research,* 2: 123–136

Johnson, C.E. and Lancaster, P. 1998. The development of more than one phonology: a case study of a Norwegian–English bilingual child. *International Journal of Bilingualism,* 2/3: 265–300

Johnson, J. and Newport, E. 1989. Critical period effects in second language learning: the influence of maturational state on the acquisition of English as a second language. *Cognitive Psychology,* 21: 60–99

Johnstone, R. 2001. *Immersion in a second or additional language at school: Evidence from international research. Report for the Scottish Executive Education Department.* Stirling: Scottish Centre for Information on Language Testing and Research

Jones, W.R. 1960. A critical study of bilingualism and nonverbal intelligence. *British Journal of Educational Psychology,* 30: 71–76

Jones, W.R. and Stewart, W.A. 1951. Bilingualism and verbal intelligence. *British Journal of Psychology,* 4: 3–8

Jorda, S. and Pilar, M. 2003. Metapragmatic awareness and pragmatic production of third language learners of English: a focus on request acts realizations. *International Journal of Bilingualism,* 7 (1): 43–69

Juan-Garau, M. and Pérez-Vidal, C. 2001. Mixing and pragmatic parental strategies in early bilingual acquisition. *Journal of Child Language*, 28: 59–86

Kachru, B. 1978. Toward structuring code-mixing: an Indian perspective. *International Journal of the Sociology of Language*, 16: 27–46

Kachru, B. 1987. The spread of English and sacred linguistic cows. *Georgetown University Round Table on Language and Linguistics*, 207–228

Kamwangamalu, Nkonko M. 2004. Bi/multilingualism in Southern Africa. In Bhatia, T.K. and Ritchie, W.C. (eds) *The handbook of bilingualism*. Malden, MA, and Oxford: Blackwell, pp. 725–741

Kanagy, R. 2001. Hai, genki desu: doing fine in a Japanese immersion classroom. In Christian, D. and Genesee, F. (eds) *Bilingual education*. Arlington, VA: TESOL

Karmiloff-Smith, A. 1992. *Beyond modularity: A developmental perspective on cognitive science*. Cambridge, MA: MIT Press

Kayser, H. 1998. *Assessment and intervention resource for Hispanic children*. San Diego, CA: Singular

Kembo, S. 1991. Language functions and language attitudes in Kenya. *English World-Wide*, 12 (2): 245–260

Kenner, C. 2004. Living in simultaneous worlds: difference and integration in bilingual script-learning. *Bilingual Education and Bilingualism*, 7 (1): 43–61

Kenner, C., Kress, G., Al-Khatib, H., Kam, R., and Tsai, Kuan-Chun. 2004. Finding the keys to biliteracy: how young children interpret different writing systems. *Language and Education*, 18 (2): 124–144

Kester, E.S. and Peña, E.D. 2002. Language ability assessment of Spanish– English bilinguals: future directions. *Practical Assessment, Research and Evaluation*, 8 (4). Retrieved 10 September 2006 from http://PAREonline.net/getvn.asp?v=8&n=4

Kiparsky, P. and Menn, L. 1977. On the acquisition of phonology. In Macnamara, J. (ed.) *Language learning and thought*. New York: Academic Press, pp. 47–48

Kissau, S. 2003. The relationship between school environment and effectiveness in French immersion. *Canadian Journal of Applied Linguistics*, 6 (1): 87–104

Köpke, B. 2004. Neurolinguistic aspects of attrition. *Journal of Neurolinguistics*, 17: 3–30

Köppe, R. and Meisel, J. 1995. Code switching in bilingual first language acquisition. In Milroy, L. and Muysken, P. (eds) *One speaker, two languages: Cross-disciplinary perspectives on code-switching*. Cambridge: Cambridge University Press

Krashen, S. 1996. *Under attack: The case against bilingual education*. Culver City, CA: Language Education Associates

Krauss, M. 1998. The condition of Native North American languages: the need for realistic assessment and action. *International Journal of the Sociology of Language*, 132: 9–21

Kuhl, P, 1980. Perceptual constancy for speech-sound categories in early infancy. In Yenikomshian, G.H., Kavanagh, J.F., and Ferguson, C.A. (eds), *Child phonology*, vol. 2, *Perception*. New York: Academic Press, pp. 41–66

Kwan-Terry, A. 2000 Language shift, mother tongue, and identity in Singapore. *International Journal of the Sociology of Language*, 143: 85–106

Lahey, M. 1992. Linguistic and cultural diversity: further problems for determining who shall be called language disordered. *Journal of Speech and Hearing Research*, 35: 638–639

Lambert, W.E. 1956. Developmental aspects of second-language acquisition: I. Associational fluency, stimulus provocativeness, and word-order influence. *Journal of Social Psycholology*, 43: 83–89

Lambert, W. 1967. A social psychology of bilingualism. *Journal of Social Issues*, 23: 91–109

Lambert, W. 1974. Culture and language as factors in learning and education. In Aboud,

F.E. and Meade, R.D. (eds) *Cultural factors in learning and education.* Bellingham, WA: Fifth Western Washington Symposium on Learning

Lambert, W.E. 1977. The effects of bilingualism on the individual: cognitive and sociocultural consequences. In Hornby, P.A. (ed.) *Bilingualism: Psychological, social and educational implications.* New York: Academic Press, pp. 15–28

Lambert, W. 1978. Psychological approaches to bilingualism, translation and interpretation. In Gerver, D. and Sinaiko, H. (eds) *Language interpretation and communication.* New York: Plenum, pp. 131–144

Lambert, W.E., Havelka, J., and Gardner, R.C. 1959. Linguistic manifestation of bilingualism. *American Journal of Psychology,* 72: 77–82

Lambert, W.E., Hodgson, C., Gardner, R.C., and Fillenbaum, S. 1960. Evaluational reactions to spoken languages. *Journal of Abnormal and Social Psychology,* 60: 44–51

Lambert, W.E. and Tucker, G.E. 1972. *Bilingual education of children: the St. Lambert experiment.* Rowley, MA: Newbury House

Landry, R.G. 1974. A comparison of second language learners and monolinguals on divergent thinking tasks at the elementary school level. *Modern Language Journal,* 58: 10–15

Langdon, H. and Saenz, T. 1996. Speech-language assessment of bilingual–bicultural students. In Langdon, H. and Saenz, T. (eds) *Language assessment and intervention with multicultural students: A guide for speech-language-hearing professionals.* Oceanside, CA: Academic Communication Associates, pp. 3–10

Langer, S. 1942. *Philosophy in a new key.* Cambridge, MA: Harvard University Press

Lanza, E. 1992. Can bilingual two-year olds code switch? *Journal of Child Language,* 19: 633–658

Lanza, E. 1997, 2004. *Language mixing in infant bilingualism.* Oxford: Clarendon Press

Laplante, B. 2000. Learning science is learning to speak science: immersion students talk to us about chemical reactions. *The Canadian Modern Language Review,* 57 (2): 245–271

Lavoie, G. and Laurendeau, M. 1960. *Tests collectifs d'intélligence générale.* Montréal: Institut de Recherches Psychologiques.

Lawson, S. and Sachdev, I. 2000. Codeswitching in Tunisia: attitudinal and behavioural dimensions. *Journal of Pragmatics* 32: 1343–1361

Leek, P. 2001. Preservice teachers' attitudes toward language diversity. Ph.D. dissertation, University of Northern Texas

Lennenberg, E. 1967. *Biological foundation of language.* New York: Wiley

Leopold, W.F. 1939. *Speech development of a bilingual child: A linguist's record.* Vol. 1: *Vocabulary growth in the first two years.* Evanston, IL: Northwestern University Press.

Leopold, W.F. 1947. *Speech development of a bilingual child: A linguist's record.* Vol. II: *Sound learning in the first two years.* Evanston, IL: Northwestern University Press

Leopold, W.F. 1949a. *Speech development of a bilingual child: A linguist's record.* Vol. III: *Grammar and general problems.* Evanston, IL: Northwestern University Press

Leopold 1949b. *Speech development of a bilingual child: A linguist's record.* Vol. IV: *Diary from age 2.* Evanston, IL: Northwestern University Press

LeSieg, T. 1974. *Wacky Wednesday.* New York: Random House

Li, D.C.S. and Lee, S. 2004. Bilingualism in East Asia. In Bhatia, T.K. and Ritchie, W.C. (eds) *The handbook of bilingualism.* Malden, MA, and Oxford: Blackwell, pp. 742–779

Li, W. 2000. Conclusion. In Li, W. (ed.) *A Bilingual Reader.* London Routledge

Li, W., Miller, N., Dodd, B., and Zhu, H. (2005) Managing linguistic diversity in the clinic: interpreters in speech-language pathology. In Ball, M. (ed.) *Clinical Sociolinguistics.* Oxford: Blackwell, pp. 193–207

Li, W. and Milroy, L. 2003. Markets, hierarchies and networks in language maintenance and language shift. In Dewaele, J.-M., Housen, A., and Li, W. (eds) *Bilingualism: Beyond basic principles*. Festschrift in Honour of Hugo Baetens Beardsmore. Clevedon: Multilingual Matters, pp. 128–140

Lidz, C. and Peña, I. 1996. Dynamic assessment: the model, its relevance as a nonbiased approach, and its application to Latino American preschool children. *Language, Speech and Hearing Services in Schools*, 27: 367–373

Lightbown, P. 1990. Process–product research on second language learning in classrooms. In Harley, B., Allen, P., Cummins, J., and Swain, M. (eds) *The development of second language proficiency*. Cambridge: Cambridge University Press

Linder, T. 1993. *Transdisciplinary play-based assessment: A functional approach to working with young children* (rev. ed.). Baltimore: Brookes

Lindgren, S.D., De Renzi, E., and Richman, L.C. 1985. Cross-national comparisons of developmental dyslexia in Italy and the United States. *Child Development*, 56: 1404–1417

Lindholm, K.J. and Padilla, A.M. 1978. Language mixing in bilingual children. *Journal of Child Language*, 5: 327–335

Little, D. 2005. The Common European Framework and the European Language Portfolio: involving learners and their judgments in the assessment process. *Language Testing*, 22 (3): 321–365

Long, M. 1990. Maturational constraints on language development. *Studies in Second Language Acquisition*, 12: 251–285

Lumley, T. 2002. Assessment criteria in a large-scale writing test: what do they really mean to the raters? *Language Testing*, 19 (3): 246–276

Lyczak, R., Fu, G.S., and Ho, A. 1976. Attitudes of Hong Kong bilinguals towards English and Chinese speakers. *Journal of Cross-Cultural Psychology*, 7 (4): 425–437

Lyster, R. 2004. Research on form-focused instruction in immersion classrooms: implications for theory and practice. *Journal of French Language Studies*, 14 (3): 321–341

McCarthy, D. 1930. *The language development of the preschool child*. Minneapolis: University of Minnesota Press

McCarthy, D. 1954. Language development in children. In L. Carmichael (ed.) *Manual of child psychology*. New York: Wiley, pp. 492–630

McCarty, T. 2002. *A place to be Navajo: Rough Rock and the struggle for self-determination in indigenous schooling*. Mahwah, NJ: Lawrence Erlbaum

McCarty, T. 2003. Revitalising indigenous languages in homogenising times. *Comparative Education*, 39 (2): 147–163

McConvell, P. 1988. Mix-im-up: Aboriginal code-switching, old and new. In M. Heller (ed.) *Codeswitching: Anthropological and sociolinguistic perspectives*. Berlin: Mouton, pp. 97–150

McConvell, P., Simpson, J., and Wigglesworth, G. 2005. Mixed codes: a comparison across the four field sites. Paper presented at the Max Planck Institute, Nijmegen, April

McConvell, P. and Thieberger, N. 2001. *State of Indigenous languages in Australia – 2001 PDF*. Australia State of the Environment Second Technical Paper Series Natural and Cultural Heritage. Canberra: Department of the Environment and Heritage

Macken, M. 1980. The child's lexical representation: the 'puzzle-puddle-pickle' evidence. *Journal of Linguistics*, 16: 1–17

Mackey, W.F. 1952. Bilingualism and education. *Pédagogie-Orientation*, 6: 135–147

Mackey, W.F. 1962. The description of bilingualism. *Canadian Journal of Linguistics*, 7: 51–85

Mackey, W.F. 2004. Bilingualism in North America. In Bhatia, T.K. and Ritchie, W.C. (eds) *The handbook of bilingualism*. Malden and Oxford: Blackwell, pp. 607–641

Mackey, W.F. and Noonan, J.A. 1952. An experiment in bilingual education. *ELT Journal* (4): 125–132

Macnamara, J. 1966. *Bilingualism and primary education*. Edinburgh: Edinburgh University Press

McLaughlin, B. 1978. *Second language acquisition in childhood*. Hillsdale, NJ: Lawrence Erlbaum

McLaughlin, B. 1984. *Second language acquisition in childhood*. Vol. 1: *Pre-school children* (2nd ed.). Hillsdale, NJ: Erlbaum

McLaughlin, B. 1985. *Second language acquisition in childhood*. Vol. 2: *School age children*. Hillsdale, NJ, and London: Lawrence Erlbaum

Macnamara, J. 1969. How can one measure the extent of a person's bilingual proficiency? In Kelly, L.G. (ed.) *Description and measurement of bilingualism*. Toronto: University of Toronto Press, pp. 80–119

McNamara, T. 1996. *Measuring second language performance*. London and New York: Longman

McNamara, T. 1998. Policy and social considerations in language assessment. *Annual Review of Applied Linguistics*, 18: 304–319

McNamara, T. 2000. *Language testing*. Oxford: Oxford University Press

MacSwan, J. 2000. The Threshold Hypothesis, semilingualism, and other contributions to a deficit view of linguistic minorities. *Hispanic Journal of Behavioral Sciences*, 221: 3–45

McWilliam, N. 1998. *What's in a word? Vocabulary development in multilingual classrooms*. Stoke-on-Trent: Trentham Books

Mahon, M., Crutchley, A., and Quinn, T. 2003. New directions in the assessment of bilingual children. *Child Language Teaching and Therapy*, 19 (3): 237–243

Martin, D., Krishnamurthy, R., Bhardwa, M., and Charles, R. 2003. Language change in young Panjabi/English children: implications for bilingual language assessment. *Child Language Teaching and Therapy*, 19 (3): 245–265

Masgoret, A. and Gardner, R. 2003. Attitudes, motivation, and second language learning: a meta-analysis. *Language Learning*, 531: 123–163

Mattes, I. and Omark, D. 1991. *Speech and language assessment for the bilingual handicapped* (2nd ed.). Oceanside, CA: Academic Communication Associates

Matthews, P. 1997. *The concise Oxford dictionary of linguistics*. Oxford: Oxford University Press

May, S. and Hill, R. 2005. Maori-medium education: current issues and challenges. *International Journal of Bilingual Education and Bilingualism*, 8 (5): 377–403

Mayer, M. and Mayer, M. 1971. *A Boy, a Dog, a Frog and a Friend*. New York: Dial Books

Meakins, F. and O'Shannessy, C. 2005. Possessing variation: age and inalienability related variables in the possessive constructions of two Australian mixed languages. *Monash University Linguistics Papers*, 4 (2): 43–63

Meisel, J. 2004. The bilingual child. In Bhatia, T.K. and Ritchie, W.C. (eds) *The handbook of bilingualism*. Malden and Oxford: Blackwell, pp. 91–113

Menn, L. 1983. Development of articulatory, phonetic, and phonological capabilities. In Butterworth, B. (ed.) *Language production*. Vol. 2: *Development, writing, and other language processes*. London: Academic Press, pp. 1–50

Menn, L. and Matthei, E. 1992. The 'two-lexicon' approach of child phonology: looking back, looking ahead. In Ferguson, C.A., Menn, L., and Stoel-Gammon, C. (eds) *Phonological development: Models, research, implications*. Timonium, MD: York Press, pp. 211–248

Miller-Guron, L. and Lundberg, I. 2000. Dyslexia and second language reading: a second bite at the apple? *Reading and Writing: An Interdisciplinary Journal*, 12: 41–61

Mills, J. 1995. Bilingual children and their assessment through mother tongue. In Verma,

M., Corrigan, K., and Firth, S. (eds) *Working with bilingual children*. Clevedon: Multilingual Matters

Mills, J. 2001. Being bilingual: perspectives of third generation Asian children on language, culture and identity. *International Journal of Bilingual Education and Bilingualism*, 4 (6): 383–402

Mkilifi, M. 1978. Triglossia and Swahili–English bilingualism in Tanzania. In Fishman, J. (ed.) *Advances in the study of societal multilingualism*. The Hague: Mouton

Morrison, J.R. 1958. Bilingualism: some psychological aspects. *Advanced Science*, 56: 287–290

Myers-Scotton, C. 2006. *Multiple voices: An introduction to bilingualism*. Malden, MA: Blackwell

Newport, E. 1990. Maturational constraints on language learning. *Cognitive Science*, 14: 11–28

Newport, E.L., Gleitman, H., and Gleitman, L.R. 1977. 'Mother, I'd rather do it myself': some effects and noneffects of maternal speech style. In Snow, C.E. and Ferguson, C.A. (eds) *Talking to children: Language input and acquisition*. New York: Cambridge University Press, pp. 109–115

Ng, B.C. in press. Linguistic pragmatism, globalization and the impact on the patterns of input in Singaporean Chinese homes. In Tan, P. and Rubdy, R. (eds) *Trading language: Of global structures and local market places*. London: Continuum

Nicholls, C. 2005. Death by a thousand cuts: indigenous language bilingual education programmes in the Northern Territory of Australia, 1972–1998. *International Journal of Bilingual Education and Bilingualism*, 8 (2&3): 160–177

Nicoladis, E. and Genesee, F. 1996. A longitudinal study of pragmatic differentiation in young bilingual children. *Language Learning*, 46: 439–464

Nicoladis, E. and Genesee, F. 1998. Parental discourse and code-mixing in bilingual children. *International Journal of Bilingualism*, 2 (1): 85–99

Ninio, A. and Snow, C.E. 1996. *Pragmatic development*. Boulder, CO: Westview Press

O'Doherty, E.F. 1958. Bilingualism: educational aspects. *Advanced Science*, 56: 282–286

OECD 1989. *Reviews of national politics for education: Turkey*. Paris: OECD

Oller, D.K., Eilers, R.A., Urgano, R., and Cobo-Lewis, A.B. 1997. Development of precursors to speech in infants exposed to two languages. *Journal of Child Language*, 24: 407–425

Olshtain, E. 1986. The attrition of English as a second language with speakers of Hebrew. In Weltens, B., De Bot, K., and Van Els, T. (eds) *Language attrition in progress*. Dordrecht: Foris Publications

Olshtain, E. 1989. Is second language attrition the reversal of second language acquisition? *Studies in Second Language Acquisition*, 11 (2) (June): 151–165

Oney, B. and Goldman, S.R. 1984. Decoding and comprehension skills in Turkish and English: effects of regularity of grapheme–phoneme correspondences. *Journal of Educational Psychology*, 76: 57–68

Oyetade, S.O. 1996. Bilingualism and ethnic identity in a Nupe–Yoruba border town in Nigeria. *Journal of Multilingual and Multicultural Development*, 17 (5): 373–384

Pakir, A. 1994. Educational linguistics: looking to the east. *Georgetown University Round Table on Languages and Linguistics*, 370–383

Paradis, J., Crago, M., Genesee, F., and Rice, M. 2003. French–English bilingual children with SLI: how do they compare with their monolingual peers? *Journal of Speech. Language, and Hearing Research*, 46 (1): 113–127

Paradis, M. 1997. The cognitive neuropsychology of bilingualism. In De Groot, A.M.B. and Kroll, J.F. (eds) *Tutorials in bilingualism: Psycholinguistic perspectives*. Mahwah, NJ: Lawrence Erlbaum, pp. 331–354

Paradis, M. 2004. *A neurolinguistic theory of bilingualism*. Amsterdam: John Benjamins

Paribakht, T.S. and Wesche, M. 1997. Vocabulary enhancement activities and reading for meaning in second language vocabulary acquisition. In Coady, J. and Huckin, T. (eds) *Second language vocabulary acquisition: A rationale for pedagogy*. Cambridge: Cambridge University Press

Pavlenko, A. 2004. 'Stop doing that, Ia komu skazala!': language choice and emotions. *Journal of Multilingual and Multicultural Development*, 25: 179–203

Pavlenko, A. 2006. *Emotions and multilinguals*. Cambridge: Cambridge University Press

Pavlovitch, M. 1920. *Le langage enfantin: Acquisition du serbe et du français par un enfant serbe*. Paris: Champion

Peal, E. and Lambert, W.E. 1962. The relation of bilingualism to intelligence. *Psychological Monographs*, 76 (27): 1–23

Pearson, B., Fernandez, S., Lewedeg, V., and Oller, K. 1997. The relation of input factors to lexical learning by bilingual infants. *Applied Psycholinguistics*, 18: 41–58

Pearson, B., Fernandez, S., and Oller, D. 1993. Lexical development in bilingual infants and toddlers: comparisons to monolingual norms. *Language Learning*, 43: 93–120

Peña, E. 1996. Dynamic assessment: the model and its language applications. In Cole, K., Dale, P., and Thal, D. (eds) *Assessment of communication and language*. Baltimore: Brookes, pp. 281–307

Peña, E.D., Bedore, L.M., and Zlatic-Giunta, R. 2002. Category-generation performance of bilingual children: the influence of condition, category, and language. *Journal of Speech, Language, and Hearing Research*, 45 (5): 938–947

Peña, E., Iglesias, A., and Lidz, C. 2001. Reducing test bias through dynamic assessment of children's word learning ability. *American Journal of Speech-Language Pathology*, 10: 138–154

Peña, E. and Quinn, R. 1997. Task familiarity: effects on the test performance of Puerto Rican and African American children. *Language, Speech and Hearing Services in Schools*, 28: 323–332

Peña, E., Quinn, R., and Iglesias, A. 1992. The application of dynamic methods to language assessment: a nonbiased procedure. *Journal of Special Education*, 26: 269–280

Pérez, B. 1998a. Literacy, diversity, and programmatic responses. In Pérez, B. (ed.) *Sociocultural contexts of language and literacy*. Mahwah, NJ: Lawrence Erlbaum, pp. 3–20

Pérez, B. 1998b. Language, literacy, and biliteracy. In Pérez, B. (ed.) *Sociocultural contexts of language and literacy*. Mahwah, NJ: Lawrence Erlbaum

Pérez, B. and Torres-Guzmán, M. 1996. *Learning in two worlds: An integrated Spanish/English biliteracy approach* (2nd ed.). White Plains, NY: Longman

Pert, S. and Letts, C. 2003. Developing an expressive language assessment for children in Rochdale with a Pakistani heritage background. *Child Language Teaching and Therapy*, 19 (3): 267–289

Petitto, L.A., Katerelos, M., Levy, B.G., Gauna, K., Tetreault, K., and Ferraro, V. 2001. Bilingual signed and spoken language acquisition from birth: implications for the mechanisms underlying early bilingual acquisition. *Journal of Child Language*, 28: 453–496

Pintner, R. and Keller, R. 1922. Intelligence tests of foreign children. *Journal of Educational Psychology*, 13: 214–222

Poplack, S. 1987. Contrasting patterns of code-switching in two communities. In Wande, E. et al. (eds) *Aspects of multilingualism*. Uppsala: Borgström, pp. 51–77

Poplack, S. 1988. Contrasting patterns of codeswitching in two communities. In M. Heller (ed.) *Codeswitching: Anthropological and sociolinguistic perspectives*. Berlin: Mouton de Gruyter

Potter, J. and Wetherell, M. 1987. *Discourse and social psychology: Beyond attitudes and behaviour*. London: Sage

Quay, S. 1992. Explaining language choice in early infant bilingualism. Paper presented at the Ninth Sociolinguistics Symposium, University of Reading, 2–4 April

Quay, S. 1995. The bilingual lexicon: implications for studies of language choice. *Journal of Child Language*, 22: 369–387

Quay, S. 1998. One parent, two languages? In Aksu Koç, A., Erguvanli-Taylan, E., Sumru Özsoy, A., and Küntay, A. (eds) *Perspectives on language acquisition: Selected papers from the VIIth International Congress for the Study of Child Language*. Istanbul: Bogaziçi University

Quebec. 1972. *Commission of Inquiry on the Position of the French Language and on Language Rights in Quebec: Language of work (Gendron Commission)*. Québec: L'Editeur Officiel du Québec

Rampton, B. 2005. *Crossing: Language and ethnicity among adolescents* (2nd ed.). Manchester: St Jerome

Rao, C. 2004. Literacy acquisition, assessment and achievement of Year Two students in total immersion in Maori programmes. *International Journal of Bilingual Education and Bilingualism*, 5 (5): 404–432

Rassool, N. 1997. Fractured or flexible identities? Life histories of 'black' diasporic women in Britain. In Safia Mirza, H. (ed.) *Black British feminism: A reader*. London: Routledge, pp. 187–204

Raven, J.C. 1956. *Coloured progressive matrices: Sets A, Ab, B*. London: Lewis

Raven, J.C. 1998. Raven's progressive matrices. In Maddox, T. (ed.) *Tests: A comprehensive reference for assessments in psychology, education and business* (5th ed.). Austin: Pro-ed

Redlinger, W. and Park, T. 1980. Language mixing in young bilinguals. *Journal of Child Language*, 7: 337–352

Reetz-Kurashige, A. 1999. Japanese returnees' retention of English-speaking skills: changes in verb usage over time. In Hansen, L. (ed.) *Second language attrition in Japanese contexts*. New York: Oxford University Press

Restrepo, M. 1998. Identifiers of predominantly Spanish-speaking children with language impairment. *Journal of Speech, Language, and Hearing Research*, 41: 1398–1411

Restrepo, M.A. and Silverman, S.W. 2001. Validity of the Spanish preschool language scale-3 for use with bilingual children. *Journal of Speech Language Pathology*, 10: 382–393

Ricciardelli, L.A. 1992. Bilingualism and cognitive development in relation to threshold theory. *Journal of Psycholinguistic Research*, 21: 301–316

Rickard-Liow, S. and Lee, L.C. 2004. Metalinguistic awareness and semi-syllabic scripts: children's spelling errors in Malay. *Reading and Writing*, 17: 7–26

Ritchie, W.C. and Bhatia, T.K. 2004. Social and psychological factors in language mixing. In Bhatia, T.K., and Ritchie, W.C. (eds) *The handbook of bilingualism*. Malden, MA, and Oxford: Blackwell, pp. 336–352

Rolstad, K. 1997. Effects of two-way immersion on the ethnic identification of third language students: an exploratory study. *Bilingual Research Journal*, 21 (1): 43–63

Romaine, S. 1995. *Bilingualism* (2nd ed.). Oxford: Blackwell

Ronjat, J. 1913. *Le développement du langage observé chez un enfant bilingue*. Paris: Libraire ancienne H. Champion

Roseberry-McKibbin, C.A. 1994. Assessment and intervention for children with limited English proficiency and language disorders. *American Journal of Speech Pathology*, 3 (3): 77–88

Roseberry-McKibbin, C. 2002. *Multicultural students with special language needs: Practical strategies for assessment and intervention* (2nd ed.). Oceanside, CA: Academic Communication Associates

Ross, S. 1998. Self-assessment in second language testing: a meta-analysis and analysis of experiential factors. *Language Testing*, 15 (1): 1–20

Rubin, H. and Turner, A. 1989. Linguistic awareness skills in grade one children in a French immersion setting. *Reading and Writing: An Interdisciplinary Journal*, 1: 73–86

Sachdev, I. and Bourhis, R.Y. 2001. Multilingual communication. In Robinson, W.P. and Giles, H. (eds) *The new handbook of language and social psychology*. New York: Wiley, pp. 407–428

Sachdev, I. and Giles, H. 2004. Bilingual accommodation. In Bhatia, T.K. and Ritchie, W.C. (eds) *The handbook of bilingualism*. Malden, MA, and Oxford: Blackwell, pp. 353–378

Saenz, T.I. and Huer, M.B. 2003. Testing strategies involving least biased language assessment of bilingual children. *Communication Disorders Quarterly*, 24 (4): 189–193

Saer, D. 1923. The effect of bilingualism on intelligence. *British Journal of Psychology*, 14: 25–38

Saer, D.J., Smith, F., and Hughes, J. 1924. *The bilingual problem*. Wrexham: Hughes and Son, p. 112

Sandilands, M.L. and Fleury, N.C. 1979. Unilinguals in des milieux bilingues: une analyse of attributions. *Canadian Journal of Behavioural Science*, 11: 164–168

Sankoff, G. 1972. Language use in multilingual societies: some alternative approaches. In Pride, J.B. and Holmes, J. (eds) *Sociolinguistics: Selected readings*. Harmondsworth: Penguin, pp. 33–51

Sanz, C. 2000. Bilingual education enhances third language acquisition: evidence from Catalonia. *Applied Psycholinguistics*, 21: 23–44

Saunders, G. 1982. *Bilingual children: Guidance for the family*. Clevedon: Multilingual Matters

Saunders, G. 1988. *Bilingual children: From birth to teens*. Clevedon and Philadelphia: Multilingual Matters

Schmid, M., Köpke, B., Keijzer, M., and Weilemar, L. 2004. *First language attrition: Interdisciplinary perspectives on methodological issues*. Amsterdam and Philadelphia: John Benjamins

Scott, S. 1973. The relation of divergent thinking to bilingualism: cause or effect?. Unpublished research report, McGill University

Scotton, C.M. and Ury, W. 1977. Bilingual strategies: the social function of code-switching. *Linguistics*, 193: 5–20

Semel, M., Wiig, V., and Secord, W. 1995. *Clinical evaluation of language fundamental skills*. Mission Viejo, CA: Author

Shinn, M., Collins, V., and Gallagher, S. 1998. Curriculum-based measurement and its use in a problem-solving model with students from minority backgrounds. In Shinn, M. (ed.) *Advanced applications of curriculum-based measurement*. New York: Guilford Press, pp. 143–197

Shohamy, E. 2006. *Language policy: Hidden agendas and new approaches*. New York: Routledge

Shore, C. 1995. *Individual differences in language development*. London: Sage

Skourtou, E. 1995. Some notes about the relationship between bilingualism and literacy concerning the teaching of Greek as a second language. *European Journal of Intercultural Studies*, 6 (2): 24–30

Skourtou, E., Kourtis-Kazoullis, V., and Cummins, J. 2006. Designing virtual learning environments for academic language development. In Weiss, J., Nolan, J., and Trifonas, P. (eds) *International handbook of virtual learning environments*. Amsterdam: Springer

Skutnabb-Kangas, T. 1981. *Bilingualism or not: The education of minorities.* Clevedon: Multilingual Matters

Slobin, D.I. (ed.) 1985–1997. *The crosslinguistic study of language acquisition.* Hillsdale, NJ: Lawrence Erlbaum

Smith, F. 1923. Bilingualism and mental development. *British Journal of Psychology*, 13: 270–282

Smith, N. 1973. *The acquisition of phonology.* Cambridge: Cambridge University Press

Smith, R. 2003. Mother tongue education and the law: a legal review of bilingualism with reference to Scottish Gaelic. *International Journal of Bilingual Education and Bilingualism*, 6 (2): 129–145

Snow, C.E., Barnes, W., Chandler, J., Goodman, I., and Hemphill, L. 1991. *Unfulfilled expectations: Home and school influences on literacy.* Cambridge, MA: Harvard University Press

Spolsky, B. 1984. A note on the dangers of terminology innovation. In Rivera, C. (ed.) *Language proficiency and academic achievement.* Clevedon: Multilingual Matters, pp. 41–43

Spolsky, B. 1985. What does it mean to know how to use a language? An essay on the theoretical basis of language testing. *Language Testing*, 2 (2): 180–191

Spratt, J.E., Seckinger, B., and Wagner, D.A. 1991. Functional literacy in Moroccan school children. *Reading Research Quarterly*, 26: 178–195

Stampe, D. 1969. The acquisition of phonetic representation. *Papers from the Fifth Regional Meeting of the Chicago Linguistic Society.* Chicago: Chicago Linguistic Society, pp. 433–444

Stampe, D. 1973. *A dissertation on natural phonology.* Doctoral dissertation, University of Chicago. New York: Garland Press

Stanovich, K.E. 1986. Matthew effects in reading: some consequences of individual differences in the acquisition of literacy. *Reading Research Quarterly*, 16: 32–71

Stevenson, D.L. and Baker, D.P. 1987. Family–school relation and the child's school performance. *Child Development*, 58: 1348–1357

Stiles, D.B. 1997. Four successful indigenous language programs. In Reyhner, J. (ed.) *Teaching indigenous languages.* Flagstaff, AZ: Northern Arizona University, pp. 148–262. Accessed at http://jan.ucc.nau.edu/~jar/TIL_21.html on 21 August 2006

Stoel-Gammon, C. and Menn, L. 1997. Phonological development: learning sounds and sound patterns. In Berko-Gleason, J. (ed.) *The development of language* (4th ed.). New York: Macmillan

Strand, S. and Demie, F. 2005. English language acquisition and educational attainment at the end of the primary school. *Educational Studies*, 13 (3): 275–291

Street, R. Jr. 1985. Participant–observer differences in speech evaluation. *Journal of Language and Social Psychology*, 4: 125–130

Swain, M. 2000. The output hypothesis and beyond: mediating acquisition through collaborative dialogue. In Lantolf, L.P. (ed.) *Sociocultural theory and second language learning.* Oxford: Oxford University Press, pp. 97–114

Swain, M. 2001. Integrating language and content teaching through collaborative tasks. *The Canadian Modern Language Review*, 58 (1): 44–63

Swain, M. and Johnson, R.K. (1997) Immersion education: a category within bilingual education. In Johnson, R.K. and Swain, M. (eds) *Immersion education: International perspectives.* Cambridge: Cambridge University Press, pp. 1–16

Swain, M. and Lapkin, S. 1991. Heritage language children in an English–French bilingual program. *The Canadian Modern Language Review*, 474: 635–641

Swain, M. and Lapkin, S. 2005. The evolving sociopolitical context of immersion education in Canada: some implications for program development. *International Journal of Applied Linguistics*, 15 (2): 169–186

Swain, M., Lapkin, S., Rowen, N., and Hart, D. 1990. The role of mother tongue literacy in third language learning. *Language Culture and Curriculum*, 3 (1): 65–81

Taeschner, T. 1983. *The sun is feminine: A study on language acquisition in bilingual children.* Berlin: Springer-Verlag

Tajfel, H. and Turner, J. 1979. An intergrative theory of intergroup conflict. In Austin, W.G. and Worchel, S. (eds) *The social psychology of intergroup relations.* Monterey: Brooks/Cole, pp. 33–53

Tamayo, J. 1987. Frequency of use as a measure of word difficulty in bilingual vocabulary test construction and translation. *Educational and Psychological Measurement*, 47: 893–902

Test, J. 2001. Bilingual acquisition in the first year: could gestures provide prelinguistic support for language differentiation? A case study. In Almgren, M., Barreña, A., Ezeizabarrena, M.-J., Idiazabal, I., and MacWhinney, B. (eds) *Research on Child Language Acquisition: Proceedings of the Eighth Conference of the International Association for the Study of Child Language.* Somerville, MA: Cascadilla Press

Thomas, W. and Collier, V. 1997. *School effectiveness for language minority students.* Washington, DC: The National Clearinghouse for Bilingual Education. Resource Collection Series, No. 9, December

Thomas, W. and Collier, V. 2002. A national study of school effectiveness for language minority students in long term academic achievement. Final report. Washington, DC: Center for Research on Education, Diversity and Excellence

Thordardottir, Alin T., Ellis Weisner, S., and Smith, Mary E. (1997). Vocabulary learning in bilingual and monolingual clinical intervention. *Child Language Teaching and Therapy*, 13 (3): 215–227

Thorndike, R., Hagen, E., and Sattler, J. 1986. *Stanford–Binet intelligence scale* (4th ed.). Chicago: Riverside

Thurstone, L.L. and Thurstone, Thelma G. 1954. *Primary mental abilities: Ages 7 to 11.* Chicago: Science Research Associates

Tipper, S.P. and McLaren, J. 1990. Evidence for efficient visual selectivity in children. In Enns, J.T. (ed.) *The development of attention: Research and theory.* New York: Elsevier, pp. 197–210

Tomiyama, M. 2000. Child second language attrition: a longitudinal case study. *Applied Linguistics*, 21 (3): 304–332

Torrance, E.P., Gowan, J.C., Wu, J.M., and Aliotti, N.C. 1970. Creative functioning of monolingual and bilingual children in Singapore. *Journal of Educational Psychology*, 61: 72–75

Tunmer, W.E. and Myhill, M.E. 1984. Metalinguistic awareness and bilingualism. In Tunmer, W.E., Pratt, C., and Merriman, M.L. (eds) *Metalinguistic awareness in children.* Berlin: Springer-Verlag, pp. 169–187

Turnbull, M., Lapkin, S., and Hart, D. 2001. Grade 3 immersion students' performance in literacy and mathematics: province-wide results from Ontario 1998–99. *The Canadian Modern Language Review*, 58 (1): 9–26

Turnbull, M.K., Lapkin, S., and Hart, D. 2003. Grade 6 French immersion students' performances on large-scale reading, writing and mathematics tests: building explanations. *Alberta Journal of Education*, 49 (1): 6–23

Tzuriel, D. 2001. *Dynamic assessment of young children.* New York: Kluwer Academic/ Plenum

Uiterwijk, H. 1994. *De bruikbaarheid van de Eindtoets Basisonderwijs voor allochtone leerlingen* [Usefulness of the final assessment at primary school test]. Arnhem: Cito.

Ukrainetz, T., Harpell, S., Walsh, C., and Coyle, C. 2000. A preliminary investigation of dynamic assessment with Native American kindergarteners. *Language, Speech, and Hearing Services in Schools*, 31: 142–154

Umbel, V.M., Pearson, B.Z., Fernandez, M.C., and Oller, D.K. 1992. Measuring bilingual children's receptive vocabulary. *Child Development*, 63: 1012–1020

Upshur, J. and Turner, C. 1999. Systematic effects in the rating of second language speaking ability: test method and learner discourse. *Language Testing*, 16 (1): 82–111

Uribe de Kellett, A. 2002. The recovery of a first language: a case study of an English/Spanish bilingual child. *International Journal of Bilingual Education and Bilingualism*, 5 (3): 162–193

Urow, C. and Sontag, J. 2001. Creating community – *Un Mundo Entero*: the inter-American experience. In Christian, D. and Genesee, F. (eds) *Bilingual Education*. Arlington, VA: TESOL

Valdes, G. and Figueroa, R. 1994. *Bilingualism and testing: A special case of bias*. Norwood, NJ: Ablex

Van den Berg, M.E. 1988. Long term accommodation of (ethno)linguistic groups toward a societal language norm. *Language and Communication*, 8 (3/4): 251–269

Van Els, T. 1986. An overview of European research on language acquisition. In Weltens, B., De Bot, K., and Van Else, T. (eds) *Language attrition in progress*. Dordrecht: Foris Publications

Veii, K. and Everatt, J. 2005. Predictors of reading among Herero–English bilingual Namibian children. *Bilingualism, Language and Cognition*, 8 (3): 239–254

Verhallen, M. and Schoonen, R. 1998. Lexical knowledge in L1 and L2 of third and fifth graders. *Applied Linguistics*, 19 (4): 452–470

Verhoeven, L. 1990. Acquisition of reading in a second language. *Reading Research Quarterly*, 25: 90–114

Verhoeven, Ludo T. 1994. Transfer in bilingual development: the Linguistic Interdependence Hypothesis revisited. *Language Learning*, 44 (3): 381–415

Verhoeven, L. 1996. Sociolinguistics in education. In Coulmas, F. (ed.) *Handbook of sociolinguistics*. Oxford: Basil Blackwell, pp. 389–404

Verhoeven, L. and Vermeer, A. 1985. Ethnic group differences in children's oral proficiency of Dutch. In Extra, G. and Vallen, T. (eds) *Ethnic minorities and Dutch as a second language*. Dordrecht: Foris Publications, pp. 105–132

Vihman, M. 1985. Language differentiation by the bilingual infant. *Journal of Child Language*, 12: 297–324

Villamil Touriño, A. 2004. Galician people in Madrid: attitudes and language maintenance. *Madrygal: Revista de Estudios Gallegos Latinos*, 7: 123–132

Vincent, C. 1996. Singing to a star: the school meanings of second generation Salvadorean students. Doctoral dissertation, George Mason University, Fairfax, VA

Volterra, V. and Taeschner, T. 1978. The acquisition and development of language by bilingual children. *Journal of Child Language*, 5: 311–326

Wagner, D.A., Spratt, J.E., and Ezzaki, A. 1989. Does learning to read in a second language always put the child at a disadvantage? Some counterevidence from Morocco. *Applied Psycholinguistics*, 10 (1): 31–48

Wang, M., Park, Y., and Lee, K.R. 2006. Korean–English biliteracy acquisition: cross-language phonological and orthographic transfer. *Journal of Educational Psychology*, 98: 148–158

Wang, Min, Perfetti, Charles A., and Liu, Ying. 2005. Chinese–English biliteracy acquisition: cross-language and writing system transfer. *Cognition*, 97 (1): 67–88

Warner, W.L., Meeker, M., and Eelis, K. 1949. *Social class in America*. Chicago: Science Research Associates

Watson, I. 1991. Phonological processing in two languages. In Bialystok, E. (ed.) *Language processing in bilingual children.* Cambridge: Cambridge University Press

Wee, L. 2003. Linguistic instrumentalism in Singapore. *Journal of Multilingual and Multicultural Development,* 24: 211–224

Weinreich, U. 1953. *Languages in contact.* New York: Linguistic Circle of New York. Reissued The Hague: Mouton, 1968

Weissberg, R. and Buker, S. 1990. *Writing up research,* Englewood Cliffs, NJ: Prentice Hall

Wellman, H.M. and Lempers, J.D. 1977. The naturalistic communicative abilities of two-year-olds. *Child Development,* 48: 1052–1057

Weltens, B. 1989. *The attrition of French as a foreign language.* Dordrecht: Foris Publications

Westby, C., Burda, A., and Mehta, Z. 2003. Asking the right questions in the right ways: strategies for ethnographic interviewing. *Asha,* 8 (4–5): 16–17

Wigglesworth, G. 1993. Bias analysis as a tool for improving rater performance in the assessment of oral English tests. *Language Testing,* 10 (3): 305–335

Wigglesworth, G. In press. Task and performance based assessment. In Shohamy, E. (ed.) *The encyclopaedia of language education.* Vol. 7: *Language testing and assessment.* Dordrecht: Springer

Wode, H. 1990. 'But grandpa always goes like this' . . . Or, the ontogeny of codeswitching. *Papers for the Workshop on Impact and Consequences.* Brussels: ESF Network on Code-Switching and Language Contact, pp. 17–50

Wölck, Wolfgang 1973. Attitudes towards Spanish and Quechua in bilingual Peru. In Shuy, R.W. (ed.) *Language attitudes: Current trends and prospects.* Washington, DC: Georgetown University Press, pp. 129–147. Reprinted in Fasold, R.W. (ed.) 1983. *Variation in the form and use of language.* Washington, DC: Georgetown University Press, pp. 370–388

Woolard, K.A. 1984. A formal measure of language attitudes in Barcelona: a note from work in progress. *International Journal of the Sociology of Language,* 47: 63–71

Yamauchi, L. and Wilhelm, P. 2001. E ola ka Hawai'I I Kon 'Olelo: Hawaiians live in their language. In Christian, D. and Genesee, F. (eds) *Bilingual Education.* Arlington, VA: TESOL

Yavas, M. and Goldstein, B. 1998. Phonological assessment and treatment of bilingual speakers. *American Journal of Speech-Language Pathology,* 7 (2): 49–60

Yelland, G.W., Pollard, J., and Mercuri, A. 1993. The metalinguistic benefits of limited contact with a second language. *Applied Psycholinguistics,* 14: 423–444

Yoshitomi, A. 1999. On the loss of English as a second language by Japanese returnee children. In Hansen, L. (ed.) *Second language attrition in Japanese contexts.* New York: Oxford University Press

Zentella, A. 1997. *Growing up bilingual: Puerto Rican children in New York.* Cambridge, MA: Blackwell

Author index

Subject index

absolute proficiency level 158–63
academic attainment 158–63
academic language proficiency 34–5, 97, 163–70
accommodation theory 118, 238–47
accuracy rate 203, 207
achievement tests 28
acquisition 40–52, 171–87, 281–7; child's complex linguistic environment 43–6; defining bilingual first-language acquisition 42–3; descriptors referring to age of acquisition 12–14; differentiation between language systems 46–8, 176–9, 180–2, 184–6; factors impacting on 41, 48–52; lexical acquisition in two languages 176–9; parental approaches to raising children bilingually 281–2; parental strategies 48–52; patterns of bilingual acquisition 282–4; phonological development in a bilingual environment 179–87; recording and transcribing data 284–6; sociolinguistic context 48–50, 171–6; strategies for raising children bilingually 286–7
activation threshold hypothesis 74–5
active bilingualism 8
additional language programmes 141–2
additive bilingualism 17, 219–20, 221, 222
additive educational practices 83, 87–94
administrative pressure 139, 147
administrative support 16–17, 124, 236, 244–5
adult repetition strategy 50, 173–4, 175
affect 108–9
African states 114
age: defining BFLA 42–3; descriptors referring to age of acquisition 12–14; and language attrition 75–6, 78–81
alphabetic writing systems 100–1

analysis and control hypothesis 68–9, 196–200
analytic rating scales 29
'Andreas', case study of 182–6
anonymity 259–60
aphasia 74
arbitrariness of language, awareness of 63–5
assessment 19–39, 58, 151–70, 275–80; of bilingual proficiency 22–3; bilingual proficiency and academic attainment 158–63; of children 33–5, 151–8; circumstantial bilinguals 32–8; classifying bilingual speakers 20–2; in the classroom 275–6; Cummins's framework 163–70; elective bilinguals 24–32; evaluating language tests 276–8; least biased assessment of children 151–8; need to test bilinguals in both languages 36–7, 104; self–assessments 37–8; specific language impairment 36–7; translated tests 56, 57, 152, 190, 278–80
assimilation 128
asymmetry in language choice 177–8
attainment, educational 158–63
attention, control of 68–9, 197–200
attitudes 13, 78, 81–2, 106–29, 236, 238–53, 274, 308–15; accommodation theory 118, 238–47; code mixing 119–23, 312; code switching 119–23, 312–14; definition 108–9; effect of bilingualism on 116–17; evaluating and measuring 109–12; healthcare professionals and 125–7; identity and 115–16, 247–52; impact of language policies on 124, 127–8; language prestige and 107, 113–15; matched-guise technique 111, 112–13, 314–15; to a minority language 41, 308–10; parents and 123–4; perceptions of language groups 311; to self and others in the community 112–13; and self-report data

Related titles from Routledge

The Bilingualism Reader
Second edition

Li Wei

From reviews of the first edition:

'A volume that would serve well as a textbook in an introductory course on bilingualism and will also prove extremely valuable to students and researchers alike.'
Language

'This book is clearly a bargain, and it is difficult to see how it could fail to become a core textbook for courses in bilingualism.'
System

'The bringing together of different fields of specialisation is enriching, yet it also brings home to the reader the great diversity of interests, opinions and agendas that exist . . . an excellent compilation and an invaluable companion.'
Language Awareness

'This outstanding collection of the key articles in the field is an essential guide for incoming students and a wonderful resource for bilingualism scholars.'
Annotated Bibliography of English Studies

The Bilingualism Reader is the definitive reader for the study of bilingualism. Designed as an integrated and structured student resource it provides invaluable editorial material that guides the reader through different sections and covers:

- definitions and typology of bilingualism
- language choice and bilingual interaction
- bilingualism, identity and ideology
- grammar of code-switching and bilingual acquisition
- bilingual production and perception
- the bilingual brain
- methodological issues in the study of bilingualism.

The second edition of this best selling volume includes nine new readings and postscripts written by the authors of the original articles, which evaluate them in the light of recent research. Critical discussion of research methods, revised graded study questions and activities, a comprehensive glossary, and an up-to-date resource list make *The Bilingualism Reader* an essential introductory text for students of linguistics, psychology and education.

Contributors: Jubin Abutalebi, Peter Auer, Jan-Petter Blom, Kees de Bot, Stefano F. Cappa, Charles A. Ferguson, Joshua A. Fishman, Fred Genesee, David W. Green, Annette M.B. de Groot, François Grosjean, John J. Gumperz, Monica Heller, Janice L. Jake, Judith F. Kroll, Li Wei, Jürgen M. Meisel, Lesley Milroy, Pieter Muysken, Carol Myers-Scotton, Loraine K. Obler, Michel Paradis, Daniela Perani, Shana Poplack, Ben Rampton, Traute Taeschner, Jyotsna Vaid, Virginia Volterra and Robert J. Zatorre.

Li Wei is Professor of Applied Linguistics at Birkbeck, University of London, UK. He is Editor of the *International Journal of Bilingualism*.

ISBN13: 978-0-415-35554-4 (hbk)
ISBN13: 978-0-415-3555-1 (pbk)

Available at all good bookshops
For ordering and further information please visit:
www.routledge.com

Related titles from Routledge

Second Language Acquisition: An Advanced Resource book
Routledge Applied Linguistics series
Kees de Bot, Wander Lowie and Marjolijn Verspoor

Second Language Acquisition, like all books in the *Routledge Applied Linguistics* series, is a comprehensive resource book that guides readers through three main sections: Section A establishes the key terms and concepts, Section B brings together influential articles, sets them in context, and discusses their contribution to the field and Section C builds on knowledge gained in the first two sections, setting thoughtful tasks around further illustrative material. Throughout the book, topics are revisited, extended, interwoven and deconstructed, with the reader's understanding strengthened by tasks and follow-up questions.

Second Language Acquisition:

- introduces the key areas in the field, including: multilingualism, the role of teaching, the mental processing of multiple languages, and patterns of growth and decline
- explores the key theories and debates and elucidates areas of controversy
- gathers together influential readings from key names in the discipline, including: Vivian Cook, William E. Dunn and James P. Lantolf, S.P. Corder, and Nina Spada and Patsy Lightbown.

ISBN13:978-0-415-33869-1 (hbk)
ISBN13:0-415-33870-7 (pbk)

Available at all good bookshops

For ordering and further information please visit:

www.routledge.com

Related titles from Routledge

English for Academic Purposes: An advanced resource book
Routledge Applied Linguistics series
Ken Hyland

English for Academic Purposes, like all books in the *Routledge Applied Linguistics* series, is a comprehensive resource book that guides readers through three main sections: Section A establishes the key terms and concepts, Section B brings together influential articles, sets them in context, and discusses their contribution to the field and Section C builds on knowledge gained in the first two sections, setting thoughtful tasks around further illustrative material. Throughout the book, topics are revisited, extended, interwoven and deconstructed, with the reader's understanding strengthened by tasks and follow-up questions.

English for Academic Purposes:

• introduces the major theories, approaches and controversies in the field

• gathers together influential readings from key names in the discipline, including: John Swales, Alastair Pennycook, Greg Myers, Brian Street and Ann Johns

• provides numerous exercises as practical study tools that encourage in students a critical approach to the subject.

Written by an experienced teacher and researcher in the field, *English for Academic Purposes* is an essential resource for students and researchers of Applied Linguistics.

ISBN13: 978-0-415-35869-9 (hbk)
ISBN13: 978-0-415-35870-5 (pbk)

Available at all good bookshops
For ordering and further information please visit:
http://www.routledge.com/rcenters/linguistics/series/ral.htm

Related titles from Routledge

Corpus-Based Language Studies: An advanced resource book
Routledge Applied Linguistics series
Anthony McEnery, Richard Xiao and Yukio Tono

Corpus-Based Language Studies, like all books in the *Routledge Applied Linguistics* series, is a comprehensive resource book that guides readers through three main sections: Section A establishes the key terms and concepts, Section B brings together influential articles, sets them in context, and discusses their contribution to the field and Section C builds on knowledge gained in the first two sections, setting thoughtful tasks around further illustrative material. Throughout the book, topics are revisited, extended, interwoven and deconstructed, with the reader's understanding strengthened by tasks and follow-up questions.

Corpus-Based Language Studies:

*   covers the major theoretical approaches to the use of corpus data
*   adopts a 'how to' approach with exercises and cases, providing students with the knowledge and tools to undertake their own corpus-based research
*   gathers together influential readings from key names in the discipline, including: Biber, Widdowson, Stubbs, Carter and McCarthy
*   supported by a website featuring long extracts for analysis by students with commentary by the authors

Written by experienced teachers and researchers in the field, *Corpus-Based Language Studies* is an essential resource for students and researchers of Applied Linguistics.

ISBN13: 978-0-415-28622-0 (hbk)
ISBN13: 978-0-415-28623-7 (pbk)

Available at all good bookshops
For ordering and further information please visit:
http://www.routledge.com/rcenters/linguistics/series/ral.htm

Related titles from Routledge

Language and Gender: An advanced resource book
Routledge Applied Linguistics series
Jane Sunderland

'This book marks a timely intervention in the field of language and gender research and provides students and researchers alike with essential primary materials. The book contains articles from a very wide range of disciplines; if you think that this book will contain all of the usual suspects, then prepare to be surprised – there are extracts on masculinity, corpus linguistics, post-structuralist linguistics, fairy tales, ELT textbooks, queer theory, and social networks. This would make an ideal textbook for gender and language courses.'
Sara Mills, *Sheffield Hallam University, UK*

Routledge Applied Linguistics is a series of comprehensive resource books, providing students and researchers with the support they need for advanced study in the core areas of English language and Applied Linguistics.

Language and Gender:

*   presents an up-to-date introduction to language and gender

*   includes diverse work from a range of cultural, including non-Western, contexts, and represents a range of methodological approaches

*   gathers together influential readings from key names in the discipline, including: Deborah Cameron, Mary Haas and Deborah Tannen

Written by an experienced teacher and researcher in the field, *Language and Gender* is an essential resource for students and researchers of Applied Linguistics.

ISBN13:978-0-41531103-8 (hbk)
ISBN13:978-0-41531104-5 (pbk)

Available at all good bookshops
For ordering and further information please visit:
http://www.routledge.com/rcenters/linguistics/series/ral.htm

Related titles from Routledge

Grammar and Context: An advanced resource book
Routledge Applied Linguistics series
Ann Hewings and Martin Hewings

Grammar and Context, like all books in the *Routledge Applied Linguistics* series, is a comprehensive resource book that guides readers through three main sections: Section A establishes the key terms and concepts, Section B brings together influential articles, sets them in context, and discusses their contribution to the field and Section C builds on knowledge gained in the first two sections, setting thoughtful tasks around further illustrative material. Throughout the book, topics are revisited, extended, interwoven and deconstructed, with the reader's understanding strengthened by tasks and follow-up questions.

Grammar in Context:

- considers how grammatical choices influence and are influenced by the context in which communication takes place

- examines the interaction of a wide variety of contexts – including socio-cultural, situational and global influences

- includes a range of different types of grammar – functional, pedagogic, descriptive and prescriptive

- explores grammatical features in a lively variety of communicative contexts, such as advertising, dinner-table talk, email and political speeches

- gathers together influential readings from key names in the discipline, including: David Crystal, M.A.K. Halliday, Joanna Thornborrow, Ken Hyland and Stephen Levey

Written by experienced teachers and researchers in the field, *Grammar in Context* is an essential resource for students and researchers of Applied Linguistics.

ISBN13: 978-0-415-31080-2 (hbk)
ISBN13: 978-0-415-31081-9 (pbk)

Available at all good bookshops
For ordering and further information please visit:
http://www.routledge.com/rcenters/linguistics/series/ral.htm